Stand Out 5

Lesson Planner

Second Edition

Staci Johnson

Rob Jenkins

HEINLE
CENGAGE Learning™

Australia · Brazil · Japan · Korea · Mexico · Singapore · Spain · United Kingdom · United States

HEINLE
CENGAGE Learning

Stand Out 5: Lesson Planner
Staci Johnson and Rob Jenkins

Publisher: Sherrise Roehr

Acquisitions Editor: Tom Jefferies

Development Editor: Michael Ryall

Director of Content and
Media Production: Michael Burggren

Product Marketing Manager: Katie Kelley

Sr. Content Project Manager: Maryellen E. Killeen

Sr. Print Buyer: Mary Beth Hennebury

Development Editor: Sarah Barnicle

Project Manager: Tunde A. Dewey

Cover / Text Designer: Studio Montage

Photo Researcher: Erika Hokanson

Illustrators: James Edwards, Scott McNeill,
S.I. International

Compositor: PrePressPMG

For product information and technology assistance, contact us at
Cengage Learning Customer & Sales Support, 1-800-354-9706

For permission to use material from this text or product,
submit all requests online at **cengage.com/permissions**
Further permissions questions can be emailed to
permissionrequest@cengage.com

ISBN-10: 1-4240-1937-0

ISBN-13: 978-1-4240-1937-3

Cengage Learning
20 Channel Center
South Boston, MA 02127
USA

Cengage Learning is a leading provider of customized learning solutions with office locations around the globe, including Singapore, the United Kingdom, Australia, Mexico, Brazil, and Japan. Locate your local office at:
international.cengage.com/region

Cengage Learning products are represented in Canada by Nelson Education, Ltd.

Visit Heinle online at **elt.heinle.com**
Visit our corporate website at **cengage.com**

Printed in China by China Translation & Printing Services Limited
2 3 4 5 6 7 11 10

ACKNOWLEDGMENTS

Elizabeth Aderman
*New York City Board of Education,
New York, NY*

Lisa Aago
Fresno Adult School, Fresno, CA

Sharon Baker
Roseville Adult School, Roseville, CA

Lillian Barredo
Stockton School for Adults, Stockton, CA

Linda Boice
*Elk Grove Adult Education,
Elk Grove, CA*

Chan Bostwick
*North Hollywood Polytechnic
Community Adult School,
Sun Valley, CA*

Debra Brooks
*Manhattan BEGIN Program,
New York, NY*

Anne Byrnes
*North Hollywood-Polytechnic
Community Adult School,
Sun Valley, CA*

Rose Cantu
John Jay High School, San Antonio, TX

Toni Chapralis
*Fremont School for Adults,
Sacramento, CA*

Melanie Chitwood
Miami-Dade College, Miami, FL

Geri Creamer
Stockton School for Adults, Stockton, CA

Stephanie Daubar
*Harry W. Brewster Technical Center,
Tampa, FL*

Marie Day
*McHenry County College,
Crystal Lake, IL*

Irene Dennis
San Antonio College, San Antonio, TX

Eileen Duffell
P.S. 64, New York, NY

Nancy Dunlap
*Northside Independent School District,
San Antonio, TX*

Gloria Eriksson
Grant Skills Center, Sacramento, CA

Marti Estrin
*Santa Rosa Junior College,
Santa Rosa, CA*

Lawrence Fish
*Shorefront YM-YWHA English
Language Program, Brooklyn, NY*

Victoria Florit
Miami-Dade College, Miami, FL

Sally Gearheart
*Santa Rosa Junior College,
Santa Rosa, CA*

Rhoda Gilbert
*New York City Board of Education,
New York, NY*

Debbie Glass
Merced Adult School, Merced, CA

Laurie Hartwick
*Lawrence High School/Adult Learning
Center, Lawrence, MA*

Kathleen Jimenez
Miami-Dade College, Miami, FL

Nancy Jordan
*John Jay High School Adult Education,
San Antonio, TX*

Renee Klosz
*Lindsey Hopkins Technical Education
Center, Miami, FL*

David Lauter
Stockton School for Adults, Stockton, CA

Patricia Long
*Old Marshall Adult Education Center,
Sacramento, CA*

Daniel Loos
Seattle Community College, Seattle, WA

Maria Miranda
*Lindsey Hopkins Technical Education
Center, Miami, FL*

Karen Moore
*Stockton School for Adults,
Stockton, CA*

George Myskiw
Malcolm X College, Chicago, IL

Dr. Betty Payne
Montgomery College, Rockville, MD

Adam Pang
*McKinley Community School for
Adults, Honolulu, HI*

Heidi Perez
*Lawrence Public Schools Adult
Learning Center, Lawrence, MA*

Marta Pitt
*Lindsey Hopkins Technical Education
Center, Miami, FL*

Sylvia Rambach
*Stockton School for Adults,
Stockton, CA*

Esther Robbins
*Prince George's Community College,
Largo, MD*

Eric Rosenbaum
*BEGIN Managed Programs,
New York, NY*

Laura Rowley
*Old Marshall Adult Education Center,
Sacramento, CA*

Stephanie Schmitter
*Mercer County Community College,
Trenton, NJ*

Amy Schneider
Pacoima Skills Center, Pacoima, CA

Sr. M. B. Theresa Spittle
Stockton School for Adults, Stockton, CA

Andre Sutton
Belmont Adult School, Los Angeles, CA

Jennifer Swoyer
*Northside Independent School District,
San Antonio, TX*

Marcia Takacs
*Coastline Community College,
Fountain Vallyey, CA*

Claire Valier
*Palm Beach County School District,
West Palm Beach, FL*

Sarah Young
*Arlington Education and Employment
Program (REEP), Arlington, VA*

Staci Johnson

Rob Jenkins

Ever since I can remember, I've been fascinated with other cultures and languages. I love to travel and every place I go, the first thing I want to do is meet the people, learn their language, and understand their culture. Becoming an ESL teacher was a perfect way to turn what I love to do into my profession. There's nothing more incredible than the exchange of teaching and learning from one another that goes on in an ESL classroom. And there's nothing more rewarding than helping a student succeed.

I love teaching. I love to see the expressions on my students' faces when the light goes on and their eyes show such sincere joy of learning. I knew the first time I stepped into an ESL classroom that this was where I needed to be and I have never questioned that resolution. I have worked in business, sales, and publishing, and I've found challenge in all, but nothing can compare to the satisfaction of reaching people in such a personal way.

We are so happy that instructors and agencies have embraced the lesson planning and project-based activities that we introduced in the first edition and are so enthusiastically teaching with **Stand Out**. It is fantastic that so many of our colleagues are as excited to be in this profession as we are. After writing over 500 lesson plans and implementing them in our own classrooms and after personal discussions with thousands of instructors all over the United States and in different parts of the world, we have found ourselves in a position to improve upon our successful model. One of the most notable things in the new edition is that we have continued to stress integrating skills in each lesson and have made this integration more apparent and obvious. To accomplish any life skill, students need to incorporate a combination of reading, writing, listening, speaking, grammar, pronunciation, and academic skills while developing vocabulary and these skills should be taught together in a lesson! We have accomplished this by extending the presentation of lessons in the book, so each lesson is more fully developed. You will also notice an extended list of ancillaries and a tighter correlation of these ancillaries to each book. The ancillaries allow you to extend practice on particular skill areas beyond the lesson in the text. We are so excited about this curriculum and know that as you implement it, you and your students will *stand out*.

Our goal is to give students challenging opportunities to be successful in their language-learning experience so they develop confidence and become independent, lifelong learners.

Staci Johnson
Rob Jenkins

ABOUT THE SERIES

The **Stand Out** series is designed to facilitate *active* learning while challenging students to build a nurturing and effective learning community.

The student books are divided into eight distinct units, mirroring competency areas most useful to newcomers. These areas are outlined in CASAS assessment programs and different state model standards for adults. Each unit in *Stand Out 5* is then divided into five lessons, a review, a research assignment, and a team project. Lessons are driven by performance objectives and are filled with challenging activities that progress from teacher-presented to student-centered tasks.

SUPPLEMENTAL MATERIALS

- The *Stand Out 5 Lesson Planner* is in full color with 60 complete lesson plans, taking the instructor through each stage of a lesson from warm-up and review through application.

- The *Stand Out 5 Activity Bank CD-ROM* has an abundance of customizable worksheets. Print or download and modify what you need for your particular class.

- The *Stand Out 5 Grammar Challenge* is a workbook that gives additional grammar explanation and practice in context.

- The *Stand Out 5 Assessment CD-ROM with ExamView®* allows you to customize pre- and post-tests for each unit as well as a pre- and post-test for the book.

- Listening scripts are found in the back of the student book and in the Lesson Planner. CDs are available with focused listening activities described in the Lesson Planner.

STAND OUT 5 LESSON PLANNER

The *Stand Out 5 Lesson Planner* is a new and innovative approach. As many seasoned teachers know, good lesson planning can make a substantial difference in the classroom. Students continue coming to class, understanding, applying, and remembering more of what they learn. They are more confident in their learning when good lesson planning techniques are incorporated.

We have developed lesson plans that are designed to be used each day and to reduce preparation time. The planner includes:

- Standard lesson progression (Warm-up and Review, Introduction, Presentation, Practice, Evaluation, and Application)

- A creative and complete way to approach varied class lengths so that each lesson will work within a class period.

- 180 hours of classroom activities
- Time suggestions for each activity
- Pedagogical comments
- Space for teacher notes and future planning
- Identification of LCP standards in addition to SCANS and CASAS standards

USER QUESTIONS ABOUT *STAND OUT*

- **What are SCANS and EFF and how do they integrate into the book?**
  SCANS is the Secretary's Commission on Achieving Necessary Skills. SCANS was developed to encourage students to prepare for the workplace. The standards developed through SCANS have been incorporated throughout the **Stand Out** student books and components.

  Stand Out addresses SCANS a little differently than do other books. SCANS standards elicit effective teaching strategies by incorporating essential skills such as critical thinking and group work. We have incorporated SCANS standards in every lesson, not isolating these standards in the work unit. All new texts have followed our lead.

  EFF, or **E**quipped **F**or the **F**uture, is another set of standards established to address students' roles as parents, workers, and citizens, with a vision of student literacy and lifelong learning. **Stand Out** addresses these standards and integrates them into the materials in a similar way to SCANS.

- **What about CASAS?** The federal government has mandated that states show student outcomes as a prerequisite to receiving funding. Some states have incorporated the **C**omprehensive **A**dult **S**tudent **A**ssessment **S**ystem (CASAS) testing to standardize agency reporting. Unfortunately, many of our students are unfamiliar with standardized testing and therefore struggle with it. Adult schools need to develop lesson plans to address specific concerns. **Stand Out** was developed with careful attention to CASAS skill areas in most lessons and performance objectives.

- **Are the tasks too challenging for my students?**
  Students learn by doing and learn more when challenged. **Stand Out** provides tasks that encourage critical thinking in a variety of ways. The tasks in each lesson move from teacher-directed to student-centered so the learner clearly understands what's expected and is willing to "take a risk." The lessons are expected to be challenging. In this way, students learn that when they work together as a learning community, anything becomes possible. The satisfaction of accomplishing something both as an

individual and as a member of a team results in greater confidence and effective learning.

- **Do I need to understand lesson planning to teach from the student book?** If you don't understand lesson planning when you start, you will when you finish! Teaching from **Stand Out** is like a course on lesson planning, especially if you use the Lesson Planner on a daily basis.

  Stand Out does *stand out* because, when we developed this series, we first established performance objectives for each lesson. Then we designed lesson plans, followed by student book pages. The introduction to each lesson varies because different objectives demand different approaches. **Stand Out's** variety of tasks makes learning more interesting for the student.

- **What is the research project?** The purpose of each research project is to empower students to seek information on the Internet, in other publications, and in their community. The resulting information will provide students with helpful and practical sources for independent research after the course.

- **What are team projects?** The final lesson of each unit is a **team project**. This is often a team simulation that incorporates the objectives of the unit and provides an additional opportunity for students to actively apply what they have learned. The project allows students to produce something that represents their progress in learning. These end-of-unit projects were created with a variety of learning styles and individual skills in mind. The team projects can be skipped or simplified, but we encourage instructors to implement them, enriching the overall student experience.

- **What do you mean by a customizable Activity Bank?** Every class, student, teacher, and approach is different. Since no one textbook can meet all these differences, the *Stand Out Activity Bank CD-ROM* allows you to customize **Stand Out** for your class. You can copy different activities and worksheets from the CD-ROM to your hard drive and then:

  - change items in supplemental vocabulary, grammar, and life skill activities;
  - personalize activities with student names and popular locations in your area;
  - extend every lesson with additional practice where you feel it is most needed.

  The Activity Bank also includes the following resources:

  - Multilevel worksheets – worksheets based on the standard worksheets described above, but at one level higher and one level lower.

- Graphic organizer templates – templates that can be used to facilitate learning. They include graphs, charts, VENN diagrams, and so on.

- Computer worksheets – worksheets designed to supplement each unit and progress from simple to complex operations in word processing; and spreadsheets for labs and computer enhanced classrooms.

- Internet worksheets – worksheets designed to supplement each unit and provide application opportunities beyond the lessons in the book.

- **Is *Stand Out* grammar-based or competency-based?** **Stand Out** is a competency-based series; however, students are exposed to basic grammar structures. We believe that grammar instruction in context is extremely important. Grammar is a necessary component for achieving most competencies; therefore it is integrated into most lessons. Students are first provided with context that incorporates the grammar, followed by an explanation and practice. At this level, we expect students to learn basic structures, but we do not expect them to acquire them. It has been our experience that students are exposed several times within their learning experience to language structures before they actually acquire them. For teachers who want to enhance grammar instruction, the *Activity Bank CD-ROM* and/or the *Grammar Challenge* workbooks provide ample opportunities.

  The six competencies that drive **Stand Out** are communication, consumer economics, community resources, health, occupational knowledge, and lifelong learning (civic responsibility replaces lifelong learning in Book 5).

- **Are there enough activities so I don't have to supplement?** **Stand Out** stands alone in providing 180 hours of instruction and activities, even without the additional suggestions in the Lesson Planner. The Lesson Planner also shows you how to streamline lessons to provide 90 hours of classwork and still have thorough lessons if you meet less often. When supplementing with the *Stand Out Activity Bank CD-ROM*, the *Assessment CD-ROM with ExamView®* and the *Stand Out Grammar Challenge* workbook, you gain unlimited opportunities to extend class hours and provide activities related directly to each lesson objective. Calculate how many hours your class meets in a semester and look to **Stand Out** to address the full class experience.

  Stand Out is a comprehensive approach to adult language learning, meeting needs of students and instructors completely and effectively.

CONTENTS

● Grammar points that are new   △ Grammar points that are being recycled   ♦ Grammar points that are presented in context

	Numeracy/ Academic Strategies	EFF	SCANS	CASAS
Pre-Unit	• Pronunciation: Enunciate clearly • Develop research skills and ideas • Take notes • Focused listening • Prepare and deliver an oral presentation • Write a personal letter/e-mail	Many EFF skills are incorporated into this unit with an emphasis on: **Communication:** • Conveying ideas in writing • Speaking so others can understand • Listening actively **Lifelong Learning:** • Learning through reasearch • Taking responsibility for learning	Many SCANS skills are incorporated in this unit with an emphasis on: • Listening • Speaking • Social • Visualization • Cultural diversity	**1:** 0.1.1, 0.1.2, 0.1.4, 7.2.1 **2:** 0.2.1, 0.2.4 **3:** 0.2.3 **RE:** 7.44
Unit 1	• Reading • Interpret meanings of words in context • Develop categories • Write a paragraph • Focused listening • Take notes from lecture/oral sources • Interpret bar graphs • Research online	Many EFF skills are incorporated into this unit with an emphasis on: **Communication:** • Reading with understanding • Observing critically **Decision-Making:** • Planning **Lifelong Learning:** • Using information and communications technololgy • Learning through research	Many SCANS skills are incorporated in this unit with an emphasis on: • Writing • Social • Negotiation • Leadership • Self-esteem • Self-management • Responsibility • Decision making	**VB:** 7.4.5 **1:** 7.4.2, 7.4.9 **2:** 4.1.9, 7.4.2 **3:** 7.4.2 **4:** 7.1.1, 7.1.2, 7.1.3, 7.4.2 **5:** 7.1.3 **RV:** 7.2.1 **RE:** 4.9.3, 7.2.1, 7.4.4, 7.4.5, 7.4.6 **TP:** 4.8.1, 4.8.5, 4.8.6
Unit 2	• Interpret meaning of idioms in context • Focused listening • Analyze and evaluate readings and budgets • Outline readings • Summarize reading passages and other sources of information • Make calculations • Create a budget	Many EFF skills are incorporated into this unit with an emphasis on: **Communication:** • Observing critically **Decision-Making:** • Using math to solve problems and communicate • Solving problems and making decisions • Planning **Lifelong Learning:** • Using information and communications technololgy • Learning through research • Reflecting and evaluating	Many SCANS skills are incorporated in this unit with an emphasis on: • Mathematics • Social • Self-management • Responsibility • Problem-solving • Decision making	**VB:** 7.4.5 **1:** 1.5.1, 4.1.4, 2.5.5 **2:** 1.6.2 **3:** 7.4.2 **4:** 1.3.2, 7.4.2 **5:** 1.6.2, 7.4.2 **RV:** 7.2.1 **RE:** 4.9.3, 7.2.1, 7.4.4, 7.4.5, 7.4.6 **TP:** 4.8.1, 4.8.5, 4.8.6

Contents

● Grammar points that are new　　△ Grammar points that are being recycled　　◆ Grammar points that are presented in context

Numeracy/ Academic Skills	EFF	SCANS	CASAS
Unit 3 • Organize sentences effectively to convey meaning • Focused listening • Read and interpret information • Scan for details • Outline prior to writing • Write two paragraph essay • Research through interview and on the computer • Make calculations • Interpret a chart	**Many EFF skills are incorporated into this unit with an emphasis on:** **Communication:** • Observing critically **Decision-Making:** • Using math to solve problems and communicate • Solving problems and making decisions • Planning **Lifelong Learning:** • Using information and communications technololgy • Learning through research • Reflecting and evaluating	**Many SCANS skills are incorporated in this unit with an emphasis on:** • Mathematics • Reading • Writing • Listening • Negotiation • Decision making	VB: 7.4.5 1: 1.9.5 2: 1.9.6 3: 1.9.8 4: 1.9.3 5: 1.9.2 RV:7.2.1 RE:4.9.3, 7.2.1, 7.4.4, 7.4.5, 7.4.6 TP:4.8.1, 4.8.5, 4.8.6
Unit 4 • Understand and use parts of speech related to root words • Focused listening • Summarize reading passages • Scan for details • Skim for general ideas • Prepare and deliver an oral presentation • Research online	**Many EFF skills are incorporated into this unit with an emphasis on:** **Communication:** • Reading with understanding **Decision-Making:** • Solving problems and making decisions • Resolving conflict and negotiating • Cooperating with others **Lifelong Learning:** • Learning through research • Reflecting and evaluating	**Many SCANS skills are incorporated in this unit with an emphasis on:** • Problem-solving • Self-management • Reading • Mathematics • Creative thinking • Responsibility • Visualization	VB:7.4.5 1: 2.1.8 2: 1.4.3 3: 1.4.5 4: 1.4.6 5: 1.4.7, 1.4.8 RV:7.2.1 RE:4.9.3, 7.2.1, 7.4.4, 7.4.5, 7.4.6 TP:4.8.1, 4.8.5, 4.8.6
Unit 5 • Analyze and use root words and related parts of speech • Focused listening • Make calculations • Interview others • Understand bar graphs • Read a spread sheet • Brainstorm • Use reference materials including a computer	**Many EFF skills are incorporated into this unit with an emphasis on:** **Communication:** • Listening actively • Observing critically **Decision-Making:** • Using math to solve problems and communicate • Solving problems and making decisions • Resolving conflict and negotiating • Cooperating with others **Lifelong Learning:** • Using information and communications technology	**Many SCANS skills are incorporated in this unit with an emphasis on:** • Mathematics • Reading • Self-esteem • Self-management • Responsibility • Problem-solving • Visualization • Decision making	VB:7.4.5 1: 3.5.8, 3.5.9 2: 3.2.3, 3.2.4 3: 3.2.3, 3.4.5 4: 3.2.3 5: 3.4.3 RV:7.2.1 RE:4.9.3, 7.2.1, 7.4.4, 7.4.5, 7.4.6 TP:4.8.1, 4.8.5, 4.8.6

CONTENTS

● Grammar points that are new   △ Grammar points that are being recycled   ◆ Grammar points that are presented in context

	Numeracy/ Academic Skills	EFF	SCANS	CASAS
Unit 6	• Understand and use synonyms • Use reference materials • Research online • Use a computer to study • Take notes • Scan for main ideas and details • Brainstorm and construct arguments	Many EFF skills are incorporated into this unit with an emphasis on: **Communication:** • Reading with understanding • Speaking so others can understand • Listening actively **Decision-Making:** • Solving problems and making decisions • Resolving conflict and negotiating • Advocating and influencing • Cooperating with others **Lifelong Learning:** • Learning through research	Many SCANS skills are incorporated in this unit with an emphasis on: • Social interaction • Negotiation • Self-management • Decision making • Writing	VB: 7.4.5 1: 1.2.4, 1.2.3, 1.2.5, 6.4.1, 6.4.3, 7.4.4 2: 1.3.1, 1.3.3 3: 1.6.3, 1.6.4, 1.7.1 4: 1.3.3 5: 1.6.3 RV: 7.2.1 RE: 4.9.3, 7.2.1, 7.4.4, 7.4.5, 7.4.6 TP: 4.8.1, 4.8.5, 4.8.6
Unit 7	• Interpret visual representations • Understand root words and suffixes • Analyze and evaluate • Understand and write directions and reports • Focused listening • Summarize reading passages	Many EFF skills are incorporated into this unit with an emphasis on: **Communication:** • Reading with understanding • Conveying ideas in writing **Decision-Making:** • Solving problems and making decisions **Lifelong Learning:** • Using information and communications technololgy • Learning through research • Reflecting and evaluating	Many SCANS skills are incorporated in this unit with an emphasis on: • Social • Problem-solving • Visualization • Creative thinking • Negotiation • Teamwork • Leadership • Reading	VB: 4.5.1, 7.4.5 1: 4.4.8, 4.5.1, 4.5.4, 4.5.6 2: 4.5.7 3: 4.5.3, 4.7.2 4: 4.8.1, 4.8.5, 4.8.6 5: 4.6.4 RV: 7.2.1 RE: 4.9.3, 7.2.1, 7.4.4, 7.4.5, 7.4.6 TP: 4.8.1, 4.8.5, 4.8.6
Unit 8	• Interpret meanings of words in context • Focused listening • Scan for details • Skim for general ideas • Identify and paraphrase information • Analyze and evaluate • Interview others • Write a paragraph • Use transitional expressions in writing • Create visual representation to brainstorm • Write a speech	Many EFF skills are incorporated into this unit with an emphasis on: **Communication:** • Reading with understanding • Conveying ideas in writing • Speaking so others can understand • Listening actively **Decision-Making:** • Advocating and influencing • Cooperating with others **Lifelong Learning:** • Learning through research • Reflecting and evaluating • Taking responsibility for learning	Many SCANS skills are incorporated in this unit with an emphasis on: • Reading • Speaking • Responsibility • Cultural diversity • Decision making	VB: 7.4.5 1: 1.5.1, 5.3.6 2: 1.6.2, 5.2.2, 5.3.2, 5.7.1, 3: 5.6.2, 5.3.8, 7.4.2 4: 1.3.2, 5.3.7, 5.7.1, 7.4.2 5: 5.1.6, 5.7.1, 7.4.2 R: 7.2.1 RE: 4.9.3, 7.2.1, 7.4.4, 7.4.5, 7.4.6 IP: 4.8.1, 4.8.5, 4.8.6

Contents

Welcome to Stand Out

Stand Out works.

And now it works even better!

Built from the standards necessary for adult English learners, *Stand Out* gives students the foundation and tools they need to develop confidence and become independent, lifelong learners.

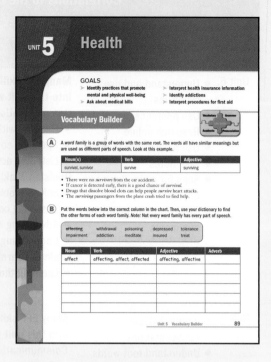

- State and federally required **life skills and competencies** are taught, helping students meet necessary benchmarks.

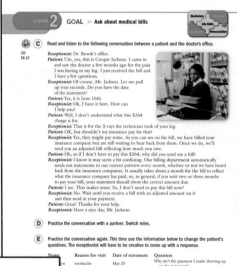

- Clearly defined **goals** provide a roadmap of learning for the student.
- **New to Level 5! The Vocabulary Builder** provides two full pages of exercises designed to draw out student knowledge of vocabulary and practice vocabulary used in each unit.

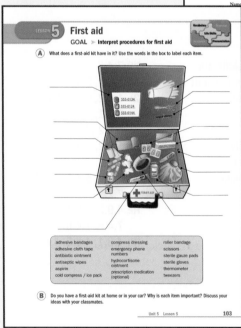

- Key **vocabulary** is introduced visually and orally.

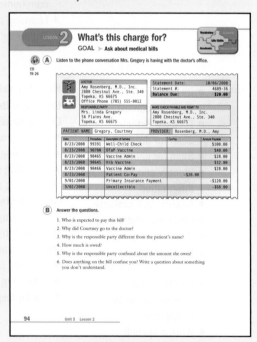

- A variety of **examples from real life**, like bills, insurance documents, contracts, newspaper ads, maps, etc. help students learn to access information and resources in their community.

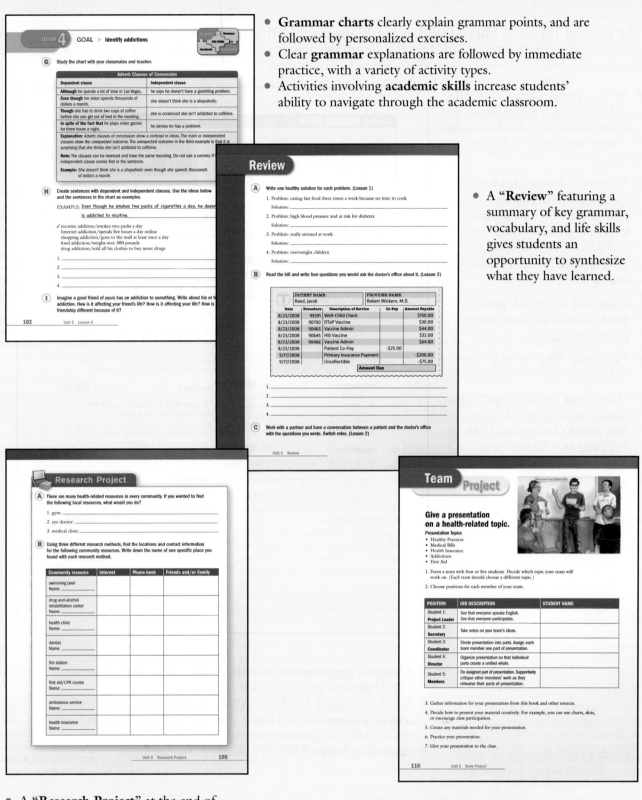

- **Grammar charts** clearly explain grammar points, and are followed by personalized exercises.
- Clear **grammar** explanations are followed by immediate practice, with a variety of activity types.
- Activities involving **academic skills** increase students' ability to navigate through the academic classroom.

- A **"Review"** featuring a summary of key grammar, vocabulary, and life skills gives students an opportunity to synthesize what they have learned.

- A **"Research Project"** at the end of each unit helps students become more competent at the academic skills needed for computer and library research.
- The **"Student Goals" Checklist** in the endmatter provides opportunities for learner self-assessment.

- **"Team Projects"** present motivating cross-ability activities which group learners of different levels together to complete a task that applies the unit objective.

The ground-breaking *Stand Out* **Lesson Planners** take the guesswork out of meeting the standards while offering high-interest, meaningful language activities, and three levels of pacing for each book.

- An **at-a-glance prep** and **agenda section** for each lesson ensure that instructors have a clear knowledge of what will be covered in the lesson.

- A complete **lesson plan** for each page in the student book is provided, following a standard lesson progression (Warm-up and Review, Introduction, Presentation, Practice, Evaluation, and Application).

- Clear, easy-to-identify **pacing guide** icons offer three different pacing strategies.

- **"Teaching Tips"** provide ideas and strategies for the classroom.

- **"Standards Correlations"** appear directly on the page, detailing how *Stand Out* meets CASAS, EFF, and SCANS standards.

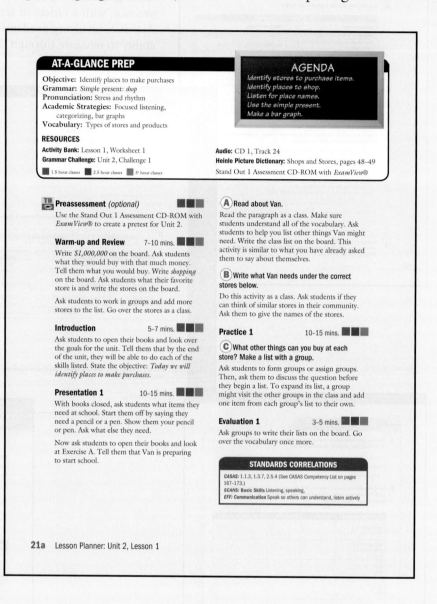

- Additional **supplemental activities** found on the *Activity Bank CD-ROM* are suggested at their point of use.
- The *Activity Bank CD-ROM* includes **reproducible multilevel activity masters** for each lesson that can be printed or downloaded and modified for classroom needs.
- **"Listening Scripts"** from the *Audio CD* are included.

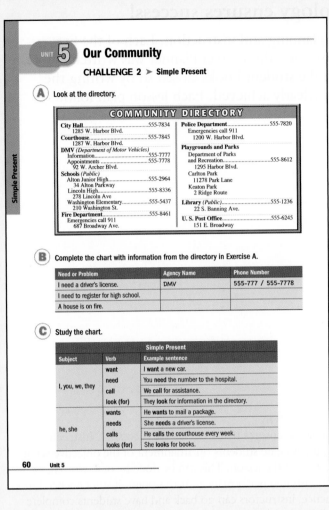

UNIT **5** **Our Community**

CHALLENGE 2 ➤ Simple Present

A Look at the directory.

COMMUNITY DIRECTORY

City Hall...............................555-7834	Police Department.....................555-7820
1285 W. Harbor Blvd.	Emergencies call 911
Courthouse...........................555-7845	1200 W. Harbor Blvd.
1287 W. Harbor Blvd.	**Playgrounds and Parks**
DMV *(Department of Motor Vehicles)*	Department of Parks
Information.....................555-7777	and Recreation...................555-8612
Appointments..................555-7778	1295 Harbor Blvd.
92 W. Archer Blvd.	Carlton Park
Schools *(Public)*	11278 Park Lane
Alton Junior High...............555-2964	Keaton Park
34 Alton Parkway	2 Ridge Route
Lincoln High......................555-8336	Library *(Public)*........................555-1236
278 Lincoln Ave	22 S. Banning Ave.
Washington Elementary.....555-5437	
210 Washington St.	U. S. Post Office......................555-6245
Fire Department..................555-8461	151 E. Broadway
Emergencies call 911	
687 Broadway Ave.	

B Complete the chart with information from the directory in Exercise A.

Need or Problem	Agency Name	Phone Number
I need a driver's license.	DMV	555-777 / 555-7778
I need to register for high school.		
A house is on fire.		

C Study the chart.

Simple Present		
Subject	Verb	Example sentence
I, you, we, they	want	I **want** a new car.
	need	You **need** the number to the hospital.
	call	We **call** for assistance.
	look (for)	They **look** for information in the directory.
he, she	wants	He **wants** to mail a package.
	needs	She **needs** a driver's license.
	calls	He **calls** the courthouse every week.
	looks (for)	She **looks** for books.

60 Unit 5

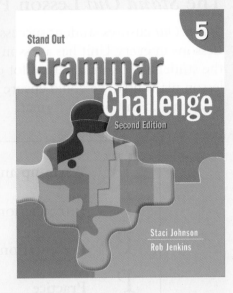

Stand Out

Grammar Challenge

Second Edition

Staci Johnson

Rob Jenkins

5

- *Grammar Challenge* workbooks include supplemental activities for students who desire even more contextual grammar and vocabulary practice.
- Clear and concise **grammar explanation boxes** provide a strong foundation for the activities.

D Complete the sentences with the correct form of the verb in the simple present.

1. Kenji _____ (need) the police immediately.
2. The women _____ (call) the hospital every hour.
3. He _____ (want) to mail a package to his mother in Columbia.
4. She _____ (look) for places to have a picnic in the city directory.
5. We _____ (call) the DMV when we buy a new car.
6. I _____ (like) the doctor on Main Street.
7. She _____ (prefer) to go to a park.
8. The nurse _____ (call) the doctor every day.
9. We _____ (eat) lunch at the restaurant on the corner.
10. The bus _____ (stops) on the corner of Main and Nutwood.
11. I _____ (visit) Marie on Saturdays.
12. My husband _____ (come) with me to the hospital.

E Write reasons why Raquel may call. What do you think?

1. (bank) Raquel needs money.
2. (dentist) Raquel
3. (shoe store) Raquel
4. (doctors) Raquel and Marie
5. (optometrist) Raquel
6. (hospital) Raquel and Mario
7. (DMV) Raquel
8. (fire department) Mario

F Write reasons why you may call a restaurant, a bank, and a rental car agency.

1. (restaurant) _____
2. (market) _____
3. (rental car agency) _____

Unit 5 **61**

- A variety of **activities** allow students develop their grammar skills and apply them.
- Written by **Rob Jenkins** and **Staci Johnson**, the *Grammar Challenge* workbooks are directly aligned to the student books.

The *Stand Out* Lesson Planner methodology ensures success!

Stand Out ensures student success through good lesson planning and instruction. Each of the five Lessons in every Unit has a lesson plan. Unlike most textbooks, the Lesson Planner was written before the student book materials. A lot of learning occurs with the student books closed so by writing the lesson plans first, we could ensure that each objective was clearly achieved. Each lesson plan follows a systematic and proven format:

W	**Warm-up and/or review**
I	**Introduction**
P	**Presentation**
P	**Practice**
E	**Evaluation**
A	**Application**

WARM-UP AND/OR REVIEW
The warm-up activities establish a context and purpose for the lesson. Exercises use previously learned content and materials that are familiar to students from previous lessons.

INTRODUCTION
In the introduction step, exercises focus the students' attention on the goals of the lesson by asking questions, showing visuals, telling a story, etc. Instructors should state the objective of the lesson and tell students what they will be doing. The objective should address what students are expected to be able to do by the end of the lesson.

PRESENTATION
The presentation activities provide students with the building blocks and skills they need to achieve the objectives set in the introduction. The exercises introduce new information to the students through visuals, realia, description, listenings, explanation, or written text. This is the time to check students' comprehension.

PRACTICE
Practice activities provide meaningful tasks for students to practice what they have just learned through different activities. These activities can be done as a class, in small groups, pairs, or individually. All of these activities are student centered and involve cooperative learning. Instructors should model each activity, monitor progress, and provide feedback.

EVALUATION
Evaluation ensures that students are successful. Instructors should evaluate students on attainment of the objective set at the start of the lesson. This can be done by oral, written, or demonstrated performance. At this point, if students need more practice, instructors can go back and have students complete additional practice activities before moving on to the application.

APPLICATION
Application activities help students apply new knowledge to their own lives or new situations. This is one of the most important steps of the lesson plan. If students can accomplish the application task, it will build their confidence to be able to use what they've learned out in the community. The Team Projects are an application of unit objectives that involves task-based activities with a product.

In addition to each lesson plan following the WIPPEA model, each unit in *Stand Out* follows this same approach. The first lesson is always an Introduction to the unit, introducing new vocabulary and the basic concepts that will be expanded upon in the unit. The following four lessons are the Presentations and Practices for the unit topic. Following the five lessons is a Review lesson, which allows students to practice everything they have already learned. In Level 5, the lesson that follows is an optional, level-appropriate Research Project that has students investigate the content of the lesson further. The final lesson is an Application for everything they learned in the unit in the form of a team project.

Text Credits

Pre-Unit
Page P10 Source: *Heinle Newbury House Dictionary of American English*, 4th edition

Unit 1
Page 7 "Educational Attainment and Earning Power for Men and Women 18 and Over" chart.
Source: U.S. Census Bureau, Current Population Survey 2006. Annual Social and Economic
Supplement.

Unit 2
Page 34 "The Four Keys to Great Credit" is used by permission. Liz Pulliam Weston is a personal finance columnist for **MSN Money** (Web site source: http://money.msn.com), where this article first appeared. Her column appears every Monday and Thursday, exclusively on *MSN Money*. She also answers reader questions in the Your Money message board.

Unit 3
Page 60 "Occupant Fatalities in 2004 by Age and Restraint Use in Passenger Vehicles"
Web site source: http://www.nhtsa.dot.gov
Page 61 "Facts on alcohol-related accidents"
Web site source: http://www.cdc.gov/ncipc/factsheets/drving.htm

Unit 4
Page 82 "Theft Prevention Newsletter" Web site source: http://www.jcsd.org/burglary_prevention.htm

Unit 5
Page 97 "Percentage of persons without health insurance, by three measurements and age group, and percentage of persons with health insurance, by coverage type and age group: United States, January, 2007–June, 2007" Source: Family Core component of the 2007 National Health Interview Survey. The estimates for 2007 are based on data collected January through June. Data are based on household interviews of a sample of the civilian non-institutionalized population.
Page 98 "Percentage of persons under 65 years of age without health insurance coverage at the time of interview, by age group and sex: United States, January, 2007–June, 2007" Source: Family Core component of the 2007 National Health Interview Survey. The estimates for 2007 are based on data collected January through June. Data are based on household interviews of a sample of the civilian non-institutionalized population.

Page 99 "Percentage of persons who lacked health insurance coverage at the time of interview, for at least part of the past year, or for more than a year, by selected demographic characteristics: United States, January, 2007–June, 2007."
Source: Family Core component of the 2007 National Health Interview Survey. The estimates for 2007 are based on data collected in January through June. Data are based on household interviews of a sample of the civilian non-institutionalized population.
Page 107 "Health Insurance Coverage of Adults 19–64 Living in Poverty, New York State (2005–2006)" Sources: Urban Institute and Kaiser Commission on Medicaid and the Uninsured estimates based on the Census Bureau's March 2006 and 2007 Current Population Survey (CPS: Annual Social and Economic Supplements). Web site source: http://www.statehealthfacts.org/comparebar.jsp?ind=131&cat=3

Unit 7
Page 143-146 "Conflict Resolution: Resolving Conflict Rationally and Effectively" Used with permission from ©Mind Tools Ltd, 1995–2008. All Rights Reserved.
Page 147 Progress report guidelines. Reprinted with permission from David A. McMurrey, author of *Power Tools for Technical Communication*, Boston: Heinle, 2001.

Unit 8
Page 158 U.S. Citizenship and Immigration Services, Web site source: www.uscis.gov
Page 163 "The Mothers' Club of Northville" Reprinted by permission of the City of Northville, MI.
Web site source: http://www.ci.northville.mi.us
Page 166 "Create Less Trash" and "In Your Home—Conserve Energy" Used with permission from Sustainable Environment for Quality of Life,
Web site source: www.seql.org
Page 167 "Carpooling—What is it?" Used with permission from Sustainable Environment for Quality of Life,
Web site source: www.seql.org

AT-A-GLANCE PREP

Objective: Get to know your classmates
Pronunciation: Enunciation
Academic Strategy: Public speaking
Vocabulary: Introductions

RESOURCES

Activity Bank: Pre-Unit, Lesson 1, Worksheet 1
Grammar Challenge 5: Pre-Unit, Challenge 1
Audio: CD Tracks 1–3

 1.5 hour classes 2.5 hour classes 3⁺ hour classes

AGENDA

Meet your classmates.
Make introductions and respond to
   introductions.
Introduce your classmates to one another.
Introduce your classmates to the class.

Stand Out 5 Assessment CD-ROM with Exam*View*®

Pre-assessment *(optional)*

Use the Stand Out 5 Assessment CD-ROM with Exam*View*® to create a pre-test for the Pre-Unit.

Warm-up and Review 5-10 mins.

As students enter your class for the first time, introduce yourself by giving them your name, saying *Nice to meet you*, and shaking their hands.

Introduction 10-20 mins.

Ask students to take out a piece of paper and number it from 1 to 4 for dictation. (To learn more about dictations, see the teaching tip on the next page.)

Dictation:

1. Liam is from France and would like to be a graphic designer.
2. Rani is from India and came here when her kids were in high school.
3. Haru just finished high school and needs to improve his writing skills.
4. Kimla came here four years ago and wants to study nursing.

State the objective: *Today you will be getting to know your classmates.*

Presentation 1 10-15 mins.

Ⓐ Read and listen to the conversation between Liam and Rani. Do you know people like them?

Ask students if they know anyone who has come to the United States to study for a career. Ask if they know anyone who has lived here for many years but is just now starting to study English.

> 🎧 **Listening Script** CD Track 1
>
> *The listening script matches the conversation in Exercise A.*

Ask a few volunteers to practice introducing themselves to you.

Practice 1 10-15 mins.

Ⓑ Using the conversation in Exercise A as an example, introduce yourself to four classmates.

Evaluation 1 5-10 mins.

Ⓒ Who are the four classmates you met? Write their names, where they are from, and something interesting you learned about them in the chart below.

Have students complete this chart on their own. Tell them that if they need to, they can talk to the students they met again to get the information correct.

STANDARDS CORRELATIONS

CASAS: 0.1.4, 7.2.1 (See CASAS Competency List on pages 187-193.)
SCANS: **Information** Acquire and evaluate information, organize and maintain information, interpret and communicate information
Interpersonal Participate as a member of a team, teach others, work with cultural diversity
Systems Monitor and correct performance
Basic Skills Reading, writing, listening, speaking

Thinking Skills Think creatively, make decisions
Personal Qualities Sociability
EFF: **Communication** Read with understanding, convey ideas in writing, speak so others can understand, listen actively, observe critically
Decision Making Plan
Interpersonal Cooperate with others

Getting to Know You

GOALS
➤ Get to know your classmates

➤ Talk about personal interests

➤ Write a personal letter

LESSON 1

Vocabulary | Grammar
Life Skills
Academic | Pronunciation

Classroom community

GOAL ➤ Get to know your classmates

Hi, my name is Liam. I am from France.

Nice to meet you, Rani. Why are you studying English?

I moved here so I could study at a university and learn how to be a graphic designer.

Agenda:
Dictation
Meet your classmates
Introduce your classmates

Nice to meet you, Liam. My name is Rani and I'm from India.

I have been here for over twenty years. I stay at home and help take care of my grandchildren while their parents work. But I finally decided to improve my English so I can help them with their school work. What about you?

CD
TR 1

A Read and listen to the conversation between Liam and Rani. Do you know people like them?
(Answers will vary.)

B Using the conversation in Exercise A as an example, introduce yourself to four classmates.

C Who are the four classmates you met? Write their names, where they are from, and something interesting you learned about them in the chart below.
(Answers will vary. Sample answers given.)

Name	Country	Interesting fact
Hamdi Mohamed	Somalia	Wants to be a doctor.

CD
TR 2

D Read and listen to the conversation between Liam, Rani, and Haru. What does Liam say to introduce Haru to Rani?

> Rani, I'd like you to meet Haru. He is from Japan and came here last year.

> It's a pleasure to meet you, Haru. You seem very young!

> Actually, I just finished high school, but my English writing still isn't good enough to go to college, so I'm going to study for one more year before I apply.

> Oh, that's smart. You remind me of my son. We came here when he was in high school, too.

E Study the expressions below.

Introduction	Responding to an introduction
I'd like to introduce you to _____.	(It's) A pleasure . . . to meet you.
I'd like you to meet _____.	. . . meeting you.
This is (friend's name) _____.	(I'm) Pleased to meet you.
Do you know _____?	(It's) Nice to meet you.
Have you met _____?	(It's) Good to meet you.

F Pair up with one of the classmates you have met. Introduce this person to four people in your class. Make sure you include the person's name, country, and an interesting fact about him or her in your introduction.

Teaching Tip

Dictation (*Listen–Repeat–Write* Method)

The purpose of dictation is for students to improve their active listening skills. In most real-world conversations, students will only hear things one time, but they should be able to get the general meaning from the phrases they catch and understand.

Dictation instructions for advanced-level students:

1. Tell students they will only be hearing each statement or question ONE time.
2. Tell them to listen FIRST with their pencils down and/or eyes closed.
3. Once they have heard the statement, tell them to say it quietly to themselves or in their heads.
4. Once they have listened to the statement and repeated it to themselves, tell them to write it down.

Dictation instructions for the teacher:

1. Read each statement once, giving students enough time to write it down. Do not repeat.
2. Once all of the statements have been read and written, read each one again, more quickly this time, just giving students enough time to make small corrections.
3. Ask students to share their dictation with a person sitting next to them and fill in what they missed or make corrections.
4. Ask volunteers to come to the board and write each statement.
5. Tell students they can come to the board and correct any mistakes they see.
6. When the class agrees that the dictation is correct, read the statements on the board yourself and indicate which statements are indeed correct and which ones still contain errors. Allow volunteers to come to the board and make corrections. Go through this process until everything on the board is correct.

Note: Students who are not familiar with this style of dictation will find it difficult at first, but, as the course progresses, they will be proud of how much their active listening skills have improved.

Presentation 2

5–10 mins.

D Read and listen to the conversation between Liam, Rani, and Haru. What does Liam say to introduce Haru to Rani?

> **Listening Script** CD Track 2
>
> *The listening script matches the conversation in Exercise D.*

E Study the expressions below.

Discuss the expressions with students. Discuss which ones are formal and which ones are informal. Then read each expression out loud and have students practice repeating it after you with correct intonation.

Practice 2

10–15 mins. ▪▪

Note: Shorter classes can practice making introductions with their family and friends at home.

F Pair up with one of the classmates you have met. Introduce this person to four people in your class. Make sure you include the person's name, country, and an interesting fact about him or her in your introduction.

Help facilitate this activity by making sure that everyone is included.

Evaluation 2

▪▪

Observe.

Presentation 3 5–10 mins.

 G Read and listen to Haru as he introduces Kimla to the class.

> 🎧 **Listening Script** CD Track 3
>
> *The listening script matches the conversation in Exercise G.*

Practice 3 10–15 mins. ■

Note: Shorter classes can do Exercise H for homework. If students are doing the exercise for homework, assign each student a different person to write about so that each student in the class gets introduced at least once.

H Choose two people that you have met in class today. Write introductions for them below. Use Haru's introduction in Exercise G as an example.

Help students choose the person they will write introductions for so that each student in the class is being written about at least once.

Evaluation 3 5–10 mins. ■

Walk around the classroom and help students. Make sure they include the appropriate information. When students have finished, they can practice reading their introductions to you. Help them with their enunciation.

Pronunciation

Enunciation

It is important for ESL/EFL students to clearly articulate words and phrases when they are having conversations or giving speeches. Help students improve their enunciation by having them speak slowly and clearly. If you have time to work individually with students, point out which words, letters, or sounds they should work on.

Application 15–25 mins. ■■■

Shorter classes who did not do Exercise H in class can choose someone they met at this class meeting and introduce the person to the class.

I Choose one of the people from Exercise H to introduce to the class.

Have each student stand in the front of the classroom or near the person he or she is introducing. Students may choose to read the introduction they wrote in their books or do it off the top of their heads.

Activity Bank

> Pre-Unit, Lesson 1, Worksheet 1: Introductions
> (listening)

📖 Refer students to *Stand Out 5 Grammar Challenge*, Pre-Unit, Challenge 1 for more practice with introductions.

Instructor's Notes

_____
_____
_____
_____
_____
_____
_____
_____
_____
_____
_____
_____
_____
_____
_____
_____
_____
_____
_____

LESSON 1   **GOAL** ▸ **Get to know your classmates**

CD
TR 3

G Read and listen to Haru as he introduces Kimla to the class.

Nice to meet you, Kimla.

I'd like you to meet Kimla. She came here with her family from Saudi Arabia four years ago. She has been studying English for three years now and would like to become a registered nurse. She hopes to apply to a nursing program at the end of this semester.

H Choose two people that you have met in class today. Write introductions for them below. Use Haru's introduction in Exercise G as an example. (Answers will vary.)

Name of classmate: _____

Information about classmate: _____

_____

_____

Name of classmate: _____

Information about classmate: _____

_____

_____

I Choose one of the people from Exercise H to introduce to the class.

What are your hobbies?

GOAL ➤ **Talk about personal interests**

A Look at the pictures of Haru, Rani, and Kimla. What do you think their personal interests are? Write them on the lines below the pictures.

playing video games   taking photographs   reading

 B Listen to the conversation between Haru, Rani, and Kimla. Then answer the questions below.

CD
TR 4

1. What kind of video games does Haru like to play? _adventure/problem solving_

2. What are three types of reading Kimla likes to do? _fiction, biographies, newspaper/magazin_

3. What kind of pictures does Rani like to take? _nature photography_

4. Where does Haru play his video games? _on the TV_

5. What doesn't Haru like to do? _reading_

6. How late does Kimla stay up reading? _until 2 in the morning_

7. Who does Haru remind Rani of? _her son_

8. What gift did Rani's son give her? _an SLR digital camera_

C Share your answers with a partner.

Objective: Talk about personal interests
Pronunciation: Enunciation
Vocabulary: Personal interests

RESOURCES

Activity Bank: Pre-Unit, Lesson 2, Worksheets 1–2
Grammar Challenge 5: Pre-Unit, Challenge 2

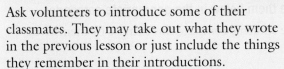

■ 1.5 hour classes ■ 2.5 hour classes ■ 3+ hour classes

AGENDA

Discuss personal interests.
Ask about personal interests.

Audio: CD Track 4

Warm-up and Review   5-10 mins. ■■■

Ask volunteers to introduce some of their classmates. They may take out what they wrote in the previous lesson or just include the things they remember in their introductions.

Pronunciation

Enunciation

Throughout the book there will be opportunities for students to give a presentation or speak out loud to the class. Teach them how important it is to speak clearly so they can be understood. Encourage students to speak slowly and clearly. As practice have each student stand up and read a sentence or two out loud. Have students focus on speaking clearly while they are reading the sentences. This is a simple exercise but it will give students an idea of how they sound to others as well as giving timid students more opportunities to practice their speech.

Introduction   10-20 mins. ■■■

Note: See the teaching tip on page P2a for a method to use while giving students a dictation.

Dictation:

1. Jason's hobbies are watching movies and playing soccer.
2. In her free time, Jenni likes to play the piano and write in her journal.
3. Kevin's personal interests are photography and digital video editing.
4. John and Maggie like to cook and throw parties.

State the objective: *Today we will talk about our personal interests.*

Presentation 1   5 mins. ■■■

 A Look at the pictures of Haru, Rani, and Kimla. What do you think their personal interests are? Write them on the lines below the pictures.

Practice 1   10-15 mins. ■■■

 B Listen to the conversation between Haru, Rani, and Kimla. Then, answer the questions below.

See the listening script on page P5a.

Evaluation 1   5 mins. ■■■

 C Share your answers with a partner.

After the students review with their partner, go over the answers as a class.

STANDARDS CORRELATIONS

CASAS: 0.2.4 (See CASAS Competency List on pages 187-193.)
SCANS: **Information** Acquire and evaluate information, interpret and communicate information
Interpersonal Participate as a member of a team, work with cultural diversity
Systems Monitor and correct performance

Basic Skills Reading, writing, listening, speaking
Thinking Skills Think creatively, make decisions
Personal Qualities Responsibility, sociability, self-management
EFF: **Communication** Read with understanding, convey ideas in writing, speak so others can understand, listen actively
Interpersonal Cooperate with others

Listening Script   CD Track 4

Haru: *So, Mrs. Morgan wants us to talk about our personal interests. What do you think she means by "personal interests?"*

Rani: *I think she means, "What do we like to do when we are not at school or not working?"*

Kimla: *I think you're right, Rani. When I'm not working or at school, I like to read. Not schoolbooks but fiction and biographies, newspapers, magazines— anything I can get my hands on. Sometimes, I'm up until two in the morning, just reading.*

Haru: *Wow, that's impressive! I hate reading, which made it pretty hard to get through my last year of high school. I like to play video games. Just like you can read for hours, I can sit and stare at a TV screen for hours, playing games. My favorite kinds of games are adventure where you have to solve problems to get to the next level.*

Rani: *I know I've said it before, but you remind me so much of my son. He likes video games, too. Although now that he has a family, he doesn't get to play them as much anymore. In my free time, I like to take pictures. My son and his wife gave me a new SLR digital camera and it takes such amazing pictures! My favorite type of photography is nature photography, so I'm outdoors a lot.*

Kimla: *That's great, Rani. The three of us have such varied interests. It's so fun to hear about what other people do when they aren't at school.*

Presentation 2   5–10 mins. ■■■

 People have many different types of interests. Look at the three categories of interests below. Can you think of some examples for each category?

Write the terms *Physical, Creative,* and *Mental/ Emotional* on the board. Ask students to give you some examples of activities that could go in each of these categories without looking in their books. Write their ideas on the board.

Practice 2   10–15 mins. ■■

Note: Shorter classes can do these exercises for homework.

 Working with a small group, put each of the activities below into the circle you think is most appropriate. Some activities may belong in more than one circle.

Draw a three circle Venn diagram and show how interests that cross over into two or three category terms can be placed where the circles intersect.

Pre-Unit, Lesson 2, Worksheet 1: List of Personal Interests

Evaluation 2   10–15 mins. ■■

Ask volunteers to come to the board and write the activities under each category head that you wrote in the presentation. Then, see if the class can come up with more examples for each category.

 Now think about your own personal interests. Write them below in the appropriate categories.

Have students complete this exercise by themselves.

Instructor's Notes

_____
_____
_____
_____
_____
_____
_____
_____
_____
_____
_____
_____
_____
_____
_____
_____
_____
_____
_____
_____

GOAL ➤ **Talk about personal interests**

D People have many different types of interests. Look at the three categories of interests below. Can you think of some examples for each category? (Answers may vary.)

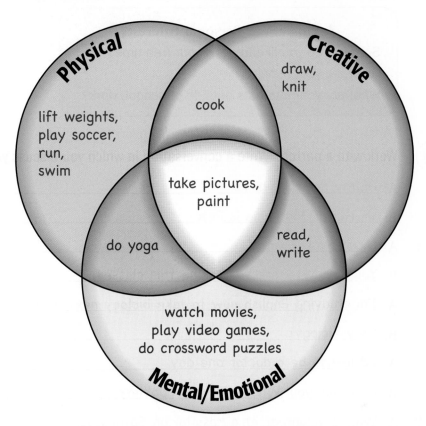

Physical
Creative

lift weights, play soccer, run, swim

cook

draw, knit

take pictures, paint

do yoga

read, write

watch movies, play video games, do crossword puzzles

Mental/Emotional

E Working with a small group, put each of the activities below into the circle you think is most appropriate. Some activities may belong in more than one circle. (Answers may vary.)

cook	lift weights	run
do crossword puzzles	paint	swim
do yoga	play soccer	take pictures
draw	play video games	watch movies
knit	read	write

F Now think about your own personal interests. Write them in the appropriate categories. (Answers will vary.)

Physical: _____

Creative: _____

Mental/Emotional: _____

GOAL ➤ **Talk about personal interests**

 How would you ask people about their personal interests? Study the phrases below.

> **Asking about Personal Interests**
> So, what do you like to do in your free time?
> What are your hobbies?
> What are your interests outside of school/work?

(Answers will vary. Sample answers given.)

 Work with a partner. Write a conversation in which you discuss your personal interests.

A: Hi. My name is Hamdi.

B: Hi, Hamdi. My name is Peter.

A: Nice to meet you.

B: You, too. Why are you taking this class?

A: I'm studying English now to take biology next year.

B: Why biology?

A: I'd like to be a doctor one day.

B: Good for you! What are your hobbies?

A: Well, I volunteer at a hospital on Saturdays.

B: I volunteer too. I work in a free food kitchen.

A: That's a nice thing to do. What do you do in your free time?

B: I like to run for exercise. I also play chess.

A: Me too! I love playing chess.

B: Maybe we can have a game after class one day.

I In a small group, discuss your personal interests. When you have finished, share what you have learned about each other with the rest of the class.

Presentation 3   5-10 mins. ■■■

G How would you ask people about their personal interests? Study the phrases below.

Go over the expressions with the class. Have them repeat after you and practice their intonation. Ask students to think back to Rani and Kimla. Ask them to imagine that they are writing a conversation in which the two women will discuss their personal interests. As a class, write a conversation on the board.

Practice 3   10-15 mins. ■

Note: Shorter classes can do this exercise for homework. Students can either create an imaginary person to have a conversation with or use a friend or family member.

H Work with a partner. Write a conversation in which you discuss your personal interests.

Evaluation 3   10-15 mins. ■

Observe and help as necessary. Have volunteer partners read their conversation in front of the class. Help students understand what a native English speaker would say in these situations.

Application   10-20 mins. ■■■

I In a small group, discuss your personal interests. When you have finished, share what you have learned about each other with the rest of the class.

Suggestion: Put students in small groups by having them *number* or *count off*. (See the Teaching Tip on this page.) This technique will ensure that students who may have never met before get to work together. When the groups have finished their discussions, ask for each group to share what they learned about its members.

Teaching Tip

Group work

The ability to work together in groups is important for students at this level. Group size should be limited to five; four is usually the ideal number of students for maximum participation. A variety of grouping strategies are suggested below. The type of strategy you use to group students should depend on the type of task they are doing.

1. Allow students to self-select groups. Students sometimes perform well with friends or people they feel comfortable with.

2. Arrange groups according to students' language level. Sometimes proficient students will excel when working in groups with other proficient students. Likewise, less proficient students won't feel intimidated by working with more proficient students and, consequently, will take more risks.

3. Arrange students in cross- or diverse-ability groups. More proficient students often enjoy helping less proficient students, and you'll have several mentors in the class instead of just one teacher.

4. Group students by having them "number off." Using this technique, students count one to four (or more depending on the desired number of groups). Students then go to the group of students that shares their "number." This grouping method ensures that students get to know students other than their friends.

5. To encourage the use of English, avoid putting students in homogeneous language groups whenever possible.

Activity Bank

Pre-Unit, Lesson 2, Worksheet 2: Personal Interests
                     Conversations
                     (listening)

Refer students to *Stand Out 5 Grammar Challenge*, Pre-Unit, Challenge 2 for more practice with conversation strategies.

AT-A-GLANCE PREP

Objective: Write a personal letter
Grammar: Error correction
Academic Strategy: Personal writing
Vocabulary: *feel like I belong, added responsibility, pretty tough, professional guidance*

RESOURCES

Activity Bank: Pre-Unit, Lesson 3, Worksheet 1
Grammar Challenge 5: Pre-Unit, Challenge 3
Suggested Realia: Personal letters

▮ 1.5 hour classes ▮ 2.5 hour classes ▮ 3+ hour classes

AGENDA

Read Liam's e-mail.
Practice vocabulary.
Discuss writing personal letters.
Read Liam's thank-you note.
Read Rani's e-mail.
Write a personal letter.

Stand Out 5 Assessment CD-ROM with Exam*View®*

Warm-up and Review   5–10 mins. ▮▮▮

Have students get in different small groups from the ones they were in during the previous class meeting and discuss their personal interests.

Introduction   5–10 mins. ▮▮▮

Note: For more information on dictations, see the teaching tip on page P2a.

Dictation:

1. I've met a lot of great friends at school and I'm really starting to feel like I belong here.
2. It was so thoughtful of you to remember us on our special day.
3. Both of our sons are married now with families of their own.
4. I really miss you and hope you can find some time to come out and visit.

State the objective: *Today you will be reading and writing personal letters.*

Presentation 1   10–15 mins. ▮▮▮

 Read the e-mail message that Liam wrote to his family.

Read Liam's letter as a class. You can read the letter out loud to the class or you can call on students to read the different paragraphs.

 This is a personal letter, not a formal letter. How can you tell that this letter is personal?

Discuss the different aspects of the letter that make it personal, such as the informal greeting, the fact that there is no return address, and informal language used throughout.

Practice 1   10–15 mins. ▮▮▮

 What do you think the following expressions mean?

Have students work in small groups to come up with the meanings for these expressions.

Evaluation 1   5–15 mins. ▮▮▮

Go over the answers as a class. As an added practice, have students write sentences using these expressions. More specifically, have them write sentences they might write in a personal letter to a friend or family member.

STANDARDS CORRELATIONS

CASAS: 0.2.3 (See CASAS Competency List on pages 187–193.)
SCANS: **Information** Acquire and evaluate information, use computers to process information (optional)
Interpersonal Participate as a member of a team, teach others, negotiate to arrive at a decision, work with cultural diversity
Systems Monitor and correct performance
Technology Apply technology to a task (optional)

Basic Skills Reading, writing
Thinking Skills Think creatively, make decisions
Personal Qualities Responsibility, sociability, self-management
EFF: **Communication** Read with understanding, convey ideas in writing
Decision Making Plan
Interpersonal Cooperate with others
Lifelong Learning Use information and communications technology (optional)

Dear friend

GOAL ➤ Write a personal letter

A Read the e-mail message that Liam wrote to his family.

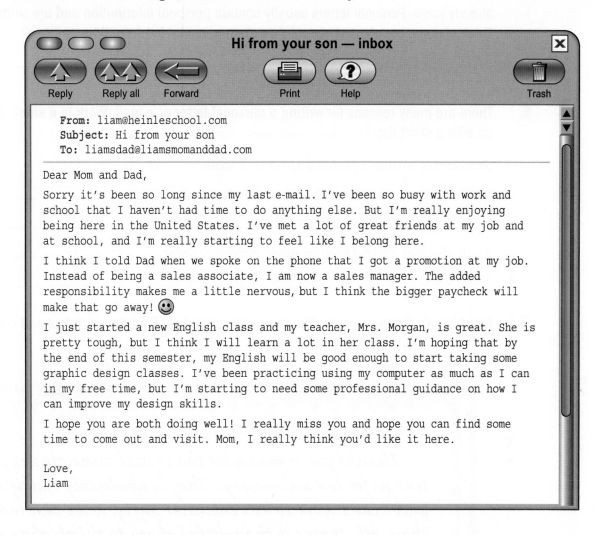

Hi from your son — inbox ☒

Reply   Reply all   Forward   Print   Help   Trash

From: liam@heinleschool.com
Subject: Hi from your son
To: liamsdad@liamsmomanddad.com

Dear Mom and Dad,

Sorry it's been so long since my last e-mail. I've been so busy with work and school that I haven't had time to do anything else. But I'm really enjoying being here in the United States. I've met a lot of great friends at my job and at school, and I'm really starting to feel like I belong here.

I think I told Dad when we spoke on the phone that I got a promotion at my job. Instead of being a sales associate, I am now a sales manager. The added responsibility makes me a little nervous, but I think the bigger paycheck will make that go away! ☺

I just started a new English class and my teacher, Mrs. Morgan, is great. She is pretty tough, but I think I will learn a lot in her class. I'm hoping that by the end of this semester, my English will be good enough to start taking some graphic design classes. I've been practicing using my computer as much as I can in my free time, but I'm starting to need some professional guidance on how I can improve my design skills.

I hope you are both doing well! I really miss you and hope you can find some time to come out and visit. Mom, I really think you'd like it here.

Love,
Liam

B This is a personal letter, not a formal letter. How can you tell that this letter is personal?

Liam writes informally about personal activities, his emotions, and signs it using "Love".

C What do you think the following expressions mean? (Answers may vary. Sample answers are given.)

1. feel like I belong I am a part of something

2. pretty tough a little difficult

3. added responsibility more duties

4. professional guidance pay someone for advice

GOAL ➤ **Write a personal letter**

D A personal letter is a letter that you write to a family member, a friend, or someone who you already know. Personal letters usually contain personal information and are written informally. Think of some people that you might write a personal letter to. Who are they?

family members and friends

E There are many reasons for writing a personal letter or e-mail. Work in a small group to come up with a short list. (Answers will vary. Sample answers are given.)

Reasons for writing a personal letter or e-mail:

1. to thank someone for a gift, a dinner, or a favor

2. to ask about someone's health

3. to say you were thinking about/miss someone

4. to make plans to get together in the future

F Read Liam's thank-you note. There are nine mistakes. Find the mistakes and correct them.

Dear Aunt Claire and Uncle Laurent,

Thanks you so much for the crystal wine glasses you sent us for our aniversary. They is absolutely beutiful and I cant wait to has a dinner party, so we can show them off. It was so thoughtful of you to think of us on our special day. I hope you are both doing well and we hopes to see you soon!

Sincerely,

Liam

Love /

are

have

G Rewrite Liam's note on a separate piece of paper. Correct the mistakes.

Presentation 2   5-10 mins. ■■■

(D) A personal letter is a letter that you write to a family member, a friend, or someone who you already know. Personal letters usually contain personal information and are written informally. Think of some people that you might write a personal letter to. Who are they?

As a class, make a list of people that personal letters could be written to.

Practice 2   10-15 mins. ■■

Note: Shorter classes can do this exercise for homework.

(E) There are many reasons for writing a personal letter or e-mail. Work in a small group to come up with a short list.

Evaluation 2   10-15 mins. ■■

As a class, create a list on the board from all the different groups' responses.

Presentation 3   5-10 mins. ■■■

Circle *thank-you note* from the list on the board if your students came up with it in Evaluation 2. If they did not think of it before, add it to the list now. Ask students when they might write thank-you notes.

Practice 3   15-20 mins. ■

Note: Shorter classes can do this exercise for homework.

(F) Read Liam's thank-you note. There are nine mistakes. Find the mistakes and correct them.

Evaluation 3   5-10 mins. ■

Go over the answers as a class.

(G) Rewrite Liam's note on a separate piece of paper. Correct the mistakes.

Refer students to *Stand Out 5 Grammar Challenge*, Pre-Unit, Challenge 3 for more practice with editing.

Instructor's Notes

Application   10-20 mins. ◼◼◼

(H) Mrs. Morgan asked her class to choose someone they had just met in class and send that person an e-mail. Read the e-mail that Rani wrote to Kimla.

Have students read the letter quietly to themselves and then discuss it as a class.

(I) Now choose one of the classmates you recently met and write this person a personal letter about yourself on a separate piece of paper.

Optional Computer Activity: If students have e-mail accounts, these letters can be written online and transmitted electronically.

Teaching Tip

Technology in the classroom

If you have access to computers, set up e-mail accounts for all the students in your class so they communicate with you as well as with one another. There are a number of free e-mail services offered on the Web, including Google™, Yahoo™ and MSN Hotmail™.

Suggestion: Print out the online form that students will have to fill out to apply for a free e-mail account. Help them fill out all the information correctly before they submit the form online. It is a good idea for students to come up with a variety of user names in advance since the ones they choose may have already been taken by other e-mail users. Discuss with them the importance of safe but easy to remember passwords.

Activity Bank

Pre-Unit, Lesson 3, Worksheet 1: Personal Letters

Teaching Tip

Correcting errors

For certain activities, it is not important to correct student errors. Since the purpose of this letter is to communicate something personal, error correction is not necessary as long as the letter's meaning can be understood by the reader.

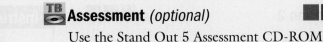

Assessment *(optional)*

Use the Stand Out 5 Assessment CD-ROM with Exam*View*® to create a post-test for the Pre-Unit.

Instructor's Notes

_____

_____

_____

_____

_____

_____

_____

_____

_____

_____

_____

_____

_____

_____

_____

_____

_____

_____

_____

_____

_____

_____

_____

_____

_____

_____

LESSON 3

GOAL ➤ **Write a personal letter**

H Mrs. Morgan asked her class to choose someone they had just met in class and send them an e-mail. Read the e-mail that Rani wrote to Kimla.

Nice to meet you!

| File | Edit | View | Isert | Format | Tools | Action | Help | Type a question here |

Reply | Reply to all | Forward | Print | Delete

From: Your friend Rani <rani@heinleschool.com>
Subject: Nice to meet you!
To: kimla@heinleschool.com

Dear Kimla,

It was so nice to meet you in class the other day. I really enjoyed learning some new things about you. I'd like to tell you a little bit more about myself.

My family came over here from India 20 years ago so that our children could finish up their education here. We wanted to give them as many opportunities as possible, and we had heard such good things about the higher education system in the United States. We have two sons, both of whom are married now with families of their own. I take care of the four grandchildren during the day before and after school.

Someday, when the kids are grown up and don't need me anymore, I would like to take some photography classes. I don't know if I will ever do anything professional with photography, but it is so intriguing to me and I would like to learn more. So that's a little bit about me.

I do hope to know you better as our class goes along. You seem like such a nice young woman, and I hope that we can be friends.

Sincerely,
Rani

I Now choose one of the classmates you recently met and write this person a personal letter about yourself on a separate piece of paper. (Answers will vary.)

Research Project

Who do you know? What do they know?

(A) *Research* is defined as "a study of information about something." *To research* something is "to study something deeply." A synonym for the verb *research* is *investigate*.

(Source: *Heinle Newbury House Dictionary of American English*, 4th edition)

(Answers will vary. See sample answer below.)

At the end of each unit in this book, you will be learning a new research strategy. Why is learning how to conduct research important? Discuss your ideas with your classmates.

To find the best information you need.

(B) Let's say you want to find out where the best Japanese restaurant is in town. How would you research this topic? Write down your ideas. (Sample answers are given.)

Ask friends who like sushi or research online.

(C) Talking to people is one of the best ways to do research. Talk to your classmates about the following topics. Write down the best ideas you get for each topic. (Answers will vary.)

1. the best place to buy a new computer: _____

_____

2. the closest bank: _____

_____

3. how to find a good babysitter: _____

_____

4. ideas for saving money: _____

_____

Share your research with your classmates.

(D) What else do you want to know? Think of a topic and then do some research! Remember to ask your classmates for ideas. (Answers will vary. Sample answer is given.)

What I want to know: _a good place for rap music_

My research findings: _____

_____

_____

AT-A-GLANCE PREP

Objective: Conduct research by talking to people
Academic Strategy: Research
Vocabulary: *research*

RESOURCES

Activity Bank: Pre-Unit, Research, Worksheet 1

AGENDA

Find information about
different topics.
Talk to your classmates.

Warm-up and Review   5-10 mins.

Have students take out the personal letters they wrote in the previous class. Ask a few volunteers to read their letters out loud. If they haven't already done so, ask them to share their letters with the classmates they wrote them to.

Introduction   1 min.

Read the research project title. State the objective: *Today you will conduct research by talking to your classmates.*

Presentation   10-15 mins.

Write the word *research* on the board and have students help you define it. Then direct them to the definition in their books.

(A) *Research* is defined as "a study of information about something." *To research* something is "to study something deeply." A synonym for the verb *research* is *investigate.*
(Source: *Heinle's Newbury House Dictionary of American English, 4th edition*)

At the end of each unit in this book, you will be learning a new research strategy. Why is learning how to conduct research important? Discuss your ideas with your classmates.

Write student ideas on the board.

(B) Let's say you want to find out where the best Japanese restaurant is in town. How would you research this topic? Write down your ideas.

Have students do this exercise by themselves and then share their ideas with the class.

Practice   10-15 mins.

(C) Talking to people is one of the best ways to do research. Talk to your classmates about the following topics. Write down the best ideas you get for each topic.

Share your research with the class.

Evaluation   5-10 mins.

Go over the responses as a class.

Application   10-15 mins.

(D) What else do you want to know? Think of a topic and then do some research! Remember to ask your classmates for ideas.

Activity Bank

Pre-Unit, Research, Worksheet 1: Talking to People

STANDARDS CORRELATIONS

CASAS: 7.4.4 (See CASAS Competency List on pages 187–193.)
SCANS: **Information** Acquire and evaluate information, organize and maintain information, interpret and communicate information
Interpersonal Participate as a member of a team, teach others, work with cultural diversity
Basic Skills Writing, listening, speaking

Personal Qualities Responsibility, sociability, self-management
EFF: **Communication** Listen actively
Interpersonal Cooperate with others, advocate and influence, resolve conflict and negotiate, guide others
Lifelong Learning Take responsibility for learning, learn through research

Objective: Introduce new vocabulary
Academic Strategies: Categorizing vocabulary, using a dictionary
Vocabulary: See lesson

RESOURCES

Dictionaries: It is recommended that each student in class have an ESL learner's dictionary or that dictionaries be made available in the classroom for students to use. Dictionaries that will be referred to in this book are the

AGENDA

Read about students in Stand Out 5.
Categorize vocabulary.
Find out what you know.
Use a dictionary.

Heinle's Newbury House Dictionary of American English and the *Collins Cobuild Intermediate* or *Advanced Dictionary of American English.*

Academic Feature: Vocabulary Builder

Each unit in *Stand Out 5* will begin with a vocabulary-building section. The purpose of this two-page section is to introduce students to many of the words they will be using in the unit lessons. Students will have a chance to see how much they already know, and they will get exposure to the new vocabulary found in the unit.

Note: All of the exercises on these two pages should be done in class, no matter the class length. Longer classes can do this lesson and then move onto Lesson 1 during the same class meeting; shorter classes may have to devote one whole class meeting to this lesson.

Introduction   5–10 mins.

State the objective: *Today we will be identifying and working with the vocabulary you will learn in this unit.*

Presentation 1   10–15 mins.

(A) Read about these students. What can you learn about each person? Discuss with a small group.

Practice 1   10–15 mins.

(B) You will study the following ideas in this unit. What do you think each expression means? Write your own thoughts.

Have students complete this exercise by themselves.

Evaluation 1   5–10 mins.

Go over students' ideas as a class. Help students arrive at the correct definition.

STANDARDS CORRELATIONS

CASAS: 7.4.5 (See CASAS Competency List on pages 187–193.)
SCANS: **Information** Acquire and evaluate information, organize and maintain information
Interpersonal Participate as a member of a team, negotiate to arrive at a decision, work with cultural diversity
Systems Understand systems, monitor and correct performance
Basic Skills Reading, writing, listening, speaking
Thinking Skills Think creatively, make decisions, see things in the mind's eye

Personal Qualities Responsibility, sociability, self-management
EFF: **Communication** Read with understanding, convey ideas in writing, speak so others can understand, listen actively
Decision Making Use math to solve problems and communicate, solve problems and make decisions, plan
Interpersonal Cooperate with others
Lifelong Learning Take responsibility for learning, reflect and evaluate, learn through research

Balancing Your Life

GOALS

➤ **Identify your learning style**

➤ **Identify a career path**

➤ **Balance your life**

➤ **Identify and prioritize goals**

➤ **Motivate yourself**

Vocabulary Builder

A Read about these students. What can you learn about each person?
Discuss with a small group.

Learning Style:
visual
Career Path:
graphic designer
Motivation:
financial

Liam

Learning Style:
visual
Career Path:
photographer
Motivation:
joy

Rani

Learning Style:
tactile
Career Path:
computer
programmer
Motivation:
fun

Haru

Learning Style:
auditory
Career Path:
registered nurse
Motivation:
time with family

Kimla

B You will study the following ideas in this unit. What do you think each expression means?
Write your own thoughts. (Answers will vary. Suggested answers are given.)

1. Learning style: <u>A person's best way of learning</u>

2. Career path: <u>The education and training to follow to achieve a career</u>

3. Motivation: <u>An idea, goal, or emotion that inspires a person</u>

Vocabulary Builder

C Below are groups of vocabulary words that you will be working with in this unit. Make your best guess as to which topic goes with each group of phrases. Write the appropriate topic on the line above each group of words.

Topics

Career Path	Learning Styles	Multiple Intelligences
Goal Setting	Motivation	

1. _Learning Styles_
   auditory
   tactile/kinesthetic
   visual

2. _Motivation_
   earning power
   pursue
   educational attainment

3. _Multiple Intelligences_
   auditory
   bodily/rhythmic
   interpersonal
   intrapersonal
   logical

4. _Multiple Intelligences_
   naturalistic
   spatial
   verbal/linguistic
   visual
   tactile/kinesthetic

5. _Goal Setting_
   achieve
   balance
   long-term
   motivate
   prioritize
   short-term

6. _Career Path_
   be flexible
   evaluate progress
   inspire
   monitor progress
   positive outlook
   support

D Put a check next to each term you are familiar with.

E Choose two new terms from Exercise C that you would like to know the meanings of. Look the items up in a dictionary. Write the word, part of speech, definition, word forms, and the example sentence—if there is one—that you find in each dictionary entry. An example has been done for you.

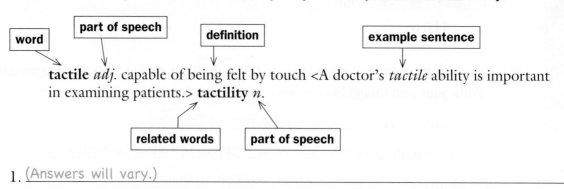

tactile *adj.* capable of being felt by touch <A doctor's *tactile* ability is important in examining patients.> **tactility** *n.*

1. _(Answers will vary.)_

2. _____

Presentation 2
5–10 mins.

C Below are groups of vocabulary words that you will be working with in this unit. Make your best guess as to which topic goes with each group of phrases. Write the appropriate topic on the line above each group of words.

Have students work with a partner to come up with topics for each group. Then go over the answers as a class.

Pronunciation

Vocabulary

When teaching students new vocabulary, pronounce each word for them several times and ask them to repeat it. Often, students may have heard the words you are introducing but have never seen them spelled out. By pronouncing a word for students, you allow students to make a connection between the word's spelling and its sound. It is also important that students learn the correct pronunciation of new words so they feel comfortable using their new vocabulary inside and outside of the classroom.

Practice 2
10–15 mins.

D Put a check next to each term you are familiar with.

E Choose two new terms from Exercise C that you would like to know the meanings of. Look the items up in a dictionary. Write the word, part of speech, definition, word forms, and the example sentence—if there is one—that you find in each dictionary entry. An example has been done for you.

Go over the example with students. Make sure they understand each part of the definition. Discuss what makes a good example sentence. (*Answer:* An example sentence helps to define or illustrate the targeted word.)

Evaluation 2
10–15 mins.

Ask volunteers to write some of their definitions on the board.

AT-A-GLANCE PREP

Objective: Identify your learning style
Academic Strategies: Active listening, note taking, active reading, finding main ideas
Vocabulary: *multiple intelligences, visual, auditory, tactile, kinesthetic, spatial, verbal, linguistic, logical, bodily, rhythmic, interpersonal, intrapersonal, naturalistic*

RESOURCES

Activity Bank: Unit 1, Lesson 1, Worksheets 1–3
Grammar Challenge 5: Unit 1, Challenge 1

■ 1.5 hour classes ■ 2.5 hour classes ■ 3⁺ hour classes

AGENDA

Discover your learning style.
Take notes.
Study multiple intelligences.
Find the main idea.
Conduct a class poll.

Audio: CD Track 5
Stand Out 5 Assessment CD-ROM with *ExamView®*

 Pre-assessment *(optional)*

Use the Stand Out 5 Assessment CD-ROM with *ExamView®* to create a pre-test for Unit 1.

Warm-up and Review   5-10 mins.

Ask students to call out new terms they learned in the previous unit. Make a list on the board. Have students make a checklist of the student book goals in their notebooks or use the list in the back of their books on pages 178–180. The checklist should list the goals as well as the page numbers where the students can find information to accomplish these goals. Show students how they can keep track on a daily or weekly basis.

Introduction   10-15 mins.

As you may have noticed in the Pre-Unit, every Introduction section will begin with dictation. Dictation will help improve students' active listening skills and teach them to correct their errors. It is also motivating and will help get students to class on time if you begin the class with it.

Dictation: **1.** Kevin learns best when he writes things down and memorizes them. **2.** My sister likes to close her eyes and listen to the teacher talking. **3.** His math teacher gives students small objects to practice addition and subtraction. **4.** I like to see everything written on the board so I can study it.

State the objective: *Today you will identify your own learning style and learn about multiple intelligences.*

(A) **Think about how you learn new skills and ideas. Do you . . .** learn through seeing? . . . learn through listening? . . . learn through moving, doing, and touching?

Have students check their learning styles individually. Take a class poll to find out how many students learn in each of the three ways. Write your findings on the board.

Presentation 1   10-15 mins.

Write *Visual, Auditory,* and *Tactile/Kinesthetic* as headings on the board. Prepare students for the listening exercise by going over the chart about learning styles. Discuss the three headings and ask students what they think the words mean.

(B) **Listen to a lecturer talk about the three learning styles and take notes. Write down any key words you hear to describe each learning style.**

Note: The listening script is on page 4a.

Have students share their notes with a classmate sitting next to them. Then, ask volunteers to come up to the board and write notes under one of three column headings.

Practice 1   5-10 mins.

(C) **Indicate the learning style next to each activity. Write V for Visual, A for Auditory, and T/K for Tactile/Kinesthetic on the line.**

Have students complete this exercise in pairs.

Evaluation 1   5 mins.

Go over the answers as a class.

(D) **Check the learning style you think best describes you.**

Have students think about the way they like to learn and answer the question. Ask: *Has anyone changed answers since Exercise A? If so, explain why.*

Note: Standards Correlations box is on the page 4a.

Learning styles

GOAL ➤ Identify your learning style

A Think about how you learn new skills and ideas. Do you . . . (Answers will vary.)

☐ learn through seeing?   ☐ learn through listening?   ☐ learn through moving, doing, and touching?

B Listen to a lecturer talk about the three learning styles and take notes. Write down any key words you hear to describe each learning style.

CD
TR 5

Visual	Auditory	Tactile/Kinesthetic
seeing	listening	moving
body language	lectures	doing, touching
facial expressions	discussions	explore surroundings
sit in front of class	listening to others	touching things
think in pictures	listen to tone, pitch, speed	moving
learn best using visuals	interpret meaning	trouble sitting still
take detailed notes	read text aloud	hands-on approach

C Indicate the learning style next to each activity. Write *V* for *Visual*, *A* for *Auditory*, and *T/K* for *Tactile/Kinesthetic* on the line.

1. touching objects __T/K__

2. watching a video __V__

3. looking at a diagram __V__

4. reading a textbook __V__

5. doing a science experiment __T/K__

6. listening to a lecture __A__

7. participating in a discussion __A__

D Check the learning style you think best describes you. (Answers will vary.)

____ visual   ____ auditory   ____ tactile/kinesthetic

E What do you think *intelligence* means? Discuss the term with a partner and write your ideas on the lines below. (Answers will vary. Sample answers are given.)

Intelligence means someone's ability to understand and remember

information and ideas.

Now look the word up in a dictionary. Write its definition below.

intelligence *n* the capacity to acquire and apply knowledge

F Read about multiple intelligences. Underline the main idea in each paragraph.

MULTIPLE INTELLIGENCES

According to psychologist Howard Gardner, there are eight different ways to show intellectual ability. These eight intelligences are described as visual/spatial, verbal/linguistic, logical/mathematical, bodily/kinesthetic, musical/rhythmic, interpersonal, intrapersonal, and naturalistic.

Visual/spatial learners tend to think in pictures. Images created in their minds help them remember information. They like to look at maps, charts, pictures, and videos. They are good at such things as reading, writing, understanding charts and graphs, building, fixing, and designing.

Verbal/linguistic learners have the ability to use language. These learners can understand what they hear and are generally good speakers. Unlike visual learners, they think in words. Verbal/linguistic learners are good at listening, speaking, writing, teaching, remembering information, and persuading others.

Logical/mathematical learners are good at using reason, logic, and numbers. They can easily make connections between pieces of information. These learners ask many questions and like experimenting. Logical/mathematical learners are good at problem solving, classifying information, figuring out relationships between abstract concepts, doing complex mathematical calculations, and working with geometric shapes.

Bodily/kinesthetic learners express themselves with their bodies through movement. They have good balance and coordination. By moving in the space around them, they can process and recall information. These learners are good at dancing, physical sports, acting, using body language, and expressing themselves with their bodies.

Musical/rhythmic learners have the ability to appreciate and produce music. They think in sounds, rhythms, and patterns. These learners can immediately appreciate and evaluate the music they hear. Musical/rhythmic learners are good at singing, playing instruments, writing music, and remembering tunes they hear.

Learners with interpersonal intelligence are good at relating to others. They can see things from the point of view of others and they can sense people's feelings. They are good at listening, working with others, communicating, and forming positive relationships with people.

Intrapersonal intelligence, not to be confused with interpersonal intelligence, is the ability to be aware of one's own feelings. These learners are good at self-reflecting, and they try to understand their own hopes, dreams, strengths, and weaknesses. They are good at recognizing their own abilities and feelings, reasoning with themselves, and understanding their role in relationship to other people.

Naturalistic intelligence has to do with understanding nature, that is, nurturing and relating information to one's surroundings. Naturalistic learners are sensitive to nature and have the ability to nurture and grow things.

Academic Skill

Note taking

Tell students that when someone is talking in an academic or training class, they should write down any important words they hear that will help them remember the information later. Refer to the teaching tip below for more information on note taking.

 Listening Script — *CD Track 5*

Do you learn best through seeing? Then you are a visual learner. Visual learners learn from body language and facial expressions. They like to sit in the front of the classroom so they can see clearly. They tend to think in pictures and learn best by looking at visuals, such as diagrams, pictures, overheads, videos, and handouts. Visual learners like to take detailed notes to help learn information.

Do you learn best by listening? Then you are an auditory learner. Auditory learners learn best by listening to lectures, participating in discussions, and listening to what others say. They also listen to tone of voice, pitch, and speed to interpret hidden meanings. Auditory learners learn best if they read texts out loud.

Do you like to learn by moving, doing, and touching? Then you are a tactile, or kinesthetic, learner. Kinesthetic learners like to actively explore their surroundings by touching things and moving. They have trouble sitting still for long periods of time. They learn best through a hands-on approach.

Teaching Tip

Note taking

Taking notes is an important academic skill that students should practice as often as they can. Explain to students that they should focus on writing down the key words and phrases of a lecture—not all of the incidental words and phrases—so that they can recall the important

(continued)

---

ideas when they look back at their notes. Using Exercise B on page 3, show students how, in the first column, the words *seeing*, *body language*, and *facial expressions* are written as notes, not complete sentences.

To demonstrate note taking, you can:

1. Have a student tell you a story and, as he or she is talking, take notes on the board.
2. Use one of the recordings from the book and, as it is playing, show students on the board how you would take notes.

Presentation 2   5-10 mins.

E **What do you think *intelligence* means? Discuss the term with a partner and write your ideas on the lines below.**

Have students come up with a definition.

Now look the word up in a dictionary. Write its definition below.

Have each pair look *intelligence* up in the dictionary and compare their definition to the dictionary's definition. Discuss the meaning as a class, focusing students on the meaning required for the reading. Also, discuss the different definitions and other word forms.

Practice 2   15-20 mins.

Note: Shorter classes can do these exercises for homework.

Ask students what they think the term *multiple intelligences* means. Go over the directions to Exercise F, telling students not to worry about the meaning of every word. Tell them to focus their attention on the main ideas.

F **Read about multiple intelligences. Underline the main idea in each paragraph.**

STANDARDS CORRELATIONS

CASAS: 7.4.2, 7.4.9 (See CASAS Competency List on pages 187-193.)
SCANS: Information Acquire and evaluate information, organize and maintain information, interpret and communicate information
Interpersonal Participate as a member of a team, work with cultural diversity
Systems Understand systems, monitor and correct performance
Technology Apply technology to a task *(optional)*
Basic Skills Reading, writing, listening, speaking

Thinking Skills Think creatively, make decisions, see things in the mind's eye
Personal Qualities Responsibility, sociability
EFF: Communication Read with understanding, speak so others can understand, listen actively, observe critically
Decision Making Solve problems and make decisions, plan
Interpersonal Cooperate with others, advocate and influence, resolve conflict and negotiate, guide others
Lifelong Learning Take responsibility for learning, reflect and evaluate

Reading for understanding

At this level, students have a high level of comprehension, but there still may be many words that they do not know. Have students focus their attention on the concepts necessary to complete the instructions for each activity rather than trying to understand every word in the exercise. In most exercises in *Stand Out 5*, it is more important for students to read for understanding and meaning than to understand each word. Tell students that when they are at home and have already completed the exercise, they can spend time looking up individual words in a dictionary.

Practice 2 *(continued)*

G Match each type of intelligence to the main idea associated with that type of intelligence. Write the letter of the corresponding main idea on the line after each type of intelligence.

Evaluation 2   10–15 mins.

Go over the answers as a class.

H Which types of intelligence do you think are strongest in you? Write down your top three in order. (For example, if you think you are mostly musical, write that one first.)

Presentation 3   5–10 mins.

Write *learning styles* on the board and have students tell you what the three learning styles are. Then write *multiple intelligences* on the board and have students help you list them. Put students into small groups and tell them they will be discussing the connection between learning styles and multiple intelligences.

Practice 3   15–20 mins.

Shorter classes can do the following exercise in written form for homework.

I How do you think the terms *learning styles* and *multiple intelligences* are related? Discuss your ideas in a small group.

Evaluation 3   5–10 mins.

Observe students as they discuss their ideas.

Application   10–20 mins.

J Take a class poll on learning styles and multiple intelligences. Which learning styles and types of intelligence are most common among your classmates?

Activity Bank

Use the template on the Activity Bank CD for students to calculate percentages and create a bar graph for their poll results.

Internet Research

The Internet activities in *Stand Out 5* help students learn more about the topics in most lessons. In this lesson, have students do an online search for *Learning Styles*. Ask them to find a quiz they can take to assess their own learning styles. They can print out results to present to a small group or the class.

Activity Bank

Unit 1, Lesson 1, Worksheet 1: Learning Styles
Unit 1, Lesson 1, Worksheet 2: Multiple Intelligences (listening)
Unit 1, Lesson 1, Worksheet 3: Class Poll—Learning Styles and Multiples Intelligences

Refer students to *Stand Out 5 Grammar Challenge*, Unit 1, Challenge 1 for practice with gerunds as objects of prepositions.

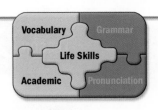

G   Match each type of intelligence to the main idea associated with that type of intelligence. Write the letter of the corresponding main idea on the line after each type of intelligence.

Intelligence

1. visual/spatial ___d___
2. verbal/linguistic ___c___
3. logical/mathematical ___h___
4. bodily/kinesthetic ___f___
5. musical/rhythmic ___e___
6. interpersonal ___g___
7. intrapersonal ___b___
8. naturalistic ___a___

Main Idea

a. nurture
b. be aware of one's feelings
c. use language
d. think in pictures
e. appreciate and produce music
f. express with movement
g. relate well to others
h. use reason, logic, and numbers

H   Which types of intelligence do you think are strongest in you? Write down your top three in order. (For example, if you think you are mostly musical, write that one first.) (Answers will vary.)

1. _____   2. _____   3. _____

I   How do you think the terms *learning styles* and *multiple intelligences* are related? Discuss your ideas in a small group. (Answers will vary. Sample answers are given.)
Learning style is how someone likes to learn. Multiple intelligences are the way in which someone best shows or uses his or her intelligence.

J   Take a class poll on learning styles and multiple intelligences. Which learning styles and types of intelligence are most common among your classmates?

(Answers will vary.)

Career planning

GOAL ➤ Identify a career path

A Do you have a job or a career? What is the difference between the two terms? Discuss the similarities and differences with a partner. Write your ideas in the chart below.

(Answers will vary. Sample answers are given.)

Job	Career
A job can be a short- or a long-term task or set of tasks done for money.	A career usually is a personal choice preceded by education and training.

B Look up the words *job* and *career* in a dictionary. Write their definitions below.

job *n* an activity performed in exchange for payment

career *n* a chosen career or life work

C Certain careers are associated with different types of the multiple intelligences you read about in the previous lesson. Look at the list of possible careers below and guess which intelligence fits each career category. Choose the type of intelligence from the box and write it in the chart.

> logical/mathematical   bodily/kinesthetic   musical/rhythmic
> interpersonal   visual/spatial   intrapersonal
> naturalistic   verbal/linguistic

Intelligence	Careers
visual/spatial	architect, engineer, interior designer, mechanic, sculptor
verbal/linguistic	journalist, lawyer, politician, teacher, translator, writer
logical/mathematical	accountant, computer programmer, doctor, researcher, scientist
bodily/kinesthetic	actor, athlete, dancer, firefighter, physical education teacher
musical/rhythmic	composer, conductor, disc jockey, musician, singer
interpersonal	businessperson, counselor, politician, salesperson, social worker
intrapersonal	philosopher, psychologist, researcher, scientist, writer
naturalistic	conservationist, farmer, gardener, scientist

Objective: Identify a career path
Academic Strategies: Active listening, note taking, analyzing a bar graph
Vocabulary: *careers, pursue, educational attainment, earning power, credential*

RESOURCES

Activity Bank: Unit 1, Lesson 2, Worksheets 1–2
Grammar Challenge 5: Unit 1, Challenge 2

■ 1.5 hour classes   ■ 2.5 hour classes   ■ 3⁺ hour classes

Audio: CD Track 6

AGENDA

Define job and career.
Match intelligence type with related careers.
Interpret information about earning power in a bar graph.
Listen to a conversation about Sonya's career path.
Choose your career path.

Warm-up and Review   5-10 mins. ■■■

Facilitate a class discussion to review the terms used to describe learning styles and multiple intelligences. Try to get as many students as possible to participate.

Introduction   5-10 mins. ■■■

Refer to the teaching tip on dictation on page P2a.

Dictation:

1. If you have a degree, you can make more money.
2. Do you have a job or a career?
3. What steps do you need to take to become a nurse?
4. People with verbal intelligence make good teachers.

State the objective: *Today, we will talk about different careers and you will identify a career path for yourself.*

Presentation 1   10-15 mins. ■■■

 Do you have a job or a career? What is the difference between the two terms? Discuss the similarities and differences with a partner. Write your ideas in the chart below.

Write the words *job* and *career* on the board and ask students to write notes in their books about the differences between the two.

 Look up the words *job* and *career* in a dictionary. Write their definitions below.

Before you define the words for students, have them look them up in the dictionary. Briefly discuss the eight intelligences that students learned in the previous lesson. Make sure they understand the meaning of each one before they go on to Exercise C.

Practice 1   10-15 mins. ■■■

 Certain careers are associated with different types of the multiple intelligences you read about in the previous lesson. Look at the list of possible careers below and guess which intelligence fits each career category. Choose the type of intelligence from the box and write it in the chart.

Have students complete this exercise with a partner.

Evaluation 1   10-15 mins. ■■□

Go over the answers as a class.

D Look back at the three types of intelligence (page 5, Exercise H) you think best describe your way of processing information. Using this information, choose two careers listed on page 6 that you would be good at or interested in. Write these two careers you might like to pursue on the lines below.

E In a small group, discuss the two careers you chose in Exercise D. What steps do you think you would need to take to pursue one of these careers? Think about the education and training these careers require. Make note of these steps.

To get students started, choose one of the careers that it seems unlikely for them to pick. Talk about what education or training might be needed for this career.

Presentation 2   5-10 mins. ■■■

F In general, the more education you have, the more money you can earn. Careers that require more education usually pay more. Look at the graph below. Which two things are compared?

Note: Use the following listening script with Exercise H on pages 8/8a.

 Listening Script   CD Track 6

Counselor: *Hi, Sonya. How are you today?*
Sonya: *A bit tired. Taking care of the kids and going to school is keeping me quite busy!*
Counselor: *I'll bet. I remember those days. Even though you get tired sometimes, doing both of those things is so worthwhile.*
Sonya: *I know it is. I just have to keep reminding myself of that!*

(continued)

Counselor: *Well, based on what we talked about in our last meeting, I would say your intelligences are most likely interpersonal as well as verbal and linguistic. Now, based on the list of careers we looked at, are there any that seem interesting to you?*
Sonya: *Actually, teacher kept jumping out at me. It showed up on the list for both of those intelligences. I have always loved working with children and helping them learn new things.*
Counselor: *Well, I think that sounds like a great career for you . . . elementary school teacher. Have you ever thought about doing that before?*
Sonya: *Not really. I never thought my English would be good enough to be a teacher. And I didn't think I could get into a school to earn a degree.*
Counselor: *Well, you are wrong on both counts. You have worked really hard and your English is getting better every day. And there are plenty of schools that would be happy to accept you as an education major.*
Sonya: *Will it be expensive?*
Counselor: *That all depends on what school you choose. But you can start at a city or community college to get your general education requirements done and then, you can transfer to a four-year school to finish up your degree and get your teaching credentials. That will definitely keep the costs down.*
Sonya: *How long will it take?*
Counselor: *Well, that all depends on you. If you can go to school full time, you could finish in four years. And I know you have little ones at home, so we can look around for some schools that offer some online classes, so you can study on your own time.*
Sonya: *I'll have to talk to my husband to see if he still needs me to work part time.*
Counselor: *If you have to, there's no reason you couldn't still work. It will just take you a little bit longer to get your degree.*
Sonya: *I wouldn't mind that. I don't want a full-time teaching job until both of my kids are in school anyway.*
Counselor: *That's smart. Your girls will appreciate having you home with them.*
Sonya: *So, what's the next step?*
Counselor: *Well, since you already have your high school diploma, let's start looking around at some local colleges where you can do your general education requirements. I'll put together a list for you and then, we can do some research on what English level you need to be at before you can apply.*
Sonya: *Sounds great. Thank you so much for all your help!*

D Look back at the three types of intelligence (page 5, Exercise H) you think best describe your way of processing information. Using this information, choose two careers listed on page 6 that you would be good at or interested in. Write these two careers you might like to pursue on the lines below. (Answers will vary.)

_____   _____

E In a small group, discuss the two careers you chose in Exercise D. What steps do you think you would need to take to pursue one of these careers? Think about the education and training these careers require. Make note of these steps. (Answers will vary. Sample answers are given.)

1. Investigate career   2. Take career courses   3. Get experience.

F In general, the more education you have, the more money you can earn. Careers that require more education usually pay more. Look at the graph below. Which two things are compared?

Median Income _____ and Education for Both Sexes 18 and Over

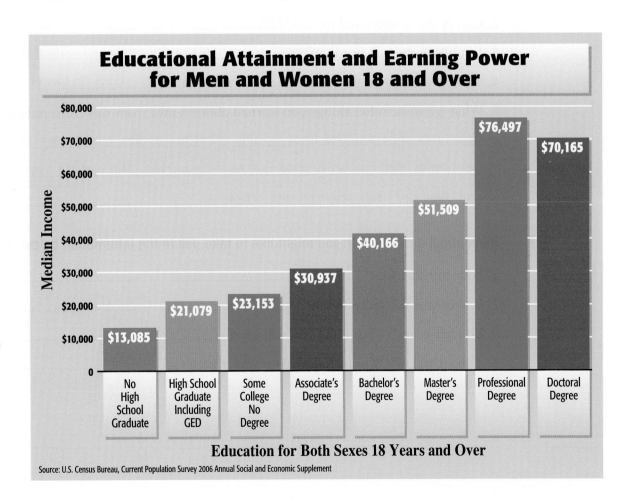

Educational Attainment and Earning Power for Men and Women 18 and Over

Median Income

No High School Graduate	$13,085
High School Graduate Including GED	$21,079
Some College No Degree	$23,153
Associate's Degree	$30,937
Bachelor's Degree	$40,166
Master's Degree	$51,509
Professional Degree	$76,497
Doctoral Degree	$70,165

Education for Both Sexes 18 Years and Over

Source: U.S. Census Bureau, Current Population Survey 2006 Annual Social and Economic Supplement

GOAL ➤ **Identify a career path**

 G With a partner, ask and answer the following questions. Use the information given in the graph on page 7. Replace the underlined words with different information from the graph.

> *A:* How much money can I make if I have <u>a master's degree</u>?
> *B:* About <u>$51,500</u>.
>
> *A:* If I want to make <u>over $70,000</u>, what education do I need?
> *B:* You need <u>a doctoral or professional degree</u>.

CD
TR 6

H Listen to the conversation between a school counselor and Sonya. Take notes on the information you hear.

1. Sonya's intelligences:

   interpersonal, verbal and linguistic

2. Career she is interested in: _teaching_

3. Education she will need: _general education requirements, education degree, teaching_ _credentials_

4. Time it will take to get her degree and credential: _four years or longer_

5. What are some other things you learned about Sonya from this conversation?

   She loves children. She likes helping them learn. She might have to work

   part time. Her English is good and getting better. She doesn't want to work

   full time until her children are grown.

I Think about a career path you might like to take. Fill in the information below. (Answers will vary.)

1. Your intelligences: _____

2. Career you are interested in: _____

3. Education and/or training you will need: _____

4. Time it will take you to follow your career path: _____

Practice 2 10-15 mins.

Note: Shorter classes can do this exercise for homework by practicing with someone at home or writing out sample conversations.

The following exercise is a fun way to get students to study the information presented in the graph. Refer to the teaching tip on this page.

G With a partner, ask and answer the following questions. Use the information given in the graph on page 7. Replace the underlined words with different information from the graph.

This activity should be fairly simple for students at this level so only do as much modeling as you think necessary for them to be able to do it on their own. You may have them sit and talk with one partner or walk around the room and talk to a variety of people.

Evaluation 2

Observe students as they talk about the graph.

Presentation 3 5 mins.

Have students look at the picture of the two women and ask them who they think each person is. Ask students what these women might be discussing. Then, focus students' attention on the information they will be listening for.

Practice 3 15-20 mins.

H Listen to the conversation between a school counselor and Sonya. Take notes on the information you hear.

Note: Refer to the Listening Script set on page 7a. Play the recording once.

Teaching Tip

Modeling

Note: Use this teaching tip with dialog exercises such as that found on page 8. In order to make sure that students understand how to do dialog practices, you may need to model the conversations for them before they work on their own. There are different levels of modeling,

(continued)

ranging from teacher-centered levels to student-centered levels:

1. Class to Class: Break the class up into two halves and have one half be Student A and the other be Student B. Teacher can participate as a member of both halves.
2. Teacher to Student: Teacher takes the role of Student A; students collectively take the role of Student B.
3. Student to Student: Students work in pairs, switching roles.

Evaluation 3 5-10 mins.

Go over the answers as a class. Once students have the correct answers written down, play the recording again.

Application 10-20 mins.

I Think about a career path you might like to take. Fill in the information below.

If students do not know the answers, ask them how they might be able to find out the information. Some students in the class may know about different careers and can share their prior knowledge with the class Your school may also have access to a school counselor who can give students more information.

Internet Research

If you have computers in your class, students may want to use the Internet to complete Exercise I. Have students research the careers they have chosen. Ask them: *How much money can you make? What are the education and experience requirements?*

Activity Bank

Unit 1, Lesson 2, Worksheet 1: Choose the Career Path

Unit 1, Lesson 2, Worksheet 2: Conversations with Counselors (listening)

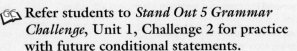 Refer students to *Stand Out 5 Grammar Challenge*, Unit 1, Challenge 2 for practice with future conditional statements.

Objective: Balance your life
Grammar: Simple verb tenses
Academic Strategy: Active listening
Vocabulary: *balance*

RESOURCES
Activity Bank: Unit 1, Lesson 3, Worksheets 1–3
Grammar Challenge 5: Unit 1, Challenge 3

■ 1.5 hour classes ■ 2.5 hour classes ■ 3⁺ hour classes

Audio: CD Track 7

AGENDA
Find out who Sonya is.
Describe yourself.
Read Sonya's paragraph.
Review simple verb tenses.
Discuss balance in your life.

Warm-up and Review   5–10 mins.

Put students in small groups and have them discuss Exercise I from the previous lesson.

Introduction   10–20 mins. ■■■

Refer to the teaching tip on page P2a for information on dictation.

Dictation:

1. If you want to be a teacher, you will need a college degree and a teaching credential.
2. Studying to be a teacher will take time away from your family.
3. Do you spend time with the people who are important to you?
4. If you could change your life somehow, what would you do?

State the objective: *Today you will meet Sonya and see how she plans to balance her life. Then you will write about balance in your own life.*

Presentation 1   10–15 mins.

Focus students' attention on the picture of Sonya and her daughter. Write on the board, *Who is Sonya?* Ask students to give you some ideas of who they think she is. Tell students they will be listening to Sonya describe herself. Play the recording.

(A) Sonya has many roles. Listen to her and take notes.

After students have listened to the recording, go over the answers as a class.

> 🎧 **Listening Script**   CD Track 7
>
> **Sonya:** *I am a wife. I am a mother. I am a sister. I am a student. I am a friend. I am a manager. I was a secretary. I will be an elementary school teacher.*

Practice 1   10–15 mins.

Have students complete these exercises on their own.

(B) Who are you? Write at least three statements.

(C) Who were you? Write at least two statements.

(D) Who will you be? Write at least two statements.

Evaluation 1   5 mins.

(E) Share and discuss your information with a partner.

STANDARDS CORRELATIONS

CASAS: 7.4.2 (See CASAS Competency List on pages 187–193.)
SCANS: Information Acquire and evaluate information, interpret and communicate information, use computers to process information *(optional)*
Interpersonal Participate as a member of a team, work with cultural diversity
Systems Monitor and correct performance
Technology Apply technology to a task *(optional)*
Basic Skills Reading, writing, listening, speaking
Thinking Skills Think creatively, make decisions, see things in the mind's eye

Personal Qualities Responsibility, sociability, self-management
EFF: Communication Read with understanding, convey ideas in writing, speak so others can understand, listen actively, observe critically
Decision Making Solve problems and make decisions, plan
Interpersonal Cooperate with others, advocate and influence, resolve conflict and negotiate, guide others
Lifelong Learning Take responsibility for learning, reflect and evaluate, use information and communications technology *(optional)*

LESSON 3 **Achieving balance**

GOAL ➤ **Balance your life**

A Sonya has many roles. Listen to her and take notes.

CD
TR 7

1. Who is Sonya? What are her roles?

a wife   a student

a mother   a friend

a sister   a manager

2. Who was she? _a secretary_

_____

3. Who will she be? _an elementary school_

teacher

B Who are you? Write at least three statements. (Answers will vary. Sample answers are given.)

I am a _brother, a son, a friend, and a student_ .

_____

_____

C Who were you? Write at least two statements.

I was a _grandson and a plumber_ .

_____

_____

Review: *Be*			
Subject	**Past**	**Present**	**Future**
I	was	am	will be
you	were	are	will be
he, she, it	was	is	will be
we	were	are	will be
they	were	are	will be

D Who will you be? Write at least two statements.

I will be a _husband, a father, and an engineer_ .

_____

_____

E Share and discuss your information with a partner.

LESSON 3

GOAL ➤ **Balance your life**

F Read what Sonya wrote and answer the questions below the paragraph with a partner.

Balance in My Life

When I was a little girl, I spent all my time playing with my two brothers. I just enjoyed doing whatever they were doing. Family was always very important to us. But as I grew older, I started working and studying more. It seemed like I was working all day, going to school every night, and studying whenever I had time. I didn't have any balance in my life. Now that I have my diploma, I don't study as much, but I still work a lot. I'm a manager at a restaurant, but I want to become an elementary school teacher. I am also a wife and a mother, and I want to spend more time with my family. So, I hope to find a job as a teacher where I can work fewer hours but still make enough money to help out. I will really enjoy being home with my family more and having more balance in my life.

---

1. How was Sonya's life different in the past from how it is now?
2. Is her life balanced right now? Why or why not?
3. What does she want to change in her life?
4. Do you think this change will make her happy? Why or why not?

(Answers are on Lesson Planner page 10a.)

Review: Simple Tenses				
Subject	**Past**	**Present**	**Future**	
I	spent	spend	will spend	more time with my brothers.
You	enjoyed	enjoy	will enjoy	being a mother.
He, She, It	studied	studies	will study	English every day.
We	put	put	will put	our studies first.
They	worked	work	will work	too many hours.

G Complete each statement about yourself using the tense and verb in parentheses.

EXAMPLE (*past*, want) I __wanted to be a firefighter.__ (Sample answers are given.)

1. (*past*, spend) I _spent time on the farm with my father_ .

2. (*present*, put) I _put money in the bank every week_ .

3. (*future*, live) I _will live in New York or Los Angeles_ .

10   Unit 1   Lesson 3

Presentation 2

10-15 mins. ■■■□

 Read what Sonya wrote and answer the questions below the paragraph with a partner.

Ask a volunteer to read Sonya's paragraph out loud. Have students answer the questions with a partner.

Answer Key for Exercise F. Answers will vary. Sample answers:

1. When Sonya was young, she spent a lot of time with her family, but now she works and studies a lot.
2. Her life isn't balanced right now because she wants to work less and she wants more time with her family.
3. She wants to find a job as a teacher, to make more money, and to work less.
4. Yes. If she makes all these changes, she will be happy because she will reach her goals.

Go over the review chart of simple tenses with the class. Based on your students' needs, spend as much or as little time as appropriate. Go over the example in Exercise G. Explain that these are open-ended statements that students must complete about themselves. Do a few examples on the board using yourself as an example.

Practice 2

10-15 mins. ■■□

Note: Shorter classes can do this exercise for homework.

 Complete each statement about yourself using the tense and verb in parentheses.

Evaluation 2

10-15 mins. ■■□

Ask volunteers to write their sentences on the board. Review the grammar chart as a class.

✍ **Refer students to** *Stand Out 5 Grammar Challenge*, **Unit 1, Challenge 3 for more practice with past, present, and future simple tenses.**

Presentation 3   5–10 mins.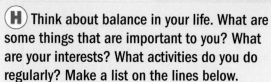

 Think about balance in your life. What are some things that are important to you? What are your interests? What activities do you do regularly? Make a list on the lines below.

Talk students through this exercise. Have them call out some other ideas of what might be important to them.

Share your list with a partner. Is there anything you can add to your list?

Practice 3   10–15 mins. ■

Note: Shorter classes can do this exercise for homework.

(I) Think about how you balanced your life in the past, how you balance it now, and what you want for the future. Answer the questions below.

Go over the questions with students and then have them complete the exercise on their own.

Evaluation 3   5–10 mins. ■

Ask volunteers to share their responses with the class.

Application   20–30 mins. ■■■

Note: Shorter classes can do the following exercise for homework.

(J) Using Sonya's paragraph in Exercise F as a writing model, write a paragraph on a piece of paper about balance in your life—past, present, and future.

(K) Share your paragraph with a partner and ask your partner for two suggestions about how to make your paragraph better. Share your thoughts on your partner's writing. Did your partner include interesting details? Write your partner's suggestions.

Before you have students complete this exercise, give suggestions of the type of advice they can tell their partner. For example, *Maybe you could state this idea more clearly,* or *Maybe you could give more details about this idea.* (On the Activity Bank CD-ROM, there is a worksheet with a list of suggestions students might give.)

Teaching Tip

Pairing students for peer-editing

Peer-editing can be difficult because not all students have learned to critically analyze texts. Pairing students of similar levels works well when students are peer-editing. If you pair students of mixed levels, one student will end up getting more out of the activity than the other. There will be some pairs who are better at peer-editing than others. Spend your time helping the pairs who need it.

Activity Bank

Unit 1, Lesson 3, Worksheet 1: Simple Verb Tenses

Unit 1, Lesson 3, Worksheet 2: Balance

Unit 1, Lesson 3, Worksheet 3: Suggestions to Improve Writing

Instructor's Notes

_____

_____

_____

_____

_____

_____

_____

_____

_____

_____

_____

_____

_____

4. (*present*, plan) I plan to be a manager one day .

5. (*future*, give) I will give money to the poor .

6. (*past*, hope) I hoped for a lot of money for myself .

7. (*past*, study) I studied engineering in my home country .

8. (*present*, work) I work on my English every day .

(H) **Think about balance in your life. What are some things that are important to you? What are your interests? What activities do you do regularly? Make a list on the lines below.**
(Answers will vary. Sample answers are given.)

play soccer   study   cook good food

visit family   play video games   practice guitar

Share your list with a partner. Is there anything you can add to your list?

(I) **Think about how you balanced your life in the past, how you balance it now, and what you want for the future. Answer the questions below.** (Answers will vary. Sample answers are below.)

1. What was important to you in the past?

   My family and friends were important in the past.

2. What is important to you now?

   Studying and playing guitar are important now.

3. Do you spend enough time on the things that are important to you now? ___No.___

4. What changes would you like to make for the future?

   I want to get more exercise in the future.

(J) **Using Sonya's paragraph in Exercise F as a writing model, write a paragraph on a piece of paper about balance in your life—past, present, and future.** (Answers will vary.)

(K) **Share your paragraph with a partner and ask your partner for two suggestions about how to make your paragraph better. Share your thoughts on your partner's writing. Did your partner include interesting details? Write your partner's suggestions.** (Sample answers are below.)

1. Write more details about the past.

2. Include more about my future hopes.

 **Setting priorities**

GOAL ➤ Identify and prioritize goals

A Read the flier and answer the questions below it.

(Answers will vary. Sample answers are below.)

1. What do you think *big picture* means?

   My view of the future

2. What is *goal setting*?

   Deciding specific things I want to accomplish

3. Would you attend the workshop described above? Why or why not?

   Yes. I don't think about long-term goals enough.

4. Think of three goals you set for yourself in the past. Write them down.

   a. Make money.   (No)

   b. Live in a big city.   (Yes)

   c. Get married.   (No.)

5. Did you achieve them? Write *yes* or *no* next to each goal.

B In a small group, discuss your answers to the questions in Exercise A.

Objective: Identify and prioritize goals
Academic Strategy: Goal setting
Vocabulary: *goal setting, big picture, long-term, short-term, prioritize, achieve, motivate*

RESOURCES

Activity Bank: Unit 1, Lesson 4, Worksheets 1–2
Grammar Challenge 5: Unit 1, Challenge 4
Audio: CD Track 8

■ 1.5 hour classes   ■ 2.5 hour classes   ■ 3+ hour classes

AGENDA

Read about a goal-setting workshop.
Take notes on a lecture.
Read about Sonya's goals.
Set and prioritize goals.

Suggested Realia: Your own personal list of goals (if you have one) or things that motivate you (e.g., pictures).

Warm-up and Review   5-10 mins.

Have students take out their paragraphs from the previous lesson and share them with a small group.

Introduction   5-10 mins.

Note: Refer to the teaching tip on dictation on page P2a to review purpose.

Dictation:

1. It is very important to set goals for your life.
2. There are many different types of goals you can set.
3. Setting and achieving goals will improve your self-confidence.
4. Have you ever set goals before?

State the objective: *Today we will learn about goal setting and you will practice identifying and prioritizing your own goals.*

Presentation 1   10-15 mins.

Use the dictation sentences as a springboard for a discussion about goals and goal setting. See what students already know and write their ideas on the board. Direct students' attention to the flier in their books. Discuss the flier and the idiomatic expressions found in it (examples: big picture, get what you want out of life, make dreams a reality).

Practice 1   10-15 mins.

(A) **Read the flier and answer the questions below it.**

Have students complete this exercise on their own.

Evaluation 1   10-15 mins.

(B) **In a small group, discuss your answers to the questions in Exercise A.**

Observe students' discussions.

Listening Script   *CD Track 8*

Goal setting is a process that makes you think about your future and helps motivate you to make that future a reality. Setting goals helps you choose the direction you want your life to go in. As you set and achieve goals, your self-confidence will improve.

The first thing you should do is to create a big picture of where you want to be in a certain number of years. Once you have created your big picture, you can make smaller or short-term goals.

In this workshop, we'd like you to focus on seven different types of goals. First are educational goals. Is there anything special you want or need to learn? Or, is there any degree you need to get to pursue your career goals? Second are career goals. How far would you like to go in your career? Third are financial goals. How much money would you like to be earning? Fourth are attitude goals. Would you like to change the way you think or act? Fifth are family goals. Do you want to have a family, increase the size of your family, or improve some of your family relationships? Sixth are physical goals. Is there anything you'd like to do to improve your health? Would you like to enter a physical competition? And, finally, pleasure goals. Are there any hobbies you'd like to do? It is important to enjoy your life so make sure you think about goals for pleasure.

It is important to spend some time thinking about all these different goals and try to choose one goal in each category that best reflects what you want to do. Then you should prioritize these goals and focus on a small number of goals at one time.

So, how do you go about setting these goals? Here are five tips that should help you to set effective goals:

1. *Set realistic goals. It is important to set a goal that you can actually achieve. It will lower your self-confidence if you set goals that are unrealistic.*
2. *Write down your goals. Writing your goals down gives them life. Try to put them in a place where you will see them every day.*
3. *Write each goal as a positive statement.*
4. *Be precise. When you set your goals, write down exact times, dates, etc. This way, it will be easy to see when you have achieved a goal.*
5. *Prioritize. When you have more than one goal, put them in order of importance. This will help you direct your attention to the most important goals and avoid feeling overwhelmed by having too much to do.*

So, now that we have talked about types of goals and tips for setting these goals, should we get down to business?

Presentation 2   15–20 mins.

Prepare students for the listening activity by reviewing the outline for their notes in their books. Ask them to tell you what they will be listening for.

C Listen to the lecture on goal setting and take notes below.

Play the listening a few times until you think students have been able to fill in most of the notes. Between listenings, have students share their answers with a partner to fill in things they may have missed. Have students complete Exercise D before you go over any of the notes.

Practice 2   5 mins.

Note: Shorter classes can do this exercise for homework.

D Answer the following questions based on the notes you took. Circle the best answer.

Evaluation 2   10–15 mins.

Go over the answers as a class. Go back to their notes and help students fill in what they may have missed or gotten wrong. You can do this using an overhead transparency or by playing the listening again.

Instructor's Notes

_____

_____

_____

_____

_____

_____

_____

_____

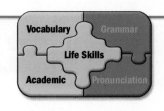

LESSON 4   **GOAL** ➤ **Identify and prioritize goals**

  C   **Listen to the lecture on goal setting and take notes below.**

CD
TR 8

Goal setting: <u>a process to make me think about the future, helps motivate me,</u>

<u>choose the direction I want to go, increase my self-confidence</u>

_____

First thing you should do: <u>Create a big picture with short term goals</u>

Types of goals:

1. <u>educational</u>   5. <u>family</u>

2. <u>career</u>   6. <u>physical</u>

3. <u>financial</u>   7. <u>pleasure</u>

4. <u>attitude</u>

Tips for setting goals:

1. <u>Set realistic goals; don't be unrealistic</u>

2. <u>Write down goals</u>

3. <u>Write goals as positive statements</u>

4. <u>Be precise about goal times and dates</u>

5. <u>Prioritize: put goals in order of importance</u>

D   **Answer the following questions based on the notes you took. Circle the best answer.**

1. Which of the following is NOT true about goal setting?
   a. It will improve your self-confidence.
   b. It helps motivate you.
   c. It makes you think about your past.
   d. It helps you choose a direction for your life.

2. What are the seven types of goals?
   a. financial, physical, attitude, pleasure, education, mental, family
   b. physical, career, family, financial, attitude, personal, education
   c. education, career, technical, financial, physical, attitude, pleasure
   d. financial, physical, career, family, education, attitude, pleasure

3. Why is it important to prioritize your goals in a list?
   a. It will be easy to know when you have achieved a goal.
   b. It will help you focus your attention on the most important goals.
   c. It gives them life.
   d. It will improve your self-confidence.

E   Sonya attended the goal-setting workshop and created a list of goals that she now keeps on her refrigerator.

The Big Picture:
I plan to be successful in my personal and professional life. I will be a highly educated elementary school teacher.

SHORT-TERM GOALS
- spend more time with my children
- exercise to reduce stress
- enroll in community college

LONG-TERM GOALS
- get my Bachelor's degree and teaching credentials
- become an elementary school teacher
- get a master's degree
- learn how to swim

F   Sonya's goals are prioritized (listed in order of importance). Do you think she put her goals in the right order? Discuss your ideas with a partner. (Answers will vary.)

G   The Big Picture: Think about where you would like to be ten years from now. Based on your thoughts, what are your long-term goals? Use the items below to help you clarify what your goals should be. (Answers will vary. Sample answers are below.)

1. Write one goal for each category.

     Education: _get a Bachelor's degree in nursing_

     Career: _become a registered nurse_

     Family: _get married by the age of 30_

     Financial: _save money for a down-payment_

     Physical: _lose 15 pounds_

     Attitude: _stay positive_

     Pleasure: _play on a soccer team_

2. Number your three most important goals above in order of priority.

3. Based on these three long-term goals, what are some short-term goals you can set in order to help you reach the long-term ones?

     Short-term goals: _get financial aid, work in a hospital, start running and lifting weights_

4. Prioritize your short-term goals. Write them in order. _See above._

Presentation 3   5-10 mins. ■■■

(E) Sonya attended the goal-setting workshop and created a list of goals that she now keeps on her refrigerator.

As a class, talk about Sonya's *big picture* and her goals.

Practice 3   5-10 mins. ■

Note: Shorter classes can do this exercise for homework.

(F) Sonya's goals are prioritized (listed in order of importance). Do you think she put her goals in the right order? Discuss your ideas with a partner.

Evaluation 3   5-10 mins. ■

Ask pairs of students to report what they discussed.

Application   10-20 mins. ■■■

(G) The Big Picture: Think about where you would like to be ten years from now. Based on your thoughts, what are your long-term goals? Use the items below to help you clarify what your goals should be.

Activity Bank

> Unit 1, Lesson 4, Worksheet 1: Goal-Setting (reading)
>
> Unit 1, Lesson 4, Worksheet 2: Goal Chart

📖 Refer students to *Stand Out 5 Grammar Challenge*, Unit 1, Challenge 4 for practice with the past perfect.

AT-A-GLANCE PREP

Objective: Motivate yourself
Grammar: Future perfect
Academic Strategies: Active listening, note taking
Vocabulary: *motivation, support, inspire, refresh, evaluate, progress, monitor, be flexible, outlook*

RESOURCES

Activity Bank: Unit 1, Lesson 5, Worksheets 1–2
Grammar Challenge 5: Unit 1, Challenge 5

■ 1.5 hour classes   ■ 2.5 hour classes   ■ 3⁺ hour classes

AGENDA

*Take notes on motivation techniques.
Complete a self-motivation checklist.
Practice using the future perfect.
Write goal statements and ideas
to motivate yourself.*

Audio: CD Track 9

Warm-up and Review   5-10 mins.

Have students take out the goals they wrote in the previous lesson in Exercise G. Have them share their short-term goals (items 3 & 4) and how they prioritized them with a small group.

Introduction   5-10 mins.

Note: Refer to the teaching tip on dictation on page P2a as needed.

Dictation:

1. I will already have become a teacher by the time my kids are in school.
2. When I turn 35, I will have been a graphic designer for five years.
3. I will have been accepted to college when I finish my last English class.
4. I will have been teaching English for 20 years when I retire.

State the objective: *Today you will learn how to motivate yourself. You will write goal statements and make a commitment to motivate yourself.*

Presentation 1   10-15 mins. ■■■

A Are you motivated to achieve your goals? Do you need someone to motivate you? Can you motivate yourself?

Define *motivation*. Define the word as a class. Encourage students to refer to their dictionaries if they are stuck or need synonyms.

B How can you motivate yourself to reach your goals? Work with a small group and make a list.

When students have finished the exercise, have them share some of their ideas with the class by writing them on the board.

Practice 1   10-15 mins.

C Listen to Mrs. Morgan's students talk about motivating themselves. Take notes about what each person says.

Note: Refer to the listening script on page 16a.

Evaluation 1   5 mins.

D What idea for getting motivated does each person have? Share what you recall with a partner.

Discuss the motivation strategies mentioned on the recording as a class.

STANDARDS CORRELATIONS

CASAS: (See CASAS Competency List on pages 187–193.)
SCANS: **Resources** Allocate time
Information Acquire and evaluate information, organize and maintain information, interpret and communicate information
Interpersonal Participate as a member of a team, negotiate to arrive at a decision, work with cultural diversity
Systems Monitor and correct performance
Basic Skills Reading, writing, listening, speaking

Thinking Skills Think creatively, make decisions, see things in the mind's eye
Personal Qualities Responsibility, sociability, self-management
EFF: **Communication** Read with understanding, convey ideas in writing, speak so others can understand, listen actively, observe critically
Decision Making Solve problems and make decisions, plan
Interpersonal Cooperate with others
Lifelong Learning Take responsibility for learning, reflect and evaluate

---

LESSON 5 Motivation

GOAL ➤ **Motivate yourself**

Vocabulary — Grammar — Life Skills — Academic — Pronunciation

 A Are you motivated to achieve your goals? Do you need someone to motivate you? Can you motivate yourself? (Answers will vary.)

Define *motivation* (your own definition or one from a dictionary): to excite or encourage someone to act

 B How can you motivate yourself to reach your goals? Work with a small group and make a list.

Ways We Can Motivate Ourselves (Answers will vary.)

Stay positive   Take classes

Choose short-term goals   Stay active

Do something you like   Talk to friends and family

Make friends with similar people   Get organized

CD
TR 9

 **C** Listen to Mrs. Morgan's students talk about motivating themselves. Take notes about what each person says.

Liam: Told friends and family to support him

Sonya: Reads books and Internet articles

Haru: Keeps a chart of goals with stickers

Rani: Have a positive attitude

Kimla: Keeps a list of goals in her planner

Mario: Set small goals to achieve

 D What idea for getting motivated does each person have? Share what you recall with a partner.

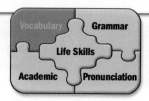

LESSON 5   **GOAL** ➤ Motivate yourself

E Below is a list of things you can do to motivate yourself toward pursuing a goal. Which of the following steps do you already do? Which of the following steps would you like to do? Put checks in the correct column. (Answers will vary.)

I already do this.	I would like to do this.	Steps to motivate yourself toward pursuing a goal
_____	_____	1. Write down your goals and put them in a place you will see them every day.
_____	_____	2. Tell family and friends about your goals so they can support you.
_____	_____	3. Tell yourself that you can do it.
_____	_____	4. Keep a positive attitude.
_____	_____	5. Be enthusiastic about your goals.
_____	_____	6. When you slow down or don't have the energy to do anything, take small steps and continue moving forward. Don't stop.
_____	_____	7. Evaluate your progress. Make a chart or do something to monitor progress.
_____	_____	8. Don't be too fixed on one approach. Be flexible and make changes when needed.
_____	_____	9. Read inspiring books.
_____	_____	10. Take some time to refresh yourself.
_____	_____	11. Exercise will help your attitude. "The better your health, the more positive your outlook."
_____	_____	12. After you are motivated, motivate others.

F One of the best ways to motivate yourself is to keep a positive attitude and remind yourself of your goals every day. Read the statements below and write the name of the person who said each statement. (Mrs. Morgan, Haru, Liam, Rani, Kimla, Sonya)

1. I will already have become a teacher by the time my kids are in school. _____Sonya_____

2. When I turn 35, I will have been a graphic designer for five years. _____Liam_____

3. By the time my grandkids go to college, I will have gone on three photography expeditions. _____Rani_____

4. I will have registered for college by the time I finish my last English class. _____Haru_____

5. I will have been a teacher of English for 20 years when I retire. _Mrs. Morgan_

6. By the time I finish my nursing program, I will have found a job at a local hospital. _____Kimla_____

16   Unit 1   Lesson 5

Listening Script *CD Track 9*

Liam: *I told my friends and family about my goals, so they could support me.*

Haru: *I keep a chart up in my room of the goals I have reached and the ones I still need to reach. When I reach a goal, I put a sticker on the chart.*

Kimla: *I made a list of all my goals and I keep it taped inside my planner, so I see it every day.*

Sonya: *I read books and look for articles on the Internet to inspire me.*

Rani: *I remind myself every morning to have a positive attitude. I tell myself, "I can do it!"*

Mario: *I set very small goals, so that I can get excited every time I achieve one.*

Presentation 2   10-15 mins.

(E) Below is a list of things you can do to motivate yourself toward pursuing a goal. Which of the following steps do you already do? Which of the following steps would you like to do? Put checks in the correct column.

Go over each statement as a class. Have students put a check in the correct column once they understand each one.

Suggestion: Put up an overhead transparency and as you go over each step, put a check in the correct column for yourself.

Practice 2   5-10 mins.

Note: Shorter classes can do this exercise for homework.

(F) One of the best ways to motivate yourself is to keep a positive attitude and remind yourself of your goals every day. Read the statements below and write the name of the person who said each statement. (Mrs. Morgan, Haru, Liam, Rani, Kimla, Sonya)

Students should be able to complete this exercise by themselves even if they don't completely understand the grammar, which will be presented in the next exercise. Play the listening from Exercise C again if students need a review of each person's motivation.

Evaluation 2   5 mins.

Go over the answers as a class.

Activity Bank

Unit 1, Lesson 5, Worksheet 1: Motivation Checklist/ Motivate Yourself

Instructor's Notes

_____
_____
_____
_____
_____
_____
_____
_____
_____
_____
_____
_____
_____
_____
_____
_____
_____
_____
_____
_____
_____
_____
_____
_____
_____
_____
_____

Presentation 3   5–10 mins. ◼◼◼

G Study the chart with your teacher.

Let students read the chart by themselves before you present it. See how much of the target structure they can figure out on their own. This is now the third time they have been exposed to the future perfect in this lesson: the dictation, the statements in Exercise E, and the grammar chart. Once you have gone over the chart as a class, create a few more examples on the board to make sure everyone understands the use of the future perfect.

Teaching Tip

Grammar charts

At this level, students should be able to read and understand grammar charts by themselves. Chart reading is a skill that they will need as they continue on to higher levels and take other academic classes. Allow students to read each chart by themselves before you present the material to the class. Encourage students to ask questions and to create their own sentences to demonstrate the targeted grammar points.

Practice 3   15–20 mins. ◼

Note: Shorter classes can do this exercise for homework.

H Mrs. Morgan's other students wrote goal statements as well. Complete each statement with the correct form of the future perfect of the verb in parentheses.

If students finish early, they can check their answers with a partner.

Evaluation 3   5–10 mins. ◼

Ask volunteers to come up and write the statements on the board. Ask the class to help you correct any mistakes.

Teaching Tip

Volunteers to the board

In the beginning of the course, you may have the same students volunteering to come to the board for each activity. As the course progresses, other students should begin to gain more confidence and volunteer as well. If, after a few weeks, some students are still not volunteering, select the students you wish to come to the board. If you think certain students may need help with the activity at the board, have them come up with a partner.

Application   10–20 mins. ◼◼◼

I Write three goal statements for yourself on a separate piece of paper.

J Now that you have written down your goals, what are you going to do to keep yourself motivated? Write down three ideas on a separate piece of paper. Share your goals and motivation with a partner.

Remind students they can look back at the list in Exercise E for ideas. Ask volunteers to come to the front of the class and share what they wrote in Exercises I and J. Remind students that they will be more motivated if they share their goals and motivations!

Activity Bank

Unit 1, Lesson 5, Worksheet 2: Future Perfect Tense

 Refer students to *Stand Out 5 Grammar Challenge*, Unit 1, Challenge 5 for more practice with the future perfect tense.

There are also two extension challenges— Extension Challenge 1 gives students practice with gerunds as direct objects, and Extension Challenge 2 gives students practice with the future perfect continuous (progressive) tense.

GOAL ➤ **Motivate yourself**

G Study the chart with your teacher.

			Future Perfect Tense		
Subject	*will have*	**Past participle**		**Future event—Time expression**
I	will have	become	a teacher	by the time my kids are in school.
He	will have	been	a graphic designer (for five years)	when he turns 35.
They	will have	found	a job	by 2015.

We use the future perfect to talk about an activity that will be completed before another time or event in the future. ____|____ present ____✗____ future to be completed (perfect) ____✗____ future event with time expression ____

Note: The order of events is not important. If the future event with the time expression comes first, use a comma.

Example: *By the time my kids are in school, I will have become a teacher.*

H Mrs. Morgan's other students wrote goal statements as well. Complete each statement with the correct form of the future perfect of the verb in parentheses.

1. By the time I graduate from high school, I (do) _____ will have done _____ 500 hours of community service.

2. I (buy) _____ will have bought _____ a new house when I retire.

3. When I turn 60, I (travel) _____ will have traveled _____ to over 20 countries.

4. We (put) _____ will have put _____ three kids through college by 2020.

5. I (become) _____ will have become _____ a successful business owner by the time I turn 40.

6. By the time I finish getting my degree, I (apply) _____ will have applied _____ to three different graduate programs.

I Write three goal statements for yourself on a separate piece of paper.

(Answers will vary.)

J Now that you have written down your goals, what are you going to do to keep yourself motivated? Write down three ideas on a separate piece of paper. Share your goals and motivation with a partner.

(Answers will vary.)

Review

A Indicate the learning style next to each activity. Write *V* for *Visual*, *A* for *Auditory*, and *T/K* for *Tactile/Kinesthetic* on the line. (Lesson 1)

1. analyzing a graph ___V___

2. listening to a discussion ___A___

3. listening to a lecture ___A___

4. participating in a dance ___T/K___

5. reading a journal article ___V___

6. touching objects ___T/K___

7. watching an online newscast ___V___

B Complete each statement with a phrase from the box. (Lesson 1)

appreciates music	relates well to surroundings
expresses oneself with movement	thinks in pictures
is aware of one's own feelings	uses language
relates well to others	uses reason, logic, and numbers

1. A naturalistic person ___relates well to surroundings___.

2. Someone with interpersonal intelligence ___relates well to others___.

3. A person who is kinesthetic ___expresses oneself with movement___.

4. A logical/mathematical person ___uses reason, logic, and numbers___.

5. A person with visual intelligence ___thinks in pictures___.

6. Someone with intrapersonal intelligence ___is aware of one's own feelings___.

7. A musical/rhythmic person ___appreciates music___.

8. A verbal/linguistic person ___uses language___.

C Interview a classmate about how the information below relates to him or her. Write his or her answers on the lines. (Lessons 2–3) (Answers will vary.)

1. Types of intelligence: _____

2. Career interests: _____

3. What is important to you now? _____

4. What changes would you like to make for your future? _____

_____

AT-A-GLANCE PREP

Objectives: All unit objectives
Grammar: All unit grammar
Academic Strategy: Reviewing
Vocabulary: All Unit 1 vocabulary

RESOURCES

Stand Out 5 Assessment CD-ROM with Exam*View*®

■ 1.5 hour classes   ■ 2.5 hour classes   ■ 3⁺ hour classes

AGENDA

Discuss unit objectives.
Complete the review.
Use unit vocabulary.

Warm-up and Review   5-10 mins.

Review the future perfect tense with students by asking volunteers to come to the board and write their goal statements from Exercise I in the previous lesson.

Introduction   5-10 mins.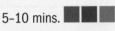

Ask students as a class to try to recall all the goals of this unit without looking back in their books. The goals for this unit include identifying your learning style, identifying a career path, balancing your life, identifying and prioritizing goals, and motivating yourself. Write all the objectives on the board from Unit 1. Show students the first page of the unit and reread the five goals together.

State the objective: *Today we will be reviewing everything you have learned in this unit and preparing for the team project.*

Presentation 1   10-15 mins.

This presentation will cover the first three pages of the review. Quickly go to the first page of each lesson. Discuss the objective of each. Ask simple questions to remind students of what they have learned.

Note: Since there is little presentation in the review, you can assign the review exercises that don't require collaboration with a partner or group for homework and go over them in class the following day.

Practice 1   20-25 mins.

Note: There are two ways to do the review:

1. Go through the exercises one at a time and, as students complete each one, go over the answers.

2. Quickly go through the instructions of each exercise, let students complete all of the exercises at once, and then go over the answers.

(A) Indicate the learning style next to each activity. Write *V* for *Visual, A* for *Auditory,* and *T/K* for *Tactile/Kinesthetic* on the line. (Lesson 1)

(B) Complete each statement with a phrase from the box. (Lesson 1)

(C) Interview a classmate about how the information below relates to him or her. Write his or her answers on the lines. (Lessons 2–3)

Evaluation 1   5-15 mins.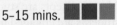

Go around the classroom and check on students' progress. Help individuals when needed. If you notice consistent errors among several students, interrupt the class and give a mini-lesson or review until students feel comfortable with the concept or point being examined.

STANDARDS CORRELATIONS

CASAS: 7.2.1 (See CASAS Competency List on pages 187–193.)
SCANS: **Resources** Allocate time
Information Acquire and evaluate information
Interpersonal Participate as a member of a team, teach others, negotiate to arrive at a decision, work with cultural diversity
Systems Monitor and correct performance
Basic Skills Reading, writing, arithmetic, listening, speaking

Thinking Skills Think creatively, make decisions, solve problems, see things in the mind's eye
Personal Qualities Responsibility, sociability, self-management
EFF: **Communication** Read with understanding, convey ideas in writing, speak so others can understand, listen actively, observe critically
Interpersonal Cooperate with others, guide others
Lifelong Learning Take responsibility for learning, reflect and evaluate

Practice 2   25–30 mins. ■■□□

D Write a paragraph about your partner on a separate piece of paper. (Lesson 3)

E Remember what you learned about goal setting. Without looking back in the unit, write four tips for setting goals. (Lesson 4)

F Walk around the classroom and ask your classmates for suggestions on how to motivate yourself. Write five ideas below. (Lesson 5)

G Choose a verb from the box below and complete each goal statement with the correct form of the future perfect. (Lesson 5)

Evaluation 2   5–15 mins. ■■□□

Go around the classroom and check on students' progress. Help individuals when needed. If you see consistent errors among several students, again, interrupt the class and give a mini-lesson or review to help students feel comfortable with the concept.

Instructor's Notes

D Write a paragraph about your partner on a separate piece of paper. (Lesson 3)

(Answers will vary.)

E Remember what you learned about goal setting. Without looking back in the unit, write four tips for setting goals. (Lesson 4) (Answers will vary. Sample answers are below.)

1. Write goals as positive statements

2. Prioritize (in order of importance)

3. Write goals where I can read them every day

4. Tell friends my goals so they can support me

F Walk around the classroom and ask your classmates for suggestions on how to motivate yourself. Write five ideas below. (Lesson 5) (Answers will vary.)

1. _____

2. _____

3. _____

4. _____

5. _____

G Choose a verb from the box below and complete each goal statement with the correct form of the future perfect. (Lesson 5)

buy and sell	raise	program
apply	compete	

1. By the time I graduate from technical school, I _____will have programmed_____ over twenty computers.

2. She _____will have bought and sold_____ at least ten properties when she retires.

3. When he turns 65, he _____will have raised_____ two amazing children.

4. They _____will have competed_____ in their first triathlon by the year 2012.

5. By the time I get my Master's Degree, I _____will have applied_____ for forty jobs at companies all over the country.

VOCABULARY REVIEW

(H) Use these words to help you complete all the exercises on this page. Some words may be used more than once.

achieve	evaluate	positive outlook
balance	inspire	prioritize
be flexible	long-term	pursue
earning power	monitor	short-term
educational attainment	motivate	support

(I) Complete each sentence with the best verb. Note that some sentences can have more than one answer. Then, work with a partner and use the five questions for a discussion.

(Answers may vary. Sample answers are given.)

1. If you _____prioritize_____ your goals, you can focus on the most important ones first.

2. Have you ever created a chart to _____evaluate_____ your progress?

3. What career do you think you might _____pursue_____?

4. How do you _____motivate_____ yourself?

5. What goals have you _____achieved_____ in the past?

6. Have you found family and friends to _____inspire_____ you?

(J) Write sentences about goal setting with the following terms. (Answers will vary. Samples are given.)

1. balance: It is important to maintain a balance of your goals.

2. be flexible: If you are flexible in your goal-setting, you will be happy.

3. positive outlook: Keep a positive outlook when working on goals.

4. achieve: Try to achieve both long- and short-term goals.

(K) Complete each phrase below. Use a word from the box above and your own words. (Sample answers are given.)

1. To improve your earning power, you should get a good education and some experience.

2. If you want to achieve your goals, you must be organized, motivated, and flexible

3. In order to best reach your long-term goals, you have to make a plan, get support, and prioritize your activities

Practice 3

25–30 mins. ▪▪▪ ▫

Vocabulary Review

(H) Use these words to help you complete all the exercises on this page. Some words may be used more than once.

(I) Complete each sentence with the best verb. Note that some sentences can have more than one answer. Then, work with a partner and use the five questions for a discussion.

(J) Write sentences about goal setting with the following terms.

(K) Complete each phrase below. Use a word from the box above and your own words.

Evaluation 3

5–15 mins. ▪▪▪ ▫

Go around the classroom and check on students' progress. Help individuals when needed. If you see consistent errors among several students, interrupt the class and give a mini-lesson or review to help students feel comfortable with the concept.

Assessment (optional)

▪▪▪ ▫

Use the Stand Out 5 Assessment CD-ROM with *ExamView®* to create a post-test for Unit 1.

AT-A-GLANCE PREP

Objective: Research information about careers

Academic Strategy: Research

RESOURCES

Web Site Addresses: Bureau of Labor Statistics

http://www.bls.gov/home.htm

http://www.bls.gov/oco/

Activity Bank: *Occupational Outlook Handbook* (reprints of each section in PDF form)

AGENDA

Use key words to conduct online research.

Use the U.S. Department of Labor's Web site to find information.

Academic Feature: Research Project

Each unit will have a research page where students are required to complete a task by conducting research. Options will be given for students to use the computer, or specifically, the Internet, as well as printed resource materials. Important resource materials for Unit 1 can be found on the Activity Bank CD-ROM.

Introduction   5–10 mins.

Remind students about the research they did in the Pre-Unit. Ask students how they did this research. Ask them to help you brainstorm other ways to research. Make a list on the board. State the objective: *Today you will research the career path you chose by using the Internet and printed material.*

Presentation   10–15 mins.

A One of the fastest ways to research something is to search the Internet. For example, you might want to know how much money you can make at a certain career. What are some key words you could use to search for this information?

As a class, talk about key words and how we use them to search for something on the Internet. If you have access to a computer connected to a projector, you can show students how to search.

Practice   15–30 mins.

B If you have access to the Internet, conduct an online search to find out the following information for the career path that you chose in Lesson 2, Exercise I.

C The U.S. Department of Labor, Bureau of Labor Statistics (http://www.bls.gov/home.htm) publishes the *Occupational Outlook Handbook* every two years. This handbook gives information about hundreds of different types of jobs. In this handbook, you will find the following types of information: the training and education needed, earnings, expected job prospects, what workers do on the job, working conditions.

The following topics are from the *Occupational Outlook Handbook*. Which one do you think would have information about your career? Underline it.

Refer to the student book page for this list of topics.

Evaluation   5–10 mins.

As a class, have each student tell you his or her career path and which topic he or she underlined.

Application   10–30 mins.

D Find the *Occupational Outlook Handbook* online at http://www.bls.gov/oco/. Search for the information about your chosen career. Print out the information to research.

STANDARDS CORRELATIONS

CASAS: 4.9.3, 7.2.1, 7.4.4, 7.4.5, 7.4.6 (See CASAS Competency List on pages 187–193.)

SCANS: **Information** Acquire and evaluate information, organize and maintain information, interpret and communicate information, use computers to process information *(optional)*

Interpersonal Participate as a member of a team, teach others, negotiate to arrive at a decision, work with cultural diversity

Systems Understand systems

Technology Select technology, apply technology to a task, maintain and troubleshoot technology *(optional)*

Basic Skills Reading, writing

Thinking Skills Creative thinking, decision making, seeing things in the mind's eye

Personal Qualities Responsibility, sociability, self-management

EFF: **Communication** Read with understanding, convey ideas in writing, observe critically

Decision Making Solve problems and make decisions, plan

Lifelong Learning Take responsibility for learning, reflect and evaluate, learn through research, use information and communications technology *(optional)*

21a   Lesson Planner: Unit 1, Research Project

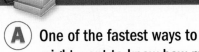

Research Project

A One of the fastest ways to research something is to search the Internet. For example, you might want to know how much money you can make at a certain career. What are some key words you could use to search for this information? (Sample answers are given.)

career, average salary, earnings, wages

B If you have access to the Internet, conduct an online search to find out the following information for the career path that you chose in Lesson 2, Exercise I.
(Answers will vary.)

Career title: _____

Training needed: _____

Education needed: _____

Possible earnings: _____

C The U.S. Department of Labor, Bureau of Labor Statistics (http://www.bls.gov/home.htm) publishes the *Occupational Outlook Handbook* every two years. This handbook gives information about hundreds of different types of jobs. In this handbook, you will find the following types of information: the training and education needed, earnings, expected job prospects, what workers do on the job, and working conditions.

The following topics are from the *Occupational Outlook Handbook*. Which one do you think would have information about your career? Underline it.

(Answers will vary.)

Management, Business, and Financial Occupations

Engineers, Life and Physical Scientists, and Related Occupations

Arts, Design, Entertainment, Sports, and Media Occupations

Education and Community and Social Service Occupations

Computer and Mathematical Occupations

Legal and Social Science Occupations

Health Diagnosing and Treating Practitioners

Health Technologists, Technicians, and Healthcare Support Occupations

Service Occupations: Cleaning, Food, and Personal

Protective Service Occupations

Sales Occupations

Office and Administrative Support Occupations

Farming, Fishing, Forestry, and Transportation Occupations

Construction Trades and Related Occupations

Installation, Maintenance, and Repair Occupations

Production Occupations

D Find the *Occupational Outlook Handbook* online at http://www.bls.gov/oco/. Search for the information about your chosen career. Print out the information to research.

Team Project

Create a personal profile.

With a team, decide on one of these project options:

a. Create a profile for yourself.
   (one profile per group member)
b. Create a profile for an imaginary person.
   (one profile per group)

1. Form a team with four or five students. Choose a position for each member of your team.

POSITION	JOB DESCRIPTION	STUDENT NAME
Student 1: **Project Leader**	See that everyone speaks English. See that everyone participates.	
Student 2: **Secretary**	Take notes on team's ideas. Write a list of items to include in profile.	
Student 3: **Designer**	Design profile.	
Student 4: **Spokesperson**	Report information to the class if team creates one profile for an imaginary person. Otherwise, prepare team members for individual presentations.	
Student 5: **Assistant**	Help the secretary and designer with their work.	

2. Discuss and decide on profile information: learning style, intelligence(s), career path, things to balance in life, short- and long-term goals, and a list of motivational strategies.*

3. Decide on the design. Organize the layout of the profile.

4. Present profile to the class.

* *Options:* If your team is creating individual profiles, work together to decide what general information will go in each person's profile as well as how to organize the profiles. Team members then complete profiles on their own.

Create a personal profile.

Each team will create a profile for an imaginary person or work together to create individual profiles for each team member. The profile will include learning style, intelligence(s), career path, things to balance, goals (big picture and short-term), and a list of motivational strategies.

The team project is the final application for the unit. It gives students a chance to show that they have mastered all of the Unit 1 objectives.

Note: Shorter classes can extend this project over two class meetings.

Stage 1   5 mins.

Form a team with four or five students. Choose a position for each member of your team.

Remind students to choose between the two project options. Then, have students decide who will lead each step as described on the student page. Provide well-defined directions on the board for how teams should proceed, but encourage creativity in each team and listen to all student ideas equally. Explain that all the students do every step as a team. Teams shouldn't go to the next stage until the previous one is complete.

Stage 2   15–20 mins.

Discuss and decide on profile information: learning style, intelligence(s), career path, things to balance in life, short- and long-term goals, and a list of motivational strategies.

Once teams have delegated tasks, have them tell the class if they are creating a profile for an imaginary person or a profile for each team member.

Stage 3   10–15 mins.

Decide on the design. Organize the layout of the profile.

To give students some suggestions, you might design two different profiles on the board so they can see how they might present their information as a poster or as a notebook (for example).

Optional Computer Activity: Students may want to use the computer to design and then create their profiles.

Stage 4   15–30 mins.

Present profile to the class.

Help teams prepare for their presentations. Suggest that each member choose a different part of the profile to present. Encourage students to be creative. The project could be composed of charts, a notebook, a poster, a slide presentation, or any combination of these media methods.

STANDARDS CORRELATIONS

CASAS: 4.8.1, 4.8.5, 4.8.6. (See CASAS Competency List on pages 187–193.)
SCANS: Resources Allocate time
Information Acquire and evaluate information, organize and maintain information, interpret and communicate information, use computers to process information
Systems Understand systems, improve and design systems
Technology Select technology, apply technology to exercise
Basic Skills Writing
Thinking Skills Think creatively, make decisions, solve problems, see things in the mind's eye, use reasoning

Personal Qualities Responsibility, self-esteem, self-management, integrity
EFF: Communication Read with understanding, convey ideas in writing, speak so others can understand, listen actively, observe critically
Decision Making Solve problems and make decisions, plan
Interpersonal Cooperate with others, advocate and influence, resolve conflict and negotiate, guide others
Lifelong Learning Take responsibility for learning, reflect and evaluate, learn through research, use information and communications technology (optional)

Objective: Introduce new vocabulary

Academic Strategies: Using context clues, using a dictionary

Vocabulary: See lesson

RESOURCES

Dictionaries: It is recommended that each student in class have an ESL learner's dictionary or that there be dictionaries available in the classroom for students to use. Dictionaries that will be referred to in this book

AGENDA

Read about Kimla's financial goals.

Define vocabulary expressions.

Use context to discover meaning.

are the *Heinle's Newbury House Dictionary of American English* and the *Collins Cobuild Intermediate* or *Advanced Dictionary of American English*.

Academic Feature: Vocabulary Builder

Each unit will begin with a vocabulary-building section. The purpose of this two-page section is to introduce students to many of the words they will be using in the unit lessons. Students will have a chance to see how much they already know, and they will get exposure to the new vocabulary found in the unit.

Note: All of the exercises on these two pages should be done in class, no matter the class length. Longer classes can do this lesson and then, move onto Lesson 1 during the same class meeting; shorter classes may have to devote one whole class meeting to this lesson.

Introduction   5–10 mins.

State the objective: *Today we will be identifying and working with the vocabulary you will study in this unit.*

Presentation 1   10–15 mins.

A Kimla sat down and made a list of her financial goals. Read what she wrote.

Read or ask a volunteer to read Kimla's goals out loud.

B What does each of the italicized expressions mean? Discuss them with your classmates.

As you discuss the vocabulary, talk about what each goal means.

Practice 1   10–15 mins.

C Some English phrases, such as *living paycheck to paycheck* or *living within your means*, have a special meaning. Often, if you try to understand the meaning of the individual words, you can understand the phrase. Talk to your classmates or use a dictionary to discover the meaning of the following expressions.

Evaluation 1   5–15 mins.

Go over the answers as a class.

STANDARDS CORRELATIONS

CASAS: 7.4.5 (See CASAS Competency List on pages 187–193.)

SCANS: **Information** Acquire and evaluate information, organize and maintain information

Interpersonal Participate as a member of a team, negotiate to arrive at a decision, work with cultural diversity

Systems Understand systems, monitor and correct performance

Basic Skills Reading, writing, listening, speaking

Thinking Skills Think creatively, make decisions, see things in the mind's eye

Personal Qualities Responsibility, sociability, self-management

EFF: **Communication** Read with understanding, convey ideas in writing, speak so others can understand, listen actively

Decision Making Use math to solve problems and communicate, solve problems and make decisions, plan

Interpersonal Cooperate with others

Lifelong Learning Take responsibility for learning, reflect and evaluate, learn through research

UNIT 2

Personal Finance

GOALS

➤ Organize your finances
➤ Reduce debt and save money
➤ Identify investment strategies

➤ Maintain good credit
➤ Protect yourself against identity theft

Vocabulary Builder

Vocabulary   Grammar
Life Skills
Academic   Pronunciation

A Kimla sat down and made a list of her financial goals. Read what she wrote.

My Financial Goals

1. I need to stop *impulse buying* and pay off my credit cards.
2. I want to stop *living paycheck to paycheck* and save enough money for a down payment on a house.
3. I want to increase my *purchasing power* by putting $200 a month into an emergency savings account.
4. I want us to start *living within our means,* so I can start giving $100 a month to charity.
5. I want to *save* $75 a month, so I can attend college next year.

B What does each of the italicized expressions mean? Discuss them with your classmates.
impulse buying = buying without a plan; living paycheck to paycheck = not saving money; purchasing power = ability to buy; living within our means = not overspending a paycheck

C Some English phrases, such as *living paycheck to paycheck* or *living within your means,* have a special meaning. Often, if you try to understand the meaning of the individual words, you can understand the phrase. Talk to your classmates or use a dictionary to discover the meaning of the following expressions. (Answers will vary.)

1. budget cut
2. buy in bulk
3. capital gains

4. commit fraud
5. counterfeit checks
6. current income

7. delinquent accounts
8. false pretenses
9. unauthorized transactions

1. reduce spending
2. buy large amounts
3. money earned as profit

4. use false information intentionally
5. fake checks
6. money earned now

7. overdue money owed
8. give untrue information
9. illegal financial deal

Vocabulary Builder

D Look at the following sentences. Try to figure out the meaning of the underlined words by reading them in context. (Answers may vary. Sample answers are given.)

1. The company declared <u>bankruptcy</u> when it ran out of money.

   Bankruptcy means _without money to pay creditors_ .

2. I took out a loan at the bank and used my house as <u>collateral</u>.

   Collateral means _property used as security for a loan_ .

3. The thought of starting a business was <u>daunting</u>, but he decided to do it anyway.

   Daunting means _intimidating or discouraging_ .

4. <u>Inflation</u> was so great that bread cost twice as much in June as it did in May.

   Inflation means _an increase in money so that prices rise beyond value_ .

5. His <u>investment</u> in the stock market has made him a millionaire.

   Investment means _to commit money to gain money_ .

6. The company has no <u>liquid</u> assets; therefore, it can't pay its bills.

   Liquid means _easily converted to cash money_ .

7. She paid the <u>penalty</u> of a large fine for cheating on her income tax returns.

   Penalty means _a punishment by law for a crime committed_ .

8. He <u>periodically</u> reviews his budget and makes changes when necessary.

   Periodically means _at regular intervals of time or date_ .

9. Putting money in the stock market might be <u>risky</u> because you could lose your money.

   Risky means _exposure to danger or damage_ .

E Look back at Kimla's financial goals in Exercise A on page 23. Using some of the new vocabulary words and phrases you have learned in this lesson, write four of your own financial goals. (Answers may vary. Sample answers are given.)

1. _I want to cut my budget._

2. _I need to stop living paycheck to paycheck._

3. _I hope to increase my current income._

4. _I will reduce my impulse buying._

Presentation 2   5-10 mins.

Show students how to find the meaning of a word by looking at an example sentence. You can use some of the expressions from Exercise A or even some of the examples in Exercise D.

Pronunciation

Vocabulary

When teaching students new vocabulary, pronounce each word for them several times and ask them to repeat it. Often, students may be familiar with the words you are introducing but have never seen them spelled out. By pronouncing the words for students, you allow students to make a connection between the words' spellings and their sounds. It is also important that students learn the correct pronunciation of new words so they feel comfortable using their new vocabulary inside and outside of the classroom.

Practice 2   10-15 mins.

D Look at the following sentences. Try to figure out the meaning of the underlined words by reading them in context.

Evaluation 2   10-15 mins.

Go over the answers as a class.

Application   5-10 mins.

E Look back at Kimla's financial goals in Exercise A on page 23. Using some of the new vocabulary words and phrases you have learned in this lesson, write four of your own financial goals.

Objective: Organize your finances
Academic Strategies: Note taking, making calculations
Vocabulary: *expense, fixed, variable, cut, live within one's means*

RESOURCES

Activity Bank: Unit 2, Lesson 1, Worksheets 1–2
Grammar Challenge 5: Unit 2, Challenge 1

 1.5 hour classes ■ 2.5 hour classes ■ 3+ hour classes

AGENDA

Assess your expenses.
Listen to a financial planner.
Study Kimla and her husband's Money Out Worksheet.
Make calculations.
Discuss fixed and variable expenses.
Create your own Money Out Worksheet.

Audio: CD Track 10
Stand Out 5 Assessment CD-ROM with *ExamView®*

Pre-assessment *(optional)*

Use the Stand Out 5 Assessment CD-ROM with *ExamView®* to create a pre-test for Unit 2.

Warm-up and Review   5-10 mins.

 A Look back at the goals you wrote in Exercise E on page 24. Rewrite the goals below, giving each one a time frame.

Have students do this exercise by themselves. While they are working, walk around the classroom and write down four student goals to use as dictation.

Introduction   10-20 mins.

Dictation: Use the four sentences you collected during the Warm-up. State the objective: *Today you will learn how to organize your finances.*

Presentation 1   10-15 mins.

 B Do you know how much money you spend a week? A month? A year? Many people are not certain of the exact amount it costs them to live. Often, people don't include the expenses that come up occasionally in their personal budgets.

Think about how you spend your money. Answer the following questions.

Go over this exercise with students and have them write their own answers. When they have finished, ask them for some ideas on how they do or would organize the money they spend.

Practice 1   10-15 mins.

 **C** Listen to a financial planner talking about how to organize personal finances. Write down the most important points the planner makes.

Prepare students for this activity by telling them they will be listening for five different suggestions. Remind them that taking notes is just writing down the important ideas, not every single word they hear. Play the recording more than once if necessary.

See listening script Exercise C on page 26a.

Evaluation 1   5-10 mins.

 D Compare your notes with a partner. Add any important points you missed.

Go over the notes with the class.

STANDARDS CORRELATIONS

CASAS: 1.5.1 (See CASAS Competency List on pages 187–193.)
SCANS: **Resources** Allocate money
Information Acquire and evaluate information, organize and maintain information, interpret and communicate information, use computers to process information *(optional)*
Interpersonal Participate as a member of a team, negotiate to arrive at a decision, work with cultural diversity
Systems Understand systems, monitor and correct performance, improve and design systems
Technology Apply technology to a task *(optional)*
Basic Skills Reading, writing, arithmetic, listening, speaking

Thinking Skills Think creatively, make decisions, solve problems, see things in the mind's eye
Personal Qualities Responsibility, sociability, self-management
EFF: **Communication** Speak so others can understand, listen actively, observe critically
Decision Making Use math to solve problems and communicate, solve problems and make decisions, plan
Interpersonal Cooperate with others, resolve conflict and negotiate
Lifelong Learning Take responsibility for learning, reflect and evaluate, use information and communications technology *(optional)*

Getting organized

GOAL ➤ Organize your finances

 A Look back at the goals you wrote in Exercise E on page 24. Rewrite the goals below, giving each one a time frame. (Answers will vary. Sample answers are given.)

EXAMPLE: By the end of next year, I will have paid off my credit cards.

1. By the end of this week, I will have cut my budget.
2. By the end of this month, I will have stopped living paycheck to paycheck.
3. By six months from now, I will have increased my income.
4. By this time tomorrow, I will have stopped my impulse buying.

 B Do you know how much money you spend a week? A month? A year? Many people are not certain of the exact amount it costs them to live. Often, people don't include the expenses that come up occasionally in their personal budgets. (Sample answers are given.)

Think about how you spend your money. Answer the following questions.

1. Did you go on a vacation last year? __YES__ How much did it cost? __$1,500__

2. Do you know how much you spend during the holidays every year? About $1,000

3. How often do you get your hair cut? 5 times/yr How much does it cost? __$150__

4. How often do you pay car insurance premiums? MONTHLY How much is each premium? __$75__

CD
TR 10

 C Listen to a financial planner talking about how to organize personal finances. Write down the most important points the planner makes.

1. Go through all financial paperwork for the past year.
2. Write all categories in which I spend money.
3. Write down how much I spend in each category per month.
4. Add up how much per year is spent for each category.
5. Divide those numbers by 12 to get average monthly spending.

D Compare your notes with a partner. Add any important points you missed.

E After meeting with a financial planner, Kimla and her husband sat down with all of their bank statements, credit card statements, ATM records, and receipts. Look at the worksheet below that they created. What do they still need to calculate?

MONEY OUT		
	Annual	**Monthly**
Mortgage/Rent	$20,400	$1,700
Home maintenance fees	$2,400	$200
Renters' insurance	$500	$41.67
Gas & Electric	$1,800	$150
Water	$240	$20
Telephone/Cell phone	$1,560	$130
Food/Restaurants	$3,600	$300
Medical/Dental	$1,020	$85
Auto expenses	$1,920	$160
Tolls/Fares/Parking	$360	$30
Clothes/Shoes	$850	$70.83
Dry cleaning	$180	$15
Hair/Manicure/Facial	$600	$50
Kids' school	$500	$41.67
Training/Education	$300	$25
Income taxes	$655	$54.58
Computer	$600	$50
Credit cards/Loans	$7,800	$650
Postage	$36	$3
Subscriptions	$24	$2
Entertainment	$600	$50
Cable/Satellite	$780	$65
Vacations	$2,000	$166.67
Hobbies	$175	$14.58
Gifts	$550	$45.83
TOTAL	$49,450	$4,120.83

Calculations

To calculate annual expenses, multiply monthly expense by 12:

250	15	55	1300
$\times 12$	$\times 12$	$\times 12$	$\times 12$
3000	180	660	15,600

To calculate monthly expenses, divide annual expense by 12:

$3000 \div 12 = 250$ $180 \div 12 = 15$

$660 \div 12 = 55$ $15,600 \div 12 = 1300$

F Calculate Kimla and her husband's annual and monthly totals.

See chart.

G Together, Kimla and her husband make about $53,000 a year before deductions. How much do they have left over? _$3550_ How much is this per month? _$295.83_ Do you think Kimla's family lives within their means? Why? or Why not? _Yes, but they should put money in a savings account._

Listening Script CD Track 10

Financial Planner: *Let's get started. The first thing you need to do is go through all of your bank statements, credit card statements, receipts—basically all of the financial paperwork you have for the past year. Next, write down all of the categories in which you spend money. Then, figure out how much you spent in each category each month. Fourth, add up how much you spent each month to find out how much you spent per year in each category. Finally, total up all these annual numbers and divide the total by 12 to find out how much you spent each month on average. If you do all these things, you'll get a good idea of your annual or yearly expenses.*

Presentation 2   5-10 mins. ■■■

 After meeting with a financial planner, Kimla and her husband sat down with all of their bank statements, credit card statements, ATM records, and receipts. Look at the worksheet below that they created. What do they still need to calculate?

Talk about the worksheet as a class, using an overhead transparency if you can. Go over each expense, making sure students understand what each one is. Then, talk about how much money Kimla and her family spend monthly or annually.

Point out which calculations are missing. Make sure students know how to do multiplication and division, using the math box to practice.

Practice 2   10-15 mins. ■■

Note: Shorter classes can do this exercise for homework.

 Calculate Kimla and her husband's annual and monthly totals.

Evaluation 2   10-15 mins. ■■

Go over the answers as a class by asking volunteers to come up and write the correct numbers on the board or overhead transparency.

Activity Bank

Unit 2, Lesson 1, Worksheet 1: Money Out

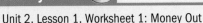 Together, Kimla and her husband make about $53,000 a year. How much do they have left over? How much is this per month? Do you think Kimla's family lives within their means?

Teaching Tip

Math

Basic calculations are a life skill that students will need to be able to do on a daily basis. Advise students to do calculations on paper before they resort to using calculators. Observe their abilities and provide supplemental review of math skills as needed.

Instructor's Notes

_____

_____

_____

_____

_____

_____

_____

_____

_____

_____

_____

_____

_____

_____

_____

_____

_____

_____

_____

Presentation 3   5-10 mins.

Write *Fixed Expenses* on the board. Ask students to help you define this term and talk about a few examples. Now write *Variable Expenses* on the board. Define this term and have students come up with examples.

Practice 3   10-15 mins. ■

(H) In Kimla and her husband's Money Out worksheet on the previous page, some expenses are *fixed* (stay the same every month) and others are *variable* (can change from month to month). With a partner, make a list of Kimla and her husband's fixed expenses and a list of their variable expenses.

Note: Shorter classes can do Exercise H for homework and review at the next class meeting.

Evaluation 3   5-10 mins. ■

Ask volunteers to come to the board and add to the lists you started in the Presentation.

(I) Look back at Kimla's financial goals on page 23. How much money does she want to start saving per month for college? For charity? For emergencies? Does she have enough money in her budget for these items? If not, what expenses do you think Kimla and her husband can cut back on? Look at the list of variable expenses you made in Exercise H and discuss your ideas with a group.

Application   10-20 mins. ■■■

(J) Create a Money Out worksheet like the one on page 26, listing all the monthly and annual expenses you have. Next to each expense, write *f* for a fixed expense or *v* for a variable expense. Look at the chart below to get you started.

Activity Bank

Unit 2, Lesson 1, Worksheet 2: Expense Sheets (template)

 Refer students to *Stand Out 5 Grammar Challenge*, Unit 2, Challenge 1 for practice with the future perfect versus the future perfect continuous (progressive).

LESSON **1** **GOAL** ➤ **Organize your finances**

H In Kimla and her husband's Money Out Worksheet on the previous page, some expenses are *fixed* (stay the same every month) and others are *variable* (can change from month to month). With a partner, make a list of Kimla and her husband's fixed expenses and a list of their variable expenses. (Answers may vary. Sample answers are below.)

Fixed	Variable
mortgage/rent, loans, subscriptions, cable TV, computer	credit cards, loans, postage, vacations, entertainment, hobbies, gifts

I Look back at Kimla's financial goals on page 23. How much money does she want to start saving per month for college? __75__ For charity? __100__ For emergencies? __200__ Does she have enough money in her budget for these items? __No__ If not, what expenses do you think Kimla and her husband can cut back on? Look at the list of variable expenses you made in Exercise H and discuss your ideas with a group. (Sample answer is given below.)
Cut back on restaurants, hobbies, and entertainment.

J Create a Money Out worksheet like the one on page 26, listing all the monthly and annual expenses you have. Next to each expense, write *f* for a fixed expense or *v* for a variable expense. Look at the chart below to get you started. (Answers will vary.)

	Annual	Monthly
Mortgage (f)		
Home maintenance fees (v)		
Homeowner's insurance (f)		
Gas & Electric (v)		
Water (v)		

Managing money

GOAL ➤ Reduce debt and save money

A Read the ad.

Do you live within your means or do you live paycheck to paycheck?

Do you owe money to a bank or another person?

Are you up to your ears in debt?

WE CAN HELP

The first thing we will help you do is make a budget. It is important to plan out your monthly expenses so you know where your money is going each month. Our advisors will help you get on track so you can make some cuts to your monthly budget. These cuts will allow you to pay off your debt faster. We'll show you how to get rid of bad debt by paying off your higher interest and long-term debts first. We'll get your credit reports for you and analyze them to see if we can help boost your credit rating. We'll also teach you some helpful tips; here's one: *Credit card interest is calculated daily, so if you make your payment earlier than the due date, you'll actually save interest!* If there are some debts that you just can't pay, we'll contact the creditors and arrange settlements for you.

How can you afford not to let us help you? **Don't hesitate.** Call us today! (800) 555-0125

B Answer the questions about the ad with a partner. (Answers will vary.)

1. Who do you think wrote this ad? _A debt reduction agency_

2. What is the purpose of this ad? (Why was it written?) _To help people in debt_

3. Would you call the number listed at the bottom of the ad? Why or why not?
   I would be concerned if their help might affect my credit rating badly.

4. The ad mentions how they would help get you out of debt. List four of their suggestions.

   a. _Make a budget._

   b. _Cut monthly budget._

   c. _Get rid of bad debt by paying off high interest/long-term debt._

   d. _Get credit reports and analyze them._

AT-A-GLANCE PREP

Objective: Reduce debt and save money
Grammar: Past perfect progressive
Academic Strategies: Identifying purpose of reading, finding details, focused listening
Vocabulary: *paycheck to paycheck, up to your ears, settlements, purpose, impulse buying, bargains, generic, deductible, in full, buy in bulk*

RESOURCES

Activity Bank: Unit 2, Lesson 2, Worksheets 1–3

 1.5 hour classes   ■ 2.5 hour classes   ■ 3+ hour classes

Grammar Challenge 5: Unit 2, Challenge 2
Audio: CD Track 11

AGENDA

Read an ad about reducing debt.
Read money-saving tips.
Listen to a conversation about Kimla and Derek's spending habits.
Practice using the past perfect progressive.
Think about ways you can save money.

Warm-up and Review   5-10 mins.

Talk about the Money Out worksheets from the previous lesson. Ask students if they filled out their worksheets at home. Discuss the challenges with filling them out, such as difficulty finding records.

Introduction   10-20 mins.

Dictation:

1. We try to live within our means every month.
2. They have been living paycheck to paycheck for the past year.
3. She doesn't know where her money goes every month.
4. He has decided to pay off all his debts by the end of next year.

State the objective: *Today you will discover ways to reduce debt and save money.*

Presentation 1   10-15 mins.

(A) Read the ad.

Let students read the ad silently. Then, ask a volunteer to read it out loud to the class. Ask students if they have any questions about the vocabulary. Try not to answer questions that students will have to answer in Exercise B.

Activity Bank

Unit 2, Lesson 2, Worksheet 1: Debt Ad Vocabulary

Practice 1   10-15 mins.

(B) Answer the questions about the ad with a partner.

Evaluation 1   5 mins.

Go over the answers as a class.

STANDARDS CORRELATIONS

CASAS: 1.6.2 (See CASAS Competency List on pages 187-193).
SCANS: **Information** Acquire and evaluate information, organize and maintain information, interpret and communicate information
Interpersonal Participate as a member of a team, negotiate to arrive at a decision, work with cultural diversity
Systems Monitor and correct performance
Basic Skills Reading, writing, listening, speaking
Thinking Skills Think creatively, make decisions

Personal Qualities Responsibility, sociability
EFF: **Communication** Read with understanding, convey ideas in writing, speak so others can understand, listen actively, observe critically
Decision Making Solve problems and make decisions, plan
Interpersonal Cooperate with others
Lifelong Learning Take responsibility for learning, reflect and evaluate, learn through research

Presentation 2   5–10 mins.

C The ad on page 28 mentions making cuts to your budget. Read the Web page below with tips on how to save money.

Go over the tips as a class.

Practice 2   10–15 mins.

Note: Shorter classes can do this exercise for homework by using the script in the back of the book.

Activity Bank

Unit 2, Lesson 2, Worksheet 2: Saving Money
(listening)

D Listen to Kimla and her husband, Derek, talk about saving money. Write *T (true)* or *F (false)* on the line before each statement.

Students may find this exercise difficult because of the grammar used in the conversation, but play it over a few times for students and see if they can discover the speakers' general meaning.

Listening Script   CD Track 11

Kimla: *Derek, I really think we need to come up with some more ways to save money.*

Derek: *More? I thought we were doing really well with our money. I'm really proud of myself for making my own coffee instead of buying it at a coffee shop and clipping coupons.*

Kimla: *Yes, you are doing a great job. But weren't you supposed to buy a used car? I thought you were looking at used cars, but then you ended up buying a new one.*

Derek: *Well, what about you and your designer clothes?*

Kimla: *At least I started buying generic-name products and turning off the air conditioner before I go to bed.*

Derek: *Um, what about your designer clothes?*

Kimla: *I know, I know, I used to be so good at looking for bargains. But I just love the designer fashions. At least I was able to call the credit card companies and lower our interest rates, so we are no longer paying on high interest cards.*

Derek: *Yeah, that was a good move. And I called the insurance company to increase our deductible so our premiums would go down.*

Kimla: *I guess you're right, Derek. We are doing a pretty good job.*

Derek: *Yep, I agree.*

Evaluation 2   10–15 mins.

Go over the answers as a class.

E Do you already follow some of the tips in the ad in Exercise C? Which ones? Put a check (✓) next to the ones you are familiar with. Which ones would you like to follow in the future? Underline these tips.

Instructor's Notes

_____

_____

_____

_____

_____

_____

_____

_____

_____

_____

_____

_____

_____

_____

_____

_____

_____

_____

_____

_____

_____

_____

GOAL ➤ **Reduce debt and save money**

C The ad on page 28 mentions making cuts to your budget. Read the Web page below with tips on how to save money.

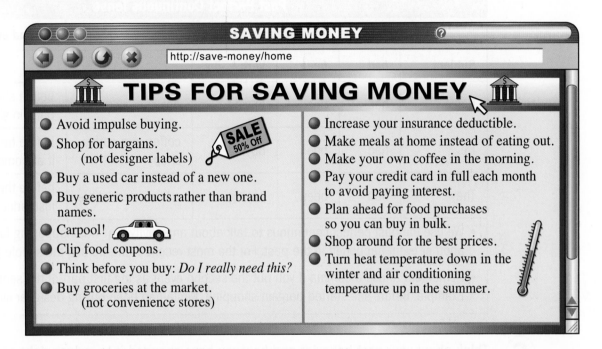

SAVING MONEY ?

http://save-money/home

TIPS FOR SAVING MONEY

- Avoid impulse buying.
- Shop for bargains.
  (not designer labels)
- Buy a used car instead of a new one.
- Buy generic products rather than brand names.
- Carpool!
- Clip food coupons.
- Think before you buy: *Do I really need this?*
- Buy groceries at the market.
  (not convenience stores)

- Increase your insurance deductible.
- Make meals at home instead of eating out.
- Make your own coffee in the morning.
- Pay your credit card in full each month to avoid paying interest.
- Plan ahead for food purchases so you can buy in bulk.
- Shop around for the best prices.
- Turn heat temperature down in the winter and air conditioning temperature up in the summer.

CD
TR 11

D Listen to Kimla and her husband, Derek, talk about saving money. Write *T (true)* or *F (false)* on the line before each statement.

_____T_____ 1. Kimla buys designer clothes.

_____F_____ 2. Derek had been buying his coffee at a coffee shop.

_____T_____ 3. Kimla had been paying high interest on credit cards.

_____F_____ 4. Derek had been looking at new cars.

_____T_____ 5. Kimla turns off the air conditioner before she goes to bed.

_____T_____ 6. Derek called the insurance to increase their deductible.

_____F_____ 7. Kimla has never bought brand name products.

_____T_____ 8. Derek clips coupons.

E Do you already follow some of the tips in the ad in Exercise C? Which ones? Put a check (✔) next to the ones you are familiar with. Which ones would you like to follow in the future? Underline these tips. (Answers will vary.)

GOAL ➤ **Reduce debt and save money**

F Study the chart with your teacher.

Past Perfect Continuous Tense					
First event in past					**Second event in past**
Subject	*had*	*been*	**Verb + -ing**		
Kimla	had	been	buying	designer clothes	before she started bargain shopping.
He	had	been	buying	coffee at a coffee shop	before he began making it at home.
They	had	been	paying	a lower deductible	before they called the insurance company.

- We use the past perfect continuous to talk about an activity that was happening for a while before another event happened in the past. For the most recent event, we use the simple past tense.

- Remember to use a comma if you put the second event as the first part of the sentence.
  Example: Before she started bargain shopping, Kimla had been buying designer clothes.

G Think about your past behavior and how you have changed it to reduce debt and save money. Write four statements. (Answers will vary.)

EXAMPLE: <u>I had been eating out for lunch every day before I started making</u>

        <u>my lunch at home.</u>

1. _____

2. _____

3. _____

4. _____

H Come up with three ways in which you are going to change your behavior to reduce debt and save money. (Answers will vary.)

EXAMPLE: <u>Tomorrow, I will start making my lunch at home.</u>

1. _____

2. _____

3. _____

Presentation 3　　　　　5-10 mins. ▪▪▫▫

F Study the chart with your teacher.

Practice 3　　　　　　　15-20 mins. ▪

Note: Shorter classes can do this exercise for homework.

G Think about your past behavior and how you have changed it to reduce debt and save money. Write four statements.

Evaluation 3　　　　　　5-10 mins. ▪

Ask volunteers to write their statements on the board. As a class, evaluate them for content and grammatical accuracy.

Application　　　　　　10-20 mins. ▪▪▫

H Come up with three ways in which you are going to change your behavior to reduce debt and save money.

Activity Bank 💿

Unit 2, Lesson 2, Worksheet 3: Past Perfect Continuous

📖 Refer students to *Stand Out 5 Grammar Challenge*, Unit 2, Challenge 2 for more practice with the past perfect continuous.

Instructor's Notes

Objective: Identify investment strategies
Academic Strategies: Outlining, writing a summary
Vocabulary: *capital gains, convert, inflation, liquid, net appreciation, penalty, purchasing power, risky, value, vehicle, worth, prevent, destroy, investment, periodically, current income, CD, capital growth, stocks, bonds, earnings*

AGENDA

Learn investment-related vocabulary.
Read about and discuss investing money.
Complete an outline.
Write a summary.

RESOURCES

Activity Bank: Unit 2, Lesson 3, Worksheets 1–2

■ 1.5 hour classes ■ 2.5 hour classes ■ 3⁺ hour classes

Grammar Challenge 5: Unit 2, Challenge 3
Suggested Realia: Money magazines (e.g., *Consumer Reports, Money, Fortune*, etc.)

Warm-up and Review   10-20 mins.

In small groups, have students discuss ways to reduce debt and save money.

Introduction   5-10 mins.

Dictation: **1.** Young investors are interested in making money over time. **2.** Older investors are more interested in earning current income. **3.** Think carefully about how soon you will need to access your money. **4.** Due to inflation, money is worth less and less every year.

State the objective: *Today you will identify different ways to invest the money you are saving.*

Presentation 1   10-15 mins.

Go over any vocabulary from the dictation that students don't understand. Some of these items will be included in Exercise A.

Practice 1   10-15 mins.

(A) In a small group, look at the following list of vocabulary words and phrases. Which words do you know? How can you find out the meaning of the ones you don't know? Discuss ways with your group and then, with your group, use those ways to find the meanings.

Evaluation 1   5-15mins.

(B) Words often have more than one meaning. It is important to know what you are listening to or reading so you can find the correct part of speech and definition for the new vocabulary word. Look at the meaning you wrote for *vehicle*. Compare your definition with this definition: *vehicle: a way in which something is accomplished.*

See if students can come up with more words that have more than one meaning but are spelled the same. Tell students these words are called *homonyms* (or more precisely, *homographs*, meaning they are spelled the same). Go over the meanings of all the words and phrases from Exercise A as a class.

Presentation 2   10-20 mins.

(C) Based on the words you defined above, what do you think the article below is about? Discuss your ideas with your classmates.

(D) Read the article about investing money.

Ask students to read the article silently. Tell them that they can read it more than one time if necessary.

STANDARDS CORRELATIONS

CASAS: 7.4.2 (See CASAS Competency List on pages 187–193.)
SCANS: **Information** Acquire and evaluate information, organize and maintain information, interpret and communicate information
Interpersonal Participate as a member of a team, teach others, work with cultural diversity
Systems Monitor and correct performance
Basic Skills Reading, writing, listening, speaking
Thinking Skills Think creatively, make decisions

Personal Qualities Responsibility, sociability, self-management
EFF: **Communication** Read with understanding, convey ideas in writing, speak so others can understand, listen actively
Decision Making Plan
Interpersonal Cooperate with others
Lifelong Learning Take responsibility for learning, reflect and evaluate, learn through research

Investing wisely

GOAL ➤ Identify investment strategies

Vocabulary | Grammar
Life Skills
Academic | Pronunciation

A In a small group, look at the following list of vocabulary words and phrases. Which words do you know? How can you find out the meaning of the ones you don't know? Discuss ways with your group and then, with your group, use those ways to find the meanings.

(Answers may vary. Dictionary definitions below.)

1. capital gains: profits from the sale of capital assets or goods

2. convert: to change into another form

3. inflation: a sharp increase in price levels because of too much available currency

4. liquid: (financial) readily converted into cash (liquid assets)

5. net appreciation: final increase after all losses are accounted for

6. penalty: a punishment by law for an offense or crime

7. purchasing power: ability of a person or group to purchase, measured by income

8. risky: involving risk or danger

9. value: an amount considered to be equivalent for something else

10. vehicle: a device for carrying passengers or goods

B Words often have more than one meaning. It is important to know what you are listening to or reading so you can find the correct part of speech and definition for the new vocabulary word. Look at the meaning you wrote for *vehicle*. Compare your definition with this definition.

vehicle: a way in which something is accomplished How to earn money through investments

C Based on the words you defined above, what do you think the article below is about? Discuss your ideas with your classmates.

D Read the article about investing money.

THE CHICKEN OR THE MARKET?

By Andrew Rothemer

I once knew a family who kept their life savings in a chicken in the freezer. My grandmother kept a stash of cash under her mattress. I think my wife has a secret hiding place in the drawer next to the bed. Where do you keep your life savings?

Investing can be risky, so many people prefer to find a safe place to put their money at home. But keeping your money in a drawer, under a mattress, or even in a chicken will eventually decrease your purchasing power. Due to inflation, money is worth less and less each year, so by not investing your money, you are actually losing money. In order to prevent inflation from destroying the value of your money, you need to invest. Let's take a look at some basic kinds of investments.

(continued)

An investment can make you money in three basic ways. First, an investment can earn *current income*. Current income is money that you receive periodically, for example, every month or every six months. An example of an investment that provides current income is a certificate of deposit (CD) because interest is paid to your account periodically. A second way that an investment can make money is through *capital growth*. This is when the amount of money you have invested grows in value over time. When you sell the investment, you get your money back plus any increase in value. Examples of capital growth investments are stocks and other assets that you own, such as your home. Finally, a third way that an investment can earn income is through a combination of current income and capital growth. Examples include rental property and stocks that pay dividends, that is, extra or bonus amounts of money.

So, which type of investment is best for you? That will depend on your age and income. Younger investors who are working and earning a steady income may not need to earn current income from their investments. They may be more interested in capital growth. On the other hand, older investors who are retired and living on limited social security and pension funds are more likely to be interested in earning current income from their investments. There are many different ways to invest your money, but let's look at five of the most widely used investment vehicles.

Probably the most popular investment vehicle is the savings account, which offers low minimum deposits, liquidity (the ability to withdraw and deposit whenever you want), and insurance protection. Because of these features, savings accounts pay relatively low interest rates. Another investment vehicle that is somewhat similar to a savings account in that it offers low interest rates and insurance protection is a certificate of deposit (CD). A CD requires that you put money in and leave it for a certain amount of time—three months, six months, a year, etc. Usually, the longer the amount of time you keep it in, the

higher the interest. CDs are not perfectly liquid because early withdrawal of funds from a CD often results in a penalty. Another type of investment is a mutual

fund where a number of investors put their money together to buy specific investments. Some mutual funds invest in stocks, some in bonds, and some in real estate. The mutual fund investor owns shares of the fund, not the actual stocks, bonds, or property purchased by the fund. Most likely, when a person thinks of investing, he or she probably thinks of the stock market. Ownership of a stock represents ownership of a *claim* on the net earnings of a company. Therefore, stock earnings depend on how well the company is doing. Stocks can be quickly converted to cash by selling them on the stock market, but because the price of stocks changes daily, there is no guarantee that you will get back the money that you paid for the stock. And finally, property or real estate is a popular investment because it can produce returns in two ways: current income and net appreciation (capital gains). You can receive current income if the property is used, such as in situations where tenants are renting it or if crops are grown on the land. Net appreciation occurs if the property increases in value during the time that you own it. A major disadvantage of real estate and rental property is that they are not very liquid; it takes time and resources to turn them into cash. It may take many months to sell a piece of property.

So, which investment will be best for you? Only you can decide. Think carefully about your financial situation, how much money you can or want to invest, and how soon you will need access to the money. I can guarantee that whatever investment vehicle you choose, you will benefit more than if you keep your cash in a chicken!

E **Discuss the following questions with a partner.** (Answers will vary.)

1. Do you invest your money? If so, how do you invest it?
2. What investment vehicles would you like to try?
3. Would you say you are conservative with your money? Why or why not?

Teaching Tip

Silent reading

Silent reading is a very important skill that should be fostered in the classroom and encouraged at home. The more silent reading activities you can provide in class, the better your students will master this skill. To encourage silent reading, you can start a small library of interesting things for students to read when they have finished an activity the rest of the class is still working on. Your library may include books, magazines, and newspapers. Alternatively, you can make it part of your daily routine to have all students spend 15 minutes per day doing silent reading.

Practice 2   5-10 mins.

E **Discuss the following questions with a partner.**

When students have finished reading the article, have them find a partner and discuss it.

Evaluation 2   10-15 mins.

Go over the article as a class, making sure students understand the general ideas covered in the article.

Activity Bank

Unit 2, Lesson 3, Worksheet 1: Investing Vocabulary Practice

Unit 2, Lesson 3, Worksheet 2: "The Chicken or the Market?" (reading comprehension)

Instructor's Notes

Evaluation 2 (continued)

(F) Use the ideas you have learned about investment strategies in this lesson to complete the sentences below. Each sentence may have more than one answer.

Tell students they can use the vocabulary they worked with in Exercise A to complete these sentences.

Presentation 3   5–10 mins. ■■□

Go over the answers as a class. Ask volunteers to come up with original sentences using the same words.

Write the word *outline* on the board and see if students can help you define it. Use the example in Exercise G to clarify the term. Ask students why outlining is an important skill.

Practice 3   15–20 mins. ■

Note: Shorter classes can do this exercise for homework and review the next class day.

(G) An outline is a way to organize the main ideas of something you have listened to or read. You can write notes or complete sentences in an outline, but do not directly copy the author's words. Based on the reading in Exercise D, complete the outline below.

Show students how some of the outline has been filled in for them and have them complete the outline by themselves.

Evaluation 3   5–10 mins. ■

Go over the answers as a class. Have students help you complete the outline on the board or on an overhead transparency.

Application   10–20 mins. ■■□

(H) A summary is a brief statement of main ideas. On a separate piece of paper, write a one-paragraph summary of the investing article using the notes from your outline.

Make sure students understand that a summary uses the main ideas of a text but omits the details.

Refer students to *Stand Out 5 Grammar Challenge*, Unit 2, Challenge 3 for practice with ability modals: *can* and *could*.

Instructor's Notes

LESSON 3   **GOAL** ➤ **Identify investment strategies**

F   Use the ideas you have learned about investment strategies in this lesson to complete the sentences below. Each sentence may have more than one answer. (Answers may vary.)

1. If you don't invest your money, you will lose _____purchasing power_____ over time.

2. The _____price/value_____ of stocks is based on the earnings of the company.

3. Savings accounts and mutual funds are not very _____profitable_____.

4. My favorite investment _____strategy_____ is _____mutual funds_____ (your own idea).

5. It is not easy to _____turn/convert/liquidate_____ real estate into cash.

6. Savings accounts are very _____popular_____. You can get the cash whenever you need it.

G   An outline is a way to organize the main ideas of something you have listened to or read. You can write notes or complete sentences in an outline, but do not directly copy the author's words. Based on the reading in Exercise D, complete the outline below.

I. Investing is risky.
   A. People like a safe place for money (home) = lower purchasing power
   B. Inflation makes money worth less and less
   C. No investment equals money losing value

II. Investments make you money.
   A. Current income (CDs)
   B. Capital growth (real estate, stocks, etc.)
   C. A combination of current income and capital growth

III. Investment type will depend on age and income.
   A. Young workers with steady income interested in capital growth
   B. Older investors interested in current income

IV. Popular investment types
   A. Savings accounts
   B. Certificates of deposit (CDs)
   C. Stocks
   D. Mutual funds
   E. Real estate/Property

H   A summary is a brief statement of main ideas. On a separate piece of paper, write a one-paragraph summary of the investing article using the notes from your outline.

(Answers may vary.)

Credit

GOAL ➤ **Maintain good credit**

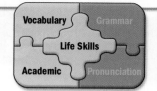

 A In a small group, discuss the following questions. (Answers will vary.)

1. What is credit?

2. What makes credit good or bad?

3. How can you find out if you have good or bad credit?

4. If you have bad credit, how can you improve it?

Refer to Lesson Planner page 34a for answers.

B Read the article below. As you read it, underline the main ideas.

THE FOUR KEYS TO GREAT CREDIT

By Liz Pulliam Weston

Your credit history can make or break you when trying to convince lenders you're a good risk. Here's how to build the best record you can—before you need it.

Getting credit when you don't have any—or when you're recovering from a credit disaster such as bankruptcy—can be daunting. Without a good credit history, it's hard to get new credit. But without credit, it's tough to build a good credit history. Tough, but far from impossible. Every day, people take steps that establish and improve their image in the eyes of lenders. So can you. Here's what you need to do:

✔ **Open checking and savings accounts.**

Having bank accounts establishes you as part of the financial mainstream. Lenders want to know you have a checking account available to pay bills, and a savings account indicates you're putting aside something for the future.

Opening bank accounts is something you can do even if you're too young to establish credit in your own name. Until you're 18, you can't legally be held to a contract, so any credit you get will have to be through an adult—either someone who cosigns a loan for you, adds you to their credit cards, or opens a joint account with you. Having bank accounts, though, gets you started on the right path and gives you practice in managing your money.

✔ **Get your credit report—if you have one.**

Next, you need to find out how lenders view you. Most lenders base their decisions on credit reports, which are compiled by for-profit companies known as credit bureaus. You are entitled to a free credit report from each of the three major bureaus each year.

Typically, a credit report includes identifying information about you, such as your name, address, social security number, and birth date. The report may also list any credit accounts or loans opened in your name, along with your payment history, account limits, and unpaid balances.

If you're young or newly arrived in the United States, you may not have a report or it may have little information. If you've had credit problems, your report will list them.

(continued)

AT-A-GLANCE PREP

Objective: Maintain good credit
Academic Strategies: Reading for understanding, outlining, summary writing
Vocabulary: *daunting, bankruptcy, mainstream, lender, omissions, delinquencies, liens, credit bureau, collateral, creditworthiness, overextended*

RESOURCES

Activity Bank: Unit 2, Lesson 4, Worksheets 1–2

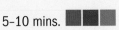 1.5 hour classes ■ 2.5 hour classes ■ 3⁺ hour classes

Grammar Challenge 5: Unit 2, Challenge 4

AGENDA

Discuss credit.

Read an online article.

Give advice.

Define new vocabulary.

Create an outline and summary.

List ways you can establish and maintain good credit.

Warm-up and Review   5-10 mins.

Have students take out their summaries from the previous lesson. Ask a volunteer to come to the board and write down one new thing they learned about investing. Tell the next volunteer that he or she has to write something new that isn't already on the board. Continue to do this until no one has anything new to write.

Introduction   5-10 mins. ■■■

Dictation:

1. Getting credit when you don't have any can be daunting.
2. Without a good credit history, it's hard to get new credit.
3. But without credit, it's tough to build a good credit history.
4. Every day, people take steps to establish and improve their image in the eyes of lenders.

State the objective: *Today you will learn about credit and how to establish and maintain good credit.*

Presentation 1   10-15 mins. ■■■

(A) **In a small group, discuss the following questions.**

These questions serve as a preview. The answers can be found in the article that students will read in Exercise B. See what students already know and try not to answer too many questions.

Exercise A answer key for the instructor:

1. Money lent to a consumer instead of immediate payment; credit-worthiness
2. Good: Keeping a bank account, pay bills on time, use credit wisely; Bad: Don't pay bills on time, max out credit cards, spend beyond your means
3. Get a credit report
4. Read credit report for errors, contact the bank or creditor or credit bureau if there are errors, pay bills on time, add positive information to your report, establish credit and use it correctly.

Practice 1   10-15 mins.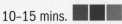

(B) **Read the article below. As you read it, underline the main ideas.**

Go over the directions with students, making sure they remember what a main idea is.

Before students start reading, review the information about the author of "The Four Keys to Great Credit" on page 35a.

STANDARDS CORRELATIONS

CASAS: 1.3.2, 7.4.2 (See CASAS Competency List on pages 187–193.)
SCANS: Information Acquire and evaluate information, organize and maintain information, interpret and communicate information
Interpersonal Participate as a member of a team, teach others, exercise leadership, negotiate to arrive at a decision, work with cultural diversity
Systems Monitor and correct performance
Technology Apply technology to a task *(optional)*
Basic Skills Reading, writing, arithmetic, listening, speaking
Thinking Skills See things in the mind's eye

Personal Qualities Responsibility, sociability, self-management
EFF: Communication Read with understanding, convey ideas in writing
Decision Making Use math to solve problems and communicate, solve problems and make decisions, plan
Interpersonal Cooperate with others
Lifelong Learning Take responsibility for learning, reflect and evaluate, learn through research, use information and communications technology *(optional)*

Unit 2, Lesson 4, Worksheet 1: "The Four Keys to
Great Credit" (Reading
Comprehension)

This worksheet contains more in-depth work with the
article in the Student Book.

Optional Internet Activity: The article in this
lesson is from an online column found on the
Web site **http://money.msn.com**. Liz Pulliam
is a columnist who is available online to answer
questions. In fact, students themselves can go
online, find the article, and come up with a few
questions to e-mail to Ms. Pullman. If she is no
longer doing her online column when students
go to the Web site, have them write questions
to the new columnist.

✔ **Fix any errors or omissions.**

Some credit reports include errors—accounts that don't belong to you or that include out-of-date or misleading information. You should read through each of your three reports and note anything that's incorrect.

Negative information, such as late payments, delinquencies, liens, and judgments against you, should be dropped after seven years. Bankruptcies can stay on your report for up to ten years.

Once you have a list of problems, ask the bureaus to investigate errors listed on their reports. You can use the form that comes with your report if you receive it by mail, or you can use the Web link if you accessed your report on the Internet.

✔ **Add positive information to your report.**

The more information you can provide about yourself, the more comfortable lenders may feel extending credit to you. In addition, certain information—such as having the same job or address for a few years—can make you appear more stable in lenders' eyes.

While this information isn't used in creating your credit score, it is often used by lenders when they make lending decisions. You may also find that your report doesn't include credit accounts or other information that it should. Here's a list of items to consider:

• Are your employer and your job title listed? If you've had the job less than two years, your previous employer and job title should be listed as well.
• Is your address listed and correct? If you've been at your current address less than two years, is your previous address listed as well?
• Is your social security number listed and correct? This is the way most lenders will identify you.
• Is your telephone number listed and correct? Many lenders may not extend credit if they can't call you to verify information.

• Does your report include all the accounts you've paid on time? Some lenders don't report regularly to credit bureaus, and some report to only one or two, rather than all three. You can ask the creditor to report the account to a bureau that doesn't list it. If the creditor refuses or doesn't respond, you can send a letter to the bureau with a copy of your latest statement and canceled checks to prove you're paying on time.

✔ **Establish credit.**

There are three common routes for establishing new credit:

1. Apply for department store and gasoline cards. These are usually easier to get than major bank credit cards.
2. Consider taking out a small personal loan from your local bank or credit union and paying the money back over time. The bank may require you to put up some collateral—such as the same amount you're borrowing, deposited into a savings account. But the loan, if reported to the credit bureaus, can still help build your credit history. Make sure that it will be reported before you borrow the money.
3. Apply for a secured credit card. These work something like the loan described above: You deposit a certain amount at a bank, and in return you're given a Visa or MasterCard with a credit limit roughly equal to the amount you deposited. You can find a list of secured cards at www.bankrate.com. Avoid any card that charges a big upfront fee for processing your application or a high annual fee.

✔ **Once you've got credit, use it right.**

Charge small amounts on each card—but never more than you can pay off each month. You need to use credit regularly to establish your credit history, but there's usually no advantage to paying interest on those charges.

(continued)

GOAL ➤ **Maintain good credit**

Once you've been approved for one card or loan, don't rush out and apply for several more. Applying for too much credit will hurt, rather than help, your score. Most people need only one or two bank cards, a gasoline card, and a department store card—acquired over a year or more—to start a solid credit history.

Pay your bills on time, all the time. This includes household bills, such as utilities and telephone, as well as your credit card bills and loans. Late payments on any of these accounts can wind up in your credit report and can really hurt your credit score—the three-digit number widely used by lenders to evaluate your creditworthiness.

Don't max out your credit cards. In fact, don't even come close. Try to avoid using more than 30% or so of the credit you have available to you—even less, if you can. Your credit score measures the difference between the credit available to you and what you're actually using. The smaller that gap, the more it hurts your score. Lenders will worry that you're becoming overextended and won't be able to pay your bills if you charge too much.

Liz Pulliam Weston is a personal finance columnist for MSN Money (http://money.msn.com), where this article first appeared. Used by permission. Her column appears every Monday and Thursday, exclusively on MSN Money. She also answers reader questions in the Your Money message board.

C **Imagine you are a financial advisor. Give your partner advice based on the following questions.**

1. What can I do to establish good credit? Apply for credit cards, take out small loans, apply for a secure card.

2. What should I look for in my credit report? Errors or omissions, negative information

3. How can I add positive information to my credit report? Check that all job information and personal data is accurate.

D **Go back through the article and underline any words or phrases you do not understand. Work with a partner and a dictionary to discover their meanings. Write them in your notebook.**

E **On a separate piece of paper, make an outline of Ms. Weston's article. Then, write a summary.** (Answers will vary.)

F **Having read the article, what are four things you need to do to help establish or maintain your credit?**

1. Open a checking and savings account.

2. Fix errors and omissions in your credit report.

3. Add positive information to your report.

4. Establish credit.

Evaluation 1   10-15 mins. ▪▪▪▫

Discuss the article as a class, helping students understand what the main ideas are. Try to refrain from going over too much vocabulary in depth since students will be doing this with a partner in Exercise D.

C Imagine you are a financial advisor. Give your partner advice based on the following questions.

Have students take turns playing the advisor and the person who needs advice.

Presentation 2   5-10 mins. ▪▪▪▫

Ask students to look back at the article and call out some words they don't understand. Start to make a list on the board. Choose one of the words and have a student look it up in a dictionary and read the definition out loud. Make sure he or she chooses the definition as it relates to the article.

Practice 2   15-20 mins. ▪▪▫▫

Note: Shorter classes can do this exercise for homework.

D Go back through the article and underline any words or phrases you don't understand. Work with a partner and a dictionary to discover their meanings. Write them in your notebook.

Evaluation 2   10-15 mins. ▪▪▫▫

Answer any questions students may have. Give them a chance to look the words up in a bilingual dictionary if they want to make sure they are confident about the meanings.

Presentation 3   5-10 mins. ▪▪▪▫

Help students begin an outline by asking them how many main sections (roman numerals) are in the article. Have them tell you what the first two sections are.

Practice 3   20-30 mins. ▪▫▫▫

Note: Shorter classes can do this exercise for homework.

E On a separate piece of paper, make an outline of Ms. Weston's article. Then, write a summary.

Evaluation 3   5-10 mins. ▪▫▫▫

Walk around the classroom and help students as they work. Remind them that everyone's outline and summary will not be exactly the same. If there's time, ask a few volunteers to share their summaries out loud.

Application   10-20 mins. ▪▪▪▫

F Having read the article, what are four things you need to do to help establish or maintain your credit?

📖 Refer students to *Stand Out 5 Grammar Challenge*, Unit 2, Challenge 4 for practice with advisability modals: *should* and *ought to*.

Instructor's Notes

_____

_____

_____

_____

_____

_____

_____

_____

_____

_____

_____

_____

_____

AT-A-GLANCE PREP

Objective: Protect yourself against identity theft
Pronunciation: Clear speech
Academic Strategies: Focused listening, identifying details, writing a summary, giving a presentation
Vocabulary: *commit fraud, good name, dumpster diving, rummage, skimming, phishing, spam, pop-up messages, reveal, divert, pretexting, false pretenses, delinquent accounts, counterfeit checks, unauthorized transactions, awareness*

■ 1.5 hour classes   ■ 2.5 hour classes   ■ 3+ hour classes

AGENDA

Listen to people discuss financial problems.
Discuss identity theft.
Listen to an interview about identity theft.
Write a summary.
Prepare a presentation.

RESOURCES

Activity Bank: Unit 2, Lesson 5, Worksheet 1
Grammar Challenge 5: Unit 2, Challenge 5
Audio: CD Tracks 12–13

Warm-up and Review   5-10 mins. ■■■

Ask volunteers to come to the board and write ideas on how to establish and maintain good credit.

Introduction   5-10 mins. ■■■

Read the following aloud: "Approximately nine million Americans have their identities stolen each year. You or someone you know may have experienced some form of identity theft."

State the objective: *Today you will learn how to protect yourself against identity theft.*

Presentation 1   5 mins. ■■■

Write *identity theft* on the board and see if students can help you define the term. You will be discussing it again in Exercise C. Have students look at the pictures in Exercise A and guess what the problems are.

Practice 1   10-15 mins. ■■■

A Listen to each of the following people talk about their financial problems. What happened? Take notes on the lines below each photo.

Evaluation 1   5-10 mins. ■■■

Go over the answers as a class.

B Have you ever had any problems with your credit similar to the ones in Exercise A? If so, what did you do about it? Tell your classmates about it.

🎧 Listening Script   CD Track 12

Man 1: *I was looking over my credit card statement last night and I noticed some charges from unfamiliar companies. When I called the companies to see what the charges were for, I found out that they were companies that I had never done business with. Apparently, someone had gotten my credit card number off of the Internet and had been using it for months to make online purchases.*

Man 2: *My cell phone bill was really expensive this month. When I looked at it closer, I realized that I had been charged for a phone number that wasn't mine. When I called the phone company to dispute it, they said that I had indeed called and added a line to my account. I told them this wasn't true, and we discovered that someone had stolen my personal information and added a phone line to my account.*

Woman: *I was in the supermarket the other day. When I tried to pay for my groceries with my ATM card, it was declined due to insufficient funds. So, then I went to an ATM machine and tried to withdraw money. My card was declined again. I called my bank and found out that someone in another state had gotten a copy of my ATM card and had withdrawn all of the money in my account.*

Presentation 2   10-15 mins. ■■■

C In a small group, discuss the following questions. Initially, students should guess at the definitions. These words will be defined later.

Tell students that they will be listening to a representative from the Federal Trade Commission (FTC) who will answer all of these questions. If students don't know what the FTC is, review the FTC Web site description on page 39a.

Note: Standards correlations are on page 39a.

GOAL ➤ **Protect yourself against identity theft**

CD
TR 12

A Listen to each of the following people talk about their financial problems. What happened? Take notes on the lines below each photo.

1. charges from unfamiliar companies on credit card statement; stolen number from Internet

2. charged for calls not made; someone stole personal information and added a phone line

3. ATM card declined; all money stolen from account

B Have you ever had any problems with your credit similar to the ones in Exercise A? If so, what did you do about it? Tell your classmates about it.

C In a small group, discuss the following questions. (Answers may vary.)

1. What is identity theft? When your financial and life information is stolen and used fraudulently.
2. What do you think the following terms mean: *dumpster diving*, *skimming*, *phishing*, and *pretexting*? Refer to listening script on page 38a for definitions
3. What are some things a person who steals your identify might do? Come up with some ideas in addition to the three from Exercise A. Use your ID to take out loans or buy a car.
4. What can you do if someone steals your identity? Notify your credit card companies, notify the police, notify credit bureau and check credit reports.

  D

CD
TR 13

Listen to an interview with a member of the Federal Trade Commission (FTC). In each question below, one answer is NOT correct. Choose the incorrect answer.

1. What is identity theft?
   a. when someone uses your credit card number without permission to buy things
   b. when someone steals your name and social security number to commit crimes
   c. when someone commits fraud using your personal information
   d. when someone asks you for your personal information

2. What are some ways thieves steal your identity?
   a. dumpster diving
   b. changing your name
   c. stealing
   d. skimming

3. An example of bank fraud is . . .
   a. when someone takes out a loan in your name.
   b. when someone gets a driver's license in your name.
   c. when someone opens an account in your name.
   d. when someone creates counterfeit checks using your account number.

4. How can you find out if your identity has been stolen?
   a. cancel credit card accounts
   b. monitor bank accounts
   c. check credit reports
   d. check my bank statements

5. What should you do if your identity has been stolen?
   a. notify creditors
   b. try to find the thief
   c. file a police report
   d. check credit reports

6. How can you help fight identity theft?
   a. donate money to the Federal Trade Commission
   b. be aware of how information is stolen
   c. monitor personal information
   d. educate friends and family about identity theft

Practice 2   10–15 mins. ■■□

 D Listen to an interview with a member of the Federal Trade Commission (FTC). In each question below, one answer is NOT correct. Choose the incorrect answer.

🎧 **Listening Script**   CD Track 13

What is identity theft? *Identity theft occurs when someone uses your personal identification information, such as your name, social security number, or credit card number, without your permission to commit fraud or other crimes.*

The FTC estimates that as many as nine million Americans have their identities stolen each year. In fact, you or someone you know may have experienced some form of identity theft. Identity theft is serious. While some identity-theft victims can resolve their problems quickly, others spend hundreds of dollars and many days repairing damage to their good name and credit record.

How do thieves steal an identity? *Identity theft starts with the misuse of your personal identification information, such as your name and social security number, credit card numbers, or other financial account information. Skilled identity thieves may use a variety of methods to get hold of your information, including: dumpster diving, skimming, and phishing. When thieves dumpster dive, they rummage through trash looking for bills or other paper with your personal information on it. When thieves employ the skimming method, they steal credit or debit card numbers by using a special storage device when processing your card. If thieves are phishing, they pretend to be financial institutions or companies and send spam or pop-up messages to get you to reveal your personal information. Often thieves change your address by completing a change-of-address form and they then divert your billing statements to another location. Identity thieves also use forms of old-fashioned methods, such as stealing wallets and purses; mail, including bank and credit card statements; pre-approved credit offers; and new checks or tax information. They steal personnel records or bribe employees who have access to them. Thieves also use false pretenses to obtain your personal information from financial institutions, telephone companies, and other sources.*

What do thieves do with a stolen identity?

Once they have your personal information, identity thieves use it in a variety of ways.

Credit card fraud: They may open new credit card accounts in your name. When they use the cards and don't pay the bills, the delinquent accounts appear on your credit report. They may change the billing address on your credit card so that you no longer receive bills and then run up charges on your account. Because your bills are now sent to a different address, it may be

(continued)

some time before you realize there's a problem. Phone or utilities fraud: They may open a new phone or wireless account in your name, or run up charges on your existing account. They may use your name to get utility services like electricity, heating, or cable TV. Bank/finance fraud: They may create counterfeit checks using your name or account number. They may open a bank account in your name and write bad checks. They may clone your ATM or debit card and make electronic withdrawals in your name, draining your accounts. They may take out a loan in your name. Government documents fraud: They may get a driver's license or official ID card issued in your name but with their picture. They may use your name and social security number to get government benefits. They may file a fraudulent tax return using your information.

Other fraud: They may get a job using your social security number. They may rent a house or get medical services using your name. They may give your personal information to police during an arrest. If they don't show up for their court date, a warrant for arrest is issued in your name.

How can you find out if your identity has been stolen? *The best way to find out is to monitor your accounts and bank statements each month and check your credit report on a regular basis. If you check your credit report regularly, you may be able to limit the damage caused by identity theft.*

What should you do if your identity is stolen? *Filing a police report, checking your credit reports, notifying creditors, and disputing any unauthorized transactions are some of the steps you must take immediately to restore your good name.*

What can you do to help fight identity theft? *Awareness is an effective weapon against many forms of identity theft. Be aware of how information is stolen and what you can do to protect yours, monitor your personal information to uncover any problems quickly, and know what to do when you suspect your identity has been stolen. You can also help fight identity theft by educating your friends, family, and members of your community.*

Evaluation 2   10–15 mins. ■■□

Go over the answers as a class.

Presentation 3   5–10 mins. ■■■□

Prepare students to write their summaries by going over the information in Exercise D. Establish the main idea or purpose of the summary and identify the supporting details. Make an outline on the board.

Practice 3   15–25 mins. ■

Note: Shorter classes can do this exercise individually for homework.

E Using the information provided from the questions in Exercise D, work with a group to write a summary about identify theft.

Evaluation 3

Walk around the classroom and help students as needed.

Application   20-30 mins.

F In your group, use your summary to prepare a presentation that will educate your classmates about identity theft. Answer the questions below.

Explain to students that they will be getting up in front of the class and giving a presentation on identity theft. Tell them to be creative and go beyond just standing up and reading their summaries. You might brainstorm with them on what they can do to make their presentations more interesting.

If time allows, have students practice their presentations with their group and then give the presentation to the class.

Activity Bank

Unit 2, Lesson 5, Worksheet 1: Identity Theft

Statement from the FTC Web site: The FTC deals with issues that touch the economic life of every American. It is the only federal agency with both consumer protection and competition jurisdiction in broad sectors of the economy. The FTC pursues vigorous and effective law enforcement; advances consumers' interests by sharing its expertise with federal and state legislatures and U.S. and international government agencies; develops policy and research tools through hearings, workshops, and conferences; and creates practical and plain-language educational programs for consumers and businesses in a global marketplace with constantly changing technologies.

Refer students to *Stand Out 5 Grammar Challenge*, Unit 2, Challenge 5 for practice with uncertainty modals: *may, might,* and *could.*

There are also two extension challenges for review of material studied. Extension Challenge 1 practices the future continuous (progressive). Extension Challenge 2 practices uncertainty future modals: *should, ought to, may, might,* and *could.*

STANDARDS CORRELATIONS

CASAS: 7.4.2 (See CASAS Competency List on pages 187–193.)
SCANS: **Resources** Allocate time, allocate materials and facility resources, allocate human resources
Information Acquire and evaluate information, organize and maintain information, interpret and communicate information
Interpersonal Participate as a member of a team, teach others, exercise leadership, negotiate to arrive at a decision, work with cultural diversity
Systems Monitor and correct performance
Basic Skills Reading, writing, listening, speaking
Thinking Skills Think creatively, make decisions, solve problems, see things in the mind's eye

Personal Qualities Responsibility, sociability, self-management
EFF: **Communication** Read with understanding, convey ideas in writing, speak so others can understand, listen actively, observe critically
Decision Making Solve problems and make decisions, plan
Interpersonal Cooperate with others, advocate and influence, resolve conflict and negotiate, guide others
Lifelong Learning Take responsibility for learning, reflect and evaluate, learn through research

LESSON 5

GOAL ➤ **Protect yourself against identity theft**

E Using the information provided from the questions in Exercise D, work with a group to write a summary about identify theft. (Answers may vary.)

_____

_____

_____

_____

_____

_____

_____

_____

_____

_____

_____

_____

F In your group, use your summary to prepare a presentation that will educate your classmates about identity theft. Answer the questions below. (Answers may vary.)

1. What information will you present to the class? _____

_____

_____

2. How will you present your information? (orally only, orally and visually, etc.)

_____

3. Who will present which part of the presentation? (Everyone in your group must participate.)

_____

_____

Review

A Roger and Rupert are brothers who live together. Complete their Money Out Worksheet below by filling in the missing numbers. (Lesson 1)

MONEY OUT		
	Annual	**Monthly**
Rent	$26,400	$2,200
Home maintenance fees	$1,800	$150
Renters' insurance	$600	$50
Gas & Electric	$2,640	$220
Water	$480	$40
Telephone/Cell phone	$1,440	$120
Food/Restaurants	$3,300	$275
Medical/Dental	$1,680	$140
Auto expenses	$10,680	$890
Clothes/Shoes	$1,125	$93.75
Hair/Manicure/Facial	$1,500	$125
Training/Education	$700	$58.33
Income taxes	$824	$68.66
Computer	$900	$75
Credit cards/Loans	$11,700	$975
Entertainment	$3000	$250
Cable/Satellite TV	$780	$65
Vacations	$500	$41.67
Gifts	$795	$66.25
TOTAL	$70,844	$5,903.66

Together, Roger and Rupert make about $72,000 a year.

1. How much do they have left over per year? ___$1,156___

2. How much do they have left over per month? ___$96.33___

3. Do you think Roger and Rupert live within their means? ___Yes___

4. What suggestions would you make for curbing their spending?

   a. ___Reduce credit card use___

   b. ___Reduce entertainment___

   c. ___Reduce auto expenses___

   d. ___Reduce hair expenses___

B Write four tips for saving money. (Lesson 2)

1. ___Make a budget___   3. ___Open a savings account___

2. ___Invest money in stocks___   4. ___Cut monthly expenses___

C Complete each statement with the past perfect continuous or the simple past. (Lesson 2)

EXAMPLE: Erika ___had been buying___ lunch every day before she ___started___ making it at home.

1. Justin ___had been charging___ (charge) his credit cards to their maximum limits before he ___cut___ (cut) them up.

AT-A-GLANCE PREP

Objectives: All unit objectives
Grammar: All unit grammar
Academic Strategy: Reviewing
Vocabulary: All Unit 2 vocabulary

RESOURCES

Stand Out 5 Assessment CD-ROM with Exam*View*®

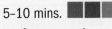 1.5 hour classes 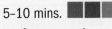 2.5 hour classes 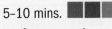 3⁺ hour classes

AGENDA

Discuss unit objectives.
Complete the review.
Use unit vocabulary.

Warm-up and Review   5–10 mins.

Have students take out a piece of paper and write down the most important things they learned about identity theft in the previous lesson. Ask volunteers to read their ideas out loud.

Introduction   5–10 mins.

Ask students as a class to try to recall all the goals of this unit without looking back in their books. The objectives for this unit include organizing your finances, reducing debt and saving money, identifying investment strategies, maintaining good credit, and protecting yourself against identity theft. Write all the goals on the board from Unit 2. Show students the first page of the unit and mention the five objectives.

State the objective: *Today we will be reviewing everything we have learned in this unit and preparing for the team project.*

Presentation 1   10–15 mins.

This presentation will cover the first three pages of the review. Quickly go to the first page of each lesson. Discuss the objective of each. Ask simple questions to remind students of what they have learned.

Note: Since there is little presentation in the review, you can assign the review exercises that don't require collaboration with a partner or group for homework and go over them in class the following day.

Practice 1   20–25 mins.

Note: There are two ways to do the review:
1. Go through the exercises one at a time and, as students complete each one, go over the answers. 2. Quickly go through the instructions of each exercise, let students complete all of the exercises at once, and then go over the answers.

 Roger and Rupert are brothers who live together. Complete their Money Out Worksheet below by filling in the missing numbers. (Lesson 1)

B Write four tips for saving money. (Lesson 2)

C Complete each statement with the past perfect continuous or simple past. (Lesson 2)

Review the example with the students.

Evaluation 1   5–10 mins.

Go around the classroom and check on students' progress. Help individuals when needed. If you see consistent errors among several students, interrupt the class and give a mini-lesson or review to help students feel comfortable with the concept.

Practice 2   25-30 mins. ■■■□

D Write four things you have learned about investing on a piece of paper. Share your ideas with a partner. Add two ideas that your partner came up with. (Lesson 3)

E Answer the following questions by yourself or with a partner. (Lesson 4)

F Read each scenario. Write what you think happened and what the person should do to fix the problem. (Lesson 5)

Evaluation 2   5-10 mins. ■■□

Go around the room and check on student progress. Help individuals when needed. If you see consistent errors among several students, interrupt the class and give a mini-lesson/review to help students feel comfortable with the concept.

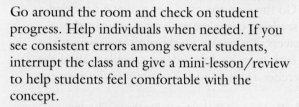

Teaching Tip

Recycling/Review

The review exercises, the research activity, and the team project are part of the recycling/review process. Students often need to be reintroduced to concepts to solidify what they have learned. Many concepts are learned and forgotten when students are engaged in learning other new concepts. This is because students learn but are not necessarily ready to acquire language concepts.

Therefore, it becomes very important to review material with students and to show them how to review it on their own. It is also important to recycle the new concepts in different contexts.

2. Before the Ingrams _____bought_____ (buy) a new car, they

_____had been leasing_____ (lease) a used one.

3. We _____had been living_____ (live) beyond our means before we

_____organized_____ (organize) our finances.

4. Before she _____researched_____ (research) insurance rates, she

_____had been spending_____ (spend) too much on auto insurance.

D **Write four things you have learned about investing on a piece of paper. Share your ideas with a partner. Add two ideas that your partner came up with. (Lesson 3)**
(Answers will vary.)

E **Answer the following questions by yourself or with a partner. (Lesson 4)** (Answers will vary.)

1. What is credit? _Financial status._

2. What can you do to establish good credit?_Open bank accounts and get credit reports._

3. What makes credit good or bad?_Good: Paying on time; Bad: Paying late or not at all_

4. How can you find out if you have good or bad credit?_Get copies of credit reports._

5. If you have bad credit, how can you improve it?_Fix errors, pay on time, establish credit._

6. What should you look for in your credit report?_Correct employers and personal information._

7. How can you add positive information to your credit report?_Include all accounts and_
creditors paid on time.

F **Read each scenario. Write what you think happened and what the person should do to fix the problem. (Lesson 5)**

1. Marika tried to withdraw money from her ATM account, which had over $1,000 in it the last time she checked it, but the bank said she had insufficient funds.

What happened? _Someone got her ATM number and password._

Solution: _She should contact her bank and the police._

2. Marco noticed some unfamiliar charges on his credit card statement.

What happened? _Someone used his credit card to make a purchase._

Solution: _Call creditor, file police report, check credit reports._

3. The IRS contacted Frankie and said he never paid income tax on a second job, which he didn't have.

What happened? _Someone stole his social security card._

Solution: _Contact the department of social security; contact employer where the_
fraud happened.

Unit 2 Review **41**

VOCABULARY REVIEW

G A *synonym* is a word that has the same meaning as another word. Look at each of the words below and choose a word from the box that is its synonym.

1. income _____earnings_____   6. good deal _____bargain_____

2. fake _____counterfeit_____   7. money due _____debt_____

3. late _____delinquent_____   8. liability _____risk_____

4. scam _____fraud_____   9. change _____convert_____

5. cost _____expense_____   10. value _____worth_____

bargain	delinquent	fraud
convert	earnings	risk
counterfeit	expense	worth
debt		

H Look back in the unit and find three new terms you learned (different from the words in the box above). Write a sentence using each of these terms. (Answers will vary.)

1. _____

2. _____

3. _____

I Complete each sentence with an appropriate vocabulary word or phrase from this unit. In many cases, more than one word or expression will work.

1. There are many ways in which people can steal your identity. Two of them are _____skimming_____ and _____pretexting_____.

2. A safe way to invest your money is by investing in CDs and mutual funds.

3. A riskier way to invest is by investing in the stock market.

4. One good way to establish credit is pay bills on time.

5. Another way is get a credit card and pay it regularly.

6. If your identity is stolen, you should file a police report, check credit reports, notify creditors

Practice 3

25–30 mins. ■■□□

Vocabulary Review

 A *synonym* is a word that has the same meaning as another word. Look at each of the words below and choose a word from the box that is its synonym.

H Look back in the unit and find three new terms you learned (different from the words in the box above). Write a sentence using each of these terms.

I Complete each sentence with an appropriate vocabulary word or phrase from this unit. In many cases, more than one word or expression will work.

Evaluation 3

5–10 mins. ■■■□

Go around the classroom and check on students' progress. Help individuals when needed. If you see consistent errors among several students, interrupt the class and give a mini-lesson or review to help students feel comfortable with the concept.

Assessment *(optional)*

■■■□

Use the Stand Out 5 Assessment CD-ROM with Exam*View*® to create a post-test for Unit 2.

Instructor's Notes

Objective: Research government agencies
Academic Strategy: Research
Vocabulary: *agency, FDIC, FTC, handbook*

RESOURCES

Suggested Realia: Telephone book, Internet, *Consumer Action Handbook* (must be ordered on-line)

Activity Bank: Research: FTC and FDIC

Academic Feature: Research Project

As with other units, students are required to complete a task by conducting research. Options will be given for students to use the Internet as well as printed resource materials. The printed resource materials can be found on the Activity Bank CD-ROM.

Introduction   5-10 mins.

State the objective: *Today you will learn how to get financial help if you ever have a consumer issue.*

Presentation   10-15 mins.

(A) In the front of the phone book, there is a section called the Blue Pages of Government Listings. These pages can help you find phone numbers of agencies that can give you financial help. Below are two of the best resources for financial help:

- FDIC (Federal Deposit Insurance Corporation)
  Consumers and Communities
- FTC (Federal Trade Commission)
  Consumer Protection

Discuss each of these agencies with your classmates and teacher.

Share your responses.

Answer Key For Exercise A:

1. The Federal Deposit Insurance Corporation (FDIC) is an independent agency created by the Congress that maintains the stability and public confidence in the nation's financial system by insuring deposits, examining and supervising financial institutions, and managing receiverships. It can help us by protecting our money in the bank and protecting us from corruption in financial institutions. It is an excellent resource for any information about consumer financial concerns such as loans and consumer news stories.

2. The FTC deals with issues that touch the economic life of every American. It is the only federal agency with both consumer protection and competition jurisdiction in broad sectors of the economy. The FTC pursues vigorous and effective law enforcement; advances consumers' interests by sharing its expertise with federal and state legislatures and U.S. and international government agencies; develops policy and research tools through hearings, workshops, and conferences; and creates practical and plain-language educational programs for consumers and businesses in a global marketplace with constantly changing technologies. It is an excellent educational source for all consumers.

Practice   10-15 mins.

(B) To get more information about each of these agencies, go to their Web sites. Click on the topics you find interesting listed in the consumer section of each site. Write down what you find.

STANDARDS CORRELATIONS

CASAS: 4.9.3, 7.2.1, 7.4.4, 7.4.5, 7.4.6 (See CASAS Competency List on pages 187–193.)
SCANS: **Information** Acquire and evaluate information, organize and maintain information, interpret and communicate information, use computers to process information *(optional)*
Interpersonal Participate as a member of a team, teach others, negotiate to arrive at a decision, work with cultural diversity
Systems Understand systems
Technology Select technology, apply technology to a task, maintain and troubleshoot technology *(optional)*

Basic Skills Reading, writing
Thinking Skills Think creatively, make decisions, see things in the mind's eye
Personal Qualities Responsibility, sociability, self-management
EFF: **Communication** Read with understanding, convey ideas in writing, observe critically
Decision Making Solve problems and make decisions, plan
Lifelong Learning Take responsibility for learning, reflect and evaluate, learn through research, use information and communications technology *(optional)*

Research Project

A In the front of the phone book there is a section called the Blue Pages of Government Listings. These pages can help you find phone numbers of agencies that can give you financial help. Below are two of the best resources for financial help:

- FDIC (Federal Deposit Insurance Corporation)
  Consumers and Communities

- FTC (Federal Trade Commission)
  Consumer Protection

Discuss each of these agencies with your classmates and teacher.

1. What does the FDIC do? How can they help me? Refer to Lesson Planner page 43a for the answers.

2. What does the FTC do? How can they help me?

B To get more information about each of these agencies, go to their Web sites. Click on the topics you find interesting listed in the consumer section of each site. Write down what you find. (Answers may vary.)

1. www.fdic.gov: You can find information about consumer news and information, loans and mortgages, banking and money, financial education and literacy, identify theft and fraud, financial privacy, community affairs.

2. www.ftc.gov: You can find information about autos, computers, Internet, credit and loans, diet and health, education and scholarships, job placement, and other consumer concerns.

C Another Web site that has very useful information for consumers is www.consumeraction.gov. Go to the Web site and order a free copy of the *Consumer Action Handbook* online.

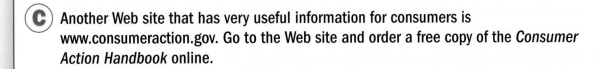

Free 2008 Consumer Action Handbook

Your new computer doesn't include a warranty. The sweater you ordered online never showed up. And the new washer you bought is noisy and leaking water. If you feel like you've just been ripped off, take action. Order your very own copy of the 2008 Consumer Action Handbook. You can expect your new Handbook to arrive within 4 weeks.

Team Project

Create a financial plan.

With a team, decide on one of these project options:

a. Create a financial plan for yourself. (one chart or poster per group member)

b. Create a financial plan for an imaginary person. (one chart or poster per group)

1. Form a team with four or five students. Choose positions for each member of your team.

POSITION	JOB DESCRIPTION	STUDENT NAME
Student 1: **Project Leader**	See that everyone speaks English. See that everyone participates.	
Student 2: **Secretary**	Take notes on team's ideas. Write a list of information that will go into financial plan.	
Student 3: **Designer**	Design financial plan.	
Student 4: **Spokesperson**	Report information to the class if team creates one plan for an imaginary person. Otherwise, assist team members with individual presentations.	
Student 5: **Assistant**	Help secretary and designer with their work.	

2. *Discuss and decide on what information should go in the financial plan: goals, organization templates for budget, plans for saving and reducing debt, names of investment vehicles, ways to protect against identity theft, and so on.

3. Organize the layout of the information for a poster.

4. Present the financial plan to the class.

* *Options:* If your team is creating individual financial plans, work together to decide what general information will go in each person's plan as well as how to organize the plans. Team members may then complete plans on their own.

C Another Web site that has very useful information for consumers is www.consumeraction. gov. Go to the Web site and order a free copy of the *Consumer Action Handbook* online.

Team Project

Create a financial plan.

Each team will create a financial plan for an imaginary person or work together to create individual financial plans for each team member. The plan should include financial goals, ways to organize finances, plans for saving money and reducing debt, places to invest, and methods to protect against identity theft.

Evaluation   5–10 mins.

Help students with the Internet activities.

The team project is the final application for the unit. It gives students a chance to show that they have mastered all of the Unit 2 objectives.

Note: Shorter classes can extend this project over two class meetings.

Stage 1   5–10 mins.

Form a team with four or five students. Choose positions for each member of your team.

Have students decide who will lead each step as described on the student page. Provide well-defined directions on the board for how

teams should proceed. Explain that all the students do every step as a team. Teams shouldn't go to the next stage until the previous one is complete.

Stage 2   15–20 mins.

Discuss and decide on what information should go in the financial plan: goals, organization templates for budget, plans for saving and reducing debt, names of investment vehicles, ways to protect against identity theft, and so on.

Once teams have delegated tasks, have them tell the class if they are creating a financial plan for an imaginary person or a plan for each team member.

Optional Computer Activity: Students may want to use the computer to design their plans.

Stage 3   10–15 mins.

Organize the layout of the information for a poster.

To give students some suggestions, you might design two different profiles on the board so they can see how they might present their information as a poster.

Stage 4   10–15 mins.

Present the financial plan to the class.

Help teams prepare for their presentations. Suggest that each member choose a different part of the plan to present.

STANDARDS CORRELATIONS

CASAS: 4.8.1, 4.8.5, 4.8.6. (See CASAS Competency List on pages 187–193.)
SCANS: **Resources** Allocate time
Information Acquire and evaluate information, organize and maintain information, interpret and communicate information, use computers to process information
Systems Understand systems, improve and design systems
Technology Select technology, apply technology to exercise
Basic Skills Writing
Thinking Skills Think creatively, make decisions, solve problems, see things in the mind's eye, use reasoning

Personal Qualities Responsibility, self-esteem, self-management, integrity
EFF: **Communication** Read with understanding, convey ideas in writing, speak so others can understand, listen actively, observe critically
Decision Making Solve problems and make decisions, plan
Interpersonal Cooperate with others, advocate and influence, resolve conflict and negotiate, guide others
Lifelong Learning Take responsibility for learning, reflect and evaluate, learn through research, use information and communications technology *(optional)*

Objective: Introduce new vocabulary
Academic Strategies: Identifying and defining vocabulary, finding synonyms
Vocabulary: See lesson

RESOURCES

Dictionaries: It is recommended that each student in class have an ESL learner's dictionary or that there be dictionaries available in the classroom for students to use. Dictionaries that will be referred to in this book

AGENDA
Describe different types of cars.
Work with synonyms.

are the *Heinle's Newbury House Dictionary of American English* and the *Collins Cobuild Intermediate* or *Advanced Dictionary of American English.*

Academic Feature: Vocabulary Builder

Each unit will begin with a vocabulary-building section. The purpose of this two-page section is to introduce students to many of the words they will be using in the unit lessons. Students will have a chance to see how much they already know, and they will get exposure to the new vocabulary found in the unit.

Note: All of the exercises on these two pages should be done in class, no matter the class length. Longer classes can do this lesson and then, move onto Lesson 1 during the same class meeting; shorter classes may have to devote one whole class meeting to this lesson.

Introduction   5-10 mins.

Ask how many students have a car. Find out how many students know how to drive. Ask a few students what kind of car they drive. (If you live in a community where most students don't drive cars, ask them if they had cars in their countries.)

State the objective: *Today we will be identifying and working with the vocabulary you will learn in this unit.*

Presentation 1   5-10 mins.

A Look at the different types of cars below. Use the terms in Exercise B to label the cars.

Practice 1   10-15 mins.

B How would you describe each car? Write your ideas next to each term below.

Evaluation 1   5-10 mins.

Go over the answers as a class.

STANDARDS CORRELATIONS

CASAS: 7.4.5 (See CASAS Competency List on pages 187–193.)
SCANS: **Information** Acquire and evaluate information, organize and maintain information
Interpersonal Participate as a member of a team, negotiate to arrive at a decision, work with cultural diversity
Systems Understand systems, monitor and correct performance
Basic Skills Reading, writing, listening, speaking
Thinking Skills Think creatively, make decisions, see things in the mind's eye

Personal Qualities Responsibility, sociability, self-management
EFF: **Communication** Read with understanding, convey ideas in writing, speak so others can understand, listen actively
Decision Making Use math to solve problems and communicate, solve problems and make decisions, plan
Interpersonal Cooperate with others
Lifelong Learning Take responsibility for learning, reflect and evaluate, learn through research

UNIT 3 — Automotive Know-How

GOALS

➤ **Purchase a car**
➤ **Maintain and repair your car**
➤ **Interpret an auto insurance policy**
➤ **Compute mileage and gas consumption**
➤ **Follow the rules of the road**

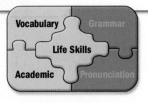

Vocabulary | Grammar
Life Skills
Academic | Pronunciation

Vocabulary Builder

A Look at the different types of cars below. Use the terms in Exercise B to label the cars.

SUV   2-door coupe   minivan   sports car   pickup truck

van   4-door sedan   convertible   station wagon

B How would you describe each car? Write your ideas next to each term below. (Answers will vary.)

1. two-door coupe: only two doors but has a back seat

2. four-door sedan: four doors for front and back seats

3. convertible: the roof is flexible and can be fully opened

4. minivan: a van with many passenger seats and windows

5. sport utility vehicle (SUV): a vehicle for driving on rough terrain

6. sports car: a car with two doors usually built for speed and handling

7. station wagon: a sedan with space in rear for more goods

8. pickup truck: generally a two-seated truck with an open rear area

9. van: a large vehicle for transporting people or goods

Unit 3   Vocabulary Builder   **45**

C Below are some suggestions for car care that you will find in this unit. Read each suggestion and replace the verb in **bold** with a synonym from the box below. Some words can be used more than once.

change	do	look at
choose	find	replace
commute	imagine	fill up

1. _____Replace_____ **Change** your air filter.

2. _____Look at_____ **Check** your oil levels.

3. _____Commute_____ **Drive** during off-peak hours.

4. _____Look at_____ **Inspect** your brakes.

5. _____Find_____ **Look for** telecommuting opportunities.

6. _____Do_____ **Perform** an oil change.

7. _____Choose_____ **Pick** your lane and stick with it.

8. _____Imagine_____ **Pretend** you're a hybrid.

9. _____Change_____ **Replace** your wipers today.

10. _____Fill up_____ **Top off** your washer fluid.

D What do the following words have in common? Write the theme below.

Theme: _Information for car insurance_

_____ accident   _____ coverage   _____ make   _____ premium

_____ bodily injury   _____ incident   _____ model   _____ uninsured motorist

_____ collision   _____ limits of liability   _____ policy   _____ VIN

E Put a check (✔) next to the terms you know in Exercise D. Circle the ones you don't know. Walk around the classroom and talk to your classmates. Find people who know the terms you have circled. (Answers will vary.)

Presentation 2   5 mins.

Remind students what a *synonym* is. (*A word having the same or nearly the same meaning.*) Ask them to give you some examples of synonyms.

Practice 2   10–15 mins.

C Below are some suggestions for car care that you will find in this unit. Read each suggestion and replace the verb in bold with a synonym from the box below. Some words can be used more than once.

Evaluation 2   10–15 mins.

Go over the answers as a class.

Presentation 3   5 mins.

D What do the following words have in common? Write the theme below.

Read the list of words out loud and ask students to guess what the theme is.

Pronunciation

Vocabulary

When teaching students new vocabulary, pronounce each word for them several times and ask them to repeat it. Often, students may be familiar with the words you are introducing but have never seen them spelled out. By pronouncing the words for students, you allow students to make a connection between the words' spellings and their sounds. It is also important that students learn the correct pronunciation of new words so they feel comfortable using their new vocabulary inside and outside of the classroom.

Practice 3   10–15 mins.

E Put a check (✓) next to the terms you know in Exercise D. Circle the ones you don't know. Walk around the classroom and talk to your classmates. Find people who know the terms you have circled.

Evaluation 3

Walk around the classroom and observe students. It is not important for them to understand all of the words because they will be working with the words again in this unit.

Objective: Purchase a car
Grammar: Information questions
Academic Strategies: Focused listening, note taking
Vocabulary: *two-door coupe, four-door sedan, station wagon, convertible, sports car, minivan, SUV, pickup truck, van*

RESOURCES

Activity Bank: Unit 3, Lesson 1, Worksheets 1–2
Grammar Challenge 5: Unit 3, Challenge 1

Audio: CD Tracks 14 and 15
Suggested Realia: Newspaper with ads for cars, copies of *Autotrader*-style journals

 1.5 hour classes   2.5 hour classes   3⁺ hour classes

AGENDA

Listen to a car salesman.
Brainstorm ways to research different types of cars.
Listen to ways Rachel researched cars.
Create a car purchase plan.

 Pre-assessment *(optional)*

Use the Stand Out Assessment CD-ROM with Exam*View®* to create a pre-test for Unit 3.

Warm-up and Review   5-10 mins.

Write *Transportation* on the board. As a class, brainstorm different types of transportation. Then take a class poll to see how many people use each type of transportation the most.

Introduction   5-10 mins.

Dictation:

1. If you want to go fast and have fun, you should drive a sports car.
2. Almost all of the families I know drive SUVs or minivans.
3. Her husband has to drive a pickup truck because of all the stuff he has to move back and forth.
4. When I was a child, my mom drove us around in a station wagon.

State the objective: *Today we will learn more about different types of cars and create a purchase plan for buying a car.*

Presentation 1   10-15 mins.

(A) **In a group, discuss the following questions.**

Have students go around in a circle and answer each question. Then, ask for some volunteers to report what they learned from their classmates.

Go over the chart in Exercise B with students and ask them what they will be listening for.

Go over the examples in the chart and ask them to guess what they might fill in for some of the boxes: *What kind of person do you think a sports car would be best for? What are the advantages of a minivan?*

Practice 1   10-15 mins.

(B) **Listen to an auto salesman who is trying to sell you a car. Take notes on what he says about the different kinds of cars.**

Note: The listening script is continued on page 48a.

Evaluation 1   5 mins.

Go over the answers as a class. Evaluation 1 is continued on the next page.

🎧 **Listening Script**   *CD Track 14*

Car Salesman: *Well, since you don't know what kind of car you are looking for, let me tell you about all the different types of vehicle on the market. Then you can decide which one will be best for you.*

First, let's talk about the four-door sedans. Sedans are a good choice for most automobile shoppers. The enclosed trunk offers security, while the rear doors allow easy entry for rear-seat passengers. Most luxury vehicles are four-door sedans because they're more comfortable than most other body styles. A smaller car is a two-door coupe. Coupes are usually driven by single adults or childless couples. Many two-door coupes have a hatchback instead of a trunk to allow large items to be carried for short distances. The rear seats are difficult to access, as the front doors must be used.

(continued)

Buying a car

GOAL ➤ Purchase a car

CD
TR 14

A In a group, discuss the following questions. (Answers will vary.)

1. Do you have a car? (If not, think of someone you know who does.)
2. Describe the car. (Include color, size, make, model, etc.)
3. How did you get the car?
4. How long have you had it?

B Listen to an auto salesman who is trying to sell you a car. Take notes on what he says about the different kinds of cars.

Vehicle	Best for	Pros	Cons
	most people	secure trunk, easy entry, comfortable	————
	single adults, childless couples	hatchback allows large items to be transported short distances	backseats are hard to access
	active family	stable, good gas mileage, low insurance rates, large interiors	————
	two people	great in good weather	not great in bad weather
	travel, weekend racing	cool looking, fun to drive	impractical for daily transport, need garage, expensive insurance
	families or cargo	handle like a car, good visibility	can't tow heavy loads
	off-road usage	handles well	gas guzzler
	towing/hauling heavy loads	now offer more seating; tows heavy weights	doesn't handle well in snow/ice, low gas mileage
	transporting a lot of people	can carry up to 15 people, can tow heavy loads	————

C   Imagine you are going to buy a new or used car. Look back at the chart in Exercise B. Which kind of car would be best for you? _____ (Answers will vary.)

Why? _____

D   Now that you have an idea which car is best for you based on the salesman's descriptions, it is a good idea to do some research on your own. What are the best ways to find out more about the car you want to buy? In a group, brainstorm ways to research different car models.

(Answers will vary.)

Ways to Research the Car I Want to Buy
Talk to people who own the same car.
Drive one at a dealer's.
Look online for reviews of the car.
Buy a consumer magazine about the car.
Ask your mechanic about the car's reputation.
Go to the manufacturer's Web site.
Talk to a dealer.
Make a list of questions before you go.

CD TR 15

E   Rachel has decided to buy a car. She has been taking the bus and riding her bike everywhere so she has saved enough money to buy the car she wants. She has decided she wants a two-door coupe. Listen to what she did to research buying a car. Write down the different things she did.

1. Made a list of all 2-door coupes for sale
2. Called family and friends to discuss the cars
3. Went to dealerships to test-drive cars
4. Did Internet research for best prices
5. Looked in newspaper and auto trader magazine
6. Test drove and brought her mechanic to look

A larger car is a station wagon. An active family will want to look at minivans, sport-utility vehicles, or station wagons. In most of the world, station wagons remain the first choice for active families. Station wagons offer the most stability, the best gas mileage, the lowest insurance rates, as well as large interiors. You won't lose your all-wheel drive either, as Subaru, Volkswagen, Audi, Volvo, and Mercedes-Benz offer all-wheel drive on all of their wagons.

Now, Let's talk about a fun car—the convertible. Most convertibles are sports cars, meaning two seats, high-performance engines, and superior handling. However, GM, Ford, Mitsubishi, and Chrysler offer a few "normal" convertibles—regular production coupes with four seats and convertible tops, such as the Chevrolet Cavalier, Pontiac Sunfire, Ford Mustang, Dodge Avenger, Chrysler Conquest, and Mitsubishi Eclipse Spyder. Luxury convertibles are available from BMW, Mercedes-Benz, Saab, and Volvo. Convertibles are great when the weather's perfect, but their drawbacks are obvious.

Here are some even more fun (and more expensive) sports cars. Sports cars were originally European two-seat roadsters designed for both daily travel and weekend racing. The term sports sedan is a more recent term to describe a four-door vehicle that handles like a sports coupe or roadster. Recently, we've seen luxury cars advertised as luxury sports sedans. Sports cars are cool and fun to drive, though impractical for daily transportation. You'll need a garage to store them in and a second mortgage to pay for their insurance. But if you've got money to burn, go for it!

Then there's the minivan. If you're constantly carting kids or cargo, a minivan may be your best choice. Most new models offer an additional fourth door on the driver's side as well as comfortable seating for seven. Minivans drive and handle just like a car, with the bonus of better visibility due to a higher center of gravity and an upright driving position. Don't look for minivans to handle your boat- or trailer-towing duties, as front wheel drive vehicles have a very limited towing capacity.

One of the most popular cars out there right now is the sport-utility vehicle or SUV. Although SUVs were designed for off-road usage, 98% of them never leave the road, fortunately for our wildernesses. If a wagon isn't for you, the car-like SUVs ride and handle significantly better than the rest. Unfortunately, they guzzle a lot of gas so you may want to think twice before buying one.

My personal favorite is the pickup truck. More new pickup trucks are sold in this country than any other type of vehicle. The smaller models now offer quad, or crew-cab four-door versions, with seating for five adults. Full-size models offer extended cabs with smaller third and fourth doors, giving access to the rear seats. Standard rear-wheel drive versions don't handle well on snow or ice without a substantial amount of weight in the rear of the truck. When equipped with towing packages with eight- or ten-cylinder engines, these rear-wheel drive vehicles can tow large boats and trailers. Full-size, two-wheel and four-wheel drive pickups get about 15 miles per gallon.

A little less common but necessary if you're transporting a lot of people is the van. If you transport large amounts of cargo or need room for more than seven adults, a full-size van is your only option. They're available with and without windows and in payload capacities of over one ton. Extended vans can seat up to 15 adult passengers. Towing packages with eight- or ten-cylinder engines will allow these rear-wheel-drive vehicles to tow large boats and trailers.

(Source: www.safecarguide.com, 2002–2003. All rights reserved.)

Evaluation 1 *(continued)*

C Imagine you are going to buy a new or used car. Look back at the chart in Exercise B. Which kind of car would be best for you? Why?

Presentation 2   10-15 mins.

D Now that you have an idea which car is best for you based on the salesman's descriptions, it is a good idea to do some research on your own. What are the best ways to find out more about the car you want to buy? In a group, brainstorm ways to research different car models.

After students brainstorm in groups, have them call out some of their ideas and make a list on the board.

Prepare students for Exercise E by reading the instructions. Point out that they will probably hear some of the same ideas they have just brainstormed.

Practice 2   10-15 mins.

E Rachel has decided to buy a car. She has been taking the bus and riding her bike everywhere so she has saved enough money to buy the car she wants. She has decided she wants a two-door coupe. Listen to what she did to research buying a car. Write down the different things she did.

Note: The listening script is on page 49a.

Evaluation 2   10-15 mins.

Have students compare the list on the board to the list in Exercise E. What are the similarities and differences? Ask them to put a check next to each step in Exercise E that they have done when looking for a car.

Rachel: *So, I finally decided that I want a two-door coupe. I think it will be the most economical for me because I am usually just driving myself places. The first thing I did was make a list of all the two-door coupes for sale. Wow, there were a lot! Then, I called all my friends and family who own coupes and asked them which cars they had. I asked them what they liked and didn't like about their cars. Once I narrowed down my list, I went out to car dealerships two weekends in a row to test-drive cars. That really helped me decide which ones I liked. At that point, there were really only two cars that I liked. So, I went home and did some Internet research to find out where I could get the best prices. I also looked in the newspaper and the Auto Trading booklet to see what used cars might be available. I realized that I was going to get a lot more for my money if I bought a used car, and it seemed like the Auto Trading booklet had some pretty good deals. So, I called up a few people to test-drive their cars. I fell in love with one of them and brought my mechanic with me to take a look. He agreed that it was in great shape and a good price. Sold! I had my new car.*

Presentation 3   5–10 mins. ■■◻

Ask students who the different people Rachel talked to were. Make a list. The list should include friends, family, car salesman, car owners, and mechanic. Ask them if there's anyone else she could have talked to. You might suggest a loan officer. Ask them to come up with some questions they might ask each of these people if they were going to buy a car. Write one or two examples on the board.

Practice 3   15–20 mins. ■◻◻

Note: Shorter classes can do this exercise for homework.

F To supplement your research, ask a variety of people for their opinions about cars. What are some questions you might ask? With a partner, create a list of questions.

Evaluation 3   5–10 mins. ■

Go over the questions that students came up with.

 Refer students to *Stand Out 5 Grammar Challenge*, Unit 3, Challenge 1 for more practice with *yes/no* and information questions.

Application   10–20 mins. ■■◻

G Create your plan to purchase a car. Write the steps you will take in the plan below.

Tell students they will be creating a plan of how they would go about purchasing a car. Remind them that a plan will need to include the steps they will take, a possible time line, and any other information they think is necessary to the plan.

 (On the Activity Bank there is a sample plan that you might want to show students as well as a blank template for them to fill in.)

Internet Research *(optional)*

Have students go to an auto-trading Web site or do a search using the phrase *cars for sale*. Have them find some ads for cars they might like. Have students print out examples of ads that impress them and ads that provide little information.

Activity Bank

Unit 3, Lesson 1, Worksheet 1: Car Ad Practice: Questions

Unit 3, Lesson 1, Worksheet 2: Car Buying Plan: Sample and Template

STANDARDS CORRELATIONS

CASAS: 1.9.5 (See CASAS Competency List on pages 187–193.)
SCANS: **Information** Acquire and evaluate information, organize and maintain information, interpret and communicate information
Interpersonal Participate as a member of a team, negotiate to arrive at a decision, work with cultural diversity
Systems Monitor and correct performance
Technology Apply technology to a task *(optional)*
Basic Skills Reading, writing, listening, speaking

Thinking Skills Think creatively, make decisions
Personal Qualities Sociability, self-management
EFF: **Communication** Convey ideas in writing, speak so others can understand, listen actively
Decision Making Solve problems and make decisions, plan
Interpersonal Cooperate with others
Lifelong Learning Learn through research, use information and communications technology *(optional)*

 LESSON 1 **GOAL** ➤ **Purchase a car**

F To supplement your research, ask a variety of people for their opinions about cars. What are some questions you might ask? With a partner, create a list of questions.
(Answers will vary. Sample answers are given.)

Friends and Family

1. What do you love about your car?

2. What do you dislike about your car?

3. What repairs have you made on the car?

Car Dealer

1. What cars do you have in my price range?

2. What cars get the best mileage?

3. Which cars handle well in snow?

Mechanic

1. Which cars are reliable?

2. Which cars rarely come in for repairs?

3. Which cars last for many years?

Loan Officer

1. What are the best interest rates?

2. How much down payment do you expect?

3. How much is it to lease a car versus buying?

G Create your plan to purchase a car. Write the steps you will take in the plan below.
(Answers will vary.)

My Car Purchase Plan
Step 1: Make a list of cars and prices I like.
Step 2: Talk to my mechanic, my friends, and dealers. Do research online and in newspapers.
Step 3: Test drive and think about what I don't like. Have mechanic check car out.

Maintenance and repair

GOAL ➤ Maintain and repair your car

A With the help of your teacher, identify the auto parts below. Write the name of each part in the corresponding box.

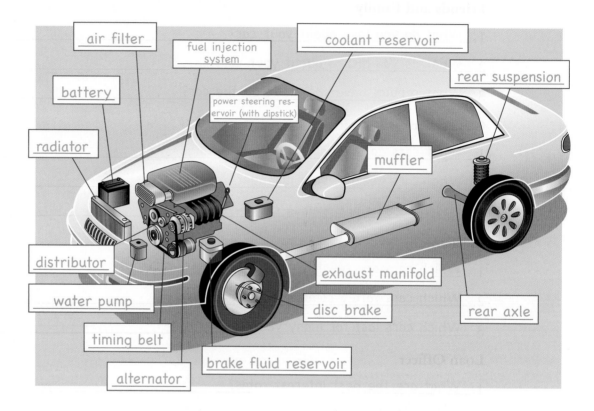

air filter

fuel injection system

coolant reservoir

rear suspension

battery

power steering reservoir (with dipstick)

radiator

muffler

distributor

exhaust manifold

water pump

disc brake

rear axle

timing belt

brake fluid reservoir

alternator

air filter	distributor	radiator
alternator	exhaust manifold	rear axle
battery	fuel injection system	rear suspension
brake fluid reservoir	muffler	timing belt
coolant reservoir	power steering reservoir	water pump
disc brake		

B What is the purpose of each part? Work with a partner and use a dictionary to define each part on a separate sheet of paper. Share your answers with other pairs.

The location of these features varies in many cars. Check specific vehicle manuals for most accurate information.

AT-A-GLANCE PREP

Objective: Maintain and repair your car
Academic Strategies: Reading, outlining, summary writing
Vocabulary: Car parts

RESOURCES
Activity Bank: Unit 3, Lesson 2, Worksheet 1
Grammar Challenge 5: Unit 3, Challenge 2

■ 1.5 hour classes   ■ 2.5 hour classes   ■ 3+ hour classes

AGENDA

Identify car parts and their purpose.
Learn how to maintain and repair your car.

Warm-up and Review   5–10 mins. ■■■

Have students take out their purchase plans from the previous lesson and share them with a partner. Ask volunteers to come to the front of the classroom and share their plans with the class.

Introduction   5–10 mins. ■■■

Dictation:

1. Maintaining your car will extend its life.
2. Finding a good mechanic may take you a long time.
3. Learning how to repair your car can be rewarding.
4. The more you know about your car, the better off you will be.

State the objective: *Today we will identify different auto parts and learn about auto maintenance and repair.*

Presentation 1   10–15 mins. ■■■

 With the help of your teacher, identify the auto parts below. Write the name of each part in the corresponding box.

Practice 1   10–15 mins. ■■■

 What is the purpose of each part? Work with a partner and use a dictionary to define each part on a separate sheet of paper. Share your answers with other pairs.

Tell students that their classmates can be a helpful resource as well as the dictionary or Internet. If you have access to computers in your classroom, let those who want to use the Internet as a resource. If students own cars, have them bring in their vehicle owner's manuals to share. Encourage students to compare location of car parts from the diagrams of their cars. Ask: *Are all parts located in the same place?*

Evaluation 1   5 mins. ■■■

Go over the answers as a class.

Note: There is a teaching resource that describes car part functions on page 51a.

STANDARDS CORRELATIONS

CASAS: 1.9.6 (See CASAS Competency List on pages 187–193.)
SCANS: **Information** Acquire and evaluate information, organize and maintain information, interpret and communicate information
Interpersonal Participate as a member of a team, teach others, exercise leadership, negotiate to arrive at a decision, work with cultural diversity
Systems Understand systems, monitor and correct performance, improve and design systems
Technology Apply technology to a task *(optional)*
Basic Skills Reading, writing, speaking

Thinking Skills Think creatively, make decisions, see things in the mind's eye
Personal Qualities Sociability, self-management
EFF: **Communication** Read with understanding, convey ideas in writing
Decision Making Plan
Interpersonal Cooperate with others
Lifelong Learning Take responsibility for learning, learn through research, use information and communications technology *(optional)*

Lesson Planner: Unit 3, Lesson 2 **50a**

Presentation 2

5-10 mins.

C Now that you know about auto parts and their importance, read this excerpt from an auto maintenance and repair guide.

Practice 2

10-15 mins.

Note: Shorter classes can do these exercises for homework.

D With a partner, answer the following questions.

Evaluation 2

5-10 mins.

Go over the answers as a class.

Teaching Resource

Car parts

Air cleaner/filter: Air is drawn through it. Contains a filter that blocks dirt before it can enter the engine.

Alternator: Takes over from the battery when the engine is running. Recharges the battery and supplies power to all electrical components.

Battery: Supplies the initial electrical power that starts the engine.

Carburetor: Most new cars now have fuel-injected engines. Older vehicles have carburetors. This gadget mixes air and fuel in the proper ratio for burning in the engine's combustion chambers.

Coolant reservoir (tank): Holds hot coolant (antifreeze) that overflows from the radiator and also draws back into the radiator as it is needed.

Distributor: Distributes high voltage electricity to the spark plugs, one at a time.

Exhaust manifold: Set of pipes, one for each cylinder, that conducts exhaust away from cylinders.

Fuel injection system: Sprays controlled amount of fuel directly into either the intake manifold or combustion chambers, resulting in a very precise air-to-fuel ratio that improves fuel economy.

Muffler: The interior "baffles" and tubes quiet the explosive release of exhaust.

Suspension system: This system receives a great deal of punishment from the roads. This system consists of shock absorbers, struts, springs, and motor mounts, tires, tie rods, ball joints, control arms, torsion bar, strut rods, spindle, axles.

(continued)

Power-steering reservoir: This reservoir contains fluid for your power-steering system. Once the reservoir cap is unscrewed, the cap will consist of a dipstick. This will identify the fluid levels.

Brake fluid reservoir: The brake fluid level can be inspected by the plastic box or bottle by the firewall on the driver side.

Disc brakes: A metal disk that spins with the wheel that the brake pad uses to pressure against to stop.

Oil dipstick: The stick that's used to check the level of the motor oil.

Rear axle: A shaft that connects the power from the transmission to the wheels.

Radiator: The device that helps to remove heat from the cooling system as coolant passes through it.

Timing belt: The timing belt is a rubber belt that drives the engine's internal components. The timing belt is not easily visible and should be replaced at the indicated mileage and time not on visual wear like a normal drive belt. If the timing belt breaks, the engine stops and costly internal engine damage can occur. The water pump on some vehicles is driven by the timing belt, and should be replaced with the timing belt replacement.

(Source: www.mycargirl.com. Used by permission.)

Instructor's Notes

_____

_____

_____

_____

_____

_____

_____

_____

_____

GOAL ➤ **Maintain and repair your car**

C Now that you know about auto parts and their importance, read this excerpt from an auto maintenance and repair guide.

How to Maintain Your Automobile

Change your air filter. A clogged air filter can affect your gas mileage as well as the performance of your engine. Change it on a regular basis.

Check your oil levels. Your engine needs a certain amount of oil to run properly, so it's important to check the oil levels regularly.

Perform an oil change. As your engine uses oil, the oil becomes dirty and should be changed at regular intervals.

Perform a timing belt inspection. A faulty timing belt can result in bent valves and other expensive engine damage. Check it at least every 10,000 miles and replace it when the manufacturer recommends doing so.

Replace your wipers today. Windshield wipers can wear out, and if they aren't working properly, they could impair your vision while on the road. Change them at least twice a year.

Perform a radiator flush. It's important to keep your radiator and cooling system clean.

Check your power steering fluid. Check your power steering fluid regularly to make sure your power steering doesn't fail.

Inspect your brakes. Protect yourself and your passengers by inspecting your brakes twice a year.

Check and fill your coolant. If your car is low on coolant, it will run hot, so make sure to check the coolant level in your radiator.

Check and replace your spark plugs. A faulty spark plug could cause poor gas mileage and/or a rough running engine and poor acceleration. Make sure to replace the spark plugs as recommended by your car's manual.

Top off your washer fluid. Make sure you have enough washer fluid so you can keep your windshield clean.

Check your wheel bolts. Check the tightness of your wheel bolts on a regular basis to make sure there is no danger of your wheels becoming loose.

D With a partner, answer the following questions.

1. What fluids need to be regularly checked? (Hint: There are four.)

   oil, power steering fluid, coolant, and washer fluid

2. Why is it important to replace windshield wipers?

   Poorly performing wipers could impair driver vision on the road.

3. Why is it bad to have a clogged air filter?

   It will affect gas mileage and performance of the engine.

4. Why should you replace your timing belt?

   A faulty belt can result in bent valves and other engine damage.

5. Why should you check your wheel bolts?

   Loose bolts might result in wheels becoming loose.

6. What could happen if you don't have enough power steering fluid?

   Power steering might fail.

E Some people can perform their own maintenance while others need the help of trained professionals. Who will do your car repairs? If you need help, how will you go about finding a reliable mechanic and getting your repairs done? Read the guide below.

GUIDE TO GETTING REPAIRS DONE

1. Ask a friend, relative, or coworker for recommendations when looking for a good auto shop or mechanic. Also, take time to find a local garage that you feel comfortable with.
2. Make a list of services you need performed or the symptoms your vehicle is experiencing so there is no misunderstanding.
3. Get more than one opinion about the repairs that need to be done.
4. Ask for a written estimate before the job is started.
5. Get more than one estimate and compare prices.
6. Ask about the warranty policy.
7. Have the mechanic show you what you need replaced and have him explain why you need to replace it.
8. Go for a test drive in your car before paying for the repairs. If something is not right with the repairs, make it understood that you are not happy. Do not pay the bill until the vehicle is repaired properly.
9. Pay with a credit card. Many credit cards offer consumer protection for fraud.
10. If you discover something is not fixed after you've paid and driven home, call the garage and explain the situation. Go back to the garage as soon as possible.

F Take out a piece of paper and number it from 1 to 10. Close your books and see how many suggestions from Exercise E you can remember. Write them down.

G Make an outline for the two guides you read: one on maintaining your automobile and one on getting repairs done.

H Using your outlines, write a two-paragraph summary of what you have learned in this lesson. Remember to include a topic sentence in each paragraph.

(Answers will vary.)

Presentation 3   5–10 mins. ■■■ ■■

E Some people can perform their own maintenance while others need the help of trained professionals. Who will do your car repairs? If you need help, how will you go about finding a reliable mechanic and getting your repairs done? Read the guide below.

Have students read the guide silently to themselves. When they have finished, go over any questions they have.

Practice 3   10–15 mins. ■

Note: Shorter classes can do this exercise for homework.

Ask students to close their books. Then read them the instructions for Exercise F.

F Take out a piece of paper and number it from 1 to 10. Close your books and see how many suggestions from Exercise E you can remember. Write them down.

Evaluation 3   5–10 mins. ■

Let students open their books and see how many they got right.

Application   10–25 mins. ■■■ ■

G Make an outline for the two guides you read: one on maintaining your automobile and one on getting repairs done.

H Using your outlines, write a two-paragraph summary of what you have learned in this lesson. Remember to include a topic sentence in each paragraph.

Have students share their paragraphs with a partner. Students should check that they understand each other's sentences and that the writing is clear.

Activity Bank

Unit 3, Lesson 2, Worksheet 1: Auto Maintenance and Repair

Refer students to *Stand Out 5 Grammar Challenge*, Unit 3, Challenge 2 for more practice with information question words and answers.

Instructor's Notes

_____

_____

_____

_____

_____

_____

_____

_____

_____

_____

_____

_____

_____

_____

_____

_____

_____

_____

Objective: Interpret an auto insurance policy
Grammar: Information questions
Vocabulary: *policy, premium, coverage, liability, period, bodily injury, collision, comprehensive, uninsured, VIN*

RESOURCES

Activity Bank: Unit 3, Lesson 3, Worksheet 1
Grammar Challenge 5: Unit 3, Challenge 3

▓ 1.5 hour classes ▓ 2.5 hour classes ▓ 3⁺ hour classes

Suggested Realia: Sample insurance policies

AGENDA

Learn about auto insurance policies.
Read Chalene's insurance policy.
Learn about different types of coverage.
Interpret Keona's policy.

Warm-up and Review   5–10 mins. ▓▓▓

(A) Discuss these questions with your classmates.

Discuss the questions as a class. You might take a poll on questions 1, 2, and 4.

Introduction   5–10 mins. ▓▓▓

Dictation: Five tips to save money on auto insurance:

1. Make sure you get all the discounts you qualify for.
2. Keep your driver's record clean and up-to-date.
3. Adjust your coverage to assume more risk.
4. Drive a low-profile car equipped with certain money-saving safety features.
5. Shop around for a good, low-cost insurance provider.

State the objective: *Today you will learn how to interpret an auto insurance policy.*

Presentation 1   10–15 mins. ▓▓▓

(B) Read what each person has to say about auto insurance policies and look at Chalene's policy below.

Talk about the policy as a class and answer any questions students might have.

Practice 1   10–15 mins. ▓▓▓

(C) Look at Chalene's policy and find each of the items below.

Evaluation 1   5 mins. ▓▓▓

Go over the answers as a class.

STANDARDS CORRELATIONS

CASAS: 1.9.8 (See CASAS Competency List on pages 187–193.)
SCANS: **Information** Acquire and evaluate information, organize and maintain information, interpret and communicate information, use computers to process information
Interpersonal Participate as a member of a team, teach others, negotiate to arrive at a decision, work with cultural diversity
Systems Monitor and correct performance
Basic Skills Reading, writing, listening, speaking

Thinking Skills Decision making
Personal Qualities Responsibility, sociability, self-management
EFF: **Communication** Read with understanding, convey ideas in writing, speak so others can understand, listen actively
Interpersonal Cooperate with others, advocate and influence, resolve conflict and negotiate, guide others
Lifelong Learning Take responsibility for learning, reflect and evaluate

Car insurance

GOAL ➤ **Interpret an auto insurance policy**

 A **Discuss these questions with your classmates.** (Answers will vary.)

1. Do you drive an automobile?
2. Do you have automobile insurance?
3. Why is it important to have auto insurance?
4. Do you understand your automobile insurance policy?
5. Is it against the law in your state to drive without insurance?

B **Read what each person says about auto insurance policies. Look at Chalene's policy below.**

"An insurance **policy** is a contract between you and the insurance company that states what the company will pay for in the event of an accident." — **Chalene**

"The insurance **premium** is the amount you pay for auto insurance for a certain period of time." — **Keona**

"**Coverage** is what is included in the insurance—what the company will pay for." — **Binata**

STANDOUT INSURANCE COMPANY

Name of Insured and Address Chalene Johnson 24573 Thatch Street Houston, TX 77042	Policy Number: 05XX 52 87D 1625 Q Policy Period: Effective Jan 13, 2009 to Jul 13, 2009
Description of Vehicle(s) **Year and Make:** 2005 Acurak **VIN:** QXXPYR18924G23794	**Annual Mileage:** 9,000 **Premium for this Policy Period:** $212.38

Coverage	Limits of Liability	Six-Month Premium
A. Bodily Injury	Each Person $100,000; Each Accident $300,000	86.92
B. Collision	Each Accident $50,000	61.43
C. Comprehensive	Each Incident $25,000	36.04
D. Uninsured Motor Vehicle Bodily Injury	Each Person $50,000; Each Accident $150,000	27.99
	TOTAL	**$212.38**

 C **Look at Chalene's policy and find each of the items below.**

1. Policy Number: 05XX 52 87D 1625 Q

2. VIN: QXXPYR18924G23794

3. Policy Premium: $212.38

4. Annual Mileage: 9,000

5. Length of Policy: six months

6. Make of Vehicle: Acurak

GOAL ➤ Interpret an auto insurance policy

D There are different types of coverage listed on insurance policies. Match each type of coverage with what it covers. Write the corresponding letter on the line.

Coverage	What it covers
1. bodily injury liability _a_	a. other people's bodily injuries or death for which you are responsible
2. property damage liability _b_	b. damage to another vehicle or property
3. collision _d_	c. loss or damage to your vehicle or the vehicle you are driving for an incident other than collision (thievery, fire, etc.)
4. medical payments _e_	d. damage to your vehicle due to an auto accident
5. comprehensive _c_	e. bodily injuries to you or your passengers caused by the accident
6. uninsured motorist's bodily injury _f_	f. bodily injury caused by another vehicle without insurance
7. uninsured motorist's property damage _g_	g. damage caused by another vehicle without insurance

E With a partner, read each scenario and decide which coverage would apply.

1. Chalene accidentally ran into a tree and damaged the front end of her car. Which coverage would apply? _____ collision _____

2. Binata was driving home from school when she hit another car. She had run through a red light, so the accident was her fault. There was no real damage to her car, but she hurt her back and had to go to the chiropractor. Also, there was significant damage to the car she hit. Which types of coverage would apply? _medical payments and property damage liability_

3. Keona and his friend Chalene were driving to work when a car hit them from behind. Then the car drove off without giving them any information. Neither Keona nor Chalene was hurt, but there was damage to Keona's car. Which coverage would apply? _uninsured motorist's property damage_

4. Keona's car got stolen from the parking lot at a movie theater. Which coverage would apply? _____ comprehensive _____

Presentation 2　　5-10 mins. ■■■□

D There are different types of coverage listed on insurance policies. Match each type of coverage with what it covers. Write the corresponding letter on the line.

Teaching Tip

Presentation: Access students' prior knowledge

Students are often already familiar with some of the information that is presented in *Stand Out 5*. When this is the case, you can rely on their prior knowledge and let them teach the class. There are several ways to illicit information from students:

1. Ask students to share what they know with a partner.
2. Have students write down what they already know.
3. Have students share what they know with the class orally or by coming to the board and writing.

Exercise D may resemble a practice exercise, but since it is in the presentation stage, it offers a chance for you to find out what students already know and teach them new concepts at the same time. For this matching exercise, see how much students can complete on their own before you give them the answers. Then, discuss each answer in detail to make sure students understand the different types of coverage.

Read the following scenarios to students and ask them what insurance coverage would apply.

1. *Imagine that you were driving to school this morning and someone stopped suddenly in front of you. You ran into their car. No one was hurt, but both cars were damaged. What coverage would apply?* (property damage liability—for the damage to the other car—and comprehensive—for the damage to your car)
2. *Imagine that your car was parked in the school parking lot and when you got out of class to go home, you noticed that someone had smashed the passenger door in with their car. What coverage would apply?* (uninsured motorist's property damage)

Practice 2　　10-15 mins. ■■□

E With a partner, read each scenario and decide which coverage would apply.

Note: Shorter classes can do this exercise for homework.

Evaluation 2　　10-15 mins. ■■□

Go over the answers as a class.

Instructor's Notes

_____

_____

_____

_____

_____

_____

_____

_____

_____

_____

_____

_____

_____

_____

_____

_____

_____

_____

_____

_____

_____

_____

Presentation 3

5-10 mins.

Have students turn back to the auto insurance policy on page 53. Ask them some questions about the policy: *What is the policy period? What vehicle is being insured? What is the six-month premium for collision coverage?* Then, ask volunteers to ask you a different question about the policy.

Practice 3

10-15 mins. ■

Note: Shorter classes can do this exercise for homework.

F Look back at Chalene's policy in Exercise B on page 53. Write a question for each answer.

Go over the instructions and example with students. Have them complete the exercise by themselves.

Evaluation 3

10-15 mins. ■

When individual students have finished, have them share their answers with a partner. When everyone has finished, ask volunteers to come to the board and write their questions. It is very likely that students will have written different questions for the same answer. Show them how more than one question can be correct.

Application

10-20 mins.

G Look at Keona's insurance policy and answer the questions that follow.

Activity Bank

Unit 3, Lesson 3, Worksheet 1: Auto Insurance Practice

Refer students to *Stand Out 5 Grammar Challenge,* Unit 3, Challenge 3 for more practice with negative questions.

F Look back at Chalene's policy in Exercise B on page 53. Write a question for each answer.

EXAMPLE: Chalene Johnson: Who is being insured through this policy?

1. $61.43: How much is collision coverage?

2. six months: How long is this policy's coverage good for?

3. 05XX 52 87D 1625 Q: What is the policy number?

4. 2005 Acurak: What is the year and make of the vehicle?

5. $212.38: What is the premium for this policy period?

6. 9,000: What is the vehicle's annual mileage?

G Look at Keona's insurance policy and answer the questions that follow.
(Answers to Exercise G may vary.)

United Automobile Association • Dallas, TX

STATE: **TX**
POLICY NUMBER: **QQP15 26 49L3798 1**
POLICY PERIOD: **September 5, 2009 to March 5, 2010**
VEHICLE(S): **2008 Fort Ficus, 2004 Chevnoret Tihoe**

NAME AND ADDRESS OF INSURED
Keona Lu
54 Plover Plaza
Galveston, TX 50472

Limits of Liability			6-Month Premium
LIABILITY			
Bodily Injury	Each Person $100,000;	Each Accident $300,000	98.12
Property Damage	Each Accident $50,000		69.07
UNINSURED MOTORISTS			
Bodily Injury	Each Person $100,000	Each Accident $300,000	27.00
Property Damage	Each Accident $50,000		21.45
PHYSICAL DAMAGE			
Comprehensive Loss	Deductible $1,000		30.92
Collision Loss	Deductible $1,000		96.41
		TOTAL:	**$342.97**

1. How many vehicles are covered by this policy?
   a. 1   (b. 2)   c. 3   d. 4

2. Where does the insured motorist live?
   a. Dallas   b. Lake Tahoe   (c. Galveston)   d. Houston

3. How much is United Automobile Association charging for liability?
   a. $98.12   b. $69.07   c. $21.45   (d. $167.19)

4. What is Keona's deductible for comprehensive loss?
   a. $96.41   b. $30.92   (c. $1,000)   d. $50,000

Gas and mileage

GOAL ➤ Compute mileage and gas consumption

 A Read and listen to the conversation between Keona and Chalene.

CD
TR 16

Keona: I can't believe the price of gasoline! I've been spending almost $60 just to fill up my tank.

Chalene: Same here. I've been trying to figure out how I can use my car less, so I save some money on gas.

Keona: Any good ideas?

Chalene: Well, I'm going to start carpooling to school two days a week, which should help. And I'm trying to combine my errands so I only go out once a week.

Keona: That sounds good. I think I'm going to look into public transportation. I have a long drive to work so maybe I can figure out how to take the train into town. I'll have to drive to the station and park, but at least I won't be driving all the way to work.

Chalene: That's a great idea!

B Can you think of some other measures Keona and Chalene can take so they won't have to use their cars so much? Write your ideas below. (Answers will vary.)

Compare prices at different gas stations/Make sure all fluids and filters in car are

checked/Check that tires are inflated properly.

C Keona wanted to see how his gas mileage was so he started keeping track of his gas consumption and driving habits in a small notebook in his car. Look at a page from his book below.

Date	Odometer	Trip	Gallons	MPG	Notes
8/7	12, 200	245 miles	13	18.85	a lot of street driving
8/15	12,475	275	14	19.64	highway driving
8/24	12,760	285	15	19	highway and street
9/1	13,020	260	14.5	17.93	

How do you think Keona might calculate his gas mileage in miles per gallon (MPG)? Create a formula and fill in the MPG column in the chart above.

Example: 245 ÷ 13 = 18.85 MPG. Divide miles driven by gallons used.

Objective: Compute mileage and gas consumption
Academic Strategies: Math calculations, focused listening, note taking
Vocabulary: *odometer, trip, MPG*

RESOURCES
Activity Bank: Unit 3, Lesson 4, Worksheets 1–3
Grammar Challenge 5: Unit 3, Challenge 4

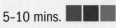 1.5 hour classes ■ 2.5 hour classes ■ 3⁺ hour classes

Audio: CD Tracks 16–17

AGENDA
Discuss ways to drive less.
Keep track of gas and mileage.
Calculate miles per gallon (MPG).
Listen to maintenance tips that help reduce gas consumption.
Discuss driving habits that save gas.
Track your own mileage.

Warm-up and Review   5-10 mins.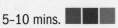

Put students in small groups and have them make a list of all the expenses associated with owning a car. Make it a game and tell them you want to see which group can come up with the longest list. When groups have finished, make a list of all their ideas on the board.

Introduction   5-10 mins. ■■

Dictation:

1. What is the best way to increase your miles per gallon? **2.** Where is the cheapest place to buy gas? **3.** What maintenance tips can help your fuel efficiency? **4.** What driving tips can help you save money on gas?

If you have time, spend some discussion time on these questions. State the objective: *Today you will learn how to compute mileage and gas consumption.*

Presentation 1   10-15 mins. ■■

(A) Read and listen to the conversation between Keona and Chalene.

> **Listening Script**   *CD Track 16*
>
> *The listening script matches the conversation in Exercise A.*

(B) Can you think of some other measures Keona and Chalene can take so they won't have to use their cars so much? Write your ideas below.

Discuss students' ideas as a class.

(C) Keona wanted to see how his gas mileage was so he started keeping track of his gas consumption and driving habits in a small notebook in his car. Look at a page from his book below.

Go over the chart as a class, making sure students understand all the vocabulary.

Practice 1   10-15 mins.

How do you think Keona might calculate his miles per gallon (MPG)? Try to come up with a calculation and fill in the MPG column in the chart above.

If necessary, help students come up with the calculation and do an example with them to get them started.

Evaluation 1   5 mins.

Go over the answers as a class.

STANDARDS CORRELATIONS

CASAS: 1.9.3 (See CASAS Competency List on pages 187-193.)
SCANS: **Information** Acquire and evaluate information
Interpersonal Participate as a member of a team, teach others, negotiate to arrive at a decision, work with cultural diversity
Systems Monitor and correct performance
Basic Skills Reading, writing, arithmetic, listening, speaking
Thinking Skills Think creatively, make decisions, solve problems, see things in the mind's eye

Personal Qualities Responsibility, sociability, self-management
EFF: **Communication** Read with understanding, convey ideas in writing, speak so others can understand, listen actively
Decision Making Use math to solve problems and communicate, solve problems and make decisions
Interpersonal Cooperate with others, resolve conflict and negotiate, guide others
Lifelong Learning Take responsibility for learning, reflect and evaluate

Presentation 2 5–10 mins.

Ask students if they know of any strategies to improve gas mileage. Brainstorm some ideas as a class.

Practice 2 10–15 mins.

D In order to improve your gas mileage, you can follow certain maintenance tips. Listen and write the five tips you hear below.

E How will each of these tips help? Listen again and write the reasons on the lines below.

F Keona followed these tips. Look at his log below and calculate the MPG and cost per mile. Did his MPG improve?

See if students can figure out how to calculate the cost per mile on their own.

Look at the cost per mile column. Which week was the cheapest? Come up with ideas how Keona can spend less per mile on gas.

Students can work in pairs or small groups to develop useful ideas for spending less on gas.

Evaluation 2 10–15 mins.

As each exercise is completed, go over the answers as a class.

 Listening Script CD Track 17

Here are five tips that should help improve your gas mileage.

1. *Get your engine tuned.*
   An improperly tuned engine hurts gas mileage by an average of 4.1 percent, according to U.S. government studies. Most important to mileage is a properly working oxygen sensor, which helps keep your engine working efficiently.

2. *Keep your tires properly inflated.*
   Underinflated tires increase resistance and make it more difficult for the engine to move your car along the road. Check your tires every time you fill the tank. The U.S. Department of Energy estimates the average person can improve their gas mileage by 3.3 percent by inflating their tires regularly.

3. *Check your air filter and replace it every 12,000 miles.*
   Cars don't just run on gasoline. They actually run on gas and oxygen. If a clogged air filter restricts the flow of air, your performance and your fuel economy suffer. The U.S. Department of Energy estimates that you could save as much as 22 cents per gallon by replacing a bad air filter.

4. *Use the right motor oil.*
   Many people think it's OK to simply put any motor oil into their engine. While your motor will continue to work with a different grade of oil, it won't work quite as efficiently. You can save a couple of cents per gallon by using the exact oil recommended for your car.

5. *Don't carry junk in your trunk.*
   Get all those newspapers, cans, and other baggage out of your car and trunk. Reducing the weight of the car increases mileage over the course of a tank of gas.

(Source: www.edmunds.com)

57a Lesson Planner: Unit 3, Lesson 4

CD
TR 17

D   In order to improve your gas mileage, you can follow certain maintenance tips. Listen and write the five tips you hear below.

Tips for improving gas mileage:

1. Get the engine tuned.

2. Keep tires properly inflated.

3. Check your air filter and replace it every 12,000 miles.

4. Use the right motor oil.

5. Don't carry junk in the trunk.

E   How will each of these tips help? Listen again and write the reasons on the lines below.

1. Improperly tuned engines hurt gas mileage.

2. Under inflated tires increase resistance and increase gas consumption.

3. If air filter is clogged, car performance and gas usage suffers.

4. The engine won't work as efficiently if the incorrect oil is used.

5. Reducing weight of the car increases mileage per gallon.

F   Keona followed these tips. Look at his log below and calculate the MPG and cost per mile. Did his MPG improve? No. His MPG did not improve.

Date	Odometer	Trip	Gallons	MPG	Cost per gallon	Cost per mile
10/5	14,687	275 miles	13	21	$3.05	.145 ¢
10/17	14,962	295	14	21	$3.07	.146 ¢
10/30	15,262	300	15	20	$2.95	.148 ¢
11/9	15,542	280	14.5	19	$3.10	.163 ¢

Look at the cost per mile column. Which week was the cheapest? Come up with ideas how Keona can spend less per mile on gas.

In terms of cost per mile, the week of 10/5 was cheapest.
In terms of actual gas paid for, the week of 11/9 was cheapest.
Ideas: Drive more slowly to reduce gas consumption.
       Reduce length of trips if possible.

G Here are some tips on how to change your driving habits in order to save gas. In a small group, discuss each tip and figure out what it means. (Answers may vary.)

1. No more drag racing. Do not speed or leave red lights too quickly.
2. Look farther down the road. Drive at a steady rate; do not speed up and slow down erratically.
3. Pick your lane and stick with it. Erratic driving increases gas consumption.
4. Pretend you're a hybrid. Try to drive economically and reduce number of trips whenever possible.
5. Carpool with classmates or coworkers. Share rides to reduce expenses for all.
6. Don't drive. Share rides and take public transportation.
7. Drive during off-peak hours. Don't drive during heavy traffic.
8. Look for telecommuting opportunities. Work from home and avoid driving.

H Keona suggested that Chalene keep track of her gas consumption and mileage. Fill in the missing numbers in her chart below.

Date	Odometer	Trip	Gallons	MPG	Cost per gallon	Cost per mile
10/5	22,758	310	15	20.7	$3.10	.15 ¢
10/20	23,068	325	16	20.3	$3.05	.15 ¢
10/30	23,393	320	15.5	20.7	$3.12	.15 ¢
11/12	23,713	280	17	16.5	$2.99	.18 ¢
11/18	23,993	275	16.5	16.7	$3.03	.18 ¢
AVERAGE		302	16	18.98	$3.06	approx .16 ¢

I Think about your own driving habits (or traveling habits if you don't own a car). Fill in the chart below as best you can and then make the calculations. (Answers will vary.)

Date	Odometer	Trip	Gallons	MPG	Cost per gallon	Cost per mile

Presentation 3   5–10 mins. ■■■

Look at the first tip in Exercise G and ask students what they think it means and why it would help them save money on gas.

Practice 3   15–20 mins. ■

 G Here are some tips on how to change your driving habits in order to save gas. In a small group, discuss each tip and figure out what it means.

Note: The entire article can be found on the Activity Bank.

1. **No more drag racing.** Gas is consumed more quickly during hard acceleration, so if you accelerate gradually from a green light, you stand to improve your mileage significantly.
2. **Look farther down the road.** Back off the accelerator if the traffic light two blocks away is red. Glide until you get the green and then accelerate moderately. This not only saves gas but also your brake pads.
3. **Pick your lane and stick with it.** Traffic studies have shown that changing lanes doesn't result in a significantly reduced travel time. It will lower your fuel consumption if you don't surge to switch lanes.
4. **Pretend you're a hybrid.** Most hybrids save gas by automatically shutting off at stoplights. Turn off your engine if you are stopped for a long period of time.
5. **Carpool with classmates or coworkers.** You can use the carpool lanes and share the driving expenses.
6. **Don't drive.** Use alternative forms of transportation such as public transportation, bicycles, or walking.
7. **Drive during off-peak hours.** Peak hours are when most people are going to or commuting from work. These are also known as "rush hours."
8. **Look for telecommuting opportunities.** Work at home using your commuter.

Evaluation 3   5–10 mins. ■

Discuss the tips as a class.

Application   10–20 mins. ■■■

H Keona suggested that Chalene keep track of her gas consumption and mileage. Fill in the missing numbers in her chart below.

I Think about your own driving habits (or traveling habits if you don't own a car). Fill in the chart below as best you can and then make the calculations.

Activity Bank

Unit 3, Lesson 4, Worksheet 1: Gas/Mileage Chart (blank template)

Unit 3, Lesson 4, Worksheet 2: Compute Mileage and Gas

Unit 3, Lesson 4, Worksheet 3: How to Change Your Driving Habits to Save Gas

Refer students to *Stand Out 5 Grammar Challenge*, Unit 3, Challenge 4 for more practice with math language.

Instructor's Notes

_____
_____
_____
_____
_____
_____
_____
_____
_____
_____
_____
_____
_____
_____

AT-A-GLANCE PREP

Objective: Follow the rules of the road
Academic Strategies: Reading tables, interpreting facts
Vocabulary: *traffic signs, pedestrians, restrained, unrestrained, occupant, fatalities, arrested, narcotics*

RESOURCES

Activity Bank: Unit 3, Lesson 5, Worksheets 1–4
Grammar Challenge 5: Unit 3, Challenge 5

■ 1.5 hour classes ■ 2.5 hour classes ■ 3⁺ hour classes

AGENDA

Discuss traffic signs and traffic laws.
Interpret information related to seat belts and safety.
Discuss alcohol-related laws and accidents.

Suggested Realia: Driver handbooks or manuals from your state RMV

Warm-up and Review   5–10 mins.

Ask students to help you brainstorm a list of fuel-saving ideas. Write them on the board. Ask students who drive if any of them use these techniques. Ask them which one(s) they will start doing.

Introduction   5–10 mins.

Dictation:

1. Driving a car comes with a lot of responsibility.
2. Following the rules of the road is very important.
3. What do you think is the most important traffic law?
4. Where can you go to find a list of traffic laws for your state?

State the objective: *Today we will learn about the rules of the road and study some facts about seat-belt safety and alcohol-related accidents.*

Presentation 1   10–15 mins.

(A) **What does each of the following signs mean? With a partner, see what you know.**

Since this is still the presentation stage, see what students already know and then talk about each sign as a class.

Practice 1   10–15 mins.

(B) **Think about the traffic laws you are familiar with. In a small group, write a law for each item below.**

Evaluation 1   5 mins. ■■■

Ask a volunteer from each group to come to the board and write one of the laws. Discuss the laws as a class.

STANDARDS CORRELATIONS

CASAS: 1.9.2 (See CASAS Competency List on pages 187–193.)
SCANS: **Information** Acquire and evaluate information, organize and maintain information, interpret and communicate information, use computers to process information *(optional)*
Interpersonal Participate as a member of a team, teach others, negotiate to arrive at a decision, work with cultural diversity
Systems Understand systems, monitor and correct performance
Technology Apply technology to a task *(optional)*
Basic Skills Reading, writing, arithmetic, listening, speaking
Thinking Skills Think creatively, make decisions, solve problems, see things in the mind's eye

Personal Qualities Responsibility, sociability, self-management
EFF: **Communication** Read with understanding, convey ideas in writing, speak so others can understand, listen actively
Decision Making Use math to solve problems and communicate, solve problems and make decisions, plan
Interpersonal Cooperate with others, advocate and influence, resolve conflict and negotiate, guide others
Lifelong Learning Take responsibility for learning, reflect and evaluate, learn through research, use information and communications technology *(optional)*

Traffic laws

GOAL ➤ **Follow the rules of the road**

Vocabulary | Grammar
Life Skills
Academic | Pronunciation

A What does each of the following signs mean? With a partner, see what you know.

two-way traffic

slippery when wet

railroad crossing

lane shifts to left

steep grade

no left turn

stoplight ahead

yield

no U-turns

divided highway ends

school crossing

merge

hospital to right

do not enter

bear right

full stop

B Think about the traffic laws you are familiar with. In a small group, write a law for each item.

EXAMPLE: yellow light: __You must slow down at a yellow light.__

1. speed limit: _You must obey the speed limit._

2. seat belts: _Everyone in the car must wear a seat belt._

3. red light: _You have to come to a full stop at a red light._

4. children: _Watch carefully for children playing on crowded neighborhood streets._

5. pedestrians: _Stop for pedestrians in a crosswalk._

6. stop sign: _You must come to a full stop at a stop sign before proceding._

7. police officer: _You must obey the directions of a police officer._

8. school bus: _Traffic behind and coming toward a school bus must stop when the bus has on flashing lights._

GOAL ➤ Follow the rules of the road

C Look back at the traffic laws you wrote for children and seat belts. The United States Department of Transportation has an organization called the National Highway Traffic Safety Administration (NHTSA) whose mission is to "save lives, prevent injuries, and reduce vehicle-related crashes." Read the data from a study NHTSA conducted and answer the questions that follow.

Occupant Fatalities in 2004 by Age and Restraint Use in Passenger Vehicles

Age group	Restrained	Percent restrained	Unrestrained	Percent unrestrained	Total	Total percent
<5	317	64	178	36	495	100
5–9	200	48	218	52	418	100
10–15	348	37	598	63	946	100
16–20	1,961	38	3,174	62	5,135	100
21–24	1,222	34	2,373	66	3,595	100
25–44	3,465	37	5,841	63	9,306	100
45–64	3,162	48	3,371	52	6,533	100
65–74	1,286	61	830	39	2,116	100
75+	2,117	69	958	31	3,075	100
Total	14,078	48	17,541	52	31,619	100

(*Source:* http://www.nhtsa.dot.gov)

1. What percentage of fatalities was unrestrained in the 21- to 24-year-old age group in 2004? ___66%___

2. How many restrained 65- to 74-year-olds died in 2004? ___1,286___

3. How many children under age five died in 2004 because they weren't restrained? ___178___

4. What is the average percentage of unrestrained passengers who died in 2004? 55% (reported)

5. How many adults over 44 died even though they were wearing seat belts? ___6,565___

D On a separate piece of paper write each question above as a statement.

EXAMPLE: Sixty-six percent of all vehicle fatalities involving 21- to 24-year-olds were unrestrained. (See answers on Lesson Planner Page 60a.)

E What traffic law was violated by the unrestrained drivers and passengers? What law was violated by the parents of the unrestrained children? Drivers, passengers, and children should all wear seat belts or restraints. This law is true in 49 of the 50 states.

Presentation 2   5–10 mins. ■■■

C Look back at the traffic laws you wrote for children and seat belts. The United States Department of Transportation has an organization called the National Highway Traffic Safety Administration (NHTSA) whose mission is to "save lives, prevent injuries, and reduce vehicle-related crashes. Read the data from a study NHTSA conducted and answer the questions that follow.

Go over the chart as a class, asking questions to make sure students understand the data that are presented. Once students understand the data, have them answer the questions by themselves. Go over the answers as a class.

Practice 2   10–15 mins. ■■

Note: Shorter classes can do this exercise for homework.

D On a separate piece of paper write each question above as a statement.

Go over the example, making sure students understand what to do.

1. In 2004, sixty-six percent of fatalities were unrestrained in the 21- to 24-year old age group.
2. In 2004, 1,286 restrained 65- to 74-year olds died.
3. In 2004, 178 children under the age of five died because they weren't restrained.
4. In fatal accidents in 2004, fifty-five percent of passengers who were unrestrained died.
5. Of adults over 44, 6,565 died in passenger vehicles even though they were wearing seat belts.

Evaluation 2   10–15 mins. ■■

Ask volunteers to write the statements on the board. Evaluate them as a class.

E What traffic law was violated by the unrestrained drivers and passengers? What law was violated by the parents of the unrestrained children?

Presentation 3

10-15 mins.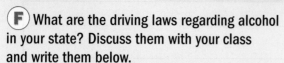

F What are the driving laws regarding alcohol in your state? Discuss them with your class and write them below.

G Read the facts on alcohol-related accidents. Check (✓) the ones that are the most surprising to you.

Read the facts as a class. Discuss which ones are the most surprising.

Practice 3

10-15 mins. ■

Note: Shorter classes can do this exercise for homework.

H With a partner, rewrite the facts above in your own words.

Go over the example with students, showing them how the fact was restated. Explain to them the purpose of the exercise is to be able to clearly explain the facts to someone else, in which case, they must first understand the facts themselves.

Evaluation 3

5-10 mins. ■

Call on different students to stand up and restate the facts.

Application

10-20 mins. ■■■

I In a small group, make a list of five driving rules that you all think are the most important. Present your list to the class.

 Note: There is a list of traffic or driving laws on the Activity Bank. To make this exercise easier, you can give students the list of laws and have them choose the five most important.

Optional Computer Activity: Go online to find the Department of Motor Vehicles (DMV) or the Registry of Motor Vehicles (RMV) for your state. Download a driver's handbook or manual.

Activity Bank

Unit 3, Lesson 5, Worksheet 1: Sample Driving Tests

Unit 3, Lesson 5, Worksheet 2: Violation Scenarios (listening)

 Refer students to *Stand Out 5 Grammar Challenge*, Unit 3, Challenge 5 for more practice with writing questions.

There are also two extension challenges. Extension Challenge 1 practices tag questions. Extension Challenge 2 practices comparative questions using *which* and *what*.

Instructor's Notes

_____

_____

_____

_____

_____

_____

_____

_____

_____

_____

_____

_____

_____

_____

_____

_____

_____

_____

F What are the driving laws regarding alcohol in your state? Discuss them with your class and write them below: (Answers will vary.)

In Texas, the limit for blood alcohol concentration is .08. However, no traceable amount

of alcohol is permitted for people under 21 years of age.

G Read the facts on alcohol-related accidents. Check (✔) the ones that are the most surprising to you. (Answers will vary.)

☐ Alcohol-related motor vehicle crashes kill someone every 31 minutes and non-fatally injure someone every two minutes.

☐ In 2005, 16,885 people in the United States died in alcohol-related motor vehicle crashes, representing 39% of all traffic-related deaths.

☐ In 2005, nearly 1.4 million drivers were arrested for driving under the influence of alcohol or narcotics.

☐ Drugs other than alcohol (e.g., marijuana and cocaine) are involved in about 18% of motor vehicle driver deaths. These other drugs are generally used in combination with alcohol.

☐ More than half of the 414 child passengers ages 14 and younger who died in alcohol-related crashes during 2005 were riding with the drinking driver.

(*Source:* http://www.cdc.gov/ncipc/factsheets/drving.htm)

H With a partner, rewrite the facts above in your own words.

EXAMPLE: Someone is killed every half an hour due to a car accident involving

alcohol.

I In a small group, make a list of five driving rules that you all think are the most important. Present your list to the class. (Answers will vary.)

Example: Drivers must yield to pedestrians.

_____

_____

_____

_____

Review

A List four different types of cars. (Lesson 1) (Answers will vary. Sample answers are given.)

1. _____SUV_____   3. _____four-door sedan_____

2. _____minivan_____   4. _____pickup truck_____

Which auto is best for you? _____sports car_____   Why? I am single and like a car
that handles well on the highway.

B Recall the auto maintenance tips you learned in Lesson 2. Write the correct verb from the box to complete each tip. You will need to use some of the verbs more than once. (Lesson 2)
(Answers will vary.)

| change | check | fill | inspect | perform | replace | top off |

1. _____Perform_____ a radiator flush.

2. _____Replace_____ your air filter. (Check/Inspect/Change)

3. _____Fill_____ your washer fluid. (Check/Top off)

4. _____Inspect_____ your wipers today. (Change/Check/Replace)

5. _____Fill_____ your power steering fluid. (Top off/Check)

6. _____Check_____ your oil levels.

7. _____Perform_____ an oil change.

8. _____Perform_____ a timing belt inspection.

9. _____Check_____ your brakes. (Inspect/Replace)

10. _____Check_____ and _____top off_____ your coolant.

11. _____Check_____ your wheel bolts. (Inspect)

C Help Gary calculate his gas mileage and how much he is spending on gas. (Lesson 4)

Date	Odometer	Trip	Gallons	MPG	Cost per gallon	Cost per mile
2/7	46,269	310	15	20.67	$3.02	.146¢
2/17	46,579	325	16	20.31	$2.90	.143¢
2/28	46,904	320	15.5	20.65	$2.95	.143¢
3/5	47,224	280	17	16.47	$3.01	.183¢
AVERAGE		308.75	15.88	19.53	$2.97	.154¢

How can Gary improve his gas mileage? With a partner, come up with five ways. (Answers will vary)

1. Drive slowly.   4. Keep tires filled.
2 Drive shorter   5. Check fluid levels
  distances.   and change filters.
3. Buy a smaller car.

AT-A-GLANCE PREP

Objectives: All unit objectives
Grammar: All unit grammar
Academic Strategy: Reviewing
Vocabulary: All Unit 3 vocabulary

RESOURCES

Stand Out 5 Assessment CD-ROM with Exam*View*®

■ 1.5 hour classes ■ 2.5 hour classes ■ 3+ hour classes

AGENDA

Discuss unit objectives.
Complete the review.
Use unit vocabulary.

Warm-up and Review 5-10 mins. ■■■

Have students take out their list of driving or traffic laws from the previous lesson. Ask a member from each group to write the list on the board. Ask the class to analyze what is written on the board to see what the lists have in common and how they differ.

Introduction 5-10 mins. ■■■

Ask students as a class to try to recall all the goals and objectives of this unit without looking back in their books. The objectives for this unit include purchasing a car, maintaining and repairing your car, interpreting an auto insurance policy, computing mileage and gas consumption, and following the rules of the road. Write all the goals or objectives on the board from Unit 3. Show students the first page of the unit and mention the five objectives. State the objective: *Today we will be reviewing everything we have learned in this unit and preparing for the team project.*

Presentation 1 10-15 mins. ■■■

This presentation will cover the first three pages of the review. Quickly go to the first page of each lesson. Discuss the objective of each. Ask simple questions to remind students of what they have learned. **Note:** Since there is little presentation in the review, you can assign the review exercises that don't require collaboration with a partner or group for homework and go over them in class the following day.

Practice 1 20-25 mins. ■■■

Note: There are two ways to do the review:
1. Go through the exercises one at a time and, as students complete each one, go over the answers. 2. Quickly go through the instructions of each exercise, let students complete all of the exercises at once, and then go over the answers.

(A) List four different types of cars. (Lesson 1) Which auto is best for you? Why?

(B) Recall the auto maintenance tips you learned in Lesson 2. Write the correct verb from the box to complete each tip. You will need to use some of the verbs more than once. (Lesson 2)

(C) Help Gary compute his gas mileage and how much he is spending on gas. (Lesson 4) . . . How can Gary improve his gas mileage? With a partner, come up with five ways.

Have students share results to help Gary improve his mileage.

Evaluation 1 5-15 mins. ■■■

Go around the classroom and check on students' progress. Help individuals when needed. If you see consistent errors among several students, interrupt the class and give a mini-lesson or review to help students feel comfortable with the concept.

STANDARDS CORRELATIONS

CASAS: 7.2.1 (See CASAS Competency List on pages 187–193.)
SCANS: Resources Allocate time
Information Acquire and evaluate information
Interpersonal Participate as a member of a team, teach others, negotiate to arrive at a decision, work with cultural diversity
Systems Monitor and correct performance
Basic Skills Reading, writing, arithmetic, listening, speaking

Thinking Skills Think creatively, make decisions, solve problems, see things in the mind's eye
Personal Qualities Responsibility, sociability, self-management
***EFF:* Communication** Read with understanding, convey ideas in writing, speak so others can understand, listen actively, observe critically
Interpersonal Cooperate with others, guide others
Lifelong Learning Take responsibility for learning, reflect and evaluate

Practice 1 (continued)   25–30 mins. ▪▪▪▫

D Read the insurance policy and answer the questions. (Lesson 3)

E On a separate piece of paper, write a summary about one of the topics given below. (Lessons 1–5)

Refer to the student book page for the topics.

Evaluation 1 (continued)   5–15 mins. ▪▪▫

Go around the classroom and check on students' progress. Help individuals when needed. If you see consistent errors among several students, interrupt the class and give a mini-lesson or review to help students feel comfortable with the concept.

Teaching Tip

Recycling/Review

The review exercises, the research activity, and the team project are part of the recycling/review process. Students often need to be reintroduced to concepts to solidify what they have learned. Many concepts are learned and forgotten when students are engaged in learning other new concepts. This is because students learn but are not necessarily ready to acquire language concepts.

Therefore, it becomes very important to review material with students and to show them how to review it on their own. It is also important to recycle the new concepts in different contexts.

Instructor's Notes

Read the insurance policy and answer the questions. (Lesson 3)

DriveRite Automotive Insurance Co., Inc.

Dung Nguyen 79563 Eastern Way Ambrose, GA 31512	Policy Number: QPX2 80 56 45F5542 6 Policy Period: 2/10/08–2/09/09	Vehicle: 2005 Folkswagin Passerine VIN: ZXYI493807T984XXX Annual Mileage: 12,500

Type of Coverage	Cost of Coverage	Limits of Liability	
A. Medical	$182.50	Each person $100,000 Each accident $300,000	
B. Liability	$175.00	Each person $100,000 Each accident $300,000	
C. Collision	$98.26	Each accident $50,000 Each person $50,000	
D. Uninsured motorist	$135.00	Each accident $150,000	
E. Comprehensive	$76.45	Each incident $25,000	

Premium: $667.21

1. Who is being insured through this insurance policy? _Dung Nguyen_

2. Where does the insured live? _Ambrose, GA_

3. How long is this policy in effect? _One year_

4. What is the total premium for Dung's policy? _$667.21_

5. How many miles does Dung drive per year? _12,500 miles_

6. Dung got in an accident last week, broke his leg, and damaged his car. Which types of coverage will pay for this? _medical, collision_

7. How much is the insurance company charging for comprehensive coverage? _$76.45_

8. If Dung's car gets stolen, how much will the insurance company pay to replace his car? _$25,000_

9. What is the most the insurance company will pay for the property damage in an accident? _$300,000_

10. How much will the insurance company pay for each person who is hurt in an accident caused by someone without insurance? _$150,000 per accident_

On a separate piece of paper, write a summary about one of these topics. (Lessons 1–5)
(Answers will vary.)
- Purchasing a Car
- Maintaining a Car
- Saving Gas
- Keeping Track of Gas Mileage
- Auto Expenditures
- Rules of the Road

VOCABULARY REVIEW

F Write the name of each car part that has a box pointing to it.

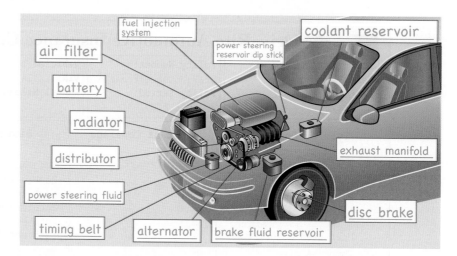

fuel injection system

coolant reservoir

air filter

power steering reservoir dip stick

battery

radiator

distributor

exhaust manifold

power steering fluid

disc brake

timing belt   alternator   brake fluid reservoir

What does each part do? With a partner, take turns describing each part and its function.

G Write a defining sentence for each of the words below. (Answers may vary.)

EXAMPLE: occupant: _An occupant is a passenger in a car._

1. premium: _The premium is the amount paid for car insurance._

2. collision: _A collision is an accident between two cars or a car and an object._

3. MPG: _MPG is miles per gallon._

4. odometer: _The odometer measures the number of miles traveled._

5. fatalities: _Fatalities are the number of deaths._

6. unrestrained: _Unrestrained indicates unprotected by a seat belt._

H Read each phrase below and match it with a vocabulary word or phrase from the unit.

EXAMPLE: restrains driver and/or passengers in an accident. _____ seat belt

1. identifies your vehicle: _VIN (Vehicle Identification Number)_

2. covers damage to another vehicle: _____ liability

3. can get clogged and affect your gas mileage: _air, gas, and/or oil filters_

4. tells you how fast you can drive on any given road: _____ speed limit

5. the different things an insurance company will pay for: _medical, collision, liability,_ _comprehensive_

6. tells you how many miles you have driven: _____ odometer

Practice 1 (continued)   25–30 mins. ■■■■

Vocabulary Review

(F) Write the name of each car part that has a box pointing to it.

Students are not given the vocabulary for this exercise. See how many parts students can fill in themselves. Then, have them work with partners to fill in anything missing. Review as a class.

What does each part do? With a partner, take turns describing each part and its function.

Have students draw diagrams if they are unfamiliar with the vocabulary. Encourage students more knowledgeable about cars to describe the various part functions.

(G) Write a defining sentence for each of the words below.

Review the example with students.

(H) Read each phrase below and match it with a vocabulary word or phrase from the unit.

Review the example with students.

Evaluation 1 (continued)   5–15 mins. ■■■■

Go around the classroom and check on students' progress. Help individuals when needed. If you see consistent errors among several students, interrupt the class and give a mini-lesson or review to help students feel comfortable with the concept.

Assessment (optional)   ■■■■

Use the Stand Out 5 Assessment CD-ROM with Exam*View*® to create a post-test for Unit 3.

Instructor's Notes

Lesson Planner: Unit 3, Vocabulary Review   **64a**

Objective: Identify ways to research

Academic Strategies: Using Internet key words, using a phone book

RESOURCES

Internet Access

Suggested Realia: Phone books, DMV driver handbooks, newspaper classifieds, auto trader publications

AGENDA

Use key words to conduct Internet research.

Use headwords to find information in a phone book.

Conduct research related to unit topics.

Academic Feature: Research Project

Each unit will have a research page where students are required to complete a task by conducting research. Options will be given for students to use the Internet as well as printed resource materials.

Introduction   5-10 mins.

Ask students what they have learned about in this unit that they would like more information on. Ask them how they would go about finding that information.

State the objective: *Today we will talk about different ways to find information and practice looking for information.*

Presentation   10-15 mins.

Tell students to imagine they just moved to your community and they need to find a school to go to. What should they do? Write all their ideas on the board (ask a friend or neighbor, go online, look up schools in the phonebook, etc.). If they suggest going online, ask them what key words they will use. If students don't understand, explain the idea of key words to them.

Practice   10-15 mins.

(A) Searching the Internet is one of the easiest ways to find information. What key words would you use to search for the following services or offices? If you don't have access to the Internet, what headwords would you look under in a phone book to find the same information? Where else could you find the information? Work with a partner to complete the chart below.

If you think your students may have trouble with this, do the first one together as a class. Make sure the difference between headwords and key words is clear to the students.

Evaluation   10-15 mins.

Go over students' ideas as a class and help them come up with more or better ideas.

Application   5-20 mins.

(B) Choose two of the items above that you want to do research on. How will you perform your research?
What specific information are you looking for?

(C) Conduct your research. What did you find? Write a summary below of the information you collected.

STANDARDS CORRELATIONS

CASAS: 4.9.3, 7.2.1, 7.4.4, 7.4.5, 7.4.6 (See CASAS Competency List on pages 187–193.)
SCANS: **Information** Acquire and evaluate information, organize and maintain information, interpret and communicate information, use computers to process information *(optional)*
Interpersonal Participate as a member of a team, teach others, negotiate to arrive at a decision, work with cultural diversity
Systems Understand systems
Technology Select technology, apply technology to a task, maintain and troubleshoot technology *(optional)*

Basic Skills Reading, writing
Thinking Skills Think creatively, make decisions, see things in the mind's eye
Personal Qualities Responsibility, sociability, self-management
EFF: **Communication** Read with understanding, convey ideas in writing, observe critically
Decision Making Solve problems and make decisions, plan
Lifelong Learning Take responsibility for learning, reflect and evaluate, learn through research, use information and communications technology *(optional)*

Research Project

A Searching the Internet is one of the easiest ways to find information. What key words would you use to search for the following services or offices? If you don't have access to the Internet, what headwords would you look under in a phone book to find the same information? Where else could you find the information? Work with a partner to complete the chart below. (Answers will vary. Sample answers are given.)

Services/Offices	Internet key words	Phone book headwords	Other places to find information
Finding cars for sale	dealer name	used cars	bulletin boards
Finding a mechanic	town name mechanic	auto repair	word of mouth
Getting tips on how to maintain your car	car maintenance tips	N/A	mechanic, car manual
Getting auto insurance quotes from different companies	auto insurance vehicle, car comparison	insurance car, vehicle, truck	word of mouth
Finding the local Department of Motor Vehicles (DMV)	DMV, town name	Check government blue pages	call information (411)
Finding out what the driving laws for your state are	driving laws, state name	DMV, government	public library, police station

B Choose two of the items above that you want to do research on. How will you perform your research?

On the Internet and in the phone book

What specific information are you looking for?

Names of auto dealers in my area

C Conduct your research. What did you find? Write a summary of the information you collected. (Answers will vary.)

_____

_____

_____

_____

_____

_____

Team Project

Auto Handbook

Create a class auto handbook.

With a team, you will create a section of an auto handbook. With the class, you will compile sections into a complete auto handbook.

1. Form a team with four or five students. Choose positions for each member of your team.

POSITION	JOB DESCRIPTION	STUDENT NAME
Student 1: **Project Leader**	See that everyone speaks English. See that everyone participates.	
Student 2: **Secretary**	Take notes on team's ideas.	
Student 3: **Designer**	Design layout of handbook section.	
Student 4: **Spokesperson**	Prepare team for presentation.	
Student 5: **Assistant**	Help secretary and designer with their work.	

2. As a class, brainstorm a list of topics to include in your auto handbook. You might include maintenance tips, directions on reading an insurance policy, and rules of the road. Count the number of teams and narrow your list of topics down to that number. Each team must choose a single topic to work on.

3. As a team, gather all the information for your group's section of the handbook.

4. Decide how you would like to present your information. You can choose pictures, lists of facts, and graphs. Be creative!

5. Create your section of the handbook.

6. Present your section of the handbook to the class.

7. Compile all the sections into one handbook.

Create a class auto handbook.

Each team will create a section of an auto handbook that will be compiled into one book at the end of the project. Sections could include different types of cars, how to buy a car, how to read an insurance policy, the rules of the road, how to keep track of gas and mileage, etc.

The team project is the final application for the unit. It gives students a chance to show that they have mastered all of the Unit 3 objectives.

Note: Shorter classes can extend this project over two class meetings.

Stage 1   5 mins.

Form a team with four or five students. Choose positions for each member of your team.

Have students decide who will lead each step as described on the student page. Provide well-defined directions on the board for how teams should proceed. Explain that all the students do every step as a team. Teams shouldn't go to the next stage until the previous one is complete.

Stage 2   10-15 mins.

As a class, brainstorm a list of topics to go in your auto handbook. You might include maintenance tips, directions on reading an insurance policy, and rules of the road. Count the number of teams and narrow your list of topics down to that number. Each team must choose a single topic to work on.

Stage 3   20-30 mins.

As a team, gather all the information for your group's section of the handbook.

Students can use their books to find information or any other resources they have access to.

Stage 4   10-15 mins.

Decide how you would like to present your information. You can choose pictures, lists of facts, and graphs. Be creative!

Ask students to try to be creative and make their section visually pleasing. (You might need to discuss what this means.)

Stage 5   30-40 mins.

Create your section of the handbook.

Optional Computer Activity: Students may want to use the computer to design their section of the handbook.

Stage 6   15-20 mins.

Present your section of the handbook to the class.

Help teams prepare for their presentations. Suggest that each team member choose a different part of the project to present.

Stage 7   10-15 mins.

Compile all the sections into one handbook.

Choose one group or one student to compile all the sections into one book and design a creative cover.

STANDARDS CORRELATIONS

CASAS: 4.8.1, 4.8.5, 4.8.6 (See CASAS Competency List on pages 187–193.)
SCANS: Resources Allocate time
Information Acquire and evaluate information, organize and maintain information, interpret and communicate information, use computers to process information
Systems Understand systems, improve and design systems
Technology Select technology, apply technology to exercise
Basic Skills Writing
Thinking Skills Think creatively, make decisions, solve problems, see things in the mind's eye, use reasoning

Personal Qualities Responsibility, self-esteem, self-management, integrity
EFF: Communication Read with understanding, convey ideas in writing, speak so others can understand, listen actively, observe critically
Decision Making Solve problems and make decisions, plan
Interpersonal Cooperate with others, advocate and influence, resolve conflict and negotiate, guide others
Lifelong Learning Take responsibility for learning, reflect and evaluate, learn through research, use information and communications technology (optional)

AT-A-GLANCE PREP

Objective: Introduce new vocabulary
Academic Strategies: Identifying a vocabulary theme, using a dictionary
Vocabulary: See lesson

RESOURCES

Dictionaries: It is recommended that each student in class have an ESL learner's dictionary or that there be dictionaries available in the classroom for students to use. Dictionaries that will be referred to in this book

AGENDA

Identify the unit theme.
Identify words by part of speech.
Write sentences.
Match phrases to definitions.

are the *Heinle's Newbury House Dictionary of American English* and the *Collins Cobuild Intermediate* or *Advanced Dictionary of American English*.

Academic Feature: Vocabulary Builder

Each unit will begin with a vocabulary-building section. The purpose of this two-page section is to introduce students to many of the words they will be using in the unit lessons. Students will have a chance to see how much they already know, and they will get exposure to the new vocabulary found in the unit.

Note: All of the exercises on these two pages should be done in class, no matter the class length. Longer classes can do this lesson and then move onto Lesson 1 during the same class meeting; shorter classes may have to devote one whole class meeting to this lesson.

Introduction   5–10 mins.

State the objective: *Today we will be identifying and working with the vocabulary you will learn in this unit.*

Presentation 1   10–15 mins.

(A) What do the following words have in common? Write the theme below.

Pronounce each word for students and have them put a check next to each word that is familiar to them. As a class, discuss what some

possible themes might be. The list leans heavily toward theft/burglary, so this topic is most likely what students will come up with.

(B) Take each word and put it in the correct column according to its part of speech. Use a dictionary if you need to.

Make sure students know the difference between a noun, verb, and adjective, which, at this level, should be review. Do the first few items together and then, have students complete the exercise on their own.

Practice 1   10–15 mins.

(C) Choose one word from each column in Exercise B. Write one sentence for each word.

Evaluation 1   5–10 mins.

Ask volunteers to write their sentences on the board. Go over the sentences as a class, making sure that students used the words correctly, both in terms of structure and meaning.

UNIT 4 Housing

GOALS
➤ **Communicate issues by phone**
➤ **Interpret rental agreements**
➤ **Identify tenant and landlord rights**
➤ **Get insurance**
➤ **Prevent theft**

Vocabulary Builder

A What do the following words have in common? Write the theme below.

Theme: _Housing crime_

abandon	dwelling	grounds	summon
burglarize	enticing	premises	theft
crime	evident	responsible	thief
disturbance	exterior	seize	weapons

B Take each word and put it in the correct column according to its part of speech.
Use a dictionary if you need to.

Noun		Verb	Adjective
crime	theft	abandon	enticing
disturbance	thief	burglarize	evident
dwelling	weapons	seize	
exterior		summon	
grounds			
premises			

C Choose one word from each column in Exercise B. Write one sentence for each word.
(Answers will vary. Sample answers are given.)

1. _The dwelling was unoccupied._

2. _They abandoned the old building._

3. _The dark building was enticing to the criminals._

D Read.

You can often tell the part of speech of a word just by looking at it. The following words are nouns. What do they have in common?

prevention   installation   expiration

The roots of these words are the verbs *prevent*, *install*, and *expire*. The suffix *-(a)tion* changes each verb into a noun. The noun form signifies the action or process of doing the action. For example, *prevention* signifies the action of preventing something.

E Following the examples in Exercise D, change each verb below into its noun form. Then, define each new word. Use your dictionary to check spelling.

Verb	Noun	Definition
1. activate	activation	making something start up or begin
2. compensate	compensation	money or goods used to reimburse
3. deteriorate	deterioration	the act of becoming less in quality
4. estimate	estimation	the act of making a judgment
5. litigate	litigation	legal action
6. possess	possession	something you own
7. terminate	termination	stopping or ending something
8. vacate	vacation	a holiday; a time of rest from work

F Without using a dictionary, try to match these phrases with their definitions.

__h__ 1. fit for human occupancy   a. advance warning written in a business letter

__a__ 2. formal written notice   b. estimate of how much one might pay for insurance

__e__ 3. full compliance   c. being gone for a long time, longer than expected

__f__ 4. housing codes   d. built well; a building in good condition

__b__ 5. insurance quote   e. completely doing what you are required to do

__c__ 6. prolonged absence   f. government regulations for building houses

__j__ 7. replacement cost   g. government rules regarding health and cleanliness

__g__ 8. sanitary regulations   h. suitable for people to live in

__d__ 9. structurally sound   i. taking up a lot of time

__i__ 10. time-consuming   j. the cost of replacing something

Vocabulary

When teaching students new vocabulary, pronounce each word for them several times and ask them to repeat it. Often, students may be familiar with the words you are introducing but have never seen them spelled out. By pronouncing the words for students, you allow students to make a connection between the words' spellings and their sounds. It is also important that students learn the correct pronunciation of new words so they feel comfortable using their new vocabulary inside and outside of the classroom.

Presentation 2   5–10 mins.

 Read.

Read this explanatory note about nouns out loud with students and discuss the concept of words having similar endings.

Academic Skill

Word Parts

Students will have a much broader vocabulary if they learn the meanings of common prefixes and suffixes:

pre-   before
over-   in excess; too much
-y   (adjective) the existence or condition of
-ness   (noun) the condition of
-ion, -sion, -tion   (nouns) the action or process of

Practice 2   15–20 mins.

E Following the examples in Exercise D, change each verb below into its noun form. Then, define each new word. Use your dictionary to check spelling.

F Without using a dictionary, match these phrases with their definitions.

If students have difficulty with a phrase, ask them to identify which words they do understand in that particular phrase and then have them work with a partner to deduce which is the definition.

Evaluation 2   10–15 mins.

Go over the answers as a class.

AT-A-GLANCE PREP

Objective: Communicate issues by phone
Grammar: Causative verbs
Pronunciation: Clear speech on the phone
Academic Strategy: Focused listening
Vocabulary: *landlord, tenant, causative*

RESOURCES

Activity Bank: Unit 4, Lesson 1, Worksheets 1–2
Grammar Challenge 5: Unit 4, Challenge 1

■ 1.5 hour classes ■ 2.5 hour classes ■ 3⁺ hour classes

AGENDA

Read about Ming Mei's problem.
Practice conversations between tenants and landlords.
Use causative verbs.
Call your landlord.

Audio: CD Tracks 18–24
Stand Out 5 Assessment CD-ROM with Exam*View*®

 Pre-assessment *(optional)* ■■■

Use the Stand Out 5 Assessment CD-ROM with Exam*View*® to create a pre-test for Unit 4.

Warm-up and Review   5–10 mins. ■■■

Ask students to take out a piece of paper and make a list of all the words and phrases they can remember from the vocabulary-building section. When they have written down everything they can think of, have them talk to a partner and try to add one or two more words and phrases to their lists. Make a class list on the board.

Introduction   5–10 mins. ■■■

Note: No dictation is in this lesson. If you would like to do dictation with your students, use the sentences from the grammar chart on page 70.

Ask students to raise their hands if they rent an apartment, house, or condo. Ask them who they pay rent to each month (landlord). Ask them to give you some reasons they might call their landlord. Make a list on the board.

State the objective: *Today we will practice communicating issues by phone.*

Presentation 1   5–10 mins. ■■■

(A) Read and listen to the phone conversation Ming Mei is having with her landlord. What is the problem? How is the landlord going to fix it?

> **Listening Script**   *CD Track 18*
>
> *The listening script matches the conversation in Exercise A.*

Practice 1   10–15 mins. ■■■

(B) Practice the conversation with a partner. Switch roles.

Pronunciation

Have a small discussion about talking on the phone. Explain how important it is to speak clearly on the phone since you cannot use facial expressions or gestures to help convey your ideas.

(C) Listen to the conversations between tenants and landlords. Take notes in the chart below.

The listening script is on page 70a.

Evaluation 1   5–10 mins. ■■■

Go over the answers as a class.

STANDARDS CORRELATIONS

CASAS: 2.1.8 (See CASAS Competency List on pages 187–193.)
SCANS: **Information** Acquire and evaluate information, organize and maintain information, interpret and communicate information
Interpersonal Participate as a member of a team, negotiate to arrive at a decision, work with cultural diversity
Systems Monitor and correct performance
Basic Skills Reading, writing, listening, speaking

Thinking Skills Think creatively, make decisions, solve problems
Personal Qualities Responsibility, sociability, self-management
EFF: **Communication** Read with understanding, convey ideas in writing, speak so others can understand, listen actively
Decision Making Solve problems and make decisions, plan
Interpersonal Cooperate with others
Lifelong Learning Take responsibility for learning, reflect and evaluate

---

I have a problem.

GOAL ➤ **Communicate issues by phone**

 A Read and listen to the phone conversation Ming Mei is having with her landlord. What is the problem? How is the landlord going to fix it?

CD
TR 18

Landlord: Hello?

Ming Mei: Hi, Mr. Martin. This is Ming Mei from the apartment on Spring Street.

Landlord: Oh, hi, Ming Mei. What's up? Is there a problem?

Ming Mei: Well, after all the rain we had this weekend, the roof has started leaking. I think there may be a pool of water still on the roof because water is leaking through our ceiling even though the rain has stopped.

Landlord: Oh, no. Has it damaged the carpet?

Ming Mei: No, we caught it right away and put a bucket down to collect the drips.

Landlord: Oh, great. Thanks for being on top of it. I'll have my handyman come over and look at the roof and your ceiling. Can you let him in around ten this morning?

Ming Mei: I have to go to work, but I can get my sister to come over.

Landlord: Great. Thanks for calling, Ming Mei.

Ming Mei: Thank you, Mr. Martin.

B Practice the conversation with a partner. Switch roles.

 C Listen to the conversations between tenants and landlords. Take notes in the chart below.

CD
TR 19-21

	Problem	Solution
Conversation 1	air-conditioning broken	install new unit; meanwhile give fans
Conversation 2	broken door handle	send handyman
Conversation 3	washing machine broken	tenant will fix and take cost off rent

GOAL ➤ **Communicate issues by phone**

D Look at the following statements from the conversation between Ming Mei and her landlord in Exercise A. Answer the questions.

I'll have my handyman come over and look at the roof and your ceiling.

1. Who is the subject of the sentence? I (the landlord)

2. Who is going to come over? my handyman (the landlord's)

I can get my sister to come over.

3. Who is the subject of the sentence? I (Ming Mei)

4. Who is going to come over? my sister (Ming Mei's)

E The grammar in the two statements in Exercise D is called causative verb structure. We use this structure when we want to indicate that the subject causes something to happen. Study the chart with your teacher.

Causative Verbs: *Get, Have, Help, Make, Let*			
Subject	**Verb**	**Noun/Pronoun**	**Infinitive (Omit *to* except with *get*.)**
He	will get	his handyman	to come.
She	had	her mom	wait for the repairperson.
The landlord	helped	me	move in.
Ming Mei	makes	her sister	pay half of the rent.
Mr. Martin	let	Ming Mei	skip one month's rent.

F Match the causative verb from Exercise E with its meaning. Two verbs have the same meaning.

Verb

  c   1. get

  c   2. have

  b   3. help

  a   4. let

  d   5. make

Meaning

a. allow

b. provide assistance

c. delegate responsibility to someone

d. require

Conversation 1
Landlord: *Hello?*
Chris: *Hi, Mrs. Kashyap. This is Chris from your apartment building on Jerome Avenue.*
Landlord: *Oh, hi, Chris. What can I do for you?*
Chris: *Well, I was hoping you might be able to get the air-conditioning fixed. It's been so hot this summer.*
Landlord: *I know. It seems like I'm hearing the same thing from all of my tenants. The issue is that the repairman can't find the parts for your unit because it is so old. So, I think I'm going to have a get a new unit installed, which could take me at least a month to do. In the meantime, I'm going to be dropping off some fans to all the tenants in your building. Would that be OK for now?*
Chris: *I guess so. When do you think you might come by?*
Landlord: *As soon as I can pick up those fans . . . before the end of the week. I'll call before I come.*
Chris: *OK. Thanks for your time, Mrs. Kashyap.*

Conversation 2
Landlord: *Hello?*
Janice: *Hi, Mrs. Sawyer. This is Janice from apartment 2B on Palo Verde.*
Landlord: *Oh, hi, Janice. How is everything going?*
Janice: *Pretty good. I was wondering if you might be able to fix the broken door handle on our bathroom. I know we talked about it when I moved in, but it's been over three months and it still isn't fixed.*
Landlord: *Oh, thank you for calling and reminding me, Janice. It completely slipped my mind. I'll send a handyman over first thing tomorrow.*
Janice: *Great, Mrs. Sawyer. Thanks!*

Conversation 3
Landlord: *Hello, is this Mr. Jessup?*
Mr. Jessup: *Sure is.*
Landlord: *Hi, it's Mr. Little. I'm returning your call from yesterday.*
Mr. Jessup: *Oh, yes, Mr. Little. Thanks for calling back. It seems that the washing machine in our building isn't working. My wife was trying to do some laundry a few days ago, and when she pulled the wet clothes out of the machine, they were still full of soap.*
Landlord: *Oh, dear. That doesn't sound right.*
Mr. Jessup: *Actually, I think I know what the problem is, but I wanted to talk to you first before I went ahead and fixed it myself.*
Landlord: *Of course. If you think you can fix it, go right ahead. I'll deduct whatever it costs you off next month's rent.*
Mr. Jessup: *Great. I'll try to fix it this afternoon, and I'll call you back to let you know if it's working again.*
Landlord: *Great, Mr. Jessup. Thanks for calling.*

Presentation 2   5–10 mins.

D Look at the following statements from the conversation between Ming Mei and her landlord in Exercise A. Answer the questions.

Do this exercise as a class. Focus first on the meaning of the sentence before you focus on the structure.

E The grammar in the two statements in Exercise D is called causative verb structure. We use this structure when we want to indicate that the subject causes something to happen. Study the chart with your teacher.

Go over the examples together and make sure students understand the structure. Causative verbs will be studied throughout this unit so just try to keep students focused on what is presented here.

Practice 2   15–20 mins. ■■

Note: Shorter classes can do this exercise for homework.

F Match the causative verb from Exercise E with its meaning. Two verbs have the same meaning.

Note: Practice 2 is continued on the next page.

 Refer students to *Stand Out 5 Grammar Challenge*, Unit 4, Challenge 1 for more practice with causative verbs: *get, have, help, make,* and *let.*

Instructor's Notes

_____
_____
_____
_____
_____
_____
_____
_____

Practice 2 (continued)

G Unscramble the words and phrases to write causative statements. Then, write a housing-related sentence of your own using the same verb.

Go over the example with students first, making sure they understand what they are supposed to do.

Evaluation 2   10–15 mins.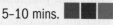

Go over the answers as a class. Ask volunteers to write their original sentences on the board.

Presentation 3   5–10 mins.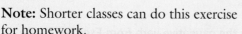

H What should you do when you call your landlord? Read the list below.

Before you focus students' attention on the list in the book, see what sort of list they can come up with as a result of their own experiences.

Practice 3   5–15 mins. ◼

Note: Shorter classes can do this exercise for homework.

I What are some problems you might have with your home that would require you to call your landlord? Brainstorm a list on a separate piece of paper with a partner.

Evaluation 3   5–10 mins. ◼

Make a comprehensive list on the board of everything the groups came up with.

Application   10–20 mins.

J With a partner, practice having phone conversations with a landlord. Use the problems you read in Exercise H and wrote for Exercise I and come up with your own solutions.

For this exercise, you can let students work with a partner and role-play a few conversations. Another option would be to divide the class in half and designate half landlords and the other half tenants. Choose one of the problems from the board and have each tenant go find a landlord to have a conversation with. Then, have them switch roles and give them a different

problem to discuss. Do this as many times as you want. To make it more realistic and to simulate a phone conversation, have students stand or sit back-to-back so they can't see one another while they are talking.

Activity Bank

Unit 4, Lesson 1, Worksheet 1: Landlord/Tenant Conversations (listening)

Unit 4, Lesson 1, Worksheet 2: Causative Verbs

Instructor's Notes

_____
_____
_____
_____
_____
_____
_____
_____
_____
_____
_____
_____
_____
_____
_____
_____
_____
_____
_____
_____
_____
_____
_____
_____

GOAL ➤ **Communicate issues by phone**

G Unscramble the words and phrases to make causative statements. Then, write a housing-related sentence of your own using the same verb. (Individual sentences will vary.)

EXAMPLE: them / had / their landlord / and leave a deposit / fill out an application

Their landlord had them fill out an application and leave a deposit.

My landlord had me paint the apartment myself and he reimbursed me.

1. to prospective renters / him / let / the apartment / show / his tenants

   His tenants let him show the apartment to prospective tenants.

(sample) _My landlord let me fix the leak myself._

2. made / my parents / a condo/ buy / me

   My parents made me buy a condo.

(sample) _I made the landlord fix the sink._

3. my boss / for me / will get / I / to write / a letter of reference

   I will get my boss to write a letter of reference for me.

(sample) _I will get my friends to help me move my furniture._

4. her husband / she / which house to rent / decide / will let

   She will let her husband decide which house to rent.

(sample) _I will let my roommate pay the utility bills._

5. find / my cousin / me / a new place to live / helped

   My cousin helped me find a new place to live.

(sample) _I helped them move out of the apartment._

H What should you do when you call your landlord? Read the list below.

1. State your name and where you live.
2. Clearly identify the problem.
3. Ask for a solution.
4. Restate the solution for clarification.

I What are some problems you might have with your home that would require you to call your landlord? Brainstorm a list on a separate piece of paper with a partner.

Sample answers: leaky roof, water in basement, insects or rodents, etc.

J With a partner, practice having phone conversations with a landlord. Use the problems you read in Exercise H and you wrote for Exercise I and come up with your own solutions.

Understand the fine print

GOAL ➤ Interpret rental agreements

A Have you ever rented a property? If so, do you remember what information was contained in your rental agreement? Make a list below. (Answers will vary. Sample answers are given.)

amount of rent	security deposit	key information
due date of rent	lease dates	return of deposit

B Rental agreements are long and contain information to protect the tenant and the landlord. Much of the agreement is about money. Read the following money-related portion of a rental agreement.

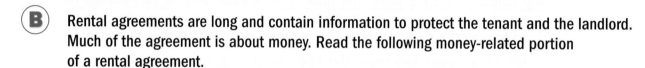

RENTAL AGREEMENT

RENT: To pay as rental the sum of $ _____ per month, due and payable in advance from the first day of every month. Failure to pay rent when due will result in the Owner taking immediate legal action to evict the Resident from the premises and seize the security deposit.

LATE FEE: Rent received after the first of the month will be subject to a late fee of 10% plus (3.00) dollars per day.

SECURITY DEPOSIT: Resident agrees to pay a deposit in the amount of $ _____ to secure Resident's pledge of full compliance with the terms of this agreement. The security deposit will be used at the end of the tenancy to compensate the Owner for any damages or unpaid rent or charges, and will be repaired at Resident's expense with funds other than the deposit.

RETURN OF DEPOSIT: Security deposits will be deposited for the Resident's benefit in a non-interest bearing bank account. Release of these deposits is subject to the provisions of State Statutes and as follows:

A. The full term of this agreement has been completed.

B. Formal written notice has been given.

C. No damage or deterioration to the premises, building(s), or grounds is evident.

D. The entire dwelling, appliance, closets, and cupboards, are clean and left free of insects; the refrigerator is defrosted; all debris and rubbish has been removed from the property; and the carpets are cleaned and left odorless.

E. Any and all unpaid charges, pet charges, late charges, extra visitor charges, delinquent rents, utility charges, etc., have been paid in full.

F. All keys have been returned, including keys to any new locks installed while Resident was in possession.

G. A forwarding address has been left with the Owner.

Thirty days after termination of occupancy, the Owner will send the balance of the deposit to the address provided by the Resident, payable to the signatories hereto, or the Owner will impose a claim on the deposit and so notify the Resident by certified letter. If such written claim is not sent, the Owner relinquishes his right to make any further claim on the deposit and must return it to the Resident provided Resident has given the Owner notice of intent to vacate, abandon, and terminate this agreement prior to the expiration of its full term, at least 7 days in advance.

C In a small group, interpret the money portion of the rental agreement. Underline things that no one in your group understands, so you can ask your teacher later.

(Answers will vary.)

AT-A-GLANCE PREP

Objective: Interpret rental agreements
Academic Strategies: Determining meaning, summarizing
Vocabulary: Rental agreement vocabulary

RESOURCES

Activity Bank: Unit 4, Lesson 2, Worksheets 1–2
Grammar Challenge 5: Unit 4, Challenge 2

■ 1.5 hour classes ■ 2.5 hour classes ■ 3⁺ hour classes

AGENDA

Interpret rental agreements.
Summarize a rental agreement.

Suggested Realia: Authentic rental agreements

Warm-up and Review   5-10 mins.

Repeat the application activity from the previous lesson regarding phone conversations.

Introduction   10-20 mins.

Warn students to listen first! These sentences are difficult.
Dictation:

1. Security deposits will be deposited for the resident's benefit in a non-interest bearing bank account.
2. Resident agrees to maintain the premises during the period of this agreement.
3. In the event repairs are needed beyond the competence of the resident, he or she is urged to arrange for professional assistance.
4. In the event that the smoke detector is missing or inoperative, the tenant must notify the landlord immediately.

State the objective: *Today we will be interpreting a rental agreement.*

Presentation 1   10-15 mins.

Ⓐ **Have you ever rented a property? If so, do you remember what information was contained in your rental agreement? Make a list below.**

Do this exercise together as a class. Make a list of students' ideas on the board as they write in their books.

Ⓑ **Rental agreements are long and contain information to protect the tenant and the landlord. Much of the agreement is about money. Read the following money-related portion of a rental agreement.**

Have students read the text silently to themselves. Then, read it out loud to them or ask volunteers to read different sections.

Practice 1   10-15 mins.

Ⓒ **In a small group, interpret the money portion of the rental agreement. Underline things that no one in your group understands, so you can ask your teacher later.**

Evaluation 1   10-20 mins. ■■■

Go over the agreement as a class.

STANDARDS CORRELATIONS

CASAS: 1.4.3 (See CASAS Competency List on pages 187–193.)
SCANS: Resources Allocate time, allocate money, allocate materials and facility resources, allocate human resources
Information Acquire and evaluate information, organize and maintain information, interpret and communicate information
Interpersonal Participate as a member of a team, teach others, negotiate to arrive at a decision, work with cultural diversity
Systems Understand systems, monitor and correct performance
Basic Skills Reading, writing, listening, speaking

Thinking Skills Make decisions, see things in the mind's eye
Personal Qualities Responsibility, sociability, self-management
EFF: Communication Read with understanding, convey ideas in writing, speak so others can understand, listen actively, observe critically
Decision Making Solve problems and make decisions, plan
Interpersonal Cooperate with others, advocate and influence, resolve conflict and negotiate, guide others
Lifelong Learning Take responsibility for learning, reflect and evaluate

Presentation 2 — 5–10 mins. ■■■ ▨

D Read the sections on maintenance and repair.

Have students read silently to themselves. Then, read it out loud to them or ask for volunteers to read different sections.

Practice 2 — 10–15 mins. ■■ ▨

E Divide into five groups. Each group will take one section from the rental agreement in Exercise D and become an "expert" on that section. Sections are marked by capital letters.

As students are doing Exercise E, walk around the classroom and help them, making sure they clearly understand the key points. Ask them how they plan to present their information and give them some suggestions on how to make their presentation interesting. No single student should be responsible for explaining all the details.

Evaluation 2 — 10–15 mins. ■■ ▨

F Summarize your section for the class.

Encourage students to ask questions of the "expert" teams.

D Read the sections on maintenance and repair.

RENTAL AGREEMENT

APPLIANCES: The above rental payment specifically EXCLUDES all appliances not permanently affixed. Appliances located at or in the property are there solely at the convenience of the Owner, who assumes no responsibility for their operation. In the event they fail to function after occupancy is started, the Resident may have them repaired at no cost to Owner or request Owner to remove them.

MAINTENANCE: Resident agrees to maintain the premises during the period of this agreement. This includes woodwork, floors, walls, furnishings and fixtures, appliances, windows, screen doors, lawns, landscaping, fences, plumbing, electrical, air-conditioning and heating, and mechanical systems. Tacks, nails, or other hangers nailed or screwed into the walls or ceilings will be removed at the termination of this agreement. Damage caused by rain, hail, or wind as a result of leaving windows or doors open, or damage caused by overflow of water, or stoppage of waste pipes, breakage of glass, damage to screens, deterioration of lawns and landscaping—whether caused by abuse or neglect—is the responsibility of the Resident.

RESIDENT'S OBLIGATIONS: The Resident agrees to meet all of Resident's obligations including:

A. Taking affirmative action to insure that nothing exists that might place the Owner in violation of applicable building, housing, and health codes.

B. Keeping the dwelling clean and sanitary; removing garbage and trash as they accumulate; maintaining plumbing in good working order to prevent stoppages and/or leakage of plumbing, fixtures, faucets, pipes, etc.

C. Operating all electrical, plumbing, sanitary, heating, ventilating, a/c, and other appliances in a reasonable and safe manner.

D. Assuring that property belonging to the Owner is safeguarded against damage, destruction, loss, removal, or theft.

REPAIRS: In the event repairs are needed beyond the competence of the Resident, he or she is urged to arrange for professional assistance. Residents are offered the discount as an incentive to make their own decisions on the property they live in. Therefore, as much as possible, the Resident should refrain from contacting the Owner except for emergencies or for repairs costing more than the discount since such involvement by the Owner will result in the loss of the discount. ANY REPAIR THAT WILL COST MORE THAN THE AMOUNT OF THE DISCOUNT MUST BE APPROVED BY THE OWNER OR THE TENANT WILL BE RESPONSIBLE FOR THE ENTIRE COST OF THAT REPAIR. Any improvement made by the tenant shall become the property of the Owner at the conclusion of this agreement.

WORKER'S WARRANTY: All parties to this agreement warrant that any work or repairs performed by the Resident will be undertaken only if he/she is competent and qualified to perform it, and the person performing the work will be totally responsible for all activities to assure they are done in a safe manner that will meet all applicable statutes. They further warrant that they will be accountable for any mishaps or accidents resulting from such work, and that they will hold the Owner free from harm, litigation, or claims of any other person.

E Divide into five groups. Each group will take one section from the rental agreement in Exercise D and become an "expert" on that section. Sections are marked by capital letters.

F Summarize your section for the class. (Answers will vary.)

G Based on what you have read so far, what do you think the rental agreement will say about each of the following items? Write your ideas. (Answers will vary.)

Gas, electric, and water: _____

Lead-based paint: _____

Phone: _____

Smoke detectors: _____

Utilities: _____

H Read the information taken from the rental agreement about the topics in Exercise G. Write the correct topic on the line that follows each section.

1. Resident agrees to install and maintain telephone service and agrees to furnish to the Owner the phone number, and any changes, within 3 days after installation.

   Phone service

2. Smoke detectors have been installed in this residence. It's the Resident's responsibility to maintain appliance including testing periodically and replacing batteries as recommended by the manufacturer. In the event the detector is missing or inoperative, the tenant has an affirmative duty to notify the landlord immediately.

   Smoke detectors

3. Resident shall be responsible for payments of all utilities, garbage, water and sewer charges, telephone, gas, or other bills incurred during his/her residency. He/She specifically authorizes the Owner to deduct amounts of unpaid bills from their deposits in the event they remain unpaid after the termination of this agreement.

   Utilities

4. Resident agrees to transfer the gas, electric, and water service charges to their name immediately upon occupancy and to make arrangements for meter readings as needed.

   Gas, electric, and water

5. Houses built before 1978 may contain lead-based paint. Lead from paint, paint chips, and dust can pose health hazards if not taken care of properly. Lead exposure is especially harmful to young children and pregnant women. Before renting pre-1978 housing, Owner must disclose the presence of known lead-based paint and lead-based paint hazards in the dwelling. Resident must also receive a federally approved pamphlet of lead-poisoning prevention.

   Lead-based paint

I With a partner, go back through the three sections of the rental agreement provided in this lesson. Make a list of all the topics. (*Hint:* There are 14 topics.) Then, on a separate piece of paper, write a statement about each topic, summarizing what the rental agreement says about it. (Refer to answers on Lesson Planner page 74a.)

Presentation 3   5-10 mins. ■■■□

G Based on what you have read so far, what do you think the rental agreement will say about each of the following items? Write your ideas.

Discuss each item as a class and encourage students to write notes in their books.

Practice 3   5-10 mins. ■□□

Note: Shorter classes can do this exercise for homework.

H Read the information taken from the rental agreement about the topics in Exercise G. Write the correct topic on the line that follows each section.

Evaluation 3   5-10 mins. ■□□

Go over the answers as a class. As you go over each answer, read the paragraph out loud and answer any questions students might have.

Application   10-20 mins. ■■□

I With a partner, go back through the three sections of the rental agreement provided in this lesson. Make a list of all the topics. (*Hint:* There are 14 topics.) Then, on a separate piece of paper, write a statement about each topic, summarizing what the rental agreement says about it.

The following are the 14 topics in the rental agreement sections:

Rent	Worker's warranty
Late fee	Phone service
Security deposit	Smoke detectors
Return of deposit	Utilities
Appliances	Gas, electric, & water
Maintenance	Lead-based paint
Resident's obligations	
Repairs	

Activity Bank

Unit 4, Lesson 2, Worksheet 1: Complete Rental Application

Unit 4, Lesson 2, Worksheet 2: Lease Agreement

 Refer students to *Stand Out 5 Grammar Challenge*, Unit 4, Challenge 2 for practice with perception verbs: *feel, hear, listen to, look at, notice, observe, see, smell,* and *watch.*

Instructor's Notes

_____
_____
_____
_____
_____
_____
_____
_____
_____
_____
_____
_____
_____
_____

AT-A-GLANCE PREP

Objective: Identify tenant and landlord rights
Grammar: Causative verb *make*
Academic Strategies: Writing definitions, comparing and contrasting
Vocabulary: *right, responsibility, advance, notice, no fault, prolonged absence, fit for human occupancy, structurally sound, monetary damages, housing code, sanitary regulation*

■ 1.5 hour classes ■ 2.5 hour classes ■ 3+ hour classes

AGENDA

Discuss rights and responsibilities of landlords and tenants.
Read about and discuss the implied warranty of habitability.

RESOURCES

Activity Bank: Unit 4, Lesson 3, Worksheet 1
Grammar Challenge 5: Unit 4, Challenge 3

Warm-up and Review   5–10 mins. ■■■

Ask students to call out things they learned about a rental agreement that they didn't know before. Discuss.

Introduction   10–20 mins. ■■■

Dictation:

1. Provide a clean apartment when the tenant moves in.
2. Keep noise to a level that will not disturb neighbors.
3. Keep the apartment and the surrounding area clean and in good condition.
4. When moving out, give landlord proper advance notice.

State the objective: *Today we will be identifying the rights and responsibilities of tenants and landlords.*

Presentation 1   10–15 mins. ■■■

Write the words *Right* and *Responsibility* on the board. Discuss the meanings as a class. As you are discussing, ask for a student to look them up in a dictionary. See how close your discussion is to the dictionary definition.

 A Define the following terms with your teacher.

Practice 1   10–15 mins. ■■■

 B As a tenant, you have rights and responsibilities, just as your landlord does. Read the list below and indicate which responsibility belongs to each person: tenant (*T*) or landlord (*L*).

Evaluation 1   5 mins. ■■■

Go over the answers as a class.

 C With a partner, restate each of the rights and responsibilities in Exercise B.

STANDARDS CORRELATIONS

CASAS: 1.4.5 (See CASAS Competency List on pages 187–193.)
SCANS: **Information** Acquire and evaluate information, interpret and communicate information
Interpersonal Participate as a member of a team, teach others, negotiate to arrive at a decision, work with cultural diversity
Systems Understand systems, monitor and correct performance
Basic Skills Reading, writing, listening, speaking

Thinking Skills Think creatively, make decisions, solve problems, see things in the mind's eye
Personal Qualities Responsibility, sociability, self-management
EFF: **Communication** Read with understanding, convey ideas in writing, speak so others can understand, listen actively, observe critically
Decision Making Solve problems and make decisions
Interpersonal Cooperate with others, resolve conflict and negotiate
Lifelong Learning Take responsibility for learning, reflect and evaluate

LESSON 3 Your rights

GOAL ➤ Identify tenant and landlord rights

A Define the following terms with your teacher. (Answers will vary.)

1. What is a *right*?

   a legal claim to something abstract or concrete

2. What is a *responsibility*?

   a duty of an individual or group to act in a certain way

B As a tenant, you have rights and responsibilities, just as your landlord does. Read the list below and indicate which responsibility belongs to each person: tenant (*T*) or landlord (*L*).

1. __L__ Provide a clean apartment when the tenant moves in.

2. __L__ Maintain common areas (hallways, stairs, yards, entryways).

3. __T__ Give the landlord permission to enter the apartment at reasonable times and with advance notice to inspect it or to make any necessary repairs.

4. __T__ Keep noise at a level that will not disturb neighbors.

5. __T__ Keep the apartment and the surrounding area clean and in good condition.

6. __T__ Notify the landlord immediately if the apartment needs repair through no fault of the tenant.

7. __T__ Notify the landlord of any anticipated prolonged absence from the apartment so he or she can keep an eye on things.

8. __T__ Pay the rent on time.

9. __L__ Provide properly working plumbing and heating (both hot and cold running water).

10. __T__ Repair any damage occurring to the apartment through the fault of the tenant, tenant's family members, or tenant's guests. Notify landlord at once of major damage.

11. __L__ Provide well-lit hallways and entryways.

12. __T__ When moving out, give landlord proper advance notice. Be sure that the apartment is in the same condition as when the tenant moved in and return the key to the landlord promptly.

C With a partner, restate each of the rights and responsibilities in Exercise B.

(Answers will vary.)

EXAMPLE: *"It is a landlord's responsibility to provide a clean apartment for the tenant. It is the tenant's right to have a clean apartment to move into."*

GOAL ➤ **Identify tenant and landlord rights**

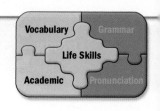

D Read about the implied warranty of habitability.

The "implied warranty of habitability" states that a landlord must keep the property in a condition fit for human occupancy. In other words, it must be a safe place for human beings to live in. Here are some questions a landlord might ask himself before he rents his property: Are there any known hazards with the property? Do the fixtures work properly? Is the building structurally sound? Does the property have any recurring problems?

If a landlord does not comply with the "implied warranty of habitability," a renter can cancel the lease, leave the premises, take the costs of repairs out of his rent, or ask for monetary damages.

In determining whether a landlord has violated the "implied warranty of habitability," courts will look at several factors:

1. Is the problem violating a housing code?
2. Is the problem violating a sanitary regulation?
3. Is the problem affecting a needed facility?
4. How long has the problem lasted?
5. How old is the building?
6. How much is the rent?
7. Has the tenant been ignoring the problem?
8. Is the tenant in any way responsible for the problem?

One or more of these factors will help the courts determine who is at fault and what the victim's rights may be.

E In a small group, discuss the following questions. (Answers will vary. Sample answers are given.)

1. If your landlord violated the implied warranty of habitability, what would you do? Discuss each of the rights of a renter listed above and decide what you would do. Take notes.

   I would send my landlord a letter of complaint and save a copy. I would wait

   30 days for a response before threatening legal action.

2. According to the list of questions that courts will ask, what are some situations in which you could take a landlord to court?

   If the problem violated a code or regulation, if the landlord doesn't comply with

   the "implied warranty of habitability"

3. Discuss some situations when you couldn't take a landlord to court. Take notes.

   If the tenant ignored the problem or was responsible for the problem.

Presentation 2

10-15 mins. ■■□

(D) Read about the implied warranty of habitability.

Have students read silently to themselves. Then, answer any questions they have.

Practice 2

10-15 mins. ■■□

(E) In a small group, discuss the following questions.

Encourage students to rely on members of their own groups.

Evaluation 2

10-15 mins. ■■□

Walk around the classroom and listen to the groups. Although this exercise is difficult, try to have students work with their groups to struggle with answers. Intervene only if their comprehension needs to be redirected.

Presentation 3   5-10 mins. ■■■□

Have students look at the pictures in Exercise F. As a class, discuss what is happening in each picture.

Practice 3   15-20 mins. ■

Note: Shorter classes can do this exercise for homework with or without a partner.

F With a partner, look at each picture below. Decide if it violates the implied warranty of habitability. Imagine that each of these situations has gone on for at least three weeks with no response from the landlord.

Evaluation 3   5-10 mins. ■

Go over the answers as a class.

Application   10-20 mins. ■■□

Go over the instructions and examples for Exercises G and H and then have students complete them on their own.

G Imagine that you are a landlord. Use the rights and responsibilities in Exercise B to write four statements using a causative verb structure.

H Imagine that you are a tenant. Look back at the rights and responsibilities in Exercise B. Write four statements using a causative verb structure.

Activity Bank

Unit 4, Lesson 3, Worksheet 1: Noisy Neighbors

📖 Refer students to *Stand Out 5 Grammar Challenge*, Unit 4, Challenge 3 for practice with relative pronouns: *who, that, when,* and *where*.

F With a partner, look at each picture below. Decide if it violates the implied warranty of habitability. Imagine that each of these situations has gone on for at least three weeks with no response from the landlord.

G Imagine that you are a landlord. Use the rights and responsibilities in Exercise B to write four statements using a causative verb structure. (Answers will vary. Sample answers are given.)

EXAMPLE: The law makes me provide a clean apartment for the tenant.

1. The law makes me maintain common areas such as the hallway.

2. The law makes me provide a clean apartment free of bugs.

3. The law makes me provide and repair plumbing. (leaky sink)

4. The law makes me keep hallways well-lit.

H Imagine that you are a tenant. Look back at the rights and responsibilities in Exercise B. Write four statements using a causative verb structure. (Answers will vary. Sample answers are given.)

EXAMPLE: The law makes me pay the rent on time.

1. The law makes me keep a clean apartment.

2. The law makes me keep music at a reasonable level.

3. The law makes me inform the landlord of known problems. (broken elevator)

4. The law makes me give the landlord advance notice if I'm moving.

LESSON 4 Insuring your home

GOAL ➤ Get insurance

A Listen to Makela and Bryce talk about the renter's insurance quote below.

CD
TR 22

Renter's Insurance Quote	
Value of Personal Property	$29,000
Deductible	$250
Liability	$100,000
Medical Payments	$1,000
Annual Premium	$220.08
Monthly Payment	$18.34

B Discuss the following questions with your classmates.

1. Do you have insurance for your property? Why or why not? (Answers will vary.)
2. What is a deductible? What is Makela's deductible? Money a person pays against a claim. ($250
3. What is the liability insurance for? If Makela causes damage or physical harm to anyone
4. What are the medical payments for? If someone gets hurt at the apartment
5. What will Makela pay per year for renter's insurance? $220.08/year (12×$18.34)

C What is the value of your personal property? Write the estimated replacement costs below.

Personal property	Typical replacement cost	Your estimated replacement cost
Personal Computer, Accessories, and Software	$1,500–$4,000	(Answers will vary.)
TV and Stereo Equipment (Home and Portable)	$500–$4,000	
Music and Movie Collection	$500–$2,000	
Furniture and Household Items	$5,000–$15,000	
Clothing and Shoes	$2,000–$4,000	
Sporting Goods	$500–$2,000	
Camera and Video Equipment	$200–$1,000	
Jewelry and Watches	$1,000	
Other (Luggage, Tools, etc.)	$1,000–$3,000	
Total Estimated Replacement Costs	$12,200–$36,000	↓

Objective: Get insurance
Academic Strategy: Supporting ideas with examples
Vocabulary: *insurance quote, estimate, replacement cost, dwelling, square footage, exterior, covering*

RESOURCES

Activity Bank: Unit 4, Lesson 4, Worksheets 1–2
Grammar Challenge 5: Unit 4, Challenge 4

■ 1.5 hour classes   ■ 2.5 hour classes   ■ 3⁺ hour classes

AGENDA

Learn about renter's insurance.
Estimate value of personal property.
Discuss differences between homeowner's and renter's insurance.
Interview classmates about insurance.

Audio: CD Track 22
Suggested Realia: Insurance policy, brochures from insurance companies

---

Warm-up and Review   5-10 mins.

Have students work in small groups to make a list of their rights and responsibilities as tenants.

Introduction   10-20 mins.

Dictation:

1. What type of insurance policy do you need?
2. How can you find an insurance company?
3. How much personal property coverage do you need?
4. How much can you spend per month on insurance?

State the objective: *Today you will learn about renter's and homeowner's insurance and how to make sure you are covered.*

Presentation 1   10-15 mins.

(A) **Listen to Makela and Bryce talk about the renter's insurance quote below.**

The listening script is on page 79a.

(B) **Discuss the following questions with your classmates.**

You can have students do this in small groups or discuss as a class.

Practice 1   10-15 mins.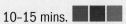

(C) **What is the value of your personal property? Write the estimated replacement costs below.**

Explain what it means to estimate and give students a few examples.

Evaluation 1   5 mins.

After students have completed Exercise C independently, have them compare the cost of their personal property with Makela and Bryce's estimated quote. Ask students to estimate if their replacement costs would be more or less. Would their own premiums be more or less? Have volunteers offer answers, but assure students that financial information need not be shared with the class. Bring in copies of your own insurance policies and premium information if possible.

STANDARDS CORRELATIONS

CASAS: 1.4.6 (See CASAS Competency List on pages 187-193.)
SCANS: **Information** Acquire and evaluate information, organize and maintain information, interpret and communicate information
Interpersonal Participate as a member of a team, teach others, negotiate to arrive at a decision, work with cultural diversity
Systems Monitor and correct performance
Basic Skills Reading, writing, arithmetic, listening, speaking

Thinking Skills Make decisions
Personal Qualities Responsibility, sociability, self-management
EFF: **Communication** Read with understanding, convey ideas in writing, speak so others can understand, listen actively
Decision Making Solve problems and make decisions, plan
Interpersonal Cooperate with others
Lifelong Learning Take responsibility for learning, reflect and evaluate

Makela: *Hey, Bryce, do you have renter's insurance?*
Bryce: *No. I keep thinking I need to get it, but I just haven't looked into it yet.*
Makela: *Well, I just called my insurance company and got a quote. Will you take a look at it and tell me what you think?*
Bryce: *How did they come up with this premium?*
Makela: *They asked a bunch of questions about the value of my personal belongings. Then they came up with the dollar amount of what it would cost to replace all my stuff.*
Bryce: *What are the medical payments for?*
Makela: *In case someone gets hurt while they are at my apartment.*
Bryce: *And what about the liability?*
Makela: *Liability covers me if I cause any damage or physical harm to anyone. I think this is required as part of the insurance.*
Bryce: *Well, $18 a month sounds pretty reasonable to me. Would it cover your belongings if someone stole them?*
Makela: *Yep. It also covers disasters like fires or a flood. I think I'm going to sign up today. You should call, too, Bryce.*
Bryce: *I think I will.*

Presentation 2   5–10 mins.

D Landlords should carry insurance for the structures they rent to others. Imagine that you own your own property. Then, imagine that you rent the same space from a landlord. How do you think homeowner's insurance is different from renter's insurance?

Discuss the differences.

Practice 2   10–15 mins.

Note: Shorter classes can do these exercises for homework.

E Read the Hahns' homeowner's insurance policy below. Then, answer the questions that follow.

You can have students answer these questions by themselves or with a partner.

F To get homeowner's insurance, the insurance company needs information about your building. Read about the Hahns' home. Then, fill in the information about your home.

Go over this list with students. Make sure they understand the different topics.

Evaluation 2   10–15 mins.

Discuss the answers to Exercise E and answer any questions students might have about Exercise F.

Instructor's Notes

LESSON 4   **GOAL** ➤ **Get insurance**

D Landlords should carry insurance for the structures they rent to others. Imagine that you own your own property. Then, imagine that you rent the same space from a landlord. How do you think homeowner's insurance is different from renter's insurance? (Answers will vary.)
Homeowner's insurance covers the whole building, covers more liability and costs more.

E Read the Hahn's homeowner's insurance policy below. Then, answer the questions that follow.

State One Insurance

Name/Address of Insured: Steve and Rosemary Hahn
7930 Inca Way, Kansas City, MO 64108

Deductible: $2,500	Annual Premium: $1,077.93
Coverage Type	**Amount of Coverage**
Dwelling	$401,000
Personal Property	$300,750
Loss of Use	$80,200
Personal Liability—Each Occurrence	$100,000
Medical Payments to Others—Each Person	$1,000

1. How much will the insurance company pay to rebuild the house? $401,000
2. How much will the insurance company pay to replace personal belongings? $300,750
3. How much will the family have to pay before the insurance company pays? $2,500
4. What is the monthly premium? $89.83

F To get homeowner's insurance, the insurance company needs information about your building. Read about the Hahn's home. Then, fill in the information about your home.

Building feature	Hahn's home	My home
Year Built	1986	(Answers will vary.)
Total Square Footage	2,378 sq. ft.	
Number of Stories	2	
Exterior Wall Construction Material	stucco on frame	
Roof Type	clay tile	
Garage or Carport	attached garage: 2-car	
Wall Partitions Construction Materials	drywall	
Wall / Floor Covering Materials	paint / wood and tile	
Number of Kitchens / Bathrooms	1 / 3	
Type of Air / Heat	central air / gas	

LESSON **4** **GOAL** ➤ **Get insurance**

G **I HAVE INSURANCE.** If you already have insurance, think about your own answers to the questions below. See possible answers in parentheses. (Answers will vary.)

1. What type of policy do you have? (homeowner's, renter's) _____

2. How long have you had your policy? (six months, two years, ten years) _____

3. What is your monthly premium? ($45, $82, $150) _____

4. How often do you review your policy in case changes need to be made? (every 3 months, once a year, never) _____

I DON'T HAVE INSURANCE. If you *don't* have insurance for your property, think about your answers to the questions below. See some possible answers in parentheses. (Answers will vary.)

1. What type of policy do you need? (homeowner's, renter's) _____

2. How can you find an insurance company? (ask a friend or family member, search online, look in the phone book) _____

3. How much personal property coverage do you need? ($5,000, $17,000, $50,000)

_____

4. How much can you spend per month on insurance? ($50, $100, $150) _____

H Using the questions in Exercise G, interview three classmates. Take notes about your interviews. Interviewees can use their own answers or choose one from the examples in parentheses. (Answers will vary.)

Name: _____ Insurance (yes/no) Type: _____

Notes: _____

Name: _____ Insurance (yes/no) Type: _____

Notes: _____

Name: _____ Insurance (yes/no) Type: _____

Notes: _____

I Write a statement about what you are going to do this week to protect yourself. (Answers will vary.)

EXAMPLE: I need renter's insurance for my personal property. This week, I'm going to go online and get quotes from three insurance companies.

80 Unit 4 Lesson 4

Presentation 3   5-10 mins. ■■■□

Model questions and answers for students. Ask a volunteer to stand up. Walk up to the volunteer and say, *Are you a renter or a homeowner?* After he or she answers, say, *Do you have insurance?* After these two questions have been answered, decide which set of questions from Exercise G you will ask based on whether the person has insurance. Explain to students what you just did and model with a few more students if necessary.

G I HAVE INSURANCE. If you already have insurance, think about your own answers to the questions below. See possible answers in parentheses.

I DON'T HAVE INSURANCE. If you don't have insurance for your property, think about your answers to the questions below. See some possible answers in parentheses.

Go over the questions with students and have them decide which set of questions to answer depending whether they carry insurance or not. Have students write answers in their books as you are reviewing the questions together.

Practice 3   15-20 mins. ■□

Note: Shorter classes can do this exercise for homework by interviewing friends or coworkers.

H Using the questions in Exercise G, interview three classmates. Take notes about your interviews. Interviewees can use their own answers or choose one from the examples in parentheses.

Evaluation 3   5-10 mins. ■

Walk around the classroom and observe students as they interview each other.

Application   10-20 mins. ■■■□

I Write a statement about what you are going to do this week to protect yourself.

Go over the example statements with students. When students have finished, ask them to stand up and read their statements to the class. You might even tell students you are going to ask them next week if they did what they said they were going to do.

Activity Bank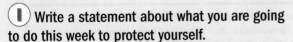

Unit 4, Lesson 4, Worksheet 1: Renter's Insurance
Unit 4, Lesson 4, Worksheet 2: Homeowner's Insurance

Refer students to *Stand Out 5 Grammar Challenge*, Unit 4, Challenge 4 for practice with passive voice verbs.

Instructor's Notes

_____
_____
_____
_____
_____
_____
_____
_____
_____
_____
_____
_____
_____
_____
_____
_____
_____
_____
_____
_____
_____
_____
_____
_____
_____
_____
_____

Objective: Prevent theft
Academic Strategy: Comparing and contrasting
Vocabulary: *burglar, burglarize, burglary, burgle, theft, thief, thieving, crime, enticing, weapons, activate, time-consuming, disturbance, summon*

RESOURCES

Activity Bank: Unit 4, Lesson 5, Worksheet 1

■ 1.5 hour classes   ■ 2.5 hour classes   ■ 3⁺ hour classes

AGENDA

Define words related to theft.
Read a newsletter about theft prevention.
Listen to a police officer.
Make a flier.

Grammar Challenge 5: Unit 4, Challenge 5
Audio: CD Tracks 23–24

Warm-up and Review   5-10 mins.

Ask students if they followed through with the statements they made in the previous lesson. For those who haven't, ask them when they are going to.

Introduction   5-10 mins.

Dictation:

1. If you don't own your home, seriously consider buying a renter's policy.
2. Your landlord will generally not be responsible for your possessions.
3. Most rental policies are available at competitive rates.
4. These policies also offer important protection against losses due to fire or storm damage.

State the objective: *Today you will learn how to prevent theft in your home.*

Presentation 1   5 mins.

Write the words *thief* and *burglar* on the board. Ask students if they can help you define them.

Ask them what the difference between the two words is. (Don't give them any answers. Just find out what they know.)

Practice 1   15-20 mins.

Ⓐ **Use a dictionary to define the words below. Include the part of speech for each word. Then, answer the questions that follow.**

Evaluation 1   5 mins.

Go over the answers as a class.

Presentation 2   5-10 mins.

Copy the chart from Exercise B on the board. Go over the instructions and come up with one example for each column as a class. Then, put students in groups to complete the exercise.

Ⓑ **You are about to read a newsletter on how to protect your home from being burglarized. What do you predict it will say about the following items? Brainstorm with a group.**

STANDARDS CORRELATIONS

CASAS: 1.4.8 (See CASAS Competency List on pages 187–193.)
SCANS: **Information** Acquire and evaluate information, organize and maintain information, interpret and communicate information, use computers to process information *(optional)*
Interpersonal Participate as a member of a team, negotiate to arrive at a decision, work with cultural diversity
Systems Monitor and correct performance
Technology Apply technology to a task *(optional)*
Basic Skills Reading, writing, listening
Thinking Skills Think creatively, make decisions, see things in the mind's eye

Personal Qualities Responsibility, sociability, self-management
EFF: **Communication** Read with understanding, convey ideas in writing, listen actively, observe critically
Decision Making Plan
Interpersonal Cooperate with others, advocate and influence, guide others
Lifelong Learning Take responsibility for learning, reflect and evaluate, learn through research, use information and communications technology *(optional)*

LESSON 5 Protecting your home

GOAL ➤ **Prevent theft**

A Use a dictionary to define the words below. Include the part of speech for each word. Then, answer the questions that follow. (Answers may vary. Sample answers are given.)

burglar: n. a house breaker, a thief

burglarize: v. to commit burglary, to break in and steal

burglary: n. the crime of breaking in with intent to commit a felony

burgle: v. to break in and steal; to burglarize

theft: n. the act of stealing

thief: n. a person who steals property

thieve: v. to steal, to take by theft

1. What is the difference between the two sets of words? The first group includes
thieving inside a house or property; the second is stealing in general

2. There are two pairs of synonyms in the groups of words above. What are they?

___burglar___ and ___thief___   ___burglarize/burgle___ and ___thieve___

B You are about to read a newsletter on how to protect your home from being burglarized. What do you predict it will say about the following items? Brainstorm with a group.
(Answers will vary. Sample answers are given.)

Light	Time	Noise
Keep lights on outside at night.	Leave your house at different times.	Play a radio or TV when you're not home.

Unit 4   Lesson 5   **81**

C Read.

Theft Prevention Newsletter

To Preserve, Protect, and Defend

Burglary Prevention

Each year in the United States, there are more than five million home burglaries. Nine out of ten of these crimes are preventable. The risk of being burglarized can be greatly reduced by taking simple steps to make your home more difficult to enter and less enticing to would-be burglars. **Remember the greatest weapons in the fight to prevent burglaries are light, time, and noise.**

(Source: http://www.jcsd.org/burglary_prevention.htm)

LIGHT

- Make sure that exterior lights are mounted out of reach so that burglars can't easily unscrew bulbs.
- Consider buying motion-sensitive lights, which are now available at relatively low prices.
- Use a variable light timer to activate lights inside your home.
- Trim trees and shrubs near doors and windows so burglars can't hide in the shadows.

TIME

Make it time-consuming for a burglar to break into your home by:

✓ installing deadbolt locks on all exterior doors.

✓ installing double key locks in doors that contain glass. This will keep a burglar from being able to open the door simply by breaking the glass and reaching through. *(Note: So that everyone in the house can get out in the event of a fire, be sure to keep the key in a designated place.)*

✓ placing additional locks on all windows and patio doors.

NOISE

- Get a dog. You don't need a large attack dog; even a small dog creates a disturbance that burglars would prefer to avoid. Remember to license and vaccinate it.
- Consider having someone care for your dogs in your home while you're away instead of boarding them.
- If you can afford it, install an alarm system that will alert neighbors of a burglar's presence. Most systems can even summon local police directly.

D Compare the ideas you brainstormed in Exercise B to the tips from the newsletter. Are there any tips you didn't think of? List them in the chart.

Light	Time	Noise
• Outside lights should be hard to reach. • Buy motion-sensitive lights. • Use a variable light timer inside. • Trim trees and shrubs.	• Install deadbolt locks. • Install double key locks in doors with glass. • Place locks on windows and patio doors.	• Get a dog. • Keep dogs at home during vacation. • Install an alarm system.

Practice 2

10-15 mins. ■■□

Note: Shorter classes can do these exercises for homework.

C Read.

D Compare the ideas you brainstormed in Exercise B to the tips from the newsletter. Are there any tips you didn't think of? List them in the chart.

Go over the concept of comparing and contrasting with students. Show them how to look at the list they made in Exercise B and compare it to what they read.

Academic Strategy

Compare and contrast

Have students compare items to see what is the same about them and contrast items to find out what is different. In this activity, students will be looking at the list that they brainstormed and comparing it to the text, looking for similarities and differences. They will write the things they missed—the differences—in their new list.

Evaluation 2

10-15 mins. ■■□

Make a comprehensive list of all the tips on the board. See if students can come up with any more. Add any additional ideas to the list.

Activity Bank

Unit 4, Lesson 5, Worksheet 1: Theft Prevention:
Compare and Contrast

Presentation 3   5–10 mins. ■■■□

Go over the instructions for Exercises E and F and ask students what they will be listening for. See if they can come up with some ideas of what they might hear.

Practice 3   15–20 mins. ■□

Note: Shorter classes can read the script and do these exercises for homework.

E Listen to the police officer talk about other tips to prevent break-ins. Write the tips below.

 Listening Script   *CD Track 23*

- *Think like a burglar. "Case" your home the way a burglar would and look for easy ways to enter your home.*
- *Be sure valuables such as guns, electronic devices, and artwork are not visible from the street.*
- *Be sure to lock up ladders and tools, which could be used to break into your home.*
- *Work together with your neighbors. Organize a Neighborhood Watch and let your neighbors know when you will be away for an extended period.*
- *While on vacation, have someone pick up your newspapers and mail, so that they do not accumulate and alert burglars to your absence.*
- *Display your house number conspicuously and have it well illuminated. This will help police and emergency personnel find your home quickly.*

(*Source:* http://www.jcsd.org/burglary_prevention.htm)

F Sometimes, all your efforts will not stop a determined burglar. It is wise to take some precautions that will help you get your property back should a criminal successfully break into your home. Listen to the police officer and take notes.

 Listening Script   *CD Track 24*

- *Make a list of your belongings. (Be sure to keep receipts, especially for expensive items like stereos and computers.) Be sure to update this list periodically.*
- *Keep copies of your inventory list and receipts in a safe-deposit box or with a friend. (This is also important in the event of a house fire.)*
- *Photographing and/or videotaping your possessions is a convenient way to keep a record of what you own.*
- *Engrave your valuables with an identification mark to deter burglary and to prove ownership should the article be stolen and recovered by the police.*
- *Be sure you have the right coverage. You may need to purchase additional coverage to protect special items like expensive jewelry or rare antiques.*
- *If you don't own your home, seriously consider buying a renter's policy. Your landlord will generally not be responsible for your possessions. Rental coverages are available at competitive rates and these policies also offer important protection against liability and losses due to fire or storm damage.*

(*Source:* http://www.jcsd.org/burglary_prevention.htm)

Evaluation 3   5–10 mins. ■

Go over the answers as a class. Either play the recordings again or allow students to look at the script in the back of their books to see if they got the answers right.

Application   10–20 mins. ■■□

G Make a flier to post in your community. Include the most important tips you learned about how to prevent theft in your home.

Optional Computer Activity: Have students create their fliers on the computer.

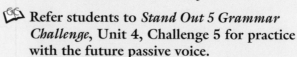 Refer students to *Stand Out 5 Grammar Challenge*, Unit 4, Challenge 5 for practice with the future passive voice.

There are also two extension challenges. Extension Challenge 1 gives practice with business letter writing and editing. Extension Challenge 2 gives practice with comparative and superlative adjectives.

GOAL ➤ **Prevent theft**

  E Listen to the police officer talk about other tips to prevent break-ins. Write the tips below.

CD
TR 23

Other tips to prevent break-ins:

1. Look at your home like a burglar (easy ways to enter, etc.)

2. Keep guns, electronic device, artwork hidden from windows.

3. Lock up tools.

4. Organize a neighborhood watch; tell each other about vacations.

5. While on vacation, have someone pick up mail and newspapers.

6. Post number clearly on house.

  F Sometimes, all your efforts will not stop a determined burglar. It is wise to take some precautions that will help you get your property back should a criminal successfully break into your home. Listen to the police officer and take notes.

CD
TR 24

1. Make a list of your belongings.

2. Keep copies of list and receipts in a safe place.

3. Photograph or videotape your possessions.

4. Engrave your valuables to prove ownership.

5. Be sure to have the right coverage for special items.

6. Renters should buy coverage for possessions.

 G Make a flier to post in your community. Include the most important tips you learned about how to prevent theft in your home.

Review

A With a partner, practice conversations between a tenant and a landlord. Practice both face-to-face and phone conversations. Use the scenarios below. (Lesson 1)

1. leaky faucet

2. broken window

3. can't pay rent on time this month

4. noisy neighbors

B Using the words provided below, write complete sentences using the causative verb structure. You may choose the verb tense to use. (Lesson 1) (Answers will vary. Sample answers are given.)

EXAMPLE: she / make / her sister / move

She made her sister move out of her apartment.

1. I / get / her / meet

I got her to meet me at the apartment.

2. they / have / their friends / wait

They had their friends wait at the bus stop.

3. Elliot / help / his father / repair

Elliot helped his father repair the sink.

4. my father / make / me / pay

My father makes me pay him $20 per month for the loan.

5. his landlord / let / him / fix

His landlord lets him fix most simple repairs.

C Make a list of five topics that can be found in a rental agreement. After each topic, write a typical statement that might be found in such an agreement. (Lesson 2) (Sample answers are given.)

EXAMPLE: _Rent: The rent must be paid on the first day of each month._

1. _Appliances: The owner assumes no responsibility for their operation._

2. _Late fee: Rent received late will be subject to a 5% late fee._

3. _Return of deposit: Security deposits will be held in an interest-bearing bank account._

4. _Worker's warranty: The person performing the work is competent and qualified._

5. _Lead-based point: Owner must reveal the presence of known lead-based paint on the property._

AT-A-GLANCE PREP

Objectives: All unit objectives
Grammar: All unit grammar
Academic Strategy: Reviewing
Vocabulary: All Unit 4 vocabulary

RESOURCES

Stand Out 5 Assessment CD-ROM with Exam*View®*

■ 1.5 hour classes ■ 2.5 hour classes ■ 3⁺ hour classes

AGENDA

Discuss unit objectives.
Complete the review.
Use unit vocabulary.

Introduction   5-10 mins.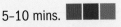

Ask students as a class to try to recall all the objectives of this unit without looking back in their books. The objectives for this unit include communicating issues by phone, interpreting rental agreements, identifying tenant and landlord rights, getting insurance, and preventing theft. Write all the objectives on the board from Unit 4. Show students the first page of the unit and mention the five objectives.

State the objective: *Today we will be reviewing everything we have learned in this unit and preparing for the team project.*

Presentation 1   10-15 mins.

This presentation will cover the first three pages of the review. Quickly go to the first page of each lesson. Discuss the objective of each. Ask simple questions to remind students of what they have learned.

Note: Since there is little presentation in the review, you can assign the review exercises that don't require collaboration with a partner or group for homework and go over them in class the following day.

Practice 1   20-25 mins.

Note: There are two ways to do the review:

1. Go through the exercises one at a time and, as students complete each one, go over the answers.

2. Quickly go through the instructions of each exercise, let students complete all of the exercises at once, and then go over the answers.

(A) With a partner, practice conversations between a tenant and a landlord. Practice both face-to-face and phone conversations. Use the scenarios below. (Lesson 1)

(B) Using the words provided below, write complete sentences using the causative verb structure. You may choose the verb tense to use. (Lesson 1)

(C) Make a list of five topics that can be found in a rental agreement. After each topic, write a typical statement that might be found in such an agreement. (Lesson 2)

STANDARDS CORRELATIONS

CASAS: 7.2.1 (See CASAS Competency List on pages 187–193.)
SCANS: Resources Allocate time
Information Acquire and evaluate information
Interpersonal Participate as a member of a team, teach others, negotiate to arrive at a decision, work with cultural diversity
Systems Monitor and correct performance
Basic Skills Reading, writing, arithmetic, listening, speaking

Thinking Skills Think creatively, make decisions, solve problems, see things in the mind's eye
Personal Qualities Responsibility, sociability, self-management
EFF: **Communication** Read with understanding, convey ideas in writing, speak so others can understand, listen actively, observe critically
Interpersonal Cooperate with others, guide others
Lifelong Learning Take responsibility for learning, reflect and evaluate

Practice 1 (continued)   25-30 mins. ■■■■

D Identify three rights that a tenant and landlord have by writing them on the lines below. (Lesson 3)

E Read the insurance policy and answer the questions. (Lesson 4)

Evaluation 1   5-15 mins. ■■■

Go around the classroom and check on students' progress. Help individuals when needed. If you see consistent errors among several students, interrupt the class and give a mini-lesson or review to help students feel comfortable with the concept.

Teaching Tip

Recycling/Review

The review exercises, the research activity, and the team project are part of the recycling/review process. Students often need to be reintroduced to concepts to solidify what they have learned. Many concepts are learned and forgotten when students are engaged in learning other new concepts. This is because students learn but are not necessarily ready to acquire language concepts.

Therefore, it becomes very important to review material with students and to show them how to review it on their own. It is also important to recycle the new concepts in different contexts.

Instructor's Notes

_____
_____
_____
_____
_____
_____
_____
_____
_____
_____
_____
_____
_____
_____
_____
_____
_____
_____
_____
_____
_____
_____
_____
_____
_____
_____
_____
_____
_____
_____
_____
_____

D Identify three rights that a tenant and landlord have by writing them on the lines below. (Lesson 3)

Tenant's Rights

1. A tenant has the right to _a clean apartment upon moving in_ .

2. _S/he has the right to clean, well-lit hallways._

3. _S/he has the right to a returned security deposit if the apartment is in good order._

Landlord's Rights

1. A landlord has the right to _enter an apartment at reasonable times_ .

2. _S/he has the right to receive the rent on time._

3. _S/he has the right to receive advance notice of tenant moving._

E Read the insurance policy and answer the questions. (Lesson 4)

INSURANCE POLICY

Deductible:	****$2,250.00****	Annual Premium:	****$989.45****

Coverage Type	Amount of Coverage
Dwelling	******$330,000
Loss of Use	*******$80,200
Medical Payments to Others—Each Person	********$1,000
Personal Liability—Each Occurrence	******$100,000
Personal Property	******$200,000

1. Is this a homeowner's or renter's policy? _Homeowner's_

   How do you know? _It includes cost of the dwelling._

2. How much will the insurance company pay to rebuild the house? _$330,000_

3. What is the annual premium? _$989.45_

4. How much will the insurance company pay to replace personal belongings?

   _$200,000_

(F) Write *T* (true) or *F* (false) in front of each theft prevention tip. (Lesson 5)

___F___ 1. Place your valuables in easy-to-see locations.

___T___ 2. Lock up anything that could be used to break into your house.

___T___ 3. Install an alarm system.

___F___ 4. Make sure you turn off all the lights when you leave your home.

___F___ 5. Install double key locks on all your windows.

___T___ 6. Let your neighbors know when you will be out of town.

VOCABULARY REVIEW

(G) Complete each question with a word or phrase from this unit. There may be more than one correct answer. (Answers will vary. Sample answers given.)

1. Have you ever been _____ a landlord _____?

2. How much _____ coverage _____ do you have for your personal property?

3. Do you have _____ renter's _____ or _____ homeowner's _____ insurance?

4. What is your monthly _____ rent _____?

5. Do you have _____ smoke detectors _____ installed in your house?

6. What would your landlord do if there were a _____ burglary _____ in your building?

(H) With a partner, ask and answer the questions in Exercise G.

(I) Without using a dictionary, define the following words. Include the part of speech. (Answers will vary.)

1. dwelling: a place to live

2. policy: a statement of the legal rules

3. right: a legal privilege

4. burglary: act of theft from a house

5. responsibility: an obligation or duty

6. prevent: to stop from happening

7. vacate: to leave

8. premium: the money to be paid by owner before insurance begins to compensate loss

(J) With a partner, write a conversation on a separate piece of paper using as many of the words from Exercise I as you can include.

Practice 1 *(continued)*   25-30 mins. ■■□□

F Write *T* (true) or *F* (false) in front of each theft prevention tip. (Lesson 5)

Vocabulary Review

G Complete each question with a word or phrase from this unit. There may be more than one correct answer.

H With a partner, ask and answer the questions in Exercise G.

I Without using a dictionary, define the following words. Include the part of speech.

Refer to the student book page for the words.

J With a partner, write a conversation on a separate piece of paper using as many of the words from Exercise I as you can include.

Evaluation 1 *(continued)*   5-15 mins. ■■□□

Go around the classroom and check on students' progress. Help individuals when needed. If you see consistent errors among several students, interrupt the class and give a mini-lesson or review to help students feel comfortable with the concept.

Have students perform the conversation they wrote for Exercise J.

TB **Assessment** *(optional)*   ■■□□

Use the Stand Out 5 Assessment CD-ROM with Exam*View*® to create a post-test for Unit 4.

AT-A-GLANCE PREP

Objective: Find reliable information
Academic Strategy: Research
Vocabulary: *reputable, reliable, source*

RESOURCES

Internet access   Local government offices

Friends and family   Local law enforcement

Academic Feature: Research Project

 The printed resource materials for this research lesson can be found on the Activity Bank CD-ROM.

Introduction   5–10 mins.

Have students brainstorm a list of all the topics they have learned about in this unit. Ask them what they would like to find more information about. State the objective: *Today's lesson is about how to find information from reliable sources.*

Presentation   10–15 mins.

Write the words *reputable*, *reliable*, and *source* on the board. Discuss the meanings of these three words and ask students what they have to do with conducting research.

(A) All of the information you find on the Internet may not be reliable. Imagine you are searching for more information about what you have learned in this unit (tenant rights, preventing theft, rental agreements, etc.). Which Web address endings below do you think contain the most reliable information? Circle your answers.

Do this exercise with students, showing them that Web addresses ending in *.gov*, *.edu*, and *.org* are probably the most reliable places to find information on the topics covered in this unit.

(That is not to say that the other sites won't have reliable information.)

Definitions of Internet domains: .com = commercial entities; .net = usually used by network providers, but not always; .org = usually nonprofit agencies; .biz = business; .edu = educational institutions; .gov = governmental agencies; .us = affiliated with the United States and its citizens but not always with the government; .tv = owned by the country of Tuvalu but in use by anyone, not exclusively for television (TV) information

Practice   10–15 mins.

(B) If you don't have access to the Internet, but you want to find out more about the following topics, where would you look for reliable information?

Evaluation   5–10 mins.

Review students' ideas as a class and vote on the best place to find information.

Application   15–20 mins.

(C) Choose one of the topics from Exercise B. Conduct research using any method you have access to, including the Internet, people you know, and local sources. Then, answer the questions below.

STANDARDS CORRELATIONS

CASAS: 4.9.3, 7.2.1, 7.4.4, 7.4.5, 7.4.6 (See CASAS Competency List on pages 187–193.)

SCANS: **Information** Acquire and evaluate information, organize and maintain information, interpret and communicate information, use computers to process information *(optional)*

Interpersonal Participate as a member of a team, teach others, negotiate to arrive at a decision, work with cultural diversity

Systems Understand systems

Technology Select technology, apply technology to a task, maintain and troubleshoot technology *(optional)*

Basic Skills Reading, writing

Thinking Skills Think creatively, make decisions, see things in the mind's eye

Personal Qualities Responsibility, sociability, self-management

EFF: **Communication** Read with understanding, convey ideas in writing, observe critically

Decision Making Solve problems and make decisions, plan

Lifelong Learning Take responsibility for learning, reflect and evaluate, learn through research, use information and communications technology *(optional)*

Research Project

A All of the information you find on the Internet may not be reliable. Imagine you are searching for more information about what you have learned in this unit (tenant rights, preventing theft, rental agreements, etc.). Which Web address endings below do you think contain the most reliable information? Circle your answers.

.com   .net   (.org)   .biz   (.edu)   (.gov)   .us   .tv

B If you don't have access to the Internet, but you want to find out more about the following topics, where would you look for reliable information? (Answers will vary.)

Tenant Rights: _Public library or a real estate dealer_

Renter's Insurance: _An insurance dealer or friends who rent_

Homeowner's Insurance: _An insurance dealer or ask friends with homes_

Rental Agreements: _A real estate dealer or public library_

Theft Prevention: _Public library or local police_

Reporting a Burglary: _Police station_

C Choose one of the topics from Exercise B. Conduct research using any method you have access to, including the Internet, people you know, and local sources. Then, answer the questions below. (Answers will vary.)

1. Which topic did you research?_____

2. Where did you find your research (specific source)? _____

_____

3. How do you know this is a reliable source? _____

_____

4. What information did you find? _____

_____

_____

_____

_____

Team Project

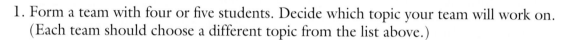

Make a presentation related to housing issues.

Presentation Topics

- Communication with a Landlord or Tenant
- Rental Agreements
- Tenant and Landlord Rights
- Renter's or Homeowner's Insurance
- Theft Prevention

1. Form a team with four or five students. Decide which topic your team will work on. (Each team should choose a different topic from the list above.)

2. Choose positions for each member of your team.

POSITION	JOB DESCRIPTION	STUDENT NAME
Student 1: **Project Leader**	See that everyone speaks English. See that everyone participates.	
Student 2: **Project Secretary**	Take notes on your team's ideas.	
Student 3: **Coordinator**	Divide presentation into parts. Assign each team member one part of the presentation.	
Student 4: **Director**	Organize a different method of presentation for each part.	
Student 5: **Advisor**	Give feedback on the presentation as each team member rehearses his/her part.	

3. Gather the information for your presentation.

4. Decide how to present your information to the class. For example, you may want to use charts, skits, or games.

5. Create any materials needed for your presentation.

6. Rehearse your presentation.

7. Give your presentation to the class.

Make a presentation related to housing issues.

Each team will prepare a presentation for the class based on one of the topics from the unit. The presentation should include information from the unit as well as from additional research.

The team project is the final application for the unit. It gives students a chance to show that they have mastered all of the Unit 4 objectives.

Note: Shorter classes can extend this project over two class meetings.

Stage 1   5–10 mins.

Form a team with four or five students. Decide which topic your team will work on. (Each team should choose a different topic from the list above.)

Make sure each team chooses a different topic.

Stage 2   15–20 mins.

Choose positions for each member of your team.

Have students decide who will lead each step as described on the student page. Provide well-defined directions on the board for how teams should proceed. Explain that all the students do every step as a team. Teams shouldn't go to the next stage until the previous one is complete.

Stage 3   15–20 mins.

Gather the information for your presentation.

Tell students to use what they learned in class and to conduct additional research.

Stage 4   15–20 mins.

Decide how to present your information to the class. For example, you may want to use charts, skits, or games.

As a class, brainstorm different methods of presentation. Try to make the list exhaustive so that every team doesn't use the same exact presentation format. Briefly discuss how some presentation methods lend themselves better to some material. Encourage the teams to use at least two different presentation methods in their presentations.

Stage 5   20–30 mins.

Create any materials needed for your presentation.

Optional Computer Activity: Students may want to use the computer to create presentation materials.

Stage 6   15–20 mins.

Rehearse your presentation.

Remind students that each team member must be involved in the presentation.

Stage 7   15–20 mins.

Give your presentation to the class.

STANDARDS CORRELATIONS

CASAS: 4.8.1, 4.8.5, 4.8.6 (See CASAS Competency List on pages 187–193.)
SCANS: **Resources** Allocate time
Information Acquire and evaluate information, organize and maintain information, interpret and communicate information, use computers to process information
Systems Understand systems, improve and design systems
Technology Select technology, apply technology to exercise
Basic Skills Writing
Thinking Skills Think creatively, make decisions, solve problems, see things in the mind's eye, use reasoning

Personal Qualities Responsibility, self-esteem, self-management, integrity
EFF: **Communication** Read with understanding, convey ideas in writing, speak so others can understand, listen actively, observe critically
Decision Making Solve problems and make decisions, plan
Interpersonal Cooperate with others, advocate and influence, resolve conflict and negotiate, guide others
Lifelong Learning Take responsibility for learning, reflect and evaluate, learn through research, use information and communications technology *(optional)*

Objective: Introduce new vocabulary
Academic Strategies: Identifying parts of speech, using a dictionary, understanding word families
Vocabulary: See lesson

RESOURCES

Dictionaries: It is recommended that each student in class have an ESL learner's dictionary or that there be dictionaries available in the classroom for students to use. Dictionaries that will be referred to in this book are

AGENDA

Understand word families.
Learn health expressions.

Heinle's Newbury House Dictionary of American English and the *Collins Cobuild Intermediate* or *Advanced Dictionary of American English.*

Academic Feature: Vocabulary Builder

Each unit will begin with a vocabulary-building section. The purpose of this two-page section is to introduce students to many of the words they will be using in the unit lessons. Students will have a chance to see how much they already know, and they will get exposure to the new vocabulary found in the unit.

Note: All of the exercises on these two pages should be done in class, no matter the class length. Longer classes can do this lesson and then move onto Lesson 1 during the same class meeting; shorter classes may have to devote one whole class meeting to this lesson.

Introduction   5-10 mins.

State the objective: *Today we will be identifying and working with the vocabulary you will learn in this unit.*

Presentation 1   5 mins.

(A) A *word family* is a group of words with the same root. The words all have similar meanings but are used as different parts of speech. Look at this example.

Practice 1   10-15 mins.

(B) Put the words below into the correct column in the chart. Then, use your dictionary to find the other forms of each word family. *Note:* Not every word family has every part of speech.

Tell students that the chart continues on page 90 in their books.

Evaluation 1   5 mins.

Go over the answers as a class.

STANDARDS CORRELATIONS

CASAS: 7.4.5 (See CASAS Competency List on pages 187–193.)
SCANS: **Information** Acquire and evaluate information, organize and maintain information
Interpersonal Participate as a member of a team, negotiate to arrive at a decision, work with cultural diversity
Systems Understand systems, monitor and correct performance
Basic Skills Reading, writing, listening, speaking
Thinking Skills Think creatively, make decisions, see things in the mind's eye

Personal Qualities Responsibility, sociability, self-management
EFF: **Communication** Read with understanding, convey ideas in writing, speak so others can understand, listen actively
Decision Making Use math to solve problems and communicate, solve problems and make decisions, plan
Interpersonal Cooperate with others
Lifelong Learning Take responsibility for learning, reflect and evaluate, learn through research

Health

GOALS

➤ Identify practices that promote mental and physical well-being

➤ Ask about medical bills

➤ Interpret health insurance information

➤ Identify addictions

➤ Interpret procedures for first aid

Vocabulary Builder

A A *word family* is a group of words with the same root. The words all have similar meanings but are used as different parts of speech. Look at this example.

Noun(s)	Verb	Adjective
survival, survivor	survive	surviving

- There were no *survivors* from the car accident.
- If cancer is detected early, there is a good chance of *survival.*
- Drugs that dissolve blood clots can help people *survive* heart attacks.
- The *surviving* passengers from the plane crash tried to find help.

B Put the words below into the correct column in the chart. Then, use your dictionary to find the other forms of each word family. *Note:* Not every word family has every part of speech.

affecting   withdrawal   poisoning   depressed   tolerance
impairment   addiction   meditate   insured   treat

Noun	Verb	Adjective	Adverb
affect	affecting, affect, affected	affecting, affective	
impairment	impairing, impair, impaired	impairing, impaired	
withdrawal	withdrawing, withdraw, withdrew	withdrawn	
addict, addiction	addicting, addict, addicted	addictive, addicting, addicted	addictively
poison	poisoning, poison, poisoned	poisoning, poisonous	poisonously
meditation	meditate, meditating, meditated	meditative	meditatively

Noun	Verb	Adjective	Adverb
depression	depressed, depressing, depress	depressed	depressingly
insurance	insured, insure, insuring	insured	
tolerance	tolerate, tolerated, tolerating	tolerant, tolerated	tolerantly
treatment	treat, treating, treated	treated	

(Answers will vary.)

 C Choose one of the word families from Exercise B that has all four parts of speech. Write a sentence using each word form. Use the example sentences in Exercise A as a model.

1. Addicts are difficult to cure.

2. Addictions to drugs and alcohol are difficult to stop.

3. The nicotine in cigarettes is addicting.

4. People can behave addictively around caffeine.

 D Each expression below is related to health. What do you think each one means? Write your ideas on the lines. (Answers will vary.)

1. mental health: the wellness of brain function

2. out of shape: your body doesn't function or look like it should

3. self-esteem: how you think about yourself

4. at risk: in danger

 E Look at the following questions. Answer the ones you feel comfortable answering. (Answers will vary.)

1. What are the major health-care issues facing your community? Which health-care issues can be categorized as mental-health issues?
   addiction, drug resistant bacteria, mental health: depression

2. Do you consider yourself in good shape? Why or why not?
   No, because I need to make my heart and body stronger.

3. Think about people who have high self-esteem. What are their traits? What are the traits of people with low self-esteem?
   High self-esteem: take care of themselves, positive
   Low: negative attitude, don't try to change

4. Do you know your family's health history? If so, what problems have faced some of your family members?
   Yes. Heart disease and cancer

Vocabulary

When teaching students new vocabulary, pronounce each word for them several times and ask them to repeat it. Often, students may be familiar with the words you are introducing but have never seen them spelled out. By pronouncing the words for students, you allow students to make a connection between the words' spellings and their sounds. It is also important that students learn the correct pronunciation of new words so they feel comfortable using their new vocabulary inside and outside of the classroom.

Practice 1 *(continued)*   5–10 mins.

Ⓒ **Choose one of the word families from Exercise B that has all four parts of speech. Write a sentence using each word form. Use the example sentences in Exercise A as a model.**

Evaluation 1 *(continued)*   10–15 mins.

Ask volunteers to write their group of sentences on the board. Analyze the sentences for meaning and grammar.

Presentation 2   10–15 mins.

Ⓓ **Each expression below is related to health. What do you think each one means? Write your ideas on the lines.**

Have students write their ideas in their books and then go over the meanings as a class.

Practice 2   10–15 mins.

Ⓔ **Look at the following questions. Answer the ones you feel comfortable answering.**

Evaluation 2   10–15 mins.

Ask volunteers to share their answers.

AT-A-GLANCE PREP

Objective: Identify practices that promote mental and physical well-being

Academic Strategies: Focused listening, note taking, writing

Vocabulary: *mental health, stress, depressed, survive, liveable, out of shape, affecting, self-esteem, obese, at risk, diabetes, prognosis, meditate, blood pressure, overworked*

RESOURCES

Activity Bank: Unit 5, Lesson 1, Worksheets 1–3
Grammar Challenge 5: Unit 5, Challenge 1

Audio: CD Track 25
Suggested Realia: newspapers, advice columns
Stand Out 5 Assessment CD-ROM with Exam*View®*

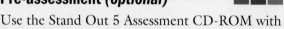 1.5 hour classes ■ 2.5 hour classes ■ 3+ hour classes

> **AGENDA**
> *Discuss your health habits.*
> *Listen to ways people handle stress.*
> *Read and give health-related advice.*
> *Read a health-related article.*
> *Create a newsletter.*

 Pre-assessment (optional)

Use the Stand Out 5 Assessment CD-ROM with Exam*View®* to create a pre-test for Unit 5.

Warm-up and Review   5–10 mins.

Ask students to take out a piece of paper and make a list of all the words and phrases they can remember from the vocabulary-building section. When they have written down everything they can think of, have them talk to a partner and try to add one or two more words and phrases to their lists. Make a class list on the board.

Introduction   5–10 mins. ■■■

Dictation:

1. Stress is a feeling that is created when we react to particular events.
2. The human body responds to stress by activating the nervous system and specific hormones.
3. Stress contributes to heart disease, high blood pressure, strokes, and other illnesses in many individuals.
4. Stress also affects the immune system, which protects us from many serious diseases.

State the objective: *Today we will identify ways to promote mental and physical well-being.*

Presentation 1   10–15 mins.

A Discuss the following questions with a small group.

Have students look at the three pictures in Exercise B. Ask them what they think they will be listening for. Before you play the recording, discuss some possible reasons for stress.

Practice 1   10–15 mins. ■■■

B Listen to the following people talk about how they handle stress. Take notes.

Note: The listening script is on page 92a.

Evaluation 1   5 mins.

Go over the answers as a class.

C Do you identify with any of these people? If yes, in what ways? If not, why not?

Discuss students' answers as a class.

STANDARDS CORRELATIONS

CASAS: 3.5.8, 3.5.9 (See CASAS Competency List on pages 187–193.)
SCANS: Resources Allocate time, allocate money, allocate materials and facility resources, allocate human resources
Information Acquire and evaluate information, organize and maintain information, interpret and communicate information, use computers to process information *(optional)*
Interpersonal Participate as a member of a team, teach others, exercise leadership, negotiate to arrive at a decision, work with cultural diversity
Systems Monitor and correct performance
Technology Select technology, apply technology to a task *(optional)*

Basic Skills Reading, writing, arithmetic, listening, speaking
Thinking Skills Think creatively, make decisions, solve problems, see things in the mind's eye
Personal Qualities Responsibility, sociability, self-management
EFF: Communication Read with understanding, convey ideas in writing, speak so others can understand, listen actively, observe critically
Decision Making Solve problems and make decisions, plan
Interpersonal Cooperate with others, advocate and influence, guide others
Lifelong Learning Take responsibility for learning, reflect and evaluate, use information and communications technology *(optional)*

91a   Lesson Planner: Unit 5, Lesson 1

Mind and body

GOAL ➤ **Identify practices that promote mental and physical well-being**

A Discuss the following questions with a small group. (Answers will vary.)

1. Do you exercise? If so, what type of exercise do you do and how often? Yes. Walking.

2. Do you eat well? On a scale of one to ten (ten being the healthiest), how healthy are the foods you eat? No. Probably a five.

3. How could you make your diet healthier? Add more vegetables. Eat less candy.

4. How much water do you drink a day? Four tall glasses.

5. Do you have a lot of stress in your life? How do you relieve stress?
   Yes. By talking with friends and walking regularly.

B Listen to the following people talk about how they handle stress. Take notes.
(Answers may vary.)

CD
TR 25

Cooper	Stephanie	Fletcher and Katie
Reason for stress:	Reason for stress:	Reason for stress:
commission-based pay	worrying about money	taking care of mother/ works long hours
How he copes with his stress:	How she copes with her stress:	How they cope with their stress:
night school	running	talking to each other
meditation		walking at night

C Do you identify with any of these people? If yes, in what ways? If not, why not?
(Answers will vary.)
Yes, I like to meditate and walk. I am taking care of a sick parent.

GOAL ➤ **Identify practices that promote mental and physical well-being**

 D "Dear Ali" is a column in the local newspaper. Ali addresses health issues. Read her column. Do you agree with her advice?

Daily Freepress News

1. Dear Ali,
I don't look forward to getting out of bed in the morning. I don't like my job. I don't like to go to school. I don't have any family around and I have very few friends. I feel like there is no reason to get up in the morning. **—Unhappy**

Dear Unhappy,
You are depressed. But that doesn't mean you can stay in bed forever. Do things that will make you want to get out of bed. Take a nice hot shower. Go for a walk. Drink some water. Eat some fresh fruit. Find something that you can look forward to. Every day, add one more thing to your day that you enjoy

doing. If you don't like your job, look for a new one. Find some classes at a nearby school that you like. Remember, we don't always like everything that we have to do in life to survive. But, if you can fill your day with at least one or two things that make you happy, it will make the rest of your day liveable.

2. Dear Ali,
I'm overweight and out of shape. I can't bear to look at myself in the mirror, and it is really affecting my self-esteem. What can I do? **—Overweight & Out of Shape**

Dear Overweight & Out of Shape,
There are only two things I can say . . . diet and exercise! The only way to lose weight and keep it off is to eat a healthy, low-calorie diet and exercise. If you can't do it by yourself, find a friend or family member to do it with you or join one of the many weight-loss programs out there. You can do it!

 E Pretend you are Ali and give advice to the following concerned people.
(Answers will vary.)

Dear Ali,
My daughter is overweight. All of the kids make fun of her at school, and I think she eats even more because she is unhappy. I try to cook healthy food at home but that doesn't seem to be helping. What can I do?
—*Mother Without a Clue*

Begin an exercise routine with her and make this a family activity.

Show her you are in this effort together. Teach her to cook and prepare

her own healthy meals.

Dear Ali,
I have a lot of stress at work. My boss pushes me pretty hard, and I want to do a good job to get ahead, but I never have any time for myself or for my family. The doctor says all the stress is giving me high blood pressure. What should I do?—*Overworked*

You need to take time for yourself and your family or you will lose your

health. Exercise together before or after work. Walk at lunchtime.

Listening Script *CD Track 25*

Cooper: *My name is Cooper and I work for a mortgage company. My job is very stressful because I work on commission and the only way I get paid is by helping people refinance their homes. If I don't help anyone, I don't make any money. The more people I help, the more money I make. I don't really like my job, so I'm going to school at night to study computer programming. Between work and school, I'm really busy and my work and studies put a lot of stress on me. One of the ways I cope with all this stress is meditation. Every morning before I leave for work, I sit outside on the porch where I can look at the trees and listen to the birds chirping. I close my eyes and breathe deeply, thinking of all the good things in my life. I picture my day at work as a productive, successful day. I picture my evening at school as a fun, eye-opening experience where I learn many new things that will help me change careers. When I open my eyes, I feel refreshed and ready to take on the day.*

Stephanie: *My name is Stephanie. I cope with my stress by exercising. I run every night after work. Running gives me time to think and use up all that built-up energy caused by stress. I work three jobs just to make enough money to pay the bills. The jobs aren't stressful, but worrying if I'm going to have enough money each month is. Running seems to be the only thing that calms my nerves.*

Fletcher: *I'm Fletcher.*
Katie: *And I'm Katie.*
Fletcher: *And the only way we can relieve our stress is by talking . . . to each other.*
Katie: *My mother is very sick and she lives with us, so I can take care of her.*
Fletcher: *And since Katie had to stop working to take care of her mother, I had to start working longer hours to make more money. Both of these things have put a lot of stress on us.*
Katie: *So, every night we take a walk around our neighborhood and talk. The fresh air is wonderful and just being able to talk about our days and our future helps us both relax. We know that we're doing the right thing by taking care of Mom, and as long as we have each other we'll be able to survive.*

Presentation 2 5–10 mins.

D "Dear Ali" is a column in the local newspaper. Ali addresses health issues. Read her column. Do you agree with her advice?

If students are unfamiliar with the concept of an advice column, explain how it works. Ask students if they have ever read any advice columns and, if so, what kind of advice was given. This is a good opportunity to bring in newspapers as realia.

Practice 2 10–15 mins.

Note: Shorter classes can do this exercise for homework.

E Pretend you are Ali and give advice to the following concerned people.

Evaluation 2 10–15 mins.

Ask volunteers to read their advice letters out loud.

Extended Practice: Give each student a note card, or have students use their own sheet of paper. Have them write a short "Dear Ali" letter. Collect the cards and pass them out to students. Make sure no one gets his or her own card. Tell students to spend a few minutes coming up with the advice they would give for the person who wrote the letter. Have each student stand up, read his or her card out loud, and then give the advice that he or she came up with. As a class, discuss if the advice is good or bad. If students think the advice isn't good, have them come up with better advice as a class.

Instructor's Notes

Presentation 3
10-15 mins. ■■□

F Danielle wrote a health-related article for her school paper. Read her article.

Have students read the article to themselves. When they finish, read the article out loud to students. Answer any vocabulary questions students might have.

Practice 3
10-15 mins. ■

Note: Shorter classes can do this exercise for homework.

G Answer the following questions.

If you want students to do this exercise individually, have them write their ideas on a piece of paper. If you want students to do this exercise in groups, have them discuss the questions.

Evaluation 3
5-10 mins. ■

Talk about the word *inspiring* and what it means. Discuss the third question as a class. Discuss what makes something *inspiring*.

Application
30-45 mins. ■■□

H With your classmates, create a health newsletter. Follow the steps below.

Let students make this newsletter as simple or as elaborate as they want. The main purpose of this exercise is for students to write an article about their health habits. But, the fact that they are "publishing their writing" gives it more of a purpose and reasons to be inspiring.

If your students need it, help them through the writing process by having them first brainstorm ideas, narrow down their ideas, write an outline, and then create a first draft. (There is a worksheet on the Activity Bank to guide them through this process.)

Optional Computer Activity: Let students type their articles and produce their newsletter on the computer.

Activity Bank

Unit 5, Lesson 1, Worksheet 1: Give Advice

Unit 5, Lesson 1, Worksheet 2: Write an Article

 Refer students to *Stand Out 5 Grammar Challenge*, Unit 5, Challenge 1 for practice with adverbial clauses of place.

Instructor's Notes

GOAL ➤ **Identify practices that promote mental and physical well-being**

 Danielle wrote a health-related article for her school paper. Read her article.

BACK ON TRACK

I think I take pretty good care of myself. But it wasn't always that way. I used to work really long hours, eat at fast-food restaurants because they were quick and easy, and I barely ever exercised. But I got a wake-up call from the doctor one day. He said I was obese and at risk for diabetes and that I might not make it to my fortieth birthday. From that day forward, I began to make changes in my life. I started by going for a walk every day. Now I go to the gym three times a week, walk six miles two days a week, and play volleyball with my family on the weekends. The day the doctor gave me that horrible prognosis, I went straight to the market and filled my cart with healthy food. I now make my lunch every day and cook healthy dinners for my family. My purse and my car are always filled with healthy snacks and water. If I ever get a craving for something really unhealthy, I let myself have one bite of it, and then I stick a piece of gum in my mouth. Although the exercise and eating habits really helped to lower my blood pressure and risk for diabetes, I still have quite a bit of stress in my life. To combat that, I make sure I take at least a half an hour a day for myself. Sometimes I meditate, sometimes I call a good friend, and other times I just sit down and read a book for pleasure.

 Answer the following questions. (Answers may vary.)

1. What forced Danielle to make changes in her life?
Her doctor told her she was at risk for diabetes because she was obese.
2. What changes did she make?
She started exercising and eating healthy foods and meditating.
3. Do you think her article is inspiring? Why or why not?
Yes, because diabetes runs in my family. She made good changes.

 With your classmates, create a health newsletter. Follow the steps below.

1. Each student writes a health article that will be inspiring to others who read it.

2. After everyone has finished his or her article, work together to edit the articles.

3. Come up with a title for your newsletter.

4. Put your newsletter together. Add artwork or photos if you want.

What's this charge for?

GOAL ➤ **Ask about medical bills**

CD
TR 26

A Listen to the phone conversation Mrs. Gregory is having with the doctor's office.

DOCTOR				
Amy Rosenberg, M.D., Inc. 2880 Chestnut Ave., Ste. 340 Topeka, KS 66675 Office Phone (785) 555-0012				

Statement Date:	10/06/2008
Statement #:	4689-36
Balance Due:	**$20.00**

RESPONSIBLE PARTY
Mrs. Linda Gregory 56 Plains Ave. Topeka, KS 66675

MAKE CHECK PAYABLE AND REMIT TO
Amy Rosenberg, M.D., Inc. 2880 Chestnut Ave., Ste. 340 Topeka, KS 66675

PATIENT NAME: Gregory, Courtney	PROVIDER: Rosenberg, M.D., Amy

Date	Procedure	Description of Service	Co-Pay	Amount Payable
8/23/2008	99391	Well-Child Check		$100.00
8/23/2008	90700	DTaP Vaccine		$40.00
8/23/2008	90465	Vaccine Admin		$28.00
8/23/2008	90645	Hib Vaccine		$32.00
8/23/2008	90466	Vaccine Admin		$28.00
8/23/2008		Patient Co-Pay	-$20.00	
9/01/2008		Primary Insurance Payment		-$120.00
9/01/2008		Uncollectible		-$68.00

B Answer the questions.

1. Who is expected to pay this bill? Mrs. Linda Gegory.

2. Why did Courtney go to the doctor? For a checkup and vaccines.

3. Why is the responsible party different from the patient's name? She is the mother.

4. How much is owed? $20.

5. Why is the responsible party confused about the amount she owes? She paid the co-pay already.

6. Does anything on the bill confuse you? Write a question about something you don't understand. Yes. I don't understand what "uncollectible" means. Who is responsible for that? (Answer will vary.)

Objective: Ask about medical bills
Pronunciation: Clear speech on the telephone
Academic Strategy: Focused listening
Vocabulary: *remit to, responsible party, procedure, co-pay, payable, code*

RESOURCES

Activity Bank: Unit 5, Lesson 2, Worksheets 1–2
Grammar Challenge 5: Unit 5, Challenge 2

◼ 1.5 hour classes   ◼ 2.5 hour classes   ◼ 3⁺ hour classes

Audio: CD Tracks 26–27
Suggested Realia: Medical bills

AGENDA

Listen to two phone conversations between patients and the doctor's office.
Practice conversations with a partner.
Write questions you would ask about a medical bill.

Warm-up and Review   5–10 mins. ◼◻◻

Have students talk about the process of creating their health newsletter. Ask them if there is any real-world application for an activity like this.

Introduction   10–20 mins. ◼◼◻

Dictation:

1. After your doctor's appointment, your doctor's office will submit a claim to your insurance company.
2. The insurance company uses the information on the claim to pay the doctor for those services.
3. A statement shows how much your doctor's office billed your insurance company for the services you received.
4. After your insurance company pays your doctor, you may need to pay the doctor any balance due.

State the objective: *Today you will practice asking questions about medical bills.*

Presentation 1   10–15 mins. ◼◼◻

 Listen to the phone conversation
Mrs. Gregory is having with the doctor's office.

Practice 1   10–15 mins. ◼◼◻

 Answer the questions.

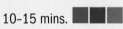 **Listening Script**   CD Track 26

Receptionist: *Good morning, Dr. Rosenberg's office.*
Mrs. Gregory: *Um, yes, this is Linda Gregory. I brought my daughter, Courtney, in a few weeks ago for her six-month checkup. I just received the bill and I have a few questions.*
Receptionist: *Yes, Mrs. Gregory. Let me pull up your records. Do you have the date of the statement?*
Mrs. Gregory: *Yes, it is October 6.*
Receptionist: *OK, I have it right here. How can I help you?*
Mrs. Gregory: *Well, I don't see why I owe $20.*
Receptionist: *That is your co-pay.*
Mrs. Gregory: *But on the statement it says that I already paid my $20 co-pay.*
Receptionist: *Yes, you're right. But when we talked to the insurance company, they told us that your co-pay is $40. You already paid $20, so you owe another $20.*
Mrs. Gregory: *$40? When did my co-pay go up to $40?*
Receptionist: *I don't know, ma'am. You'll have to call your insurance company to find out.*
Patient: *OK. So all I owe right now is $20?*
Receptionist: *Yes.*
Patient: *OK. Thank you for your time.*

Tell the class that insurance forms and medical bills are often difficult to understand. Encourage students to call their doctors' offices or their insurance companies if there is something on a bill they don't understand.

STANDARDS CORRELATIONS

CASAS: 3.2.4 (See CASAS Competency List on pages 187–193.)
SCANS: Information Acquire and evaluate information, organize and maintain information, interpret and communicate information
Interpersonal Participate as a member of a team, teach others, exercise leadership, negotiate to arrive at a decision, work with cultural diversity
Systems Monitor and correct performance
Basic Skills Reading, writing, arithmetic, listening, speaking
Thinking Skills Think creatively, make decisions, solve problems, see things in the mind's eye

Personal Qualities Responsibility, sociability, self-management
EFF: Communication Read with understanding, convey ideas in writing, speak so others can understand, listen actively, observe critically
Decision Making Solve problems and make decisions, plan
Interpersonal Cooperate with others, advocate and influence, resolve conflict and negotiate, guide others
Lifelong Learning Take responsibility for learning

Evaluation 1   5 mins. ■■□

Go over the answers as a class.

Presentation 2   5-10 mins. ■■□

🎧 Listening Script   CD Track 27

The listening script matches the conversation in Exercise C.

C Read and listen to the following conversation between a patient and the doctor's office.

Practice 2   10-15 mins. ■■□

Note: Shorter classes can do these exercises for homework.

D Practice the conversation with a partner. Switch roles.

E Practice the conversation again. This time use the information below to change the patient's questions. The receptionist will have to be creative to come up with a response.

Model this activity for students by practicing with a volunteer.

Evaluation 2   10-15 mins. ■■□

Walk around the classroom and listen to students' conversations. When students have finished, ask volunteer pairs to perform their conversations for the class.

Pronunciation

Speaking on the phone

Remind students that when speaking on the phone, they need to enunciate clearly. To help them improve this skill, have students stand back-to-back when practicing conversations in pairs.

CD
TR 27

C Read and listen to the following conversation between a patient and the doctor's office.

Receptionist: Dr. Brook's office.

Patient: Um, yes, this is Cooper Jackson. I came in and saw the doctor a few months ago for the pain I was having in my leg. I just received the bill and I have a few questions.

Receptionist: Of course, Mr. Jackson. Let me pull up your records. Do you have the date of the statement?

Patient: Yes, it is June 16th.

Receptionist: Ok, I have it here. How can I help you?

Patient: Well, I don't understand what this $264 charge is for.

Receptionist: That is for the X-rays the technician took of your leg.

Patient: OK, but shouldn't my insurance pay for that?

Receptionist: Yes, they might pay some. As you can see on the bill, we have billed your insurance company but are still waiting to hear back from them. Once we do, we'll send you an adjusted bill reflecting how much you owe.

Patient: Oh, so if I don't have to pay this $264, why did you send me a bill?

Receptionist: I know it may seem a bit confusing. Our billing department automatically sends out statements to our current patients every month, whether or not we have heard back from the insurance companies. It usually takes about a month for the bill to reflect what the insurance company has paid, so, in general, if you wait two or three months to pay your bill, your statement should show the correct amount due.

Patient: I see. That makes sense. So, I don't need to pay this bill now?

Receptionist: No. Wait until you receive a bill with an adjusted amount on it and then send in your payment.

Patient: Great! Thanks for your help.

Receptionist: Have a nice day, Mr. Jackson.

D Practice the conversation with a partner. Switch roles.

E Practice the conversation again. This time use the information below to change the patient's questions. The receptionist will have to be creative to come up with a response.

Name	Reason for visit	Date of statement	Question
Jenna Lyn	toothache	May 25	Why isn't the payment I made showing up on the statement?
Javier Bardo	headaches	December 2	Do you offer discounted services? I don't have health insurance.
Kim Jensen	skin rash	March 14	Why do I have to pay more than my co-pay?
Young Lee	ingrown toenail	July 7	Why didn't my insurance pay for the procedure?

GOAL ➤ **Ask about medical bills**

F) Look at the bill below. Write five questions you would ask someone at the doctor's office.
(Answers may vary. Sample questions are given below.)

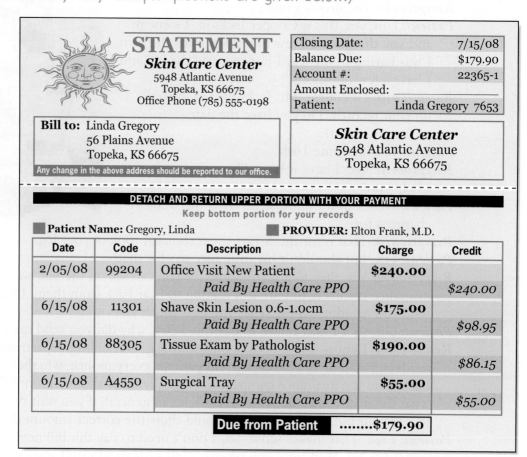

Date	Code	Description	Charge	Credit
2/05/08	99204	Office Visit New Patient	**$240.00**	
		Paid By Health Care PPO		*$240.00*
6/15/08	11301	Shave Skin Lesion 0.6-1.0cm	**$175.00**	
		Paid By Health Care PPO		*$98.95*
6/15/08	88305	Tissue Exam by Pathologist	**$190.00**	
		Paid By Health Care PPO		*$86.15*
6/15/08	A4550	Surgical Tray	**$55.00**	
		Paid By Health Care PPO		*$55.00*

1. When was this bill due?

2. Why does the Health Care PPO pay less than the charge?

3. Who is the doctor?

4. What is a pathologist?

5. Can I pay a smaller amount over 3 months?

G) Go over the bill with your teacher to make sure you understand everything on it.

H) Find a partner (receptionist) and have a conversation, asking him or her the questions you wrote above. Switch roles.

Presentation 3   5-10 mins. ■■■

Ask students a few simple questions about the bill in Exercise C. Don't answer any of their questions or give them any information that you think they might need.

Practice 3   5-10 mins. ■

Note: Shorter classes can do this exercise for homework.

F Look at the bill below. Write five questions you would ask someone at the doctor's office.

Evaluation 3   5-10 mins. ■

As a class, go over the questions students wrote and try to answer the questions together.

G Go over the bill with your teacher to make sure you understand everything on it.

Application   10-20 mins. ■■■

H Find a partner (receptionist) and have a conversation, asking him or her the questions you wrote above. Switch roles.

Activity Bank 🔊

Unit 5, Lesson 2, Worksheet 1: Conversations with the Doctor's Office (listening)

Unit 5, Lesson 2, Worksheet 2: Medical Bills

📖 Refer students to *Stand Out 5 Grammar Challenge*, Unit 5, Challenge 2 for practice with adverbial clauses of time.

Objective: Interpret health insurance information
Academic Strategy: Interpreting bar graphs and tables
Vocabulary: *insured, uninsured, percentage*

RESOURCES

Activity Bank: Unit 5, Lesson 3, PDF and Worksheet 1
Grammar Challenge 5: Unit 5, Challenge 3

■ 1.5 hour classes   ■ 2.5 hour classes   ■ 3⁺ hour classes

AGENDA

Discuss health insurance.
Interpret a bar graph.
Interpret a table.
Recreate a graph or chart.

Warm-up and Review   5–10 mins.

Have students repeat the application from the previous lesson, this time with a different partner.

Introduction   5–10 mins.

Before beginning the dictation, have students practice writing large numbers and percentages down. Allow students to use numerals in dictation rather than spelling out the numbers.

Dictation:

1. From January to June, 2007, 42.5 million people didn't have health insurance.
2. The percentage of children under age 18 years old who were uninsured in the first six months of 2007 was 8.6%.
3. In the first six months of 2007, 14% of employed adults had been uninsured for more than a year.
4. Since 1997, there has been a decreasing trend in the percentage of children who were uninsured.

State the objective: *Today you will interpret graphs and tables about health insurance coverage.*

Presentation 1   15–20 mins.

(A) What do you know about health insurance? In a small group, try to answer the following questions. If you need more help, talk to other groups.

(B) Read the bar graph about the insured and uninsured and answer the questions.

Practice 1   10–15 mins.

(C) Ask your partner questions about the information presented in the graph. Use the questions from Exercise B as examples.

Evaluation 1

Observe pair work.

Activity Bank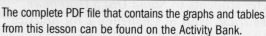

The complete PDF file that contains the graphs and tables from this lesson can be found on the Activity Bank.

(*Source:* Health Insurance Coverage: Early Release of Estimates from the National Health Interview Survey, January–June, 2007, by Robin A. Cohen, Ph.D., and Michael E. Martinez, M.P.H., Division of Health Interview Statistics, National Center for Health Statistics)

STANDARDS CORRELATIONS

CASAS: 3.2.3 (See CASAS Competency List on pages 187–193.)
SCANS: **Resources** Allocate time, allocate human resources
Information Acquire and evaluate information, organize and maintain information, interpret and communicate information, use computers to process information (*optional*)
Interpersonal Participate as a member of a team, exercise leadership, negotiate to arrive at a decision, work with cultural diversity
Systems Understand systems, monitor and correct performance, improve and design systems
Technology Select technology, apply technology to a task (*optional*)
Basic Skills Reading, writing, arithmetic, listening, speaking

Thinking Skills Think creatively, make decisions, solve problems, see things in the mind's eye
Personal Qualities Responsibility, sociability, self-management
EFF: **Communication** Read with understanding, convey ideas in writing, speak so others can understand, listen actively, observe critically
Decision Making Use math to solve problems and communicate, plan
Interpersonal Cooperate with others, advocate and influence, resolve conflict and negotiate, guide others
Lifelong Learning Take responsibility for learning, reflect and evaluate, learn through research, use information and communications technology (*optional*)

 LESSON 3

Health insurance

GOAL ➤ **Interpret health insurance information**

A What do you know about health insurance? In a small group, try to answer the following questions. If you need more help, talk to other groups. (Answers will vary.)

1. Is it mandatory in your state to have health insurance?
2. What happens if you go to the doctor's or hospital without health insurance?
3. What is the difference between an HMO and a PPO?
4. Name four health insurance companies.

B Read the bar graph about the insured and uninsured and answer the questions.

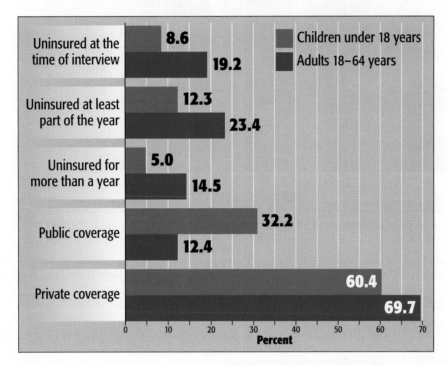

Percentage of persons without health insurance, by three measurements and age group, and percentage of persons with health insurance, by coverage type and age group: United States, January, 2007–June, 2007

(*Source:* Family Core component of the 2007 National Health Interview Survey. The estimates for 2007 are based on data collected January through June. Data are based on household interviews of a sample of the civilian non-institutionalized population.)

1. What percentage of adults is insured? 82.1%
2. Of the uninsured people, what percentage of children was uninsured for more than a year? 5%
3. What percentage of adults has private insurance? 69.7%
4. What percentage of children has public coverage? 32.2%

C Ask your partner questions about the information presented in the graph. Use the questions from Exercise B as examples. (Answers will vary. Sample questions are given.)

What percent of adults were uninsured at the time of the interview?

When was this interview conducted?

Vocabulary Grammar
Life Skills
Academic Pronunciation

D Read the graph and complete the sentences below.

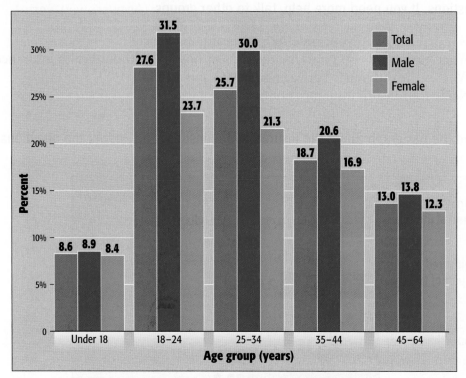

Percentage of persons under 65 years of age without health insurance coverage at the time of interview, by age group and sex: United States, January, 2007–June, 2007

(*Source:* Family Core component of the 2007 National Health Interview Survey. The estimates for 2007 are based on data collected January through June. Data are based on household interviews of a sample of the civilian non-institutionalized population.)

1. Of both sexes, the ____males____ are the most uninsured.

2. Out of all the age groups, the ____18–24____ -year-olds are the most uninsured.

3. ____8.6%____ of children are uninsured.

4. ____91.4%____ of children are insured.

5. ____16.9%____ of women ages 35–44 are uninsured.

6. _____ of people in my age group are uninsured. (Answers will vary.)

E Write three more sentences about the statistics in the graph. (Answers will vary. Sample answers are given.)

1. 25.7% of adults 25–34 are uninsured. _____

2. 86.2% of men 45–64 are insured. _____

3. People 18–24 are the least insured. _____

Presentation 2   5-10 mins. ■■■☐

Go over the graph with students. Make sure they understand how to read it. Ask them a few questions to check for understanding, such as, *What percentage of females aged 45 to 64 don't have health insurance coverage?*

Practice 2   10-15 mins. ■■☐

Note: Shorter classes can do these exercises for homework.

(D) Read the graph and complete the sentences below.

(E) Write three more sentences about the statistics in the graph.

Evaluation 2   5-10 mins. ■■☐

Ask volunteers to write their sentences on the board. Have students compare the sentences with the information presented in the graph.

Presentation 3   5–10 mins.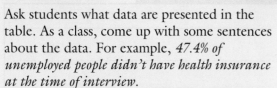

Ask students what data are presented in the table. As a class, come up with some sentences about the data. For example, *47.4% of unemployed people didn't have health insurance at the time of interview.*

On the board, brainstorm some questions students might ask about the data in the table. For example, *What percentage of people with a high school diploma have been uninsured for more than a year?*

Practice 3   15–20 mins.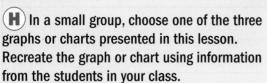

Note: Shorter classes can do these exercises for homework.

F Look at the data in the table below and write six questions based on the data.

G Interview three students using the questions you wrote.

Evaluation 3   5–15 mins. ▮

Observe.

Application   20–30 mins. ▮▮▮

H In a small group, choose one of the three graphs or charts presented in this lesson. Recreate the graph or chart using information from the students in your class.

Activity Bank 💿

Unit 5, Lesson 3, PDF: Health Insurance

Unit 5, Lesson 3, Worksheet 1: Doing Research

Refer students to *Stand Out 5 Grammar Challenge*, Unit 5, Challenge 3 for practice with adverbial clauses of reason.

LESSON 3

GOAL ➤ Interpret health insurance information

F Look at the data in the table below and write six questions based on the data.
(Answers will vary. Sample questions are given below.)

Selected characteristic	Uninsured[1] at the time of interview	Uninsured[1] for at least part of the year[2]	Uninsured[1] for more than a year[2]
RACE/ETHNICITY	**PERCENT** (standard error)		
Hispanic or Latino	31.4 (1.11)	35.6 (1.17)	25.8 (1.08)
Non-Hispanic			
White, single race	10.2 (0.37)	13.7 (0.42)	7.1 (0.31)
Black, single race	14.4 (0.65)	17.8 (0.74)	9.6 (0.57)
Asian, single race	13.0 (1.57)	15.7 (1.71)	9.4 (1.26)
Other races & multiple races	23.6 (4.52)	28.8 (4.26)	11.3 (1.84)
EDUCATION[3]			
Less than high school	31.2 (1.06)	35.1 (1.10)	26.1 (1.07)
High school diploma or GED[4]	19.1 (0.55)	22.3 (0.60)	14.8 (0.50)
More than high school	10.4 (0.36)	14.3 (0.41)	7.0 (0.29)
EMPLOYMENT STATUS[5]			
Employed	17.9 (0.48)	22.3 (0.52)	13.8 (0.45)
Unemployed	47.4 (2.16)	51.8 (2.11)	33.5 (2.06)
Not in workforce	19.9 (0.77)	23.6 (0.83)	14.5 (0.62)

Percentage of persons who lacked health insurance coverage at the time of interview, for at least part of the past year, or for more than a year, by selected demographic characteristics: United States, January, 2007–June, 2007.

[1]A person was defined as uninsured if he or she did not have any private health insurance, Medicare, Medicaid, State Children's Health Insurance Program (SCHIP), state-sponsored or other government-sponsored health plan, or military plan.
[2]A year is defined as the 12 months prior to interview.
[3]Education and marital status are shown only for persons aged 18 years and over.
[4]GED is General Educational Development high school equivalency diploma.
[5]Employment status is shown only for persons 18–64 years of age.

(*Source:* Family Core component of the 2007 National Health Interview Survey. The estimates for 2007 are based on data collected in January through June. Data are based on household interviews of a sample of the civilian non-institutionalized population.)

G Interview three students using the questions you wrote.

H In a small group, choose one of the three graphs or charts presented in this lesson. Recreate the graph or chart using information from the students in your class.

Answers for Exercise F:
1. What percent of employed people have been uninsured for more than one year?
2. Which ethnic group was least insured at the time of the interview?
3. Does education make a difference to how much insurance you have?
4. What percent of people with only a GED had insurance part of last year?
5. What percent of uninsured were not in the workforce at the time of the interview?
6. Which racial/ethnic group was insured 92.9% of the time for more than one year?

Addictions

GOAL ➤ **Identify addictions**

Ⓐ Look up the word *addiction* in a dictionary. Write the definition and an example sentence that uses the word. (Answers will vary. Sample answer is given.)

addiction *n.* _the state of being addicted compulsively to something_

He has an addiction to lying.

Ⓑ Work with a partner and brainstorm a list of addictions. (Answers will vary.)

Nicotine, alcohol, cocaine, coffee, heroin, chocolate, shopping, food, etc.

Ⓒ Match the words below to their correct definitions and write the complete sentences on another piece of paper. Use a dictionary if you need to.

1. Tolerance is __g__.

2. Impairment is __f__.

3. Substance addiction is __b__.

4. Physiological dependence is __j__.

5. A twelve-step program is __c__.

6. Psychological dependence is __d__.

7. Process addiction is __e__.

8. Detoxification is __h__.

9. Withdrawal is __a__.

10. An addict is __i__.

a. the process of giving up a substance or activity to which a person has become addicted

b. a condition in which a person is dependent on some chemical substance, such as cocaine or heroin

c. a plan for overcoming an addiction by going through twelve stages of personal development

d. a condition in which a person requires certain activities or the intake of some substance in order to maintain mental stability

e. a condition in which a person is dependent on some type of behavior, such as gambling or shopping

f. an inability to carry on normal, everyday functions because of an addiction

g. the ability of the body to endure a certain amount of a substance

h. the process of adjusting to the absence of some substance or activity that a person has become addicted

i. a person physically or emotionally dependent on a substance or an activity

j. a condition in which a person's body requires certain behaviors or the intake of some substance, without which it will become physically ill

Objective: Identify addictions
Grammar: Adverb clauses of concession
Academic Strategies: Defining words, using a dictionary
Vocabulary: *addiction, tolerance, impairment, substance, physiological, psychological, process, detoxification, withdrawal*

RESOURCES
Activity Bank: Unit 5, Lesson 4, Worksheets 1–2
Grammar Challenge 5: Unit 5, Challenge 4

■ 1.5 hour classes ■ 2.5 hour classes ■ 3⁺ hour classes

AGENDA

Define addiction.

Learn vocabulary related to addictions.

Distinguish between substance and process addictions.

Work with adverb clauses of concession.

Write about an addiction.

Warm-up and Review   10-15 mins.

Have students take out their graphs from the previous lesson. Ask volunteers from each group to present the graph to the class.

Introduction   5-10 mins.

Dictation:

1. She spends over $500 a month on clothes and shoes.
2. He likes to go to the horse races every weekend and place bets.
3. Her brother plays video games with his friends for more than three hours a day.
4. They exercise at least four hours a day, six days a week.

State the objective: *Today we will identify different addictions and discuss vocabulary associated with addictions.*

Presentation 1   10-15 mins.

A Look up the word *addiction* in a dictionary. Write the definition and an example sentence that uses the word.

Have students do this exercise by themselves and then go over the definitions and example sentences as a class.

Ask students to look back at their dictation sentences. Ask them if they think the people described in these sentences have addictions.

B Work with a partner and brainstorm a list of addictions.

Once students have completed their lists, make a comprehensive list on the board.

Practice 1   10-15 mins.

C Match the words below to their correct definitions and write the complete sentences on another piece of paper. Use a dictionary if you need to.

STANDARDS CORRELATIONS

CASAS: (See CASAS Competency List on pages 187–193.)
SCANS: **Information** Acquire and evaluate information, organize and maintain information, interpret and communicate information
Interpersonal Participate as a member of a team, negotiate to arrive at a decision, work with cultural diversity
Systems Monitor and correct performance
Basic Skills Reading, writing, arithmetic, listening, speaking

Thinking Skills Think creatively, make decisions, solve problems, see things in the mind's eye
Personal Qualities Responsibility, sociability, self-management
EFF: **Communication** Read with understanding, convey ideas in writing, speak so others can understand, listen actively, observe critically
Decision Making Solve problems and make decisions, plan
Interpersonal Cooperate with others
Lifelong Learning Take responsibility for learning, reflect and evaluate

Evaluation 1 5 mins. ■■□□

Go over the answers as a class.

Practice 1 *(continued)*

D Look at the list of addictions below. Which ones are substance (S) addictions and which ones are process (P) addictions? Circle your choice.

Presentation 2 5–10 mins. ■■■□

E In a small group, discuss the following questions.

Once students have discussed the questions in groups, discuss them as a class.

Practice 2 10–15 mins. ■■□□

Note: Shorter classes can do this exercise for homework.

F Read the statements below. Do you think each person has an addiction problem? Circle *yes* or *no* and then give a reason for your answer.

Have students do this exercise by themselves.

Evaluation 2 10–15 mins. ■■□□

Put students in small groups and have them discuss their answers. Tell them there are no right or wrong answers, especially since there are not many details given.

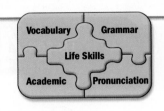

D Look at the list of addictions below. Which ones are substance (S) addictions and which ones are process (P) addictions? Circle your choice.

Addictions		
alcohol ⓈP	food ⓈP	shopping S Ⓟ
caffeine ⓈP	gambling S Ⓟ	video games S Ⓟ
prescription medicine ⓈP	surfing the Internet S Ⓟ	work S Ⓟ
illegal drugs ⓈP	smoking (nicotine) ⓈP	

E In a small group, discuss the following questions. (Answers will vary.)

1. Why do people become addicts? Either physical or psychological dependence.

2. What can you do if you are addicted to something? Seek help from a doctor.

3. What can you do to help a friend or family member who is addicted to something?
Support them. Give them information about recovery programs.

F Read the statements below. Do you think each person has an addiction problem? Circle *yes* or *no* and then give a reason for your answer. (Answers will vary.)

1. Although my uncle Gerry sold his car to spend more time gaming in Las Vegas, he says he doesn't have a gambling problem.
   Addiction: ⓨes no **Reason:** A car is needed to work and live. This is an irresponsible choice.

2. Even though her sister spends thousands of dollars a month on her credit cards, she doesn't think she is a shopaholic.
   Addiction: ⓨes no **Reason:** If you outspend your budget, you have out of control spending.

3. Danielle is convinced she isn't addicted to caffeine although she has to drink two cups of coffee before she can get out of bed in the morning.
   Addiction: ⓨes no **Reason:** If you need to consume something before you can take action, you are an addict.

4. In spite of the fact that Fletcher plays video games for three hours a night instead of doing his homework, he denies he has a problem.
   Addiction: yes ⓝo **Reason:** Maybe he has difficulty with schoolwork and he is avoiding it.

G Study the chart with your classmates and teacher.

Adverb Clauses of Concession	
Dependent clause	**Independent clause**
Although he spends a lot of time in Las Vegas,	he says he doesn't have a gambling problem.
Even though her sister spends thousands of dollars a month,	she doesn't think she is a shopaholic.
Though she has to drink two cups of coffee before she can get out of bed in the morning,	she is convinced she isn't addicted to caffeine.
In spite of the fact that he plays video games for three hours a night,	he denies he has a problem.

Explanation: Adverb clauses of concession show a contrast in ideas. The main or independent clauses show the unexpected outcome. The unexpected outcome in the third example is that it is surprising that she thinks she isn't addicted to caffeine.

Note: The clauses can be reversed and have the same meaning. Do not use a comma if the independent clause comes first in the sentence.

Example: *She doesn't think she is a shopaholic even though she spends thousands of dollars a month.*

H Create sentences with dependent and independent clauses. Use the ideas below and the sentences in the chart as examples. (Answers will vary.)

EXAMPLE: <u>Even though he smokes two packs of cigarettes a day, he doesn't think he</u>

<u>is addicted to nicotine.</u>

 nicotine addition/smokes two packs a day
Internet addiction/spends five hours a day online
shopping addiction/goes to the mall at least once a day
food addiction/weighs over 300 pounds
drug addiction/sold all his clothes to buy more drugs

1. <u>Even though she spends 5 hours a day online, she denies an Internet addiction.</u>

2. <u>Although he goes to the mall at least once a day, he is convinced he doesn't have a shopping addiction.</u>

3. <u>In spite of the fact that she weighs over 300 pounds, she denies a food addiction.</u>

4. <u>Though he sold all his clothes to buy more drugs, he doesn't think he has a drug addiction.</u>

I Imagine a good friend of yours has an addiction to something. Write about his or her addiction. How is it affecting your friend's life? How is it affecting your life? How is your friendship different because of it? (Answers will vary.)

Presentation 3   10-15 mins. ▪▪▪

G Study the chart with your classmates and teacher.

To help students better understand the meaning of the sentences, have them come up with a few of their own and write them on the board for the class to analyze.

Practice 3   10-15 mins. ▪

Note: Shorter classes can do this exercise for homework.

H Create sentences with dependent and independent clauses. Use the ideas below and the sentences in the chart as examples.

Evaluation 3   10-15 mins. ▪

Have volunteers write their sentences on the board for the class to see.

Application   10-20 mins. ▪▪▪

I Imagine a good friend of yours has an addiction to something. Write about his or her addiction. How is it affecting your friend's life? How is it affecting your life? How is your friendship different because of it?

The reason for the imaginary addiction is to raise students' comfort level. You may decide to make this a lighthearted exercise by suggesting they write about something funny, for example, an addiction to chocolate or an addiction to learning English.

Give students an example by talking about one of your own addictions.

Example description of an addiction: *I am addicted to exercise. The first thing I do when I wake up in the morning is go for a run. When I get to work, I park as far away from the building as possible, so I have to walk far to get to my office. Every hour, I take five minutes and do something . . . stretching, jumping jacks, push-ups. During my lunch break, I walk up and down the stairs for 40 minutes. After work, I go for a two-hour bike ride. My family and friends complain that I am too skinny. They also say I never have enough time to spend with them because I am always exercising. My coworkers complain that I never have lunch*

with them. I really like the way I look and feel. But maybe I need to start exercising less. What do you think?

Activity Bank

Unit 5, Lesson 4, Worksheet 1: Substance Abuse and
                                Addiction (reading)

Unit 5, Lesson 4, Worksheet 2: Adverb Clauses of
                                Concession

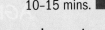 Refer students to *Stand Out 5 Grammar Challenge*, Unit 5, Challenge 4 for more practice with adverb clauses of concession.

Instructor's Notes

_____

_____

_____

_____

_____

_____

_____

_____

_____

_____

_____

_____

_____

_____

_____

_____

_____

_____

AT-A-GLANCE PREP

Objective: Interpret procedures for first aid
Academic Strategy: Problem solving
Vocabulary: *first-aid kit items, burn, choking, poisoning, open wound, head injury, shock, external bleeding, strike, treat*

RESOURCES

Activity Bank: Unit 5, Lesson 5, Worksheet 1
Grammar Challenge 5: Unit 5, Challenge 5

■ 1.5 hour classes   ■ 2.5 hour classes   ■ 3⁺ hour classes

AGENDA

Label items in a first-aid kit.
Determine appropriate first-aid procedures for various injuries.

Suggested Realia: First-aid kit, items from a first-aid kit

Warm-up and Review   5-10 mins.

Ask students if they have had or been part of a medical emergency. Encourage a class discussion about the nature of the emergency, what they did, what the results were, etc.

Introduction   5-10 mins.

Dictation:

1. If someone has been poisoned, you should not give him anything to eat or drink.
2. Do not give a choking victim water.
3. If someone is in shock, you should not raise his or her head.
4. Do not put any creams or grease on burned skin.

State the objective: *Today we will talk about first-aid kits and interpret first-aid procedures.*

Tell students that the information in this lesson doesn't take the place of a good first aid class. Encourage students to take a first aid and/or a CPR (Cardio Pulmonary Resuscitation) class at their local hospital or fire station or community college. Classes are often free or inexpensive to take.

Presentation 1   10-15 mins.

With books closed, write *First-Aid Kit* on the board and have students help you brainstorm what they might find in a first-aid kit. Don't give them any answers; just see what they can come up with. If you brought items to class with you, you might show a few of them and see if students know what they are called.

Practice 1   5-10 mins.

(A) What does a first-aid kit have in it? Use the words in the box to label each item.

Evaluation 1   10-15 mins.

(B) Do you have a first-aid kit at home or in your car? Why is each item important? Discuss your ideas with your classmates.

STANDARDS CORRELATIONS

CASAS: 3.4.3 (See CASAS Competency List on pages 187–193.)
SCANS: **Resources** Allocate materials and facility resources, allocate human resources
Information Acquire and evaluate information, organize and maintain information, interpret and communicate information
Interpersonal Participate as a member of a team, teach others, serve clients and customers, exercise leadership, negotiate to arrive at a decision, work with cultural diversity
Systems Monitor and correct performance
Basic Skills Reading, writing, listening, speaking

Thinking Skills Think creatively, make decisions, solve problems, see things in the mind's eye
Personal Qualities Responsibility, sociability, self-management
EFF: **Communication** Read with understanding, convey ideas in writing, speak so others can understand, listen actively, observe critically
Decision Making Solve problems and make decisions, plan
Interpersonal Cooperate with others, advocate and influence, resolve conflict and negotiate, guide others
Lifelong Learning Take responsibility for learning, reflect and evaluate, learn through research

 LESSON **5**

First aid

GOAL ➤ **Interpret procedures for first aid**

A What does a first-aid kit have in it? Use the words in the box to label each item.

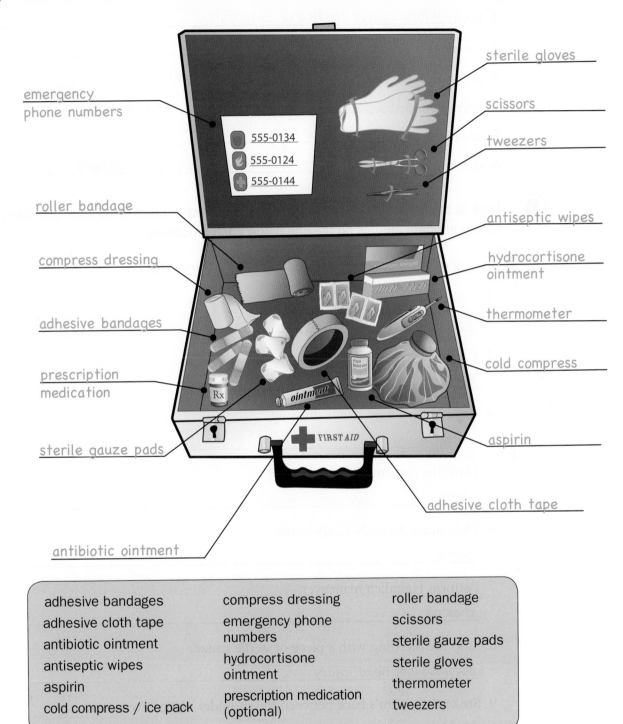

emergency phone numbers

sterile gloves

scissors

tweezers

555-0134
555-0124
555-0144

roller bandage

antiseptic wipes

compress dressing

hydrocortisone ointment

thermometer

adhesive bandages

prescription medication

cold compress

sterile gauze pads

aspirin

adhesive cloth tape

antibiotic ointment

adhesive bandages	compress dressing	roller bandage
adhesive cloth tape	emergency phone numbers	scissors
antibiotic ointment	hydrocortisone ointment	sterile gauze pads
antiseptic wipes		sterile gloves
aspirin	prescription medication (optional)	thermometer
cold compress / ice pack		tweezers

B Do you have a first-aid kit at home or in your car? Why is each item important? Discuss your ideas with your classmates. (Answers will vary.)

C Define the following injuries. (Answers may vary.)

1. burn: <u>injury caused by fire or chemicals</u>

2. choking: <u>something caught in airway</u>

3. poisoning: <u>dangerous chemical, drink, or food ingested</u>

4. open wound: <u>injury where layers below skin are exposed</u>

5. head injury: <u>injury to head area</u>

6. shock: <u>injury to body where blood pressure drops and systems begin to stop functioning</u>

D Look at the list of first-aid procedures below. Which injuries does each one apply to? Write the appropriate injuries on the line below each procedure.

1. Call 911. <u>choking, poisoning, head injury, shock</u>

2. Call Poison Control.

   <u>poisoning</u>

3. Control external bleeding.

   <u>open wound, head injury</u>

4. Cover with a light gauze dressing.

   <u>burn</u>

5. Have the person lie down.

   <u>shock</u>

6. Help maintain body temperature.

   <u>shock</u>

7. Perform Heimlich maneuver.

   <u>choking</u>

8. Stop the bleeding with a piece of sterile gauze.

   <u>open wound, head injury</u>

9. Strike the victim's back between the shoulder blades five times.

   <u>choking</u>

10. Treat wounds.

    <u>burn, open wound, head injury</u>

Presentation 2   5-10 mins. ■■■

Pronounce the injuries one at a time and ask if students know what each one is. It is OK to discuss them a bit but not too much since students will be writing formal definitions in Practice 2.

Practice 2   15-20 mins. ■■

Note: Shorter classes can do these exercises for homework.

(C) Define the following injuries.

Encourage students to use dictionaries to complete this exercise.

(D) Look at the list of first-aid procedures below. Which injuries does each one apply to? Write the appropriate injuries on the line below each procedure.

Evaluation 2   10-15 mins. ■■

Go over the injuries as a class. Do not go over the answers to Exercise D. Students will do this by themselves in Practice 3.

Presentation 3   15-20 mins. ■■■

Go over the chart as a class, discussing each procedure and the *do's* and *don'ts*. Demonstrate some of the procedures if you need to.

Present instructions for Exercise E to students. Show them how to find each procedure from Exercise D in the chart and see if they wrote the correct injuries on the lines.

Practice 3   10-15 mins. ■

Note: Shorter classes can do this exercise for homework.

E Read the chart below. Compare the information with your answers in Exercise D. Were you right?

Evaluation 3   ■

Walk around the classroom and help students as needed.

Application   10-20 mins. ■■■

F Divide the class into victims and good citizens. All "victims" should write one of the injuries from page 104 on an index card or piece of paper. Walk up to another student in the classroom and show him or her your card. Ask him or her what he or she would do. All "good citizens" should tell victims what you can do to help his or her injury.

Read the directions together. Then ask a few volunteers to demonstrate this activity before students do it by themselves. Have students switch roles so they have an opportunity to both be a victim and to give first aid advice.

Activity Bank

Unit 5, Lesson 5, Worksheet 1: First-Aid Kit

Refer students to *Stand Out 5 Grammar Challenge*, Unit 5, Challenge 5 for practice with adverbial clauses of purpose and manner.

There are also two extension challenges. Extension Challenges 1 and 2 both give practice with adverbial clauses of condition.

LESSON 5 **GOAL** ➤ **Interpret procedures for first aid**

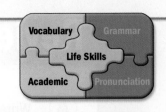

 Read the chart below. Compare the information with your answers in Exercise D. Were you right?

First-Aid Procedures*		
Injury	**Do**	**Don't**
burn	Run cold water over burn area for 15 minutes. Cover the burn with a light gauze dressing. If blisters pop, apply a light antibiotic ointment and cover with light gauze dressing.	**Don't** put any creams or greases on the burned area. **Don't** pop any blisters. **Don't** use an ice pack.
choking	Call 911. Strike the victim's back between the shoulder blades five times. Perform Heimlich maneuver.	**Don't** give water to the person.
poisoning	Call 911 (if person is unconscious or having trouble breathing). Call Poison Control (800-222-1222).	**Don't** induce vomiting. **Don't** give the person anything to eat or drink.
open wound	Stop the bleeding with a piece of sterile gauze. Wash with soap and water (if minor), apply a thin layer of antibiotic ointment, and cover with a bandage.	**Don't** remove any object protruding from injury. **Don't** wash or apply ointment to a large, deep wound.
head injury	Call 911 if person is unconscious or drowsy. Treat wounds. Ice a small bump.	**Don't** leave the person alone, especially when sleeping. Instead, wake up every two to three hours and have the person answer simple questions.
shock	Call 911. Have the person lie down. Control external bleeding. Help maintain body temperature.	**Don't** raise the person's head. **Don't** give the person food or drink.

* Not all first-aid procedures for each injury are listed.

F Divide the class into victims and good citizens. All "victims" should write one of the injuries from page 104 on an index card or piece of paper. Walk up to another student in the classroom and show him or her your card. Ask him or her what he or she would do. All "good citizens" should tell victims what you can do to help his or her injury.

EXAMPLE:
Victim: (Shows Good Citizen card that reads "Choking.")
Good Citizen says to Victim: "I'm going to call 911. Then, I'm going to strike your back five times between your shoulder blades. If that doesn't work, I'm going to perform the Heimlich maneuver. I will not give you water."

Review

Write one healthy solution for each problem. (Lesson 1) (Answers may vary. Sample answers are given.)

1. Problem: eating fast food three times a week because no time to cook

   Solution: _prepare food in advance_

2. Problem: high blood pressure and at risk for diabetes

   Solution: _lose weight, exercise_

3. Problem: really stressed at work

   Solution: _meditate, talk to boss, exercise_

4. Problem: overweight children

   Solution: _family should exercise together_

Read the bill and write four questions you would ask the doctor's office about it. (Lesson 2)
(Answers will vary. Sample questions are given.)

PATIENT NAME: Reed, Jacob			PROVIDER NAME: Robert Wickern, M.D.	
Date	**Procedure**	**Description of Service**	**Co-Pay**	**Amount Payable**
8/23/2008	99391	Well-Child Check		$150.00
8/23/2008	90700	DTaP Vaccine		$30.00
8/23/2008	90465	Vaccine Admin		$44.00
8/23/2008	90645	Hib Vaccine		$32.00
8/23/2008	90466	Vaccine Admin		$64.00
8/23/2008		Patient Co-Pay	-$25.00	
9/17/2008		Primary Insurance Payment		-$200.00
9/17/2008		Uncollectible		-$75.00
			Amount Due	

1. _How much does the patient owe?_
2. _Why is $75 uncollectible?_
3. _Who do I pay?_
4. _When is this bill due?_

Work with a partner and have a conversation between a patient and the doctor's office with the questions you wrote. Switch roles. (Lesson 2)

AT-A-GLANCE PREP

Objectives: All unit objectives
Grammar: All unit grammar
Academic Strategy: Reviewing
Vocabulary: All Unit 5 vocabulary

RESOURCES

Stand Out 5 Assessment CD-ROM with Exam*View*®

■ 1.5 hour classes ■ 2.5 hour classes ■ 3⁺ hour classes

AGENDA

Discuss unit objectives.
Complete the review.
Use unit vocabulary.

Warm-up and Review   5-10 mins.

Ask students if they've examined their first aid kit at home since the previous lesson. Have them name items that are different in their kits at home that weren't discussed in the lesson. Ask them to think about medical emergencies they've experienced and discuss what equipment might have been helpful at that time.

Introduction   5-10 mins. ■■■

Ask students as a class to try to recall all the objectives of this unit without looking back in their books. The objectives for this unit include identifying practices that promote mental and physical well-being, asking about medical bills, interpreting health insurance information, identifying addictions, and interpreting procedures for first aid. Write all the objectives on the board from Unit 5. Show students the first page of the unit and mention the five objectives.

State the objective: *Today we will be reviewing everything we have learned in this unit and preparing for the team project.*

Presentation 1   10-15 mins. ■■■

This presentation will cover the first three pages of the review. Quickly go to the first page of each lesson. Discuss the objective of each. Ask simple questions to remind students of what they have learned.

Note: Since there is little presentation in the review, you can assign the review exercises that don't require collaboration with a partner or group for homework and go over them in class the following day.

Practice 1   20-25 mins. ■■■

Note: There are two ways to do the review:

1. Go through the exercises one at a time and, as students complete each one, go over the answers.

2. Quickly go through the instructions of each exercise, let students complete all of the exercises at once, and then go over the answers.

(A) Write one healthy solution for each problem. (Lesson 1)

(B) Read the bill and write four questions you would ask the doctor's office about it. (Lesson 2)

(C) Work with a partner and have a conversation between a patient and the doctor's office with the questions you wrote. Switch roles. (Lesson 2)

Evaluation 1   5-15 mins.

Go around the classroom and check on students' progress. Help individuals when needed. If you see consistent errors among several students, interrupt the class and give a mini-lesson or review to help students feel comfortable with the concept.

Practice 1 *(continued)*   25-30 mins. ■■■□

D Read the bar graph. Then, answer the questions below it. (Lesson 3)

E Write sentences on a separate piece of paper combining the ideas below. (Lesson 4)

F Write down six injuries you learned about in this unit. In a group, discuss the first-aid procedures for each injury in Exercise F. (Lesson 5)

Evaluation 1 *(continued)*   ■■■□

Go around the classroom and check on students' progress. Help individuals when needed. If you see consistent errors among several students, interrupt the class and give a mini-lesson or review to help students feel comfortable with the concept.

Teaching Tip

Recycling/Review

The review exercises, the research activity, and the team project are part of the recycling/review process. Students often need to be reintroduced to concepts to solidify what they have learned. Many concepts are learned and forgotten when students are engaged in learning other new concepts. This is because students learn but are not necessarily ready to acquire language concepts.

Therefore, it becomes very important to review material with students and to show them how to review it on their own. It is also important to recycle the new concepts in different contexts.

Instructor's Notes

D Read the bar graph. Then, answer the questions below it. (Lesson 3)

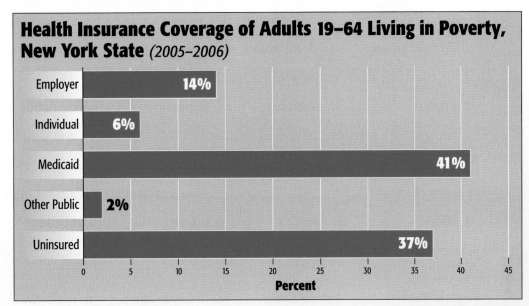

Health Insurance Coverage of Adults 19–64 Living in Poverty, New York State *(2005–2006)*

Employer — **14%**
Individual — **6%**
Medicaid — **41%**
Other Public — **2%**
Uninsured — **37%**

Percent (0, 5, 10, 15, 20, 25, 30, 35, 40, 45)

(*Sources:* Urban Institute and Kaiser Commission on Medicaid and the Uninsured estimates based on the Census Bureau's March 2006 and 2007 Current Population Survey (CPS: Annual Social and Economic Supplements). Web site: http://www.statehealthfacts. org/comparebar.jsp?ind=131&cat=3)

1. What percentage of adults is uninsured? _____37%_____

2. What percentage of adults is insured by their employers? _____14%_____

3. What percentage of adults is on Medicaid? _____41%_____

4. What percentage of adults has insurance coverage? _____63%_____

E Write sentences on a separate piece of paper combining the ideas below. (Lesson 4)

EXAMPLE: nicotine addiction/smokes two packs of cigarettes a day

Even though he smokes two packs of cigarettes a day, he doesn't think he

is addicted to nicotine.

1. exercise addiction/works out 3 times a day
2. sleeping addiction/sleeps 11 hours a night
3. food addiction/eats all day long
4. coffee addiction/drinks 4 cups a day

F Write down six injuries you learned about in this unit. In a group, discuss the first-aid procedures for each injury in Exercise F. (Lesson 5) (Answers may vary.)

_____burns_____   _____shock_____   _____poisoning_____

_____head injury_____   _____choking_____   _____open wound_____

VOCABULARY REVIEW

G Choose the correct word for each sentence.

1. _____Meditation_____ helps me relax when I've had a long day at work.

   a. Detoxification (b.) Meditation c. Tolerance d. Depression

2. They think she has a sleeping-pill _____addiction_____.

   a. process b. insurance c. depression (d.) addiction

3. If you are with someone who is in _____shock_____, you should call 911.

   (a.) shock b. out of shape c. meditation d. treatment

4. How would you _____treat_____ someone who has a head injury?

   a. affect (b.) treat c. impair d. insure

5. Jared's body has built up a _____tolerance_____ to alcohol since he has been drinking for so long.

   (a.) tolerance b. substance c. detoxification d. withdrawal

H Give two examples of each of the following items. (Answers will vary.)

1. Substance addictions: _____heroin_____ _____caffeine_____

2. Process addictions: _____shopping_____ _____gambling_____

3. First-aid kit items: _____cold compress_____ _____antibiotic ointment_____

4. Items on a medical bill: _____co-pay_____ _____uncollectible_____

I Write original sentences for each of the following terms. (Answers will vary.)

1. uninsured: _There are many uninsured people 18–24 years old._

2. at risk: _Trying drugs puts you at risk for addiction._

3. self-esteem: _People with high self-esteem often are healthy._

4. responsible party: _The responsible party pays the bills._

5. survive: _Call 911 to survive a bad car accident._

Practice 1 (continued)   25–30 mins. ■■■□

Vocabulary Review

G Choose the correct word for each sentence.

H Give two examples of each of the following items.

I Write original sentences for each of the following terms.

Evaluation 1 (continued)   ■■■□

Go around the classroom and check on students' progress. Help individuals when needed. If you see consistent errors among several students, interrupt the class and give a mini-lesson or review to help students feel comfortable with the concept.

TB **Assessment** (optional)   ■■■□

Use the Stand Out 5 Assessment CD-ROM with Exam*View*® to create a post-test for Unit 5.

AT-A-GLANCE PREP

Objective: Find health-related resources
Academic Strategy: Research
Vocabulary: See lesson

RESOURCES

Suggested Realia: Internet, telephone book

AGENDA

*Research health-related resources
in the community.
Use three different research methods.*

Academic Feature: Research

Each unit will have a research page where students are required to complete a task by conducting research. Options will be given for students to use the Internet as well as printed resource materials. The printed resource materials can be found on the Activity Bank CD-ROM.

Introduction   1 min.

State the objective: *Today we will find health-related resources in our community using different research methods.*

Presentation   10–15 mins.

(A) There are many health-related resources in every community. If you wanted to find the following local resources, what would you do?

Have students complete this exercise individually and then discuss it as a class.

Practice   15–20 mins.

(B) Using three different research methods, find the locations and contact information for the following community resources. Write down the name of one specific place you found with each research method.

This exercise gives students a chance to conduct research in three different ways, at least one of which they can do in the classroom.

Evaluation   10–15 mins.

Have students share what they learned with the class.

STANDARDS CORRELATIONS

CASAS: 4.9.3, 7.2.1, 7.4.4, 7.4.5, 7.4.6 (See CASAS Competency List on pages 187–193.)
SCANS: **Information** Acquire and evaluate information, organize and maintain information, interpret and communicate information, use computers to process information *(optional)*
Interpersonal Participate as a member of a team, teach others, negotiate to arrive at a decision, work with cultural diversity
Systems Understand systems
Technology Select technology, apply technology to a task, maintain and troubleshoot technology *(optional)*

Basic Skills Reading, writing
Thinking Skills Think creatively, make decisions, see things in the mind's eye
Personal Qualities Responsibility, sociability, self-management
EFF: **Communication** Read with understanding, convey ideas in writing, observe critically
Decision Making Solve problems and make decisions, plan
Lifelong Learning Take responsibility for learning, reflect and evaluate, learn through research, use information and communications technology *(optional)*

Research Project

A There are many health-related resources in every community. If you wanted to find the following local resources, what would you do?

1. gym: _____

2. eye doctor: _____

3. medical clinic: _____

B Using three different research methods, find the locations and contact information for the following community resources. Write down the name of one specific place you found with each research method.

Community resource	Internet	Phone book	Friends and/or Family
swimming pool Name: _____			
drug-and-alcohol rehabilitation center Name: _____			
health clinic Name: _____			
dentist Name: _____			
fire station Name: _____			
first aid/CPR course Name: _____			
ambulance service Name: _____			
health insurance Name: _____			

Team Project

Give a presentation on a health-related topic.

Presentation Topics
- Healthy Practices
- Medical Bills
- Health Insurance
- Addictions
- First Aid

1. Form a team with four or five students. Decide which topic your team will work on. (Each team should choose a different topic.)

2. Choose positions for each member of your team.

POSITION	JOB DESCRIPTION	STUDENT NAME
Student 1: **Project Leader**	See that everyone speaks English. See that everyone participates.	
Student 2: **Secretary**	Take notes on your team's ideas.	
Student 3: **Coordinator**	Divide presentation into parts. Assign each team member one part of presentation.	
Student 4: **Director**	Organize presentation so that individual parts create a unified whole.	
Student 5: **Members**	Do assigned part of presentation. Supportively critique other members' work as they rehearse their parts of presentation.	

3. Gather information for your presentation from this book and other sources.

4. Decide how to present your material creatively. For example, you can use charts, skits, or encourage class participation.

5. Create any materials needed for your presentation.

6. Practice your presentation.

7. Give your presentation to the class.

Give a presentation on a health-related topic.

Each team will prepare a presentation for the class based on one of the topics from the unit. The presentation should include information from the unit as well as from additional research.

The team project is the final application for the unit. It gives students a chance to show that they have mastered all the Unit 5 objectives.

Note: Shorter classes can extend this project over two class meetings.

Stage 1   5-10 mins.

Form a team with four or five students. Decide which topic your team will work on. (Each team should choose a different topic.)

Stage 2   10-15 mins.

Choose positions for each member of your team.

Have students decide who will lead each step as described on the student page. Provide well-defined directions on the board for how teams should proceed. Explain that all the students do every step as a team. Teams shouldn't go to the next stage until the previous one is complete.

Stage 3   15-20 mins.

Gather information for your presentation from this book and other sources.

Tell students to use what they learned in class as well as gather any additional research they can.

Stage 4   10-15 mins.

Decide how to present your material creatively. For example, you can use charts, skits, or encourage class participation.

As a class, brainstorm different methods of presentation. Try to make the list exhaustive so that every team doesn't use the same presentation format. Briefly discuss how some presentation methods lend themselves better to some material. Encourage the teams to use at least two different presentation methods in their presentations.

Stage 5   15-20 mins.

Create any materials needed for your presentation.

Anticipate materials students might need for the presentation such as health magazines, computer print outs, poster board, glue and markers.

Optional Computer Activity: Students may want to use the computer to create presentation materials.

Stage 6   20-30 mins.

Practice your presentation.

Remind students that each team member must be involved in the presentation.

Stage 7   15-20 mins.

Give your presentation to the class.

STANDARDS CORRELATIONS

CASAS: 4.8.1, 4.8.5, 4.8.6 (See CASAS Competency List on pages 187–193.)
SCANS: Resources Allocate time
Information Acquire and evaluate information, organize and maintain information, interpret and communicate information, use computers to process information
Systems Understand systems, improve and design systems
Technology Select technology, apply technology to exercise
Basic Skills Writing
Thinking Skills Think creatively, make decisions, solve problems, see things in the mind's eye, use reasoning

Personal Qualities Responsibility, self-esteem, self-management, integrity
EFF: **Communication** Read with understanding, convey ideas in writing, speak so others can understand, listen actively, observe critically
Decision Making Solve problems and make decisions, plan
Interpersonal Cooperate with others, advocate and influence, resolve conflict and negotiate, guide others
Lifelong Learning Take responsibility for learning, reflect and evaluate, learn through research, use information and communications technology *(optional)*

AT-A-GLANCE PREP

Objective: Introduce new vocabulary
Academic Strategies: Categorizing vocabulary, using a dictionary
Vocabulary: See lesson.

RESOURCES

Dictionaries: It is recommended that each student in class have an ESL learner's dictionary or that there be dictionaries available in the classroom for students to use. Dictionaries that will be referred to in this book are the *Heinle's Newbury House Dictionary of American English* and the *Collins Cobuild Intermediate* or *Advanced Dictionary of American English*.

Academic Feature: Vocabulary Builder

Each unit will begin with a vocabulary-building section. The purpose of this two-page section is to introduce students to many of the words they will be using in the unit lessons. Students will have a chance to see how much they already know, and they will get exposure to the new vocabulary found in the unit.

Note: All of the exercises on these two pages should be done in class, no matter the class length. Longer classes can do this lesson and then move onto Lesson 1 during the same class meeting; shorter classes may have to devote one whole class meeting to this lesson.

Introduction
1 min.

State the objective: *Today we will be identifying and working with the vocabulary you will learn in this unit.*

Presentation 1
5 mins.

Talk about the picture as a class. Ask students what they see, what is happening, etc.

Practice 1
10–15 mins.

(A) Using the words in the box below, discuss the picture with a partner. Look up the words you do not know in a dictionary.

Evaluation 1
10–15 mins.

Talk about the picture as a class. Have students use the words from the box. Ask students which words they had to look up in a dictionary and make sure they understand the meanings.

STANDARDS CORRELATIONS

CASAS: 7.4.5 (See CASAS Competency List on pages 187–193.)
SCANS: **Information** Acquire and evaluate information, organize and maintain information
Interpersonal Participate as a member of a team, negotiate to arrive at a decision, work with cultural diversity
Systems Understand systems, monitor and correct performance
Basic Skills Reading, writing, listening, speaking
Thinking Skills Think creatively, make decisions, see things in the mind's eye

Personal Qualities Responsibility, sociability, self-management
EFF: **Communication** Read with understanding, convey ideas in writing, speak so others can understand, listen actively
Decision Making Use math to solve problems and communicate, solve problems and make decisions, plan
Interpersonal Cooperate with others
Lifelong Learning Take responsibility for learning, reflect and evaluate, learn through research

Retail

GOALS

➤ Do product research
➤ Purchase goods and services by phone and Internet

➤ Interpret product guarantees and warranties
➤ Return a product
➤ Sell a product

Vocabulary Builder

Vocabulary | Grammar
Life Skills
Academic | Pronunciation

 A Using the words in the box below, discuss the picture with a partner. Look up the words you do not know in a dictionary. (Answers will vary.)

EXAMPLE: *This woman is asking the salesperson about the product warranty.*

convince	exchange	free of charge	guarantee
make	model	policy	quality
receipt	refund	research	return
review	transaction	warranty	

Vocabulary Builder

B Look at the following goals in this unit. Then, look back at the words and phrases from Exercise A. Decide which words and phrases go with each goal. Write them on the lines after each goal. (Some words and phrases can be used with more than one goal.)

1. Do product research: _make, review, model, free of charge, policy, research,_ _warranty, guarantee, quality_

2. Purchase goods and services by phone and Internet: _receipt, transaction,_ _free of charge, policy, model, transaction_

3. Interpret product guarantees and warranties: _receipt, exchange, refund, policy,_ _warranty, guarantee, quality, return_

4. Return a product: _receipt, review, exchange, refund, policy, guarantee, return_

5. Sell a product: _convince, warranty, guarantee, quality, review, free of charge_

C Knowing a synonym for an unfamiliar word will often help you better understand its meaning. Find synonyms for the words below in a dictionary or thesaurus.

Word	Synonym
1. allege	claim
2. conform	comply
3. convince	persuade
4. exchange	give back to/take another of same value
5. fault	error
6. guarantee	promise
7. malfunction	break down
8. model	type
9. quality	value
10. refund	money given back
11. research	investigation
12. return	give/take back
13. review	opinion/look over

Presentation 2 5-10 mins.

Go over the instructions to Exercise B with students, briefly discussing each goal. Do an example or two with students before they complete the exercise on their own. For example, ask *Which goal or goals does* convince *fit into?* (Sell a product or Purchase goods and services by phone and Internet)

Pronunciation

Vocabulary

When teaching students new vocabulary, pronounce each word for them several times and ask them to repeat it. Often, students may be familiar with the words you are introducing but have never seen them spelled out. By pronouncing the words for students, you allow students to make a connection between the words' spellings and their sounds. It is also important that students learn the correct pronunciation of new words so they feel comfortable using their new vocabulary inside and outside of the classroom.

Practice 2 10-15 mins.

B Look at the following goals in this unit. Then, look back at the words and phrases from Exercise A. Decide which words and phrases go with each goal. Write them on the lines after each goal. (Some words and phrases can be used with more than one goal.)

Evaluation 2 5-10 mins.

Go over the answers as a class.

Practice 3 10-15 mins.

C Knowing a synonym for an unfamiliar word will often help you better understand its meaning. Find synonyms for the words below in a dictionary or thesaurus.

Remind students what a synonym is. Ask them to see if they can come up with any on their own before turning to a dictionary or thesaurus.

Evaluation 3 5-10 mins.

Go over the answers as a class.

Instructor's Notes

_____
_____
_____
_____
_____
_____
_____
_____
_____
_____
_____
_____
_____
_____
_____
_____
_____
_____
_____
_____
_____
_____
_____
_____
_____
_____
_____
_____
_____
_____
_____
_____
_____
_____

AT-A-GLANCE PREP

Objective: Do product research
Academic Strategies: Focused listening,
  writing a review
Vocabulary: *research, review, make, model, quality*

RESOURCES

Activity Bank: Unit 6, Lesson 1, Worksheets 1–2
Grammar Challenge 5: Unit 6, Challenge 1
Audio: CD Track 28

 1.5 hour classes   2.5 hour classes   3⁺ hour classes

AGENDA

*Listen to a conversation between
  a salesperson and a customer.
Read product reviews.
Research a product.*

Suggested Realia: Consumer magazines, printouts from
  Web sites with reviews
Stand Out 5 Assessment CD-ROM with Exam*View*®

Pre-assessment *(optional)*

Use the Stand Out 5 Assessment CD-ROM with
Exam*View*® to create a pre-test for Unit 6.

Warm-up and Review   5 mins.

Ask students to think about big purchases
they have made within the last year (car,
house, computer, camera, etc.). Ask volunteers
to share what they bought and where they
bought it.

Introduction   5-10 mins.

Dictation:

1. How long will the battery last if I start with a
   full charge?
2. With this plan, how many minutes do I get
   per month?
3. Are nights and weekends free and what time
   do they start?
4. Are calls to my friends and family on the same
   network free?

After completing the dictation, ask students what
these questions pertain to. (cell phones)

State the objective: *Today, we'll be doing product
research.*

Ask students how many of them did research
before they made the purchase they discussed in

the Warm-up and Review. Ask them what kind
of research they did and how they did it.

Presentation 1   10-15 mins.

Write the word *bed* on the board. Ask students to
raise their hands if they have bought a bed before.
Ask them what they would want to find out before
buying a bed. Write their ideas on the board.
(price, comfort, stain-proof, pillow top, etc.)

(A) Imagine you are going to buy the following
products. In a group, discuss what information you
need to research before you make your purchases.
Write you ideas on the line beside each item.

Practice 1   10-15 mins.

(B) Listen to the conversation Maya is having
with the salesperson. What does she want to
know about the patio set? Write her questions
below. Some questions are embedded.

Note: The listening script is on page 114a.

Evaluation 1   5 mins.

Go over the answers as a class.

(C) How did the salesperson answer the
questions above? Discuss these answers with
your classmates.

STANDARDS CORRELATIONS

CASAS: 1.2.5, 7.4.4 (See CASAS Competency List on pages 187–193.)
SCANS: **Information** Acquire and evaluate information
Interpersonal Participate as a member of a team, teach others, work
with cultural diversity
Systems Understand systems, monitor and correct performance, improve
and design systems
Technology Select technology, apply technology to a task
Basic Skills Reading, writing, listening, speaking

Thinking Skills Think creatively, make decisions
Personal Qualities Responsibility, sociability, self-management
EFF: **Communication** Read with understanding, convey ideas in writing,
speak so others can understand, listen actively, observe critically
Decision Making Solve problems and make decisions, plan
Interpersonal Cooperate with others, advocate and influence, guide others
Lifelong Learning Take responsibility for learning, reflect and evaluate,
learn through research, use information and communications technology

How much is it?

GOAL ➤ Do product research

A Imagine that you are going to buy the following products. In a group, discuss what information you need to research before you make your purchases. Write your ideas on the line next to each item.

1. a bed: price, standards, warranty, quality

2. a refrigerator: size, price, features: freezer, ice maker, energy use

3. a television: size, price, warranty, installation fee

4. a cell phone: price, monthly payments, minutes, plan, features

5. an air conditioner: price, size, energy usage

6. a car: price, style, MPG, gas usage, repair records, review

CD
TR 28

B Listen to the conversation Maya is having with the salesperson. What does she want to know about the patio set? Write her questions below. Some questions are embedded.

1. Could you answer some questions about patio furniture?

2. Is it lightweight? Easy to move?

3. How can I clean it?

4. I wasn't sure if it had to be re-sanded or what.

5. How does teak hold up in bad weather?

6. How much does this set (with table, umbrella, and 4 chairs) cost?

7. Can I use it (this 20% off coupon)?

8. Does it come with a warranty?

C How did the salesperson answer the questions above? Discuss these answers with your classmates.

D Look at the list of ways to research a product. Which methods have you used before?
(Answers will vary.)
- Ask friends and family
- Ask the salesperson
- Go online and read product reviews
- Read a consumer magazine

E Maya went online to research the patio furniture she saw in the store. Read the product reviews she found.

U-RATE-IT

http://U-Rate-It/patio_furniture

U-RATE-IT *Patio Furniture Reviews from Actual Buyers* ADD YOUR RATING

AcmeFurniture   4 REVIEWS

★★☆☆☆ *Good-Looking, But Poor Quality*
The cushions are almost flat after a few sittings. The fabric started pilling and I thought we could remove the fabric to wash it, but that's not the case. It stains easily. Not for outdoors or indoors. Not worth spending your money on.

★☆☆☆☆ *Not for Outdoors*
This set is NOT for outdoor use. We bought this set in June, and by the end of the summer it looked TERRIBLE. Our patio gets late afternoon sun, and after a month the wood stain started to fade. We are going to stain it with deck stain to try to make it last another year. But for the amount we paid, we are very disappointed in the quality.

★★★★★ *Love It!*
I bought this set in May and absolutely LOVE it! It is under a gazebo and

gets wet from the rain, but I haven't had any splitting or mold that the other people are talking about. If it rains, you just have to put the seat cushions up so they can dry...simple. It's comfortable and I would buy it again! Maybe some other people got a "bad batch" or something. Love it!

★★★☆☆ *You Get What You Pay For*
I purchased this beautiful set for our open-air, roofless patio about three weeks ago. So far, it has endured California weather. The wood is too thin to endure year-round exposure. Even the owner's manual suggests covering it when not in use. Our plan is to enjoy it now and stash it away in the garage after summer. This set was on sale at the time we made the purchase, and I'm glad I didn't pay full price. If you want longevity and to worry less about your wood furniture, spend a little more for the heavier woods. I would give 5 stars for the "look," and 2 ¾ stars for "quality." If we had paid full price for this set, it would have made its way back to the store.

F Based on the reviews, would you buy this patio furniture if it were on sale? Why or why not? Which review made the biggest impression on you? Why? (Answers will vary.)

_____

_____

_____

G Think of something you have bought recently. Write a review for it on a separate piece of paper. (Answers will vary.)

Listening Script *CD Track 28*

Maya: *Excuse me, could you answer some questions for me about the patio furniture?*
Salesperson: *Sure, which set are you looking at?*
Maya: *This teak set.*
Salesperson: *One of our best sellers. How can I help?*
Maya: *Well, I saw it online and was reading the reviews, so I wanted to see what you thought.*
Salesperson: *Sure.*
Maya: *I want to know if it's comfortable.*
Salesperson: *Well, why don't you sit down and see for yourself?*
Maya: *(pause) Yeah, it is pretty comfortable. Is it lightweight, easy to move?*
Salesperson: *I think it's pretty lightweight for wood. Why don't you move the table a bit and see what you think?*
Maya: *(pause) Not bad. It's definitely lighter than it looks. How can I clean it?*
Salesperson: *A damp cloth should do just fine. And when the stain starts to fade, you can just get a brush and some teak oil to brighten it up again.*
Maya: *Oh, good. That was the next thing I was going to ask you. I've never owned teak before so I wasn't sure if it had to be re-sanded or what.*
Salesperson: *If you keep on top of it with the oil, it shouldn't need re-sanding.*
Maya: *Great. So, how does teak hold up in bad weather?*
Salesperson: *Just fine. The sun will cause the fading, but we already talked about how to fix that. It's heavy enough that it won't get blown by wind. And it does just fine in the rain.*
Maya: *Good to know. So, how much does this set, with the table, umbrella, and four chairs, cost?*
Salesperson: *$1,450.*
Maya: *And I got this 20-percent-off coupon in the mail. Can I use it?*
Salesperson: *Sure. That will bring the price down to around $1,160.*
Maya: *OK. Oh, and one more thing. Does it come with a warranty?*
Salesperson: *Yep, a 90-day manufacturer's warranty against any product defects.*
Maya: *Great. I'll talk it over with my husband and then we'll make a decision. Thanks for your help.*
Salesperson: *No problem. That's what I'm here for!*

Presentation 2   10–15 mins.

 Look at the list of ways to research a product. Which methods have you used before?

E Maya went online to research the patio furniture she saw in the store. Read the product reviews she found.

Have students read the reviews to themselves. Then, go over them as a class.

Practice 2   10–15 mins.

Note: Shorter classes can do these exercises for homework.

F Based on the reviews, would you buy this patio furniture if it were on sale? Why or why not? Which review made the biggest impression on you? Why?

Have students answer these questions with a partner.

G Think of something you have bought recently. Write a review for it on a separate piece of paper.

Evaluation 2   10–15 mins.

Ask volunteers to read their reviews out loud.

Instructor's Notes

_____

_____

_____

_____

_____

_____

_____

_____

_____

_____

_____

_____

_____

Presentation 3   5–10 mins. ■■■□

(H) Imagine you are buying a new refrigerator. What questions would you ask before you made your decision to purchase a particular model? Write some ideas below.

Do this exercise as a class.

(I) Think about the refrigerator in your home. Answer the following questions. (If you don't know the answer, make it up.)

Go over each question and have students write their own answers on the lines.

Practice 3   15–20 mins. ■

(J) In order to research different refrigerator models, talk to your classmates. Ask them the questions you wrote in Exercise H as well as the ones in Exercise I.

Evaluation 3   5–10 mins. ■

(K) Based on your product research, what kind of refrigerator would you buy?

Application   10–20 mins. ■■■

(L) Choose one of the items from Exercise A to purchase. Do product research by reading reviews on the Internet or talking to your classmates. What did you find out about this product? Write some of the things you learned below.

Students can do this exercise in pairs or small groups.

Activity Bank

Unit 6, Lesson 1, Worksheet 1: Product Reviews

Unit 6, Lesson 1, Worksheet 2: Product Research

Refer students to *Stand Out 5 Grammar Challenge*, Unit 6, Challenge 1 for practice with adjective clauses with subject pronouns.

H   Imagine that you are buying a new refrigerator. What questions would you ask before you made your decision to purchase a particular model? Write some ideas below.

1. What are the special features of this refrigerator?

2. How much freezer space is there?

3. Can I see a cheaper refrigerator and a more expensive one?

I   Think about the refrigerator in your home. Answer the following questions. (If you don't know the answer, make it up.) (Answers will vary.)

1. What is the make and model? _____

2. How much did it cost? _____

3. Where did you buy it? _____

4. How is the quality? _____

5. Have you ever had any problems with it? _____

6. Did it come with a warranty? _____

7. What do you like about it? _____

8. What do you not like about it? _____

J   In order to research different refrigerator models, talk to your classmates. Ask them the questions you wrote in Exercise H as well the ones in Exercise I.

K   Based on your product research, what kind of refrigerator would you buy?

(Answers will vary.)

L   Choose one of the items from Exercise A to purchase. Do product research by reading reviews on the Internet or talking to your classmates. What did you find out about this product? Write some of the things you learned below.

(Answers will vary.)

_____

_____

Shopping from home

GOAL ➤ Purchase goods and services by phone and Internet

Vocabulary — Grammar

Life Skills

Academic — Pronunciation

A Take a class poll. How many of your classmates shop online? How many of your classmates order from catalogs? (Answers will vary.)

B Look at the page from a housewares catalog. Find each of the following pieces of information for each product: item name, item description, item price, and item number.

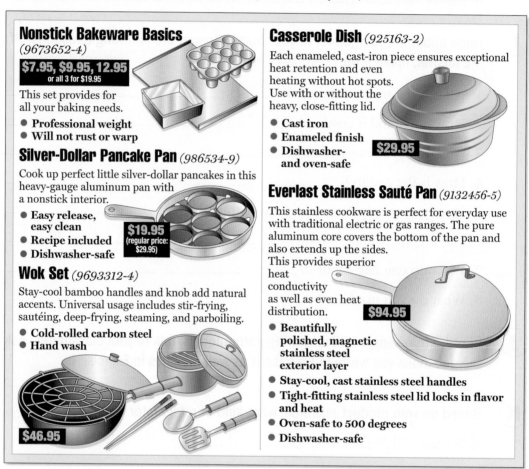

Nonstick Bakeware Basics (9673652-4)

$7.95, $9.95, 12.95 or all 3 for $19.95

This set provides for all your baking needs.
- Professional weight
- Will not rust or warp

Silver-Dollar Pancake Pan (986534-9)

Cook up perfect little silver-dollar pancakes in this heavy-gauge aluminum pan with a nonstick interior.
- Easy release, easy clean
- Recipe included
- Dishwasher-safe

$19.95 (regular price: $29.95)

Wok Set (9693312-4)

Stay-cool bamboo handles and knob add natural accents. Universal usage includes stir-frying, sautéing, deep-frying, steaming, and parboiling.
- Cold-rolled carbon steel
- Hand wash

$46.95

Casserole Dish (925163-2)

Each enameled, cast-iron piece ensures exceptional heat retention and even heating without hot spots. Use with or without the heavy, close-fitting lid.
- Cast iron
- Enameled finish
- Dishwasher- and oven-safe

$29.95

Everlast Stainless Sauté Pan (9132456-5)

This stainless cookware is perfect for everyday use with traditional electric or gas ranges. The pure aluminum core covers the bottom of the pan and also extends up the sides. This provides superior heat conductivity as well as even heat distribution.

$94.95

- Beautifully polished, magnetic stainless steel exterior layer
- Stay-cool, cast stainless steel handles
- Tight-fitting stainless steel lid locks in flavor and heat
- Oven-safe to 500 degrees
- Dishwasher-safe

  C Listen to four phone conversations between salespeople and customers who are buying items from this catalog page. Complete the chart below based on what you hear.

CD
TR 29

	Item	Total cost	Method of payment
1.	Casserole dish	$32.42	Versa
2.	Silver-dollar Pancake Pan	$21.60	Discovery
3.	2 Everlast Stainless Saute Pans	$205.57	Discovery
4.	Nonstick Bakeware Muffin Pan	$14.02	MisterCard

Objective: Purchase goods and services by phone and Internet

Academic Strategies: Focused listening, critical thinking

Vocabulary: *lightweight, withstand the elements, fabric pilling, stain, longevity*

RESOURCES

Activity Bank: Unit 6, Lesson 2, Worksheet 1

Grammar Challenge 5: Unit 6, Challenge 2

■ 1.5 hour classes   ■ 2.5 hour classes   ■ 3+ hour classes

Audio: CD Track 29

Suggested Realia: Store, mail-order, and online catalog pages

AGENDA

Read a catalog page.

Listen to customers order products on the phone.

Review the process of shopping online.

Warm-up and Review   5-10 mins.

Have students get in small groups and talk about things they have researched before they purchased something. Ask them to tell their group members how they did their research and what they found.

Introduction   5-10 mins.

Dictation:

1. Does the product come with a warranty?
2. Have you ever had any problems with it?
3. Did you shop around for the best price?
4. Would you buy the same product again?

State the objective: *Today you will practice buying things by phone and Internet.*

Presentation 1   10-15 mins.

(A) Take a class poll. How many of your classmates shop online? How many of your classmates order from catalogs?

Ask students who raise their hands for either question what catalogs they shop from and what online stores they buy from. Discuss the benefits to buying online or from catalogs.

(B) Look at the page from a housewares catalog. Find each of the following pieces of information for each product: item name, item description, item price, and item number.

Practice 1   10-15 mins.

(C) Listen to four phone conversations between salespeople and customers who are buying items from this catalog page. Complete the chart below based on what you hear.

The listening script is on page 117a.

Evaluation 1   5 mins.

Go over the answers as a class.

For more practice, have students work with a partner to practice ordering items from the catalog.

STANDARDS CORRELATIONS

CASAS: 1.3.1, 1.3.3 (See CASAS Competency List on pages 187–193.)

SCANS: **Resources** Allocate time, allocate money, allocate materials and facility resources, allocate human resources

Information Acquire and evaluate information, organize and maintain information, interpret and communicate information, use computers to process information

Interpersonal Participate as a member of a team, teach others, serve clients and customers, exercise leadership, negotiate to arrive at a decision, work with cultural diversity

Systems Understand systems, monitor and correct performance, improve and design systems

Technology Select technology, apply technology to a task, maintain and troubleshoot technology

Basic Skills Reading, writing, arithmetic, listening, speaking

Thinking Skills Think creatively, make decisions, solve problems, see things in the mind's eye

Personal Qualities Responsibility, sociability, self-management

EFF: **Communication** Read with understanding, convey ideas in writing, speak so others can understand, listen actively, observe critically

Decision Making Use math to solve problems and communicate, solve problems and make decisions, plan

Interpersonal Cooperate with others, advocate and influence, resolve conflict and negotiate, guide others

Lifelong Learning Take responsibility for learning, reflect and evaluate, learn through research, use information and communications technology

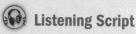

Conversation 1
Salesperson: *Cook-It-Right Catalog Sales. Would you like to order something from our catalog?*
Customer: *Yes, I'd like to order item number 925163-2.*
Salesperson: *How many?*
Customer: *Just one, please.*
Salesperson: *OK, your total will be $32.42 with tax. Will you be paying with Versa, MisterCard, or Discovery today?*
Customer: *Versa.*
Salesperson: *Great. I'll need the number and expiration date whenever you're ready.*

Conversation 2
Salesperson: *Cook-It-Right Catalog Sales. Would you like to order something from our catalog?*
Customer: *Yes, I'd like to order item number 986534-9.*
Salesperson: *How many?*
Customer: *Just one, please.*
Salesperson: *OK, your total will be $21.60. Will you be paying with Versa, MisterCard, or Discovery today?*
Customer: *You don't take American Expression?*
Salesperson: *Sorry, ma'am. No.*
Customer: *OK, I'll pay with Discovery.*
Salesperson: *Great. I'll need the number and expiration date whenever you're ready.*

Conversation 3
Salesperson: *Cook-It-Right Catalog Sales. Would you like to order something from our catalog?*
Customer: *Yes, I'd like to order item number 9132456-5.*
Salesperson: *How many?*
Customer: *Two, please.*
Salesperson: *OK, your total will be $205.57 with tax and shipping. Will you be paying with Versa, MisterCard, or Discovery today?*
Customer: *Discovery.*
Salesperson: *Great. I'll need the number and expiration date whenever you're ready.*

Conversation 4
Salesperson: *Cook-It-Right Catalog Sales. Would you like to order something from our catalog?*
Customer: *Yes, I'd like to order item number 9673652-4.*
Salesperson: *All three pieces?*
Customer: *Just the muffin pan, please.*
Salesperson: *OK, your total will be $14.02 with tax. Will you be paying with Versa, MisterCard, or Discovery today?*
Customer: *MisterCard.*
Salesperson: *Great. I'll need the number and expiration date whenever you're ready.*

Presentation 2   5–10 mins.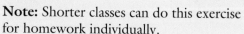

D With your teacher, review the process of making a purchase online. Look for each step in the screen shots below.

Practice 2   10–15 mins.

Note: Shorter classes can do this exercise for homework individually.

E In a group, discuss the pros and cons of buying something online. Make two lists on a separate piece of paper.

Instructor's Notes

_____

_____

_____

_____

_____

_____

_____

_____

_____

_____

_____

_____

_____

_____

GOAL ➤ **Purchase goods and services by phone and Internet**

Vocabulary / Grammar / Life Skills / Academic / Pronunciation

D With your teacher, review the process of making a purchase online. Look for each step in the screen shots below.

1. Find the Web site you want to buy something from.
2. Perform a search.
3. Look at the results of your search.
4. Narrow down the results to one item.
5. Make purchase.

E In a group, discuss the pros and cons of buying something online. Make two lists on a separate piece of paper. (Answers will vary. Sample answers are below)

Pros: convenient, easy to compare prices, pay by credit card is usually safe

Cons: can't see product, may be unreliable Web site, shipping costs

GOAL ➤ **Purchase goods and services by phone and Internet**

F What kinds of things are good to buy on the Internet? _books, DVDs, games, dishware,_

some clothes

G With a partner, create a list of specific items that could be sold in a catalog or online.

(Answers will vary.)

1. Decide what type of items you could sell.
2. On a separate piece of paper, create art, descriptions, and prices for at least five items.

H Exchange your page with another pair of students. Have a conversation about purchasing the new items with your partner. One of you should be a sales representative explaining your products. Sit back-to-back to simulate selling and purchasing on the phone.

I Do an Internet search to find items similar to the ones on the catalog page in Exercise B. Follow the steps in Exercise D to find the items you want.

If you don't have computer access, answer the following questions. (Answers will vary.)

1. What would you like to buy online? _____

2. What words will you type in to search for that item? _____

3. Do you know of an online store that sells this item? _____

4. Once you click on the store that sells your item, what information will you look for?

_____

_____

5. How will you decide if you are going to purchase the item? What information will you consider?

_____

_____

Practice 2 (continued)

(F) What kinds of things are good to buy on the Internet?

Evaluation 2   10–15 mins. ■■□

Go over students' ideas as a class, asking volunteers to write pros and cons on the board.

Presentation 3   1 min. ■■■

Go over the instructions to Exercise G.

Practice 3   15–20 mins. ■

Note: Shorter classes can do this exercise for homework.

(G) With a partner, create a list of specific items that could be sold in a catalog or online.

Evaluation 3   ■

Walk around the classroom and help students as needed.

Application   10–20 mins. ■■■

Note: Students will need a catalog page to look at if they didn't create one in Practice 3. If necessary, they can use the catalog page on page 114. If possible, bring in sample catalogs for students to use.

(H) Exchange your page with another pair of students. Have a conversation about purchasing the new items with your partner. One of you should be a sales representative. Sit back-to-back to simulate selling and purchasing on the phone.

Ideally, the student playing the sales representative would have Internet access and could practice searching for something online.

(I) Do an Internet search to find items similar to the ones on the catalog page. Follow the steps in Exercise D to find the items you want.

If students don't have computer access, have students complete the alternate questions 1–5 in Exercise I to the best of their ability.

Activity Bank 💿

Unit 6, Lesson 2, Worksheet 1: Catalog Shopping

📖 Refer students to *Stand Out 5 Grammar Challenge*, Unit 6, Challenge 2 for practice with adjective clauses with object pronouns.

Instructor's Notes

_____
_____
_____
_____
_____
_____
_____
_____
_____
_____
_____
_____
_____
_____
_____
_____
_____
_____
_____
_____
_____
_____
_____
_____
_____
_____
_____
_____
_____
_____
_____
_____

AT-A-GLANCE PREP

Objective: Interpret product guarantees and warranties
Academic Strategy: Making inferences
Vocabulary: *guarantee, warranty, free of charge, faults, defects in workmanship, foregoing, alleging, conform, deems, malfunctions*

RESOURCES

Activity Bank: Unit 6, Lesson 3, Worksheets 1–2

 1.5 hour classes ■ 2.5 hour classes ■ 3⁺ hour classes

Grammar Challenge 5: Unit 6, Challenge 3

> ## AGENDA
> *Read and answer questions about a product warranty.*
> *Work with legal language used in warranties.*
> *Choose the best answer about a product guarantee.*
> *Write a guarantee.*

Warm-up and Review   5-10 mins. ■■■

Repeat the application activity from the previous lesson. Have students work with a different student than they did in the previous lesson.

Introduction   5-10 mins. ■■■

Dictation:

1. We will not be undersold by our competitors.
2. Our products are backed by our no-hassle warranty.
3. They guarantee their products for two years from purchase date.
4. The warranty covers only defects arising under normal use.

State the objective: *Today you will be interpreting product warranties and guarantees.*

Presentation 1   10-15 mins. ■■■

(A) Think about the following situations and make some decisions with a partner.

Once students have had a chance to discuss the situations with a partner, discuss each one as a class.

(B) A *warranty* or *guarantee* is a written promise by a company to replace or repair a product free of charge within a certain time period after purchase if it has any defects. Read the following warranty for home-stereo speakers.

Point out to students that guarantees and warranties are basically the same. In fact, if you look both words up in the dictionary, the definitions are almost identical.

Practice 1   5 mins.

(C) Answer the following questions about the warranty.

Evaluation 1   5 mins.

Go over the answers as a class.

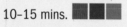

STANDARDS CORRELATIONS

CASAS: 1.6.3, 1.6.4 (See CASAS Competency List on pages 187–193.)
SCANS: **Information** Acquire and evaluate information, interpret and communicate information
Interpersonal Participate as a member of a team, teach others, negotiate to arrive at a decision, work with cultural diversity
Systems Understand systems, monitor and correct performance
Basic Skills Reading, writing, listening, speaking
Thinking Skills Think creatively, make decisions, solve problems, see things in the mind's eye

Personal Qualities Responsibility, sociability, self-management
EFF: **Communication** Read with understanding, convey ideas in writing, speak so others can understand, listen actively, observe critically
Decision Making Solve problems and make decisions, plan
Interpersonal Cooperate with others, advocate and influence, resolve conflict and negotiate, guide others
Lifelong Learning Take responsibility for learning, reflect and evaluate

119a Lesson Planner: Unit 6, Lesson 3

Is this under warranty?

GOAL ➤ **Interpret product guarantees and warranties**

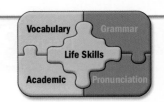

 A Think about the following situations and make some decisions with a partner.

What would you do if . . . (Answers will vary. Sample answers are given.)

1. the air-conditioning in your car wasn't cold enough? Take it to a mechanic.

2. your printer stopped working one week after you bought it? Take it back to the store.

3. the speaker on your cell phone didn't work? Take it back to the store, go online for help with problems.

4. you washed a new shirt according to the care instructions on the tag and it shrank? Take it back to the store for a refund.

B A *warranty* or *guarantee* is a written promise by a company to replace or repair a product free of charge within a certain time period after purchase if it has any defects. Read the following warranty for home-stereo speakers.

> This product is guaranteed against all defects in workmanship and materials for two years following purchase. All it takes to ensure complete coverage is to register your purchase. Once you have warranty-registered your product, the nearest service center can respond rapidly and directly to you.

 C Answer the following questions about the warranty.

1. Where do you take your product if something goes wrong?

   the nearest service center

2. How long is the product guaranteed?

   2 years

3. What do you need to do to make sure you receive the warranty for the product?

   register the product

4. Does the warranty cover your dropping and breaking the product?

   probably not: it covers defects, not damage

GOAL ➤ Interpret product guarantees
and warranties

D Warranties are often worded with legal language that can be difficult to understand. Look at the example below and see how it can be restated more clearly.

> Seller warrants to the original customers purchasing products from Seller that all such products, under normal use and operation, will be free from defects in materials and workmanship affecting form, fit, and function.

In other words . . .

The seller says that if I use this product under normal conditions, as it was meant to be used, there won't be any problems with it.

E Restate each sentence below in your own words.

1. Any claims alleging failure of products to conform to the foregoing warranty may be made only by the customer who purchased the product.

    Return or refund requests made because the product didn't function

    as promised can only be made by the original purchaser.

2. The foregoing warranty only applies while the product is being used in the original machine with the original hardware and software configuration.

    The company promise is only valid while the item is used as intended with the

    original computer programs and parts.

3. Seller, at its option, will repair, replace, or provide a credit or refund of either the original purchase price less a restock fee or current fair market value, whichever is less, for any product Seller deems to be defective.

    The seller will make the decision to fix, match, give credit or refund at the selling

    price minus a charge for taking it back, or the current price depending on which is
    less if the seller sees that the product is imperfect.

4. The above warranties cover only defects arising under normal use and do not include malfunctions or failures from misuse, neglect, alteration, abuse, improper installation, or acts of nature.

    The warranty previously stated only covers flaws that show up with normal wear

    and doesn't consider breakdowns or errors in function from breakage, accidents,
    drops or poor installment.

5. Removal of the labeling on products will void all warranties.

    If you remove the original labels from the items, the warranty or promise

    will not be honored.

Presentation 2

5-10 mins. ◼◼◻

 Warranties are often worded with legal language that can be difficult to understand. Look at the example below and see how it can be restated more clearly.

Go over the example and show students how to arrive at the general meaning of a warranty.

Practice 2

15-20 mins. ◼◻

Note: Shorter classes can do this exercise for homework.

 Restate each sentence below in your own words.

Students can work in pairs if necessary. Tell students they can use dictionaries, but all they need to gather is the general idea of each sentence. Consequently, they don't need to understand every word.

Evaluation 2

10-15 mins. ◼◻

Go over students' ideas as a class. If you have time, have volunteers write their restatements on the board. Have the class vote on which ones they think are the most accurate.

Instructor's Notes

Lesson Planner: Unit 6, Lesson 3   **120a**

Presentation 3

5 mins.

Go over the instructions for the next two exercises.

Practice 3

10-15 mins.

Note: Shorter classes can do these exercises for homework.

F Read the following guarantee from a printer company.

G Choose the best answer.

Evaluation 3

5-10 mins.

Go over the answers as a class.

Application

10-20 mins.

H With a partner, choose a product from the list below and write your own guarantee. Use the ideas from the three warranties you have read in this lesson, but use your own words.

To help students get started, brainstorm some ideas of what should be included in a warranty as a class.

Activity Bank

Unit 6, Lesson 3, Worksheet 1: Warranties

Unit 6, Lesson 3, Worksheet 2: Sample Complaint Letter

Refer students to *Stand Out 5 Grammar Challenge*, Unit 6, Challenge 3 for practice with adjective clauses using *when*, *where*, or *why*.

Instructor's Notes

GOAL ➤ Interpret product guarantees and warranties

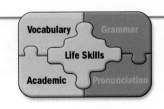

 F Read the following guarantee from a printer company.

OUR NO-HASSLE GUARANTEE

Our products are backed the way they are built—the best in the industry. Our no-hassle printer guarantee gives you excellent product support with no worries, no hassles. Now you can enjoy the benefit of a substitute printer if your printer fails during the first 30 days of use.

We will send a replacement printer to you within 48 hours of your request for any printer that fails to meet the factory specifications or fails to power up upon delivery within 30 days of your invoice date. No hassles. Upon receipt of your no-hassle replacement printer, you must return your defective printer to us. Your defective printer will be exchanged for the same make and model, or for a printer of equal value. In addition, if your printer has three separate quality issues, which are documented with our technical support team, within one year from the date of your invoice, we will permanently replace your defective printer with a new printer of equal or greater value.

 G Choose the best answer.

1. You can receive a substitute printer if your printer doesn't work during the first
   a. 48 hours.   (b.) 30 days.   c. week.

2. How soon will you receive your substitute printer?
   (a.) 48 hours   b. 30 days   c. one week

3. When you receive your replacement printer, you must
   (a.) return the defective printer.   b. do nothing.   c. call the company.

4. If you have three problems with your printer during the first year, the company will
   a. fix your printer for free.   b. refund your money.   (c.) permanently replace the printer.

 H With a partner, choose a product from the list below and write your own guarantee. Use the ideas from the three warranties you have read in this lesson, but use your own words.

digital camera   bicycle   cell phone   washing machine

(Answers will vary.)

Returns and exchanges

GOAL ➤ **Return a product**

 A Think of some things you have returned to the stores where you bought them. What did you return and why? Discuss your experiences with your classmates.

 B Read and listen to the conversation.

CD
TR 30

Sales Associate: Can I help you with something?
Customer: Yes, I'd like to return these shoes. I wore them around my house on the carpet for a few days and they are still uncomfortable. The salesman who sold them to me insisted they would stretch out and soften up, but they haven't. I'd like to get my money back.
Sales Associate: I'm afraid I can't give you your money back. These were on sale and we don't offer refunds for sale items.
Customer: Can I exchange them?
Sales Associate: Yes, you can exchange them for something of equal value.
Customer: OK, I'll do that. Let me look around for a bit.
Sales Associate: Take your time.

 C Listen to each question and write the correct answer. (Answers will vary.)

CD
TR 31

1. Some shoes

2. They are uncomfortable.

3. No, it won't.

4. The shoes were on sale and the store doesn't refund sale items.

5. The customer can exchange them for something of equal value.

6. Yes, she does.

AT-A-GLANCE PREP

Objective: Return a product
Academic Strategy: Focused listening
Vocabulary: *return, exchange, refund, valid photo ID, original form of payment, issued, policy*

RESOURCES

Activity Bank: Unit 6, Lesson 4, Worksheet 1
Grammar Challenge 5: Unit 6, Challenge 4

■ 1.5 hour classes ■ 2.5 hour classes ■ 3⁺ hour classes

Audio: CD Tracks 30–32

AGENDA

Listen to customers returning items.

Interpret return policies.

Practice conversations about returning or exchanging a product.

Warm-up and Review   5-10 mins. ■■■

Ask volunteers to take out the warranties they wrote from the previous lesson and share them out loud with the class. It their warranties are short, ask volunteers to write them on the board.

Introduction   5-10 mins. ■■■

Dictation:

1. An original sales receipt is required for a full refund.
2. If you find a lower price at any of our competitors, we will meet that price.
3. Without a receipt, returns can be made for store credit.
4. Some items cannot be returned if opened.

State the objective: *Today we will practice returning products.*

Presentation 1   10-15 mins. ■■■

 Think of some things you have returned to the stores where you bought them. What did you return and why? Discuss your experiences with your classmates.

 Read and listen to the conversation.

> **Listening Script**   *CD Track 30*
>
> *The listening script matches the conversation in Exercise B.*

Practice 1   10-15 mins. ■■■

 Listen to each question and write the correct answer.

Tell students they will be listening to questions about the conversation in Exercise B. Tell them to write short answers to the questions they hear.

> **Listening Script**   *CD Track 31*
>
> 1. *What is the customer trying to return?*
> 2. *Why is she returning them?*
> 3. *Will the store give the customer her money back?*
> 4. *Why not?*
> 5. *What does the sales associate say the customer can do?*
> 6. *Does the customer seem satisfied?*

Evaluation 1   5 mins. ■■■

Go over the answers as a class.

STANDARDS CORRELATIONS

CASAS: 1.3.3 (See CASAS Competency List on pages 187-193.)
SCANS: **Resources** Allocate human resources
Information Acquire and evaluate information, interpret and communicate information
Interpersonal Participate as a member of a team, teach others, serve clients and customers, exercise leadership, negotiate to arrive at a decision, work with cultural diversity
Systems Monitor and correct performance
Basic Skills Reading, writing, listening, speaking

Thinking Skills Think creatively, make decisions, solve problems, see things in the mind's eye
Personal Qualities Responsibility, sociability, self-management
EFF: **Communication** Read with understanding, convey ideas in writing, speak so others can understand, listen actively, observe critically
Decision Making Solve problems and make decisions, plan
Interpersonal Cooperate with others, advocate and influence, resolve conflict and negotiate, guide others
Lifelong Learning Take responsibility for learning, reflect and evaluate

Presentation 2   5-10 mins. ■■■□

Discuss return policies. Ask students what they think most stores require in order to return or exchange something. Make a list.

Practice 2   10-15 mins. ■■□

Note: Shorter classes can do these exercises for homework.

(D) Read each return policy and the statements below it. Circle *T* (true) or *F* (false).

(E) Look back at all the false statements. (*Hint:* There are five.) On a separate sheet of paper, rewrite each statement, making it true.

Evaluation 2   10-15 mins. ■■□

Go over the answers as a class.

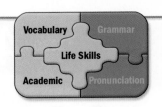

D   Read each return policy and the statements below it. Circle *T* (true) or *F* (false).

> Thank you for shopping at Nico's. Return or exchange for merchandise within 2 weeks with tags attached and/or in original packaging. Original sales receipt is required for full refund. Final sale on all sale items.

1. You can exchange sale items.   T   (F)
2. You need an original sales receipt for a refund.   (T)   F

> Valid photo ID required for all returns (except for credit card purchases), exchanges, and to receive and redeem store credit. With a receipt, a full refund in the original form of payment, except payments made with checks, will be issued for new and unread books and unopened music within 4 days. For merchandise purchased with a check, a store credit will be issued within the first 7 days. Without an original receipt, a store credit issued by mail will be offered at the lowest selling price. With a receipt, returns of new and unread books and unopened music from our Web site can be made for store credit. Textbooks after 14 days or without a receipt are not returnable. Used books are not returnable.

3. If you pay with a check, you can get cash back.   T   (F)
4. You cannot return used books.   (T)   F
5. If you have a receipt, you can get a refund on unopened music within four days.   (T)   F
6. If you don't have a receipt, you can exchange an item.   T   (F)

> All returns and exchanges must be new, unused, and have original packaging and accessories. Some items cannot be returned if opened. For our full return and exchange policy, visit the store or log onto our Web site. For a gift receipt, bring this receipt back to any store within 90 days. Ask about receipt look-up.

7. All opened items can be exchanged.   T   (F)

> We will not be undersold. Guaranteed! If you find a lower price at any of our competitors, we will meet that price.

8. This store will offer you a lower price than its competitors.   T   (F)

E   Look back at all the false statements. (*Hint:* There are five.) On a separate piece of paper, rewrite each statement, making it true.

1. You cannot exchange sale items.
3. If you pay with a check, you can get store credit.
6. Without a receipt, store credit will be issued.
7. Some items cannot be returned if opened.
8. This store will match the low prices of competitors.

CD
TR 32

(F) Listen to six conversations and write the corresponding conversation number in front of the reason each person gave for returning the product. Then write what product the person returned.

Conversation #	Reason for returning or exchanging item	Was item returned or exchanged?
5	bought the wrong package	exchanged
6	already have them	exchanged
1	bad reception	exchanged
2	don't fit right	exchanged
3	broken	exchanged
4	doesn't work with computer	returned

(G) **Write two reasons you might return each of the items listed below.** (Answers will vary.)

1. digital video camera

   a. _screen doesn't work_   b. _not enough features_

2. gallon of milk

   a. _sour_   b. _already opened_

3. pair of pants

   a. _too large/small_   b. _defective zipper_

4. laptop computer

   a. _too slow_   b. _programs don't stay on_

5. sunglasses

   a. _not dark enough_   b. _pinch nose_

6. textbook

   a. _wrong edition_   b. _already written in_

(H) **Divide the class into two halves—clerks and customers.**

Clerks should help each customer with his or her return.

Customers should choose one item from Exercise G to return or exchange. Use one of the reasons you came up with. Have at least three conversations with different clerks or customers and then switch roles.

Presentation 3 — 5-10 mins.

Go over the reasons listed in Exercise F for why someone might return something. Ask students what sort of items might be returned for these reasons.

Practice 3 — 15-20 mins.

Note: Shorter classes can do this exercise for homework by using the script in the back of their books.

F Listen to six conversations and write the corresponding conversation number in front of the reason each person gave for returning the product. Then write what product the person returned.

 Listening Script — CD Track 32

Conversation 1
Sales Associate: *Can I help you with something?*
Customer: *Yes, I'd like to exchange this phone for a different one.*
Sales Associate: *Is something wrong with it?*
Customer: *Well, I can't hear the person on the other end very well when I'm at my house or at work. Basically, that makes the phone useless to me.*
Sales Associate: *Yeah, that's not good. Let's get you another one and see if it works better.*
Customer: *Thanks.*

Conversation 2
Sales Associate: *How can I help you?*
Customer: *I bought these pants here last week and I didn't have time to try them on. When I got home and put them on, I realized they are too small. Can I try on a larger size?*
Sales Associate: *Let me see if we have them in stock. (pause) You're in luck! Here, let me get you a fitting room.*

Conversation 3
Sales Associate: *Can I help you with something?*
Customer: *Yes, I ordered these glasses online and when I received them in the mail, they were broken. I thought it would be easier to return them to the store rather than trying to ship them back.*
Sales Associate: *Good idea. Unfortunately, we are all out of this style right now. Would you like me to give you a credit and then we'll call you when they come in?*
Customer: *Could I get something different?*
Sales Associate: *Certainly. Why don't you look around and I'll hold them up here at the counter for you.*
Customer: *Great.*

(continued)

Conversation 4
Sales Associate: *What can I do for you today?*
Customer: *Well, I got this printer home and realized it doesn't work with my computer. I called tech support and they told me I never should've been sold this printer because it doesn't come with a driver to make it work with my computer.*
Sales Associate: *I'm sorry about that. Would you like to shop around for another printer?*
Customer: *No, I think I just want my money back.*
Sales Associate: *As long as you have your receipt, we can definitely do that.*
Customer: *Here it is.*

Conversation 5
Customer: *Hi. I need to exchange these baby diapers for a larger size. I accidentally bought the wrong ones.*
Sales Associate: *No worries. Why don't you go ahead and pick out the size you need. Then come back and I'll do the exchange for you.*
Customer: *Perfect. Thanks!*

Conversation 6
Sales Associate: *Can I help you with something?*
Customer: *Yes, I was given these three books as a gift last week and I actually already have them.*
Sales Associate: *Do you have a receipt?*
Customer: *I don't.*
Sales Associate: *OK, well let me see how much they were and you can pick out something of equal value to exchange with them.*
Customer: *Sounds great. Thank you.*

Evaluation 3 — 5-10 mins.

Go over the answers as a class.

Application — 10-20 mins.

G Write two reasons you might return each of the items listed below.

H Divide the class into two halves—clerks and customers.

Clerks should help each customer with his or her return.

Customers should choose one item from Exercise G to return or exchange. Use one of the reasons you came up with. Have at least three conversations with different clerks or customers and then switch roles.

Activity Bank

Unit 6, Lesson 4, Worksheet 1: Returns and Exchanges

 Refer students to *Stand Out 5 Grammar Challenge*, Unit 6, Challenge 4 for practice with the reduction of adjective clauses to adjective phrases.

AT-A-GLANCE PREP

Objective: Sell a product
Grammar: Appositives
Vocabulary: *convince, face value, appositive*

RESOURCES

Activity Bank: Unit 6, Lesson 5, Worksheets 1–2
Grammar Challenge 5: Unit 6, Challenge 5

■ 1.5 hour classes ■ 2.5 hour classes ■ 3⁺ hour classes

AGENDA

Read classified ads.
Work with appositives.
Write an ad.

Suggested Realia: Printouts from Web sites where people sell or auction things, other publications (local newspapers, flyers in the mail, etc.)

Warm-up and Review   10–15 mins. ■■■

Repeat the application in Exercise H from the previous lesson, giving students more practice with returning or exchanging different items.

Introduction   5–10 mins. ■■■

Dictation:

1. These tickets, the best seats in the house, are selling for face value.
2. This car, a sporty red convertible, will make you feel like royalty.
3. This brown leather couch, a part of our family for years, will be the most comfortable piece of furniture you have ever sat on.
4. This bike, a great, fun means of transportation, will get you around in style.

State the objective: *Today we will discuss how to sell a product.*

Presentation 1   10–15 mins. ■■■

 If you were not going to go out physically to buy something in an actual store, where would you shop? Brainstorm ideas with a partner.

Have students come up with places where they could find ads selling products.

 If you were going to sell some items you owned, what would they be? Make a list on a separate piece of paper.

Ask students to share what they might sell.

Practice 1   10–15 mins. ■■■

 Read each of the ads below and think about the following questions.

You can do this activity in a variety of ways:

1. Have students do just as the instructions say and then go over the answers in Evaluation 1.
2. Have students work with a partner and ask each other the questions.
3. Have students work in small groups and discuss the questions for each ad.

Evaluation 1   5 mins. ■■■

Go over the answers as a class.

GOAL ➤ Sell a product

A If you were not going to go out physically to buy something in an actual store, where would you shop? Brainstorm ideas with a partner. (Answers will vary.)

From a catalog form, on the phone, on the Internet

B If you were going to sell some items you owned, what would they be? Make a list on a separate piece of paper.

Books, clothes, dishes, knitting, car

C Read each of the ads below and think about the following questions.

1. What is for sale? a car, a coach, concert tickets, a bicycle
2. How is the seller trying to convince you to buy it? (Answers will vary.)
3. Would you consider buying any of the items in the ads? Why or why not?
   (Answers will vary.)

This car, <u>a sporty red convertible,</u> will make you feel like royalty. **Rare Red Dino 1973 Ferrari 246 GTS.** Right-hand drive, 50,000 miles before restoration, 10,500 miles after. One owner. Serious inquiries only. (784) 555-9712

Looking for a great place to sit? Watch movies? Chat with friends? This brown leather couch, <u>a part of our family for years,</u> will be the most comfortable piece of furniture you have ever sat on. Come sit on it today. $890. (732) 555-3337

I bought too many tickets for the Taylor Band.

These tickets, <u>the best seats in the house,</u> are selling for face value. I have a total of eight available tickets but will sell them separately. From $60. E-mail me at tix@redhouse.com

Save on gas!
Buy a bicycle! This bike, <u>a fun means of transportation,</u> will get you around in style. In great shape and only six months old. Take it for a test ride. $275. spin@buyitcheap.com

D Read about appositives with your classmates and teacher.

	Appositives	
Noun or Noun Phrase	**Appositive**	**Remainder of sentence (Predicate)**
The ad,	**the one with all the great pictures,**	makes me want to buy those dishes.
That computer,	**the fastest machine in the store,**	sells for over $2,000.

Explanation:
• An appositive is a noun or noun phrase that renames another noun next to it in a sentence.
• The appositive adds extra descriptive detail, explains, or identifies something about the noun.
• An appositive can come before or after the noun phrase it is modifying.

Example: *A helpful gift, money is always appreciated by a newly married couple.*

Note: Appositives are usually set off by commas.

E Find and underline the appositives in the ads on the previous page. There is one appositive in each ad.

F Complete each of the statements below with an appositive. (Answers will vary.)

EXAMPLE: Her dress, _____a really fancy gown_____, got the attention of every customer in the room.

1. That used car, _____an old, rusty sedan_____, will probably be for sale for quite a while.

2. Used pots and pans, _____the ones from your mom_____, are hard to sell without the matching lids.

3. Two round-trip plane tickets, _____the winning prize_____, can be used to travel anywhere in the United States.

4. The MP3 player, _____a convenient source of music_____, can hold over 2,000 songs.

5. Those leather shoes, _____imports from Italy_____, have many more years of walking in them.

6. This restaurant, _____a place for home-cooking_____, will make you money as soon as you open the doors.

7. That set of suitcases, _____the largest in the store_____, will carry enough clothing and accessories for two weeks of traveling.

8. Her Web site, _____an attractive and accessible page_____, is an online store with tons of gently worn clothes for sale.

Presentation 2   10-15 mins.

D Read about appositives with your classmates and teacher.

E Find and underline the appositives in the ads on the previous page. There is one appositive in each ad.

Do Exercise E as a class. Ask students to find each appositive by themselves and then ask the entire class for the correct answer. If necessary for more clarification, discuss each appositive and point out what makes it an appositive (as opposed to an adjective clause).

Teaching Tip

Appositive vs. adjective clause

An appositive renames a noun, usually with a description, but it does not include any verbs and it must include another noun.

For example:

The ad, <u>the one with all the great pictures</u>, makes me want to buy those dishes.

The ad, <u>part of my favorite cooking magazine</u>, makes me want to buy those dishes.

An adjective clause usually includes a relative pronoun and must include a verb.

For example:

The ad <u>that I saw in that magazine</u> makes me want to buy those dishes.

The ad, <u>where the girl is cooking in her new kitchen</u>, makes me want to buy those dishes.

Practice 2   10-15 mins.

Note: Shorter classes can do this exercise for homework.

F Complete each of the statements below with an appositive.

Evaluation 2   10-15 mins.

Ask volunteers to write their sentences on the board. As you go over each statement, ask other volunteers to read what they wrote out loud. This will enable students to see that there is more than one possibility for each restatement.

Presentation 3

5-10 mins.

G If you wanted to buy the following things (not in a store), where would you look?

Do this exercise as a class. Make sure you exhaust all the possibilities of places to sell things (Penny Saver, eBay, Craig's List, local newspaper, etc.).

Practice 3

10-15 mins.

Note: Shorter classes can do these exercises for homework.

H Imagine that you are going to sell something. Answer the questions below.

I Write three statements with appositives that you would use in your advertisement.

Evaluation 3

5-10 mins.

Ask volunteers to share their answers with the class.

Application

10-20 mins.

J On another piece of paper, write an ad to sell your product. Find an attractive photo or create a drawing to draw attention to your ad.

Optional Computer Activity: Have students create their ads on the computer.

K Share your ad with your classmates. See if you can find anyone who would buy what you are selling.

If you have a smaller class, ask each student to read his or her ad out loud. Ask the other students in the class to make a note to themselves if they might be interested in buying the product. When students have finished reading their ads out loud, have them walk around and talk to the students whose products they might be interested in buying.

For a larger class, have students post their ads around the room and let students walk around and read the ads, looking for something they might be interested in buying.

Activity Bank

Unit 6, Lesson 5, Worksheet 1: Radio Ads (listening)
Unit 6, Lesson 5, Worksheet 2: Appositives

Refer students to *Stand Out 5 Grammar Challenge*, Unit 6, Challenge 5 for more practice with appositives.

There are also two extension challenges. Extension Challenge 1 gives practice using adjective clauses with *whose*. Extension Challenge 2 offers practice with adjective clauses that modify indefinite pronouns.

Instructor's Notes

_____
_____
_____
_____
_____
_____
_____
_____
_____
_____
_____
_____
_____
_____
_____
_____
_____
_____
_____
_____
_____
_____

G If you wanted to buy the following things (not in a store), where would you look?

(Answers will vary.)

1. car: _Internet, Autotrader, classified ads_

2. shoes: _Internet, catalog_

3. CDs (music): _online, magazine_

4. furniture: _catalog, Internet_

H Imagine that you are going to sell something. Answer the questions below.

(Answers will vary.)

1. What would you sell? _____

2. What would you say to make your product sound appealing?

_____

3. How much would you sell it for? _____

4. Where would you place your ad? _____

5. How would you want people to contact you? _____

I Write three statements with appositives that you would use in your advertisement.

1. _(Answers will vary.)_____

2. _____

3. _____

J On another piece of paper, write an ad to sell your product. Find an attractive photo or create a drawing to draw attention to your ad. (Answers will vary.)

K Share your ad with your classmates. See if you can find anyone who would buy what you are selling.

Review

A Imagine that you are going to buy a used car. Write four questions you would ask car owners who want to sell their car. (Lesson 1) (Questions will vary. Sample questions are below.)

1. What repairs have been done?

2. How often do you replace the oil?

3. Did you buy this car new?

4. How old are the tires?

B Ask your classmates the questions you wrote in Exercise A. Write some of their responses below. When your classmates ask you their questions, you can talk about your own car or a car you are familiar with. (Lesson 1) (Answers will vary.)

_____

_____

_____

C Imagine that you are going to buy a product online. Write a short paragraph about the steps you will need to take to buy the product. (Lesson 2) (Answers will vary. Sample answer is given)

First, I will go online. On the Internet I will go to may favorite Web site for clothing. Next, I will search for "hoodies" or sweatshirts. After that, I will choose the look and color I like. Finally, I will choose the one with the best price and pay for it with my credit card.

_____

D Look back at the sample catalog on page 116. With a partner, practice buying and selling three of the items listed on the page. (Lesson 2) (Conversations will vary.)

E Write a conversation about one of the items on page 116. Continue on another piece of paper if needed. (Lesson 2) (Answers will vary.)

Salesperson: How can I help you today?

Customer: Hi, I'm interested in buying a wok.

Salesperson: We have a good one here for $46.95.

Customer: Oh, that's expensive. Does it come with a warranty?

Salesperson: Yes, it comes with a one year warranty and a steamer.

Customer: That sounds reasonable. I'll take this wok set.

AT-A-GLANCE PREP

Objectives: All unit objectives
Grammar: All unit grammar
Academic Strategy: Reviewing
Vocabulary: All Unit 6 vocabulary

RESOURCES

Stand Out 5 Assessment CD-ROM with Exam*View*®

■ 1.5 hour classes　■ 2.5 hour classes　■ 3⁺ hour classes

Warm-up and Review　5-10 mins.

Review appositives with students. Have students write a few examples in groups and then share them with the class.

Introduction　5-10 mins.

Ask students as a class to try to recall all the objectives of this unit without looking back in their books. The objectives for this unit include doing product research, purchasing goods and services by phone and Internet, interpreting product guarantees and warranties, returning a product, and selling a product. Write all the objectives on the board from Unit 6. Show students the first page of the unit and mention the five objectives.

State the objective: *Today we will be reviewing everything we have learned in this unit and preparing for the team project.*

Presentation 1　10-15 mins.

This presentation will cover the first three pages of the review. Quickly go to the first page of each lesson. Discuss the objective of each. Ask simple questions to remind students of what they have learned.

Note: Since there is little presentation in the review, you can assign the review exercises that don't require collaboration with a partner or group for homework and go over them in class the following day.

Practice 1　20-25 mins.

Note: There are two ways to do the review:
1. Go through the exercises one at a time and, as students complete each one, go over the answers.
2. Quickly go through the instructions of each exercise, let students complete all of the exercises at once, and then go over the answers.

(A) Imagine that you are going to buy a used car. Write four questions you would ask car owners who want to sell their car. (Lesson 1)

(B) Ask your classmates the questions you wrote in Exercise A. Write some of their responses below. When your classmates ask you their questions, you can talk about your own car or a car you are familiar with. (Lesson 1)

(C) Imagine that you are going to buy a product online. Write a short paragraph about the steps you will need to take to buy the product. (Lesson 2)

(D) Look back at the sample catalog on page 116. With a partner, practice buying and selling three of the items listed on the page. (Lesson 2)

(E) Write a conversation about one of the items on page 116. Continue on another piece of paper if needed. (Lesson 2)

Evaluation 1　5-15 mins.

Go around the classroom and check on students' progress. Help individuals when needed. If you see consistent errors among several students, interrupt the class and give a mini-lesson or review to help students feel comfortable with the concept.

STANDARDS CORRELATIONS

CASAS: 7.2.1 (See CASAS Competency List on pages 187–193.)
SCANS: **Resources** Allocate time
Information Acquire and evaluate information
Interpersonal Participate as a member of a team, teach others, negotiate to arrive at a decision, work with cultural diversity
Systems Monitor and correct performance
Basic Skills Reading, writing, arithmetic, listening, speaking

Thinking Skills Think creatively, make decisions, solve problems, see things in the mind's eye
Personal Qualities Responsibility, sociability, self-management
EFF: **Communication** Read with understanding, convey ideas in writing, speak so others can understand, listen actively, observe critically
Interpersonal Cooperate with others, guide others
Lifelong Learning Take responsibility for learning, reflect and evaluate

Practice 1 *(continued)*   25-30 mins. ▪▪▪▫

F Read the following warranty and circle *T* (true) or *F* (false). (Lesson 3)

G Working in pairs, practice asking questions about returning items. One student is a customer and one is a clerk. Switch roles. Use the following return policy to explain the rules. (Lesson 4)

H Write appositives to complete each statement below. (Lesson 5)

I Using one of the statements in Exercise H, write an ad for the product on another piece of paper. Include an appositive somewhere in the ad. (Lesson 5)

Evaluation 1 *(continued)*   5-10 mins. ▪▪▪▫

Go around the classroom and check on students' progress. Help individuals when needed. If you see consistent errors among several students, interrupt the class and give a mini-lesson or review to help students feel comfortable with the concept.

Teacher Tip

Recycling/Review

The review exercises, the research activity, and the team project are part of the recycling/review process. Students often need to be reintroduced to concepts to solidify what they have learned. Many concepts are learned and forgotten when students are engaged in learning other new concepts. This is because students learn but are not necessarily ready to acquire language concepts.

Therefore, it becomes very important to review material with students and to show them how to review it on their own. It is also important to recycle the new concepts in different contexts.

(F) Read the following warranty and circle *T* (true) or *F* (false). (Lesson 3)

> CLARICO warrants this product against defects in material and workmanship under normal use and service for one year from the original purchase date. CLARICO will repair or replace the defective product covered by this warranty. Please retain the dated sales receipt as evidence of the date of purchase. You will need it for any warranty service. In order to keep this warranty in effect, the product must have been handled and used as described in the instructions accompanying this warranty. This warranty does not cover any damage due to accident, misuse, abuse, or negligence.

1. This warranty is good for two years.   T   (F)
2. CLARICO will replace your product if it gets stolen.   T   (F)
3. You need your receipt to get service under this warranty.   (T)   F
4. This warranty covers product defects.   (T)   F

(G) Working in pairs, practice asking questions about returning items. One student is a customer and one is a clerk. Switch roles. Use the following return policy to explain the rules. (Lesson 4) (Questions and answers will vary.)

> Valid photo ID required for all returns (except for credit card purchases), exchanges, and to receive and redeem store credit. With a receipt, a full refund in the original form of payment, except payments made with checks, will be issued for new and unread books and unopened music within 4 days. For merchandise purchased with a check, a store credit will be issued within the first 7 days. Without an original receipt, a store credit issued by mail will be offered at the lowest selling price. With a receipt, returns of new and unread books and unopened music from our Web site can be made for store credit. Textbooks after 14 days or without a receipt are not returnable. Used books are not returnable.

1. return books with the original receipt
2. return textbooks after three weeks

3. return two calendars without a receipt
4. exchange CDs that have not been opened

(H) Write appositives to complete each statement below. (Lesson 5) (Answers will vary.)

1. This pre-owned car, _____ a four-door sedan _____, has been thoroughly inspected and is in tip-top shape.

2. This laptop computer, _____ the lightest on the market _____, still has a two-year warranty.

3. Two theater tickets, _____ the most expensive in town _____, can be used any weeknight in the month of August.

4. The bicycle, _____ a red, ten-speed _____, has barely been ridden.

(I) Using one of the statements in Exercise H, write an ad for the product on another piece of paper. Include an appositive somewhere in the ad. (Lesson 5) (Answers will vary.)

VOCABULARY REVIEW

 J **Use the following words in a sentence.** (Answers will vary.)

1. allege: <u>The salesperson alleged that this computer was the best for $1000.</u>

2. guarantee: <u>The guarantee stated that all parts were covered.</u>

3. quality: <u>The quality of the product should be guaranteed.</u>

4. convince: <u>Salespeople convince customers to buy new things.</u>

5. malfunction: <u>If the computer malfunctions, we will replace it.</u>

6. policy: <u>Our policy is to refund gifts with store credit.</u>

 K **Share your sentences with a partner. Write your partner's best sentence below.**

<u>(Answers will vary.)</u>

 L **Match each word to its synonym.**

Word	**Synonym**
1. return <u>h</u>	a. claim
2. refund <u>e</u>	b. promise
3. model <u>g</u>	c. match
4. guarantee <u>b</u>	d. replace
5. exchange <u>d</u>	e. reimburse
6. convince <u>f</u>	f. persuade
7. conform <u>c</u>	g. type
8. allege <u>a</u>	h. take back

Practice 1 (continued)   25–30 mins. ■■■□

Vocabulary Review

(J) Use the following words in a sentence.

(K) Share your sentences with a partner. Write your partner's best sentence below.

(L) Match each word below to its synonym.

Evaluation 1 (continued)   ■■□□

Go around the classroom and check on students' progress. Help individuals when needed. If you see consistent errors among several students, interrupt the class and give a mini-lesson or review to help students feel comfortable with the concept.

Assessment (optional)   ■■■□

Use the Stand Out 5 Assessment CD-ROM with Exam*View*® to create a post-test for Unit 6.

Objective: Research placing an ad
Academic Strategy: Research

RESOURCES

Printed information from the Internet on how to place an ad in the newspaper or online auction site.

Internet access

Activity Bank: Research—How to compare product information from an online source

AGENDA

Come up with ways to sell various items.

Find out what is involved in different ways to sell items.

Academic Feature: Research Project

Each unit will have a research page where students are required to complete a task by conducting research. Options will be given for students to use the Internet as well as printed resource materials. The printed resource materials can be found on the Activity Bank CD-ROM.

Introduction   5–10 mins.

Ask students the following questions and have a brief discussion. *What did you learn about in this unit that you would like to know more about? How can you find out more about these topics?*

State the objective: *Today we will talk about different ways to sell things and research how to place an ad.*

Presentation   10–15 mins.

A There are quite a few ways to sell things. What items might you try to sell using the following methods?

B Can you think of other ways to sell something? Write down your ideas.

Practice   10–15 mins.

There are materials on the Activity Bank to help students compare products online. They should keep the features they compare in mind when they consider listing an item online.

C Imagine that you are going to sell something. Find out what is involved in using the two methods below. Write notes after each method. (*Ideas:* How much does it cost to place the ad? How long will the ad stay up? How many words can you write?)

Evaluation   5–10 mins.

Have students share their research with the class.

STANDARDS CORRELATIONS

CASAS: 4.9.3, 7.2.1, 7.4.4, 7.4.5, 7.4.6 (See CASAS Competency List on pages 187–193.)
SCANS: **Information** Acquire and evaluate information, organize and maintain information, interpret and communicate information, use computers to process information *(optional)*
Interpersonal Participate as a member of a team, teach others, negotiate to arrive at a decision, work with cultural diversity
Systems Understand systems
Technology Select technology, apply technology to a task, maintain and troubleshoot technology *(optional)*

Basic Skills Reading, writing
Thinking Skills Think creatively, make decisions, see things in the mind's eye
Personal Qualities Responsibility, sociability, self-management
EFF: **Communication** Read with understanding, convey ideas in writing, observe critically
Decision Making Solve problems and make decisions, plan
Lifelong Learning Take responsibility for learning, reflect and evaluate, learn through research, use information and communications technology *(optional)*

Research Project

A **There are quite a few ways to sell things. What items might you try to sell using the following methods?** (Answers will vary.)

1. Placing an ad in the newspaper: _furniture, car, appliances, pets_

2. Having a yard sale: _pots & pans, toys, dishes, books, machines_

3. Posting a sign on the sale item: _car, house, farm equipment, vegetables grown, furniture_

4. Placing an ad at a local community center, church, or library: _furniture, car, service, books_

5. Listing the item on an online auction site: _jewelry, computer, art_

B **Can you think of other ways to sell something? Write down your ideas.**

Email to friends, post sign in laundromat, post sign on telephone pole, put flyer in mailboxes or on people's front step

C **Imagine that you are going to sell something. Find out what is involved in using the two methods below. Write notes after each method.** (*Ideas:* **How much does it cost to place the ad? How long will the ad stay up? How many words can you write?**) (Answers will vary.)

Placing an ad in the newspaper: _____

_____

_____

_____

_____

_____

Listing an item on an online auction site: _____

_____

_____

_____

_____

_____

_____

Team Project

Create an online or catalog-only store.

1. Form a team with four or five students. Choose positions for each member of your team.

POSITION	JOB DESCRIPTION	STUDENT NAME
Student 1: **Project Leader**	See that everyone speaks English. See that everyone participates.	
Student 2: **Secretary**	Take notes on your team's ideas.	
Student 3: **Designer**	Design layout of catalog or Web page.	
Student 4: **Director**	Assign each team member one part of presentation. Organize presentation so that individual parts create a unified whole.	
Student 5: **Assistant**	Help secretary and designer with their work.	

2. Decide the name of your store and what you will sell. Select a variety of items to sell.

3. Create the following items for your store: catalog or Web pages, the store's return policy, and a warranty/guarantee policy.

4. Prepare a poster that contains all of the information in Steps 2 and 3.

5. Present your store's catalog pages or Web pages to the class.

Team Project

Create an online or catalog-only store.

Each team will create a store where they will sell things over the Internet or by a catalog. For each store, the students must create a catalog page or a Web page. Then they must write a return policy and warranty of the items they carry in their store.

The team project is the final application for the unit. It gives students a chance to show that they have mastered all of the Unit 6 objectives.

Note: Shorter classes can extend this project over two class meetings.

Stage 1   5 mins.

Form a team with four or five students. Choose positions for each member of your team.

Have students decide who will lead each step as described on the student page. Provide well-defined directions on the board for how teams should proceed. Explain that all the students do every step as a team. Teams shouldn't go to the next stage until the previous one is complete.

Stage 2   5 mins.

Decide the name of your store and what you will sell. Select a variety of items to sell.

Ask the spokesperson of each team to report this information to the class.

Stage 3   20-30 mins.

Create the following items for your store: a catalog or Web page(s), the store's return policy, and a warranty/guarantee policy.

Stage 4   15-20 mins.

Prepare a poster that contains all of the information in Steps 2 and 3.

Optional Computer Activity: Students may want to use the computer to design their catalog page or Web pages.

Stage 5   15-20 mins.

Present your store's catalog pages or Web pages to the class.

Help teams prepare for their presentations. Suggest that each member choose a different part of the project to present to the class.

STANDARDS CORRELATIONS

CASAS: 4.8.1, 4.8.5, 4.8.6. (See CASAS Competency List on pages 187–193.)
SCANS: Resources Allocate time
Information Acquire and evaluate information, organize and maintain information, interpret and communicate information, use computers to process information
Systems Understand systems, improve and design systems
Technology Select technology, apply technology to exercise
Basic Skills Writing
Thinking Skills Think creatively, make decisions, solve problems, see things in the mind's eye, use reasoning

Personal Qualities Responsibility, self-esteem, self-management, integrity
EFF: Communication Read with understanding, convey ideas in writing, speak so others can understand, listen actively, observe critically
Decision Making Solve problems and make decisions, plan
Interpersonal Cooperate with others, advocate and influence, resolve conflict and negotiate, guide others
Lifelong Learning Take responsibility for learning, reflect and evaluate, learn through research, use information and communications technology (optional)

Objective: Introduce new vocabulary

Academic Strategies: Identifying and defining vocabulary, finding word families, using a dictionary

Vocabulary: See lesson

RESOURCES

Dictionaries: It is recommended that each student in class have an ESL learner's dictionary or that there be dictionaries available in the classroom for students to use. Dictionaries that will be referred to in this book are the *Heinle's Newbury House Dictionary*

AGENDA

Label and describe technology.
Illustrate and define vocabulary.
Find nouns and adjectives in word families.

---

of American English and the *Collins Cobuild Intermediate* or *Advanced Dictionary of American English*.

Academic Feature: Vocabulary Builder

Each unit will begin with a vocabulary-building section. The purpose of this two-page section is to introduce students to many of the words they will be using in the unit lessons. Students will have a chance to see how much they already know, and they will get exposure to the new vocabulary found in the unit.

Note: All of the exercises on these two pages should be done in class, no matter the class length. Longer classes can do this lesson and then move onto Lesson 1 during the same class meeting; shorter classes may have to devote one whole class meeting to this lesson.

Introduction   5–10 mins.

Ask students what types of technology they have in their homes. Get them started by writing *telephone* on the board.

State the objective: *Today we will be identifying and working with the vocabulary you will learn in this unit.*

Presentation 1   5–10 mins.

Get students started on Exercise A by reviewing the directions and then describing the purpose of one or two items together. Have them complete Exercise A for Practice 1.

Practice 1   10–15 mins.

Ⓐ Use the terms in the box below to label each item you might find in an office. Under each item, write a brief description of its purpose.

Evaluation 1   5 mins.

Go over the answers as a class. Ask students if they see any of these items in the classroom. If so, have them point them out. Also, ask if they have any of these items at home or at work.

STANDARDS CORRELATIONS

CASAS: 4.5.1, 7.4.5 (See CASAS Competency List on pages 187–193.)
SCANS: Information Acquire and evaluate information, organize and maintain information
Interpersonal Participate as a member of a team, negotiate to arrive at a decision, work with cultural diversity
Systems Understand systems, monitor and correct performance
Basic Skills Reading, writing, listening, speaking
Thinking Skills Think creatively, make decisions, see things in the mind's eye
Personal Qualities Responsibility, sociability, self-management

EFF: Communication Read with understanding, convey ideas in writing, speak so others can understand, listen actively
Decision Making Use math to solve problems and communicate, solve problems and make decisions, plan
Interpersonal Cooperate with others
Lifelong Learning Take responsibility for learning, reflect and evaluate, learn through research

---

The Office

GOALS

➤ **Identify and use technology**
➤ **Resolve technology problems**
➤ **Establish an organizational system**

➤ **Identify and resolve problems at work**
➤ **Report progress**

Vocabulary Builder

Vocabulary | Grammar
Life Skills
Academic | Pronunciation

A Use the terms in the box below to label each item you might find in an office. Under each item, write a brief description of its purpose. (Answers may vary.)

business telephone	fax machine	LCD projector	photocopier
~~laptop computer~~	flash drive	paper shredder	printer
external hard drive	label maker	PDA	scanner

laptop computer: process

information, create reports

and do Internet research

external hard drive:

provides more memory,

exchanges information.

business telephone:

allows hold, transfers

calls, conference calls

photocopier:

makes copies,

collates papers

paper shredder;

destroys sensitive

personal documents

flash drive: provides

extra storage/

memory for computer

printer: prints

documents

and photos

scanner: scans photos,

art, documents for

saving to computer

Vocabulary Builder

fax machine: sends copies of docs on phone line

PDA: stores calendar, contact information, emails

label maker: prints sticky labels

LCD projector: projects images and slide shows from computer

B A great way to remember vocabulary is to draw a picture of the items you are learning. Look up the following words if you don't know them and draw a picture for each one. (Remember to look for the definition that is related to technology.)

(Drawings will vary.)

handset	cable	port	memory card

C These three technology terms cannot be easily drawn. Write a definition for each one.

1. troubleshoot: to search for the solution of a technical problem

2. paper jam: paper caught in the workings of a machine

3. feed: to put paper into the proper machine area

D Look at the verbs in the chart below. Find the nouns and adjectives in the verbs' word families. (*Hint:* Not every verb has an adjective in its family.)

Verb	Noun	Adjective
compete	competition	competitive
collaborate	collaboration	collaborative
avoid	avoidance	avoidance
accommodate	accomodation	accommodating
compromise	compromise	compromising
motivate	motivation	motivational
resolve	resolution	resolute

Presentation 2   5–10 mins.

Go over the instructions to Exercises B, C, and D.

Pronunciation

Vocabulary

When teaching students new vocabulary, pronounce each word for them several times and ask them to repeat it. Many times, students may be familiar with the words you are saying but have never seen them spelled out. By pronouncing the words for students, you allow students to make a connection between the words' spellings and their sounds. It is also important that students learn the correct pronunciation of new words so they feel comfortable using their new vocabulary inside and outside of the classroom. Remember to point out which letters are silent when pronounced aloud.

Practice 2   10–15 mins.

B A great way to remember vocabulary is to draw a picture of the items you are learning. Look up the following words if you don't know them and draw a picture for each one. (Remember to look for the definition that is related to technology.)

C These three technology terms cannot be easily drawn. Write a definition for each one.

D Look at the verbs in the chart below. Find the nouns and adjectives in the verbs' word families. (*Hint:* Not every verb has an adjective in its family.)

Evaluation 2   10–15 mins.

Go over the answers as a class.

AT-A-GLANCE PREP

Objective: Identify and use technology
Academic Strategy: Paraphrasing
Vocabulary: *power supply, USB, port, firewire, cable, document, feeder*

RESOURCES

Activity Bank: Unit 7, Lesson 1, Worksheet 1
Grammar Challenge 5: Unit 7, Challenge 1

 1.5 hour classes   2.5 hour classes   3⁺ hour classes

AGENDA

Connect a printer.
Connect an external hard drive.
Use a fax machine.
Write instructions.

Suggested Realia: Computer, hard drive, printer, scanner, technology manuals

Stand Out 5 Assessment CD-ROM with *ExamView*®

 Pre-assessment *(optional)*

Use the Stand Out 5 Assessment CD-ROM with *ExamView*® to create a pre-test for Unit 7.

Warm-up and Review   5–10 mins.

Ask students to write a list of the vocabulary they learned in the vocabulary-building lessons without looking back in their books. Have them share their list with a partner and try to add more words to their list. For extra practice, have them discuss what each word means.

Introduction   5–10 mins.

Dictation:

1. Make sure it is plugged in and turned on.
2. Put less than 50 sheets of paper in the paper tray.
3. Select the document you want to print.
4. Click on the word *Print* in the print dialog box.

Ask students this question once the dictation is complete: *Two pieces of technological equipment are being discussed in these instructions. What are they?*

State the objective: *Today we will interpret and follow instructions for connecting and using technology.*

Presentation 1   10–15 mins.

Ask students what kinds of technology they have in their homes. *Raise your hand if you have a computer. Raise your hand if you have a printer.* Ask the same questions about technology they use at work. Have a discussion about who uses the technology in both of these places. Ask them who set up the technology.

A **Read the instructions for connecting a printer.**
Go over the instructions as a class.

Practice 1   10–15 mins.

B **Reread the instructions until you completely understand them. Then, in your own words, tell a partner how to connect a printer to a computer. (If you have a computer and printer in your classroom, you can explain the steps as you do them.)**

If you think students need more practice, have them work with several different partners, doing the exercise as many times as necessary.

Note: See page 136a for a teaching tip on paraphrasing.

Evaluation 1   5–10 mins.

Ask a few volunteers to explain the directions to the class without looking at their books.

STANDARDS CORRELATIONS

CASAS: 4.4.8, 4.5.1, 4.5.4, 4.5.6 (See CASAS Competency List on pages 187–195.)
SCANS: **Information** Acquire and evaluate information, organize and maintain information, interpret and communicate information
Interpersonal Participate as a member of a team, teach others, exercise leadership, work with cultural diversity
Systems Understand systems, monitor and correct performance, improve and design systems
Technology Select technology, apply technology to a task

Basic Skills Reading, writing, listening, speaking
Thinking Skills Think creatively, make decisions
Personal Qualities Responsibility, sociability, self-management
EFF: **Communication** Read with understanding, convey ideas in writing, speak so others can understand, listen actively
Interpersonal Cooperate with others, guide others
Lifelong Learning Take responsibility for learning, reflect and evaluate, use information and communications technology

---

How do you turn it on?

GOAL ➤ Identify and use technology

Vocabulary
Grammar
Life Skills
Academic
Pronunciation

A Read the instructions for connecting a printer.

Instructions for Connecting Your Printer

1. Take the **printer** out of the box and set it next to your **computer**.

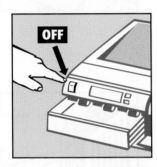

2. Make sure the printer is **off**.

3. Plug the **power supply cord** into the back of the printer and then plug it into the wall socket.

4. Plug one end of the **USB cable** into the **USB port** on the back of the printer. Plug the other end into the **USB port** on the computer.

B Reread the instructions until you completely understand them. Then, in your own words, tell a partner how to connect a printer to a computer. (If you have a computer and printer in your classroom, you can explain the steps as you do them.)

GOAL ➤ Identify and use technology

C Connecting an external hard drive is similar to connecting a printer. Match each of the instructions below to the correct picture. Then, label each computer part in the diagrams below with the bold words from the instructions.

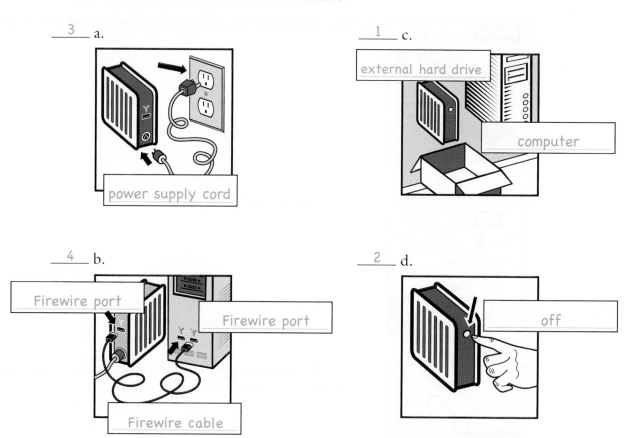

3 a.

power supply cord

1 c.

external hard drive

computer

4 b.

Firewire port

Firewire port

Firewire cable

2 d.

off

1. Take the **external hard drive** out of the box and set it next to your **computer**.

2. Make sure the external hard drive is **off**.

3. Plug the **external power supply** into the back of the external hard drive and then plug it into the wall socket.

4. Plug one end of the **firewire cable** into the **firewire port** on the back of the external hard drive. Plug the other end into the **firewire port** on the computer.

Presentation 2   5 mins.

Go over the instructions for Exercise C.

Practice 2   10-15 mins.

Note: Shorter classes can do this exercise for homework.

C Connecting an external hard drive is similar to connecting a printer. Match each of the instructions below to the correct picture. Then, label each computer part in the diagrams below with the bold words from the instructions.

Extra Practice: Now that students have completed two exercises related to connecting pieces of hardware, have them close their books and take out a sheet of paper. Have them write and illustrate the instructions for connecting something to a computer, either a printer or an external hard drive.

Even Better Practice: Set up a computer somewhere in the classroom where students can practice connecting something to it—a printer, a hard drive, a scanner, etc. Have students work in pairs to practice connecting the external component to the computer.

Evaluation 2   10-15 mins.

Go over the answers as a class.

Activity Bank

Unit 7, Lesson 1, Worksheet 1: Technology Instructions

 Refer students to *Stand Out 5 Grammar Challenge*, **Unit 7, Challenge 1 for practice with nouns: phrases, pronouns, and clauses.**

Instructor's Notes

Presentation 3   5-10 mins. ■■■□

Look at the fax machine together and go over all the parts.

Practice 3   15-20 mins. ■

Note: Shorter classes can do this exercise for homework.

D Read the excerpt from a fax machine manual and answer the questions that follow it.

Evaluation 3   5-10 mins. ■

Go over the answers as a class.

Application   10-20 mins. ■■■

E Look back at the list of technology items on pages 133-134. Choose one item that you are familiar with and write a list of instructions with illustrations. Review instructions with a partner for clarity.

Have students share their completed instructions with the class.

D Read the excerpt from a fax machine manual and answer the questions that follow it.

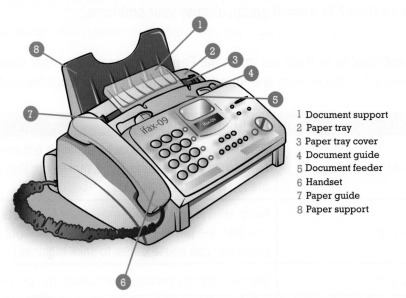

1 Document support
2 Paper tray
3 Paper tray cover
4 Document guide
5 Document feeder
6 Handset
7 Paper guide
8 Paper support

QUICK START

This chapter gives you a brief introduction to the basic functions of the fax machine. Please refer to the rest of the manual for more detailed instructions.

SENDING A FAX

1. Place the document to be sent (up to 15 pages) in the document feeder.
2. Dial the number in one of the following ways:
a. Dial the number and press start.
b. Lift the handset, dial the number, and press start.
c. Push the speakerphone button, dial the number, and press start.
d. Press and hold the one-touch button. *(See one-touch dialing on page 15.)*
e. Press the speed-dial button, enter a speed-dial code, and press start. *(See speed dialing on page 16.)*

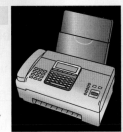

RECEIVING A FAX

There are three modes for receiving faxes:

1. FAX mode: The fax machine will answer the phone, detect fax tones, and receive the fax.
2. AUTO answer mode: The telephone rings for a certain number of rings and then switches to fax receiving.
3. TEL answer mode: You must manually receive the fax:
a. Answer the phone.
b. If you hear a fax tone, press the start button.
c. Once you hear the fax tones from both machines, hang up the phone to receive the fax.

1. When sending a fax, how many different ways are there to dial? _____5_____

2. Which method doesn't require pushing the start button? _____d_____

3. How many pages can you fax at once? _____15_____

4. How many ways are there to receive a fax? _____3_____

5. Which mode requires that you answer the phone? _____TEL answer mode_____

E Look back at the list of technology items on pages 133–134. Choose one item that you are familiar with and write a list of instructions with illustrations. Review instructions with a partner for clarity. (Answers will vary.)

LESSON 2

How do you fix it?

GOAL ➤ **Resolve technology problems**

A Think of some problems you have had in the past with technology. What were the problems? How did you fix them? In a small group, discuss your problems.
(Sample problems: jammed paper, no ink, computer slow, lost documents)

B Carla is having trouble with her fax machine. For some reason, no paper comes out when she tries to receive a fax. Read what she found in her manual under *troubleshooting*.

Problem	Solution
Paper jams during printing.	Remove the jammed paper by pulling it out smoothly. If the paper tears while you are removing it, make sure that no small pieces are left inside the machine.
Paper sticks together.	Make sure you don't have more than 40 sheets in the paper tray. Take the paper out, fan the pages, and put them back in. (Humidity can cause pages to stick together.)
Paper won't feed.	Remove any obstructions from inside the printer.
Multiple sheets of paper feed at the same time.	When loading the paper, do not force the paper down into the printer. If multiple sheets have caused a paper jam, clear it.

C Answer the questions based on the troubleshooting guide.

1. What should you do if paper tears while you are removing it from the printer?
   Make sure there are no small torn pieces left in the machine.

2. How many sheets can the paper tray hold? No more than 40.

3. What causes pages to stick together? Humidity.

4. What should you do if the paper won't feed? Remove obstructions or blockages
   from inside the printer.

5. What should you do if there is a paper jam? Remove the paper by pulling gently
   and smoothly.

D Based on the information above, what are three suggestions you might give Carla?

1. Check to see if the paper is jammed.

2. Check if the paper is stuck together; fan the pages.

3. Look to see if multiple pages fed at one time; remove.

AT-A-GLANCE PREP

Objective: Resolve technology problems
Academic Strategies: Solving problems and making decisions
Vocabulary: *paper jam, feed, fan, humidity, obstructions, force, faded, splotchy, cartridge, toner, LCD screen, resolution, display, compartment*

RESOURCES

Activity Bank: Unit 7, Lesson 2, Worksheet 1
Grammar Challenge 5: Unit 7, Challenge 2

 1.5 hour classes   2.5 hour classes 3⁺ hour classes

Audio: CD Track 33
Suggested Realia: Technology manuals

AGENDA

Troubleshoot fax machine problems.
Listen to employees.
Troubleshoot problems with a digital camera.
Troubleshoot problems with a label maker.
Ask classmates for help.

Warm-up and Review   5-10 mins.

Ask volunteers to stand up and give the class instructions on using technology.

Introduction   5-10 mins.

Dictation:

1. When loading the paper, do not force the paper down into the printer.
2. If you are using batteries, check that they are inserted correctly.
3. Make sure the tape compartment cover has been closed.
4. If the paper tears while you are removing it, make sure that no small pieces are left inside the machine.

State the objective: *Today we will learn how to resolve technology problems.*

Presentation 1   10-15 mins.

(A) Think of some problems you have had in the past with technology. What were the problems? How did you fix them? In a small group, discuss your problems.

(B) Carla is having trouble with her fax machine. For some reason, no paper comes out when she tries to receive a fax. Read what she found in her manual under *troubleshooting*.

Go over the manual excerpt as a class.

Practice 1   10-15 mins.

(C) Answer the questions based on the troubleshooting guide.

Have students do this exercise by themselves.

(D) Based on the information above, what are three suggestions you might give Carla?

Evaluation 1   5 mins.

Go over the answers as a class.

STANDARDS CORRELATIONS

CASAS: 4.5.7 (See CASAS Competency List on pages 187–193.)
SCANS: **Information** Acquire and evaluate information, interpret and communicate information
Interpersonal Participate as a member of a team, teach others, exercise leadership, negotiate to arrive at a decision, work with cultural diversity
Systems Understand systems, monitor and correct performance
Technology Maintain and troubleshoot technology
Basic Skills Reading, writing, listening, speaking
Thinking Skills Think creatively, make decisions, solve problems, see things in the mind's eye

Personal Qualities Responsibility, sociability, self-management
EFF: **Communication** Read with understanding, convey ideas in writing, speak so others can understand, listen actively, observe critically
Decision Making Solve problems and make decisions
Interpersonal Cooperate with others, advocate and influence, resolve conflict and negotiate, guide others
Lifelong Learning Take responsibility for learning, reflect and evaluate, learn through research

Presentation 2 5-10 mins.

Go over the instructions for Exercises E and F (separately).

Practice 2 10-15 mins.

 E Listen to the conversations between employees at a small printing company. Write the problems and suggestions for fixing them in the chart below.

🎧 Listening Script CD Track 33

Conversation 1

Aaron: *Hey, Linda, could you help me for a second?*
Linda: *Sure. What do you need?*
Aaron: *Something is wrong with my printer. The pages are coming out faded and splotchy.*
Linda: *Hmm. Sounds like a problem with your toner. Did you take it out and shake it?*
Aaron: *I tried that. It didn't help.*
Linda: *Well, then you probably need to replace the cartridge. When is the last time you changed it?*
Aaron: *I have no idea. Maybe six months ago?*
Linda: *Yep, that's probably the issue. Put another one in and see if that helps.*
Aaron: *Thanks, Linda.*

Conversation 2

Preston: *Oh, Mark, I'm so glad you were walking by.*
Mark: *What's up?*
Preston: *For some reason, my computer won't turn on.*
Mark: *That's strange.*
Preston: *I know. It was working just fine before lunch.*
Mark: *Did you check to make sure the power cord is plugged in?*
Preston: *No. Let me check. (pause) Boy, do I feel stupid. I must have knocked it out with my foot.*
Mark: *Happens to the best of us.*
Preston: *Thanks.*

(continued)

Conversation 3

Kim: *Claudia, do you know anything about this photocopier?*
Claudia: *I know a bit. Try me.*
Kim: *Well, it's just not working. When I push the green button, nothing happens.*
Claudia: *Is it plugged in?*
Kim: *Yep.*
Claudia: *Did you check to make sure there is paper in the paper tray?*
Kim: *Yep, it has plenty.*
Claudia: *What about the toner?*
Kim: *I didn't check the toner. How do I do that?*
Claudia: *Well, you can see on the display right here how much toner is left in the cartridge. Yep, it looks like it's low. This copier won't even try to make copies if the toner is too low. If you put a new toner cartridge in, that should solve your problem.*
Kim: *Thanks, Claudia.*

F Maya has to take pictures for her job as a home appraiser. She is having some problems with her digital camera. Look at her manual below and match each problem to its possible solution.

Evaluation 2 10-15 mins.

Go over the answers as a class.

Presentation 3 1 min.

Go over the instructions for Exercise G.

Practice 3 15-20 mins.

Note: Shorter classes can do this exercise for homework.

G Read the troubleshooting guide for the label maker. Fill in the best answer for each question and statement on the next page.

Note: Questions and answer choices for Exercise G are found on student book page 140.

 E Listen to the conversations between employees at a small printing company. Write the problems and suggestions for fixing them in the chart below.

CD
TR 33

Problem	Suggestions
Pages are faded and splotchy from printer.	1. Take out toner and shake. 2. Replace the cartridge.
Computer won't turn on.	1. Check that power cord is plugged in.
Photocopier not working.	1. Plug in. 2. Paper in tray. 3. Check the toner.

 F Maya has to take pictures for her job as a home appraiser. She is having some problems with her digital camera. Look at her manual below and match each problem to its possible solution.

Problem

1. Camera will not operate. __b__
2. Camera won't take any more pictures or video. __d__
3. Only a few pictures will fit on the memory card. __e__
4. Battery loses its charge quickly. __c__
5. Pictures won't display on the LCD screen. __a__

Solution

a. Turn LCD screen on.
b. Turn camera on.
c. Replace battery.
d. Clear memory card.
e. Take pictures at a lower resolution.

 G Read the troubleshooting guide for the label maker. Fill in the best answer for each question and statement on the next page.

Problem	Solution
1. The display stays blank after you have turned on the machine.	Check that the AC adaptor is connected correctly. If you are using batteries, check that they are inserted correctly. If the batteries are low, replace them.
2. The machine doesn't print or the printed characters are blurred.	Check that the tape cassette has been inserted properly. If the tape cassette is empty, replace it. Make sure the tape compartment cover has been closed.
3. The text files that you stored in the memory are no longer there.	Replace the batteries.
4. A blank horizontal line appears through the printed label.	Clean the printhead.
5. Striped tape appears.	You have reached the end of the tape. Replace the tape cassette with a new one.

1. You should clean the printhead when
   - ○ a. striped tape appears.
   - ● b. a horizontal line appears.
   - ○ c. the display is blank.

2. When your files from memory are no longer there, you should
   - ○ a. connect the AC adaptor.
   - ○ b. clean the printhead.
   - ● c. replace the batteries.

3. What can you do if the printed characters are blurred?
   - ● a. Replace the tape cassette.
   - ○ b. Replace the batteries.
   - ○ c. Clean the printhead.

4. What does striped tape mean?
   - ○ a. The printhead is dirty.
   - ● b. The tape cassette needs to be replaced.
   - ○ c. The tape compartment needs to be closed.

H In a small group, ask for help with the technology problems below. Write down their suggestions in the chart below. (Answers will vary. Sample answers are given.)

Problem	Suggestions
My fax machine won't send a fax.	Check the phone connection. Check the power switch.
There is no dial tone on my telephone.	Check the phone jack. Press the receiver button again.
My printer won't print.	Check the toner. Check the plug.
My paper shredder won't shred.	Check the electric cord.
The copier keeps jamming.	Fan the paper. Look for small pieces stuck in copier.

I Share the suggestions you received with your other classmates. Which suggestions are the best? (Answers will vary.)

Evaluation 3   5-10 mins. ■

Go over the answers to Exercise G as a class.

Application   10-20 mins. ■■■

(H) In a small group, ask for help with the technology problems below. Write down their suggestions in the chart below.

Prepare students for this activity by having them look at the conversations from Practice 2. (The listening script can be found in the back of their books.) You can also create a sample conversation on the board. Encourage students to have a complete conversation, not just one that starts right off with the problem. Offer this example below if needed.

Student 1: _____, *can you help me with something?*

Student 2: *Sure.*

Student 1: *I can't get my fax machine to send a fax.*

Student 2: *Hmm, that's strange. Is there paper in the tray?*

Student 1: *Yes, that's the first thing I checked.*

Student 2: *Maybe there's a paper jam.*

Student 1: *I didn't even think to open up the machine. (pause) Yep, it looks like a small piece of paper is stuck in there. That should fix the problem. Thanks, _____.*

(I) Share the suggestions you received with your other classmates. Which suggestions are the best?

Activity Bank

Unit 7, Lesson 2, Worksheet 1: Troubleshoot
                            Technology (listening)

📖 Refer students to *Stand Out 5 Grammar Challenge*, Unit 7, Challenge 2 for practice with noun clauses as objects of prepositions.

Instructor's Notes

_____

_____

_____

_____

_____

_____

_____

_____

_____

_____

_____

_____

_____

_____

_____

_____

_____

_____

_____

_____

_____

_____

_____

_____

_____

_____

_____

_____

_____

_____

_____

_____

Objective: Establish an organizational system
Academic Strategy: Organizing paperwork
Vocabulary: *organize, reorganize, purchase orders, alphabetical order, hanging files, liabilities*

RESOURCES

Activity Bank: Unit 7, Lesson 3, Worksheet 1
Grammar Challenge 5: Unit 7, Challenge 3

■ 1.5 hour classes   ■ 2.5 hour classes   ■ 3⁺ hour classes

AGENDA

Group items.
Organize files.
Describe organizational problems and solutions.

Suggested Realia: Hanging file folders, file folders, labels, label maker (anything used for organizing)

Warm-up and Review   5–10 mins.

Ask students to share something new they learned in Lesson 2. Make a comprehensive list on the board as students are sharing.

Introduction   5–10 mins.

Dictation: Read all or as many of the tips below as you want.

Tips for Staying Organized

1. Put each item away after each use so you won't waste time searching for it when you really need it.
2. Set up a box in each room and use it for your clutter. Before it overflows, clean it out so it's ready to start collecting more stuff.
3. Use clear containers to store stuff. Seeing what's inside will save you a lot of time.
4. Keep a small container in a convenient place to hold keys, glasses, and wallets.
5. Schedule weekly bill-paying and paperwork sessions.
6. Keep files well categorized, alphabetized, and up-to-date.

State the objective: *Today we will practice establishing organizational systems.*

Presentation 1   10–15 mins.

(A) One way of organizing things is by putting similar items in groups. How would you organize this supply closet? Discuss your solutions with your classmates.

Practice 1   10–15 mins.

(B) On a separate piece of paper, reorganize the supply closet. Do a simple drawing of the closet with shelves and cabinets and show where you would keep each item.

Evaluation 1   5–10 mins.

Go over students' ideas as a class.

STANDARDS CORRELATIONS

CASAS: 4.5.3, 4.7.2 (See CASAS Competency List on pages 187–193.)
SCANS: **Resources** Allocate materials and facility resources
Information Acquire and evaluate information, organize and maintain information
Interpersonal Participate as a member of a team, teach others, exercise leadership, negotiate to arrive at a decision, work with cultural diversity
Systems Understand systems, monitor and correct performance, improve and design system
Basic Skills Reading, writing, arithmetic, listening, speaking

Thinking Skills Think creatively, make decisions, solve problems, see things in the mind's eye
Personal Qualities Responsibility, sociability, self-management
EFF: **Communication** Read with understanding, convey ideas in writing, speak so others can understand, listen actively, observe critically
Decision Making Solve problems and make decisions, plan
Interpersonal Cooperate with others, advocate and influence, resolve conflict and negotiate, guide others
Lifelong Learning Take responsibility for learning, reflect and evaluate

Files and folders

GOAL ➤ Establish an organizational system

Vocabulary · Grammar · Life Skills · Academic · Pronunciation

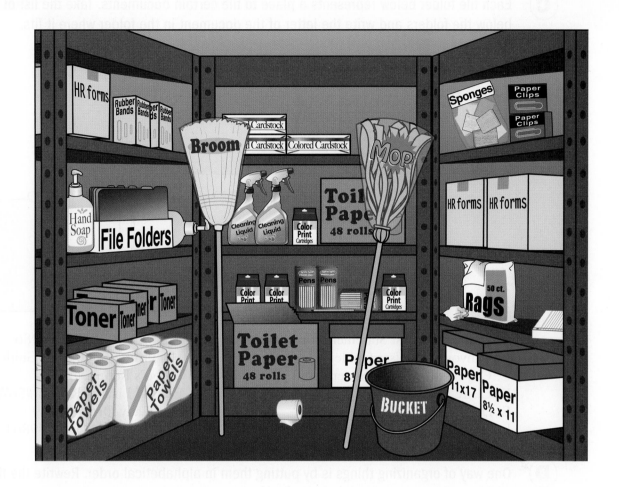

A One way of organizing things is by putting similar items in groups. How would you organize this supply closet? Discuss your solutions with your classmates.

Cleaning supplies/Bathroom supplies/Office supplies

B On a separate piece of paper, reorganize the supply closet. Do a simple drawing of the closet with shelves and cabinets and show where you would keep each item.

(Answers may vary.)

Cleaning supplies	Office supplies	Bathroom supplies
Paper towels	HR forms	Hand soap
Cleaning liquid	File folders	Toilet paper
Sponges	Toner	Cleaning liquid
Rags	Colored card stock	(also in cleaning supplies)
Bucket	Color print cartridges	Paper towels
Broom	Pens	(also in cleaning supplies)
Mop	Paper	
	Paper clips	

GOAL ➤ **Establish an organizational system**

C Each file folder below represents a place to file certain documents. Take the list of documents below the folders and write the letter of the document in the folder where it fits.

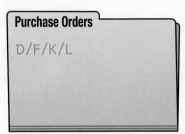

Purchase Orders
D/F/K/L

Bank Statements
A/C

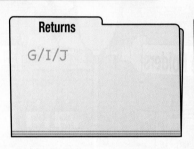

Returns
G/I/J

Manuals
B/E/H

A. Bank of the East Statement for March
B. Canyon i867 User Guide
C. City National Bank Statement for April
D. Claire's Order #7654
E. Delpi Photo Plus Manual
F. Dresses 'n' More Order #7625

G. Fancy Pants Return #7986
H. HL Printer 5000 User Guide
I. Jimbo's Return #7893
J. Leapin' Lizards Return #5678
K. Pink Lady Order #6879
L. Sunshine Girls Order #9864

D One way of organizing things is by putting them in alphabetical order. Rewrite the list of folders from above in alphabetical order.

1. Bank Statements
2. Manuals
3. Purchase Orders
4. Returns

E Organize the purchase orders and returns in Exercise C in numerical order. List them in order below.

Purchase Orders

1. #6879 (Pink Lady)
2. #7625 (Dresses n' More)
3. #7654 (Claire's)
4. #9864 (Sunshine Girls)

Returns

1. #5678 (Leapin' Lizards)
2. #7893 (Jimbo's)
3. #7986 (Fancy Pants)

Presentation 2 5-10 mins. ■■□

C Each file folder below represents a place to file certain documents. Take the list of documents below the folders and write the letter of the document in the folder where it fits.

Help students get started on this exercise and then let them finish by themselves.

Practice 2 10-15 mins. ■■□

Note: Shorter classes can do these exercises for homework.

D One way of organizing things is by putting them in alphabetical order. Rewrite the list of folders from above in alphabetical order.

E Organize the purchase orders and returns in Exercise C in numerical order. List them in order below.

Evaluation 2 10-15 mins. ■■□

Go over the answers as a class. Ask students what things they have at home that are filed or could be filed. Ask students to share some specific examples.

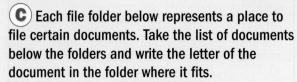

Presentation 3

10-15 mins.

F Lars knows he needs to get some organizing done in his home office. Read about his problem and solution.

Read about Lars as a class. Discuss his problem and solution. Ask: *Do you think it's a good solution? Why or why not? Is there one solution that is best? Or do different solutions work for different people?*

Practice 3

15-20 mins.

Note: Shorter classes can do this exercise for homework.

G In a small group, come up with organizing solutions for these problems.

Evaluation 3

10-15 mins. ▪

Have groups share their solutions. See how many people came up with the same solution. Vote on which solutions are the most creative.

Application

10-20 mins. ▪▪▪

H Think of an organizational problem you have at home, perhaps in your refrigerator, pantry, or garage. Describe the problem below and write out a detailed solution.

Activity Bank

Unit 7, Lesson 3, Worksheet 1: Organize it!

Refer students to *Stand Out 5 Grammar Challenge*, **Unit 7, Challenge 3 for practice with noun clauses as complements.**

F Lars knows he needs to get organized in his home office. Read about his problem and solution.

> **Problem:** My financial papers are very disorganized. They are in huge piles on my desk and in piles in my desk drawers.
>
> **Solution:** I'm going to buy hanging files and file folders. The tabs on my hanging files will be labeled as follows: Bank Accounts, Credit Cards, Income, Investments, Retirement Accounts, Liabilities, Insurance, Real Estate, and Tax Returns. Each hanging folder will be a different color and inside there will be file folders of that same color. For example, in my Bank Account file there will be a file folder for each of the three banks where I have accounts. Inside those folders, I will keep my bank statements and any papers related to that account.

G In a small group, come up with organizing solutions for these problems.
(Answers will vary. Sample answers below)

1. **Problem:** There are over 300 books scattered about the office, in bookshelves, on people's desks, and on the floor next to desks.

   Solution: Set up an office library in a hallway or spare room where everyone can have access to it.

2. **Problem:** Supply closet has supplies everywhere; nothing can be found.

   Solution: Organize the supply closet with clear labels and categories.

3. **Problem:** Papers are very disorganized; there are stacks of papers everywhere.

   Solution: Sort papers into active, inactive, and throw out piles. Sort into separate files. Maintain files daily.

H Think of an organizational problem you have at home, perhaps in your refrigerator, pantry, or garage. Describe the problem below and write out a detailed solution.

(Answers will vary. See Exercise F for an example.)

_____

_____

_____

_____

What's the problem?

GOAL ➤ Identify and resolve problems at work

 A Answer the following questions with a partner. (Answers will vary.)

1. What is *conflict resolution*? To solve a problem or argument.
2. Where are some places that conflicts might occur? The office, between businesses and relatives
3. Who are some people that you might have conflicts with? Boss, coworkers, roommates
4. Think about the ways you handle conflicts with people. What would you say your personal style of behavior is when speaking to people in conflict? Not very aggressive.

B As you read the article on the next few pages, think about the following questions. When you have finished, come back and answer them. (Answers may vary. See sample answers on LP page 144a.)

1. What are the three benefits to resolving conflict?
2. What can happen if conflict is not handled effectively?
3. What are the five different conflict styles in Thomas and Kilmann's theory?
4. What does *IBR* stand for? What are the six steps of the IBR approach?
5. What are the five steps for resolving conflict?

Conflict Resolution: Resolving Conflict Rationally and Effectively

In many cases, conflict in the workplace just seems to be a fact of life. We've all seen situations where different people with different goals and needs have come into conflict. And we've all seen the often intense personal animosity that can result.

The fact that conflict exists, however, is not necessarily a bad thing: As long as it is resolved effectively, it can lead to personal and professional growth.

The good news is that by resolving conflict successfully, you can solve many of the problems that it has brought to the surface, as well as getting benefits that you might not at first expect:

1. **Increased understanding**: The discussion needed to resolve conflict expands people's awareness of the situation, giving them an insight into how they can achieve their own goals without undermining those of other people;

2. **Increased group cohesion**: When conflict is resolved effectively, team members can develop stronger mutual respect and a renewed faith in their ability to work together;

3. **Improved self-knowledge**: Conflict pushes individuals to examine their goals in close detail, helping them understand the things that are most important to them, sharpening their focus, and enhancing their effectiveness.

However, if conflict is not handled effectively, the results can be damaging. Conflicting goals can quickly turn into personal dislike. Teamwork breaks down. Talent is wasted as people disengage from their work. And it's easy to end up in a vicious downward spiral of negativity and recrimination. If you're to keep your team or organization working effectively, you need to stop this downward spiral as soon as you can. To do this, it helps to understand two of the theories that lie behind effective conflict-resolution techniques.

Understanding the Theory: *Conflict Styles*

In the 1970s, Kenneth Thomas and Ralph Kilmann identified five main styles of dealing with conflict that vary in their degrees of cooperativeness and assertiveness.

Competitive: People who tend towards a competitive style take a firm stand and know what they want. They usually operate from a position of power, drawn from things like title, rank, expertise, or persuasive ability. This style can be useful when there is an emergency and a decision needs to be made fast; when the decision is unpopular; or when defending against someone who is trying to exploit the situation selfishly. However, it can leave people feeling bruised, unsatisfied, and resentful when used in less urgent situations.

(Continued)

Objective: Identify and resolve problems at work
Academic Strategies: Analyzing reading, defining vocabulary, writing a summary
Vocabulary: See the article.

RESOURCES

Activity Bank: Unit 7, Lesson 4, Worksheets 1–4
Grammar Challenge 5: Unit 7, Challenge 4

■ 1.5 hour classes   ■ 2.5 hour classes   ■ 3⁺ hour classes

AGENDA

Discuss and read about conflict resolution.
Define new vocabulary.
Write a summary.

Warm-up and Review   5-10 mins. ■■■

Have students form small groups and discuss the organizational problems they wrote about in the previous lesson. Have them ask their classmates for suggestions on how to better organize.

Introduction   1 min. ■■■

Note: No dictation is included due to the length of the reading in this lesson. However, if you choose to do a dictation, choose a few sentences from the reading. Additionally, there are only two presentations in this lesson.

State the objective: *Today we will read and analyze an article on resolving conflicts.*

Presentation 1   10-15 mins. ■■■

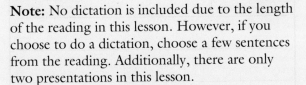 **Answer the following questions with a partner.**

After students complete Exercise A, go over the questions in Exercise B with students to help prepare them for the reading.

Practice 1   20-30 mins. ■■■

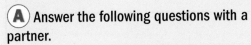 **As you read the article on the next few pages, think about the following questions. When you have finished, come back and answer them.**

Have students read the article silently.

Note: The article takes up all three pages of the lesson, not leaving much room for activities. See suggestions on the next page for activities you might want to do to help students better understand the reading. Also, there are more comprehension and vocabulary-building activities on the Activity Bank CD-ROM.

Evaluation 1   10-15 mins. ■■■

Once students have read the article, make sure they come back to the questions in Exercise B. Go over the answers as a class.

Sample answers:
1. Increased understanding, increased group cohesion, and improved self-knowledge
2. Conflicting goals can turn into personal dislike. Teamwork can break down. Talent can be wasted if people disengage from their work. Increasing negativity and recrimination in the workplace may result.
3. Competitive, collaborative, compromising, accomodating, avoiding
4. I(Interest)–B(Based) R(Relational) approach. The six steps are: 1. Make sure that good relationships are the first priority. 2. Keep people and problems separate. 3. Pay attention to the interests being presented. 4. Listen first; talk second. 5. Set out the "facts." 6. Explore options together.
5. The steps are: 1. Set the scene. 2. Gather information. 3. Agree on the problem. 4. Brainstorm possible solutions. 5. Negotiate a solution.

STANDARDS CORRELATIONS

CASAS: 4.8.1, 4.8.5, 4.8.6 (See CASAS Competency List on pages 187-193.)
SCANS: Information Acquire and evaluate information, organize and maintain information, interpret and communicate information
Interpersonal Teach others, work with cultural diversity
Systems Monitor and correct performance
Basic Skills Reading, writing, listening, speaking
Thinking Skills Think creatively, make decisions, see things in the mind's eye

Personal Qualities Responsibility, sociability, self-management
EFF: Communication Read with understanding, convey ideas in writing, speak so others can understand, listen actively, observe critically
Decision Making Plan
Interpersonal Cooperate with others, advocate and influence, resolve conflict and negotiate, guide others
Lifelong Learning Take responsibility for learning, reflect and evaluate, learn through research

Teaching Tip

Highlighting or taking notes while reading

The article in this lesson is long and complicated, but it is very similar to something students might read in a textbook in their college classes. The entire article is available on the Activity Bank CD-ROM, so you can print it out for students. A way to make the material easier to digest is to break it up into smaller pieces, having students read and analyze one piece at a time before moving on to the next. Show students how to go through the article by starting with the first part and reading it out loud. Tell them what you would highlight or take notes on. Once they have seen an example, have them do it themselves for the next section.

Teaching Tip

Jigsaw

One way to turn the reading into a cooperative learning activity would be to break up the pieces and assign each group one part. Each group will then be responsible for understanding its part and teaching it to the rest of the class.

Collaborative: People tending towards a collaborative style try to meet the needs of all people involved. These people can be highly assertive but, unlike the competitor, they cooperate effectively and acknowledge that everyone is important. This style is useful when you need to bring together a variety of viewpoints to get the best solution; when there have been previous conflicts in the group; or when the situation is too important for a simple trade-off.

Compromising: People who prefer a compromising style try to find a solution that will at least partially satisfy everyone. Everyone is expected to give up something, and the compromiser also expects to relinquish something. Compromise is useful when the cost of conflict is higher than the cost of losing ground, when equal strength opponents are at a standstill, and when there is a deadline looming.

Accommodating: This style indicates a willingness to meet the needs of others at the expense of the person's own needs. The accommodator often knows when to give in to others, but can be persuaded to surrender a position even when it is not warranted. This person is not assertive but is highly cooperative. Accommodation is appropriate when the issues matter more to the other party, when peace is more valuable than winning, or when you want to be in a position to collect on this "favor" you gave. However, people may not return favors, and overall this approach is unlikely to give the best outcomes.

Avoiding: People tending towards this style seek to evade the conflict entirely. This style is typified by delegating controversial decisions, accepting default decisions, and not wanting to hurt anyone's feelings. It can be appropriate when victory is impossible, when the controversy is trivial, or when someone else is in a better position to solve the problem. However, in many situations this is a weak and ineffective approach to take.

Understanding the Theory: *The Interest-based Relational Approach*

Once you understand the different styles, you can use them to think about the most appropriate approach (or mixture of approaches) for the situation you're in. You can also think about your own instinctive approach and learn how you need to change this if necessary.

The second theory is commonly referred to as the Interest-Based Relational (IBR) Approach. This conflict-resolution strategy respects individual differences while helping people avoid becoming too entrenched in a fixed position. In resolving conflict using this approach, you follow these rules:

1. **Make sure that good relationships are the first priority.** As far as possible, make sure that you treat the other calmly and that you try to build mutual respect. Do your best to be courteous to one-another and remain constructive under pressure.
2. **Keep people and problems separate.** Recognize that in many cases the other person is not just "being difficult"—real and valid differences can lie behind conflictive positions. By separating the problem from the person, real issues can be debated without damaging working relationships.
3. **Pay attention to the interests that are being presented.** By listening carefully you'll most likely understand why the person is adopting his or her position.
4. **Listen first; talk second.** To solve a problem effectively, you have to understand *where the other person is coming from* before defending your own position.
5. **Set out the "facts."** Agree and establish the objective, observable elements that will have an impact on the decision.
6. **Explore options together.** Be open to the idea that a third position may exist, and that you can get to this idea jointly.

By following these rules, you can often keep contentious discussions positive and constructive. This helps to prevent the antagonism and dislike which so often causes conflict to spin out of control.

Using the Tool: *A Conflict-Resolution Process*

Based on these approaches, a starting point for dealing with conflict is to identify the overriding conflict style employed by yourself, your team, or your organization. Look at the circumstances and think about the style that may be appropriate. Then use the process below to resolve the conflict.

(Continued)

Step One: Set the scene.

Make sure that people understand that the conflict may be a mutual problem, which may be best resolved through discussion and negotiation rather than through raw aggression. If you are involved in the conflict, emphasize the fact that you are presenting your perception of the problem. Use active listening skills to ensure you hear and understand others' positions and perceptions. And make sure that when you talk, you're using an adult, assertive approach rather than a submissive or aggressive style.

Step Two: Gather information.

Here you are trying to get to the underlying interests, needs, and concerns of the other people involved. Ask for the other people's viewpoints and confirm that you respect their opinions and need their cooperation to solve the problem. Try to understand their motivations and goals and see how your actions may be affecting them.

Step Three: Agree on the problem.

This sounds like an obvious step, but often different underlying needs, interests, and goals can cause people to perceive problems very differently. You'll need to agree on the problems that you are trying to solve before you'll find a mutually acceptable solution. Sometimes different people will see different but interlocking problems—if you can't reach a common perception of the problem, then, at the very least, you need to understand what the other people see as the problem.

Step Four: Brainstorm possible solutions.

If everyone is going to feel satisfied with the resolution, it will help if everyone has had fair input in generating solutions. Brainstorm possible solutions and be open to all ideas, including ones you never considered before.

Step Five: Negotiate a solution.

By this stage, the conflict may be resolved—both sides may better understand the position of the other, and a mutually satisfactory solution may be clear to all.

There are three guiding principles here: *Be Calm, Be Patient, Have Respect.* Managed in the wrong way, real and legitimate differences between people can quickly spiral out of control, resulting in situations where cooperation breaks down and the team's mission is threatened. This is particularly the case when the wrong approaches to conflict resolution are used.

To calm these situations down, it helps to take a positive approach to conflict resolution, where discussion is courteous and nonconfrontational, and the focus is on issues rather than on individuals. If this is done, then, as long as people listen carefully and explore facts, issues, and possible solutions properly, conflict can often be resolved effectively.

(Source: Used with permission from ©Mind Tools Ltd, 1995–2008, All rights reserved.)

C On another piece of paper, make a list of all the vocabulary words in the article that are unfamiliar to you. Choose ten that are the most important to your understanding of the article. Define them and write example sentences. (Answers will vary.)

D Choose one of the following topics and write a one-paragraph summary. (Answers will vary.)

1. Thomas and Killman's five conflict styles
2. The IBR approach
3. The five steps of the conflict-resolution process

Presentation 2   10-15 mins. ■■ ■ ■

Have students do the first part of Practice 2 (writing the list of words). When they have finished, have them call out all the unfamiliar words and make a comprehensive list on the board.

Practice 2   15-20 mins. ■

Note: Shorter classes can do this exercise for homework.

Ⓒ On another sheet of paper, make a list of all the vocabulary words in the article that are unfamiliar to you. Choose ten that are the most important to your understanding of the article. Define them and write example sentences.

Evaluation 2   15-20 mins. ■

Call on students to write their original sentences on the board. If some students are still unclear of a word's meaning, even after they have seen a student's example sentence, ask the sentence creator to define the word for the class.

Application   10-20 mins. ■■ ■

Ⓓ Choose one of the following topics and write a one-paragraph summary.

Before students begin the exercise, discuss the tips for writing a good summary.

Teaching Tip

Writing a summary

1. Make a brief outline of the important points you want to include in your summary.
2. Identify the main idea and write it first.
3. Identify only the most important supporting points and omit unnecessary details.
4. Use your own words, but don't include your own ideas or comments.
5. Present the ideas in the order in which they were discussed in the article.
6. Remind the reader that you are summarizing someone else's ideas by using citation expressions. (The author . . . says that, states that, explains that, points out that, mentions that, emphasizes that, argues that, maintains that, highlights the fact that, concludes that . . . .)

Activity Bank

Unit 7, Lesson 4, Worksheet 2: Conflict
                         Resolution—Vocabulary
Unit 7, Lesson 4, Worksheet 3: Conflict
                         Resolution—Scenarios

 Refer students to *Stand Out 5 Grammar Challenge*, Unit 7, Challenge 4 for practice with noun clauses as subjects.

Instructor's Notes

_____
_____
_____
_____
_____
_____
_____
_____
_____
_____
_____
_____
_____
_____
_____
_____
_____
_____
_____
_____
_____
_____
_____

AT-A-GLANCE PREP

Objective: Progress report
Grammar: Noun clauses as objects
Academic Strategy: Writing a progress report
Vocabulary: *long-term, in progress, cost-effective, effective*

RESOURCES
Activity Bank: Unit 7, Lesson 5, Worksheets 1–2
Grammar Challenge 5: Unit 7, Challenge 5

■ 1.5 hour classes ■ 2.5 hour classes ■ 3⁺ hour classes

Warm-up and Review   5-10 mins.

Discuss the article from the previous lesson. Ask students to write down three things they learned and then share them with the class.

Introduction   5-10 mins.

Dictation:

1. He has started on the project and will have it completed by June.
2. She put a team together to help her prepare the presentation by the end of the week.
3. They delegated the tasks to three teams of employees.
4. His supervisor asked him to head the new research project.

State the objective: *Today you will learn how to write a progress report.*

Presentation 1   10-15 mins.

 Maria's supervisor has asked her to write a progress report about a long-term project she is working on. Read the guidelines he gave her.

Go over the guidelines as a class.

B Read part of Maria's report. Is she following the guidelines so far?

Practice 1   5 mins.

C What does Maria still need to include in her report?

Evaluation 1   5 mins.

Go over the answers as a class.

STANDARDS CORRELATIONS

CASAS: 4.6.4 (See CASAS Competency List on pages 187–193.)
SCANS: **Resources** *(optional)* Allocate time, allocate money, allocate materials and facility resources, allocate human resources
Information Acquire and evaluate information, organize and maintain information, interpret and communicate information, use computers to process information
Interpersonal Participate as a member of a team, teach others, serve clients and customers, exercise leadership, negotiate to arrive at a decision, work with cultural diversity
Systems Understand systems, monitor and correct performance, improve and design systems

Technology Select technology, apply technology to a task, maintain and troubleshoot technology
Basic Skills Reading, writing, arithmetic, listening, speaking
Thinking Skills Think creatively, make decisions, solve problems, see things in the mind's eye
Personal Qualities Responsibility, sociability, self-management
EFF: **Communication** Read with understanding, convey ideas in writing
Decision Making Solve problems and make decisions, plan
Lifelong Learning Take responsibility for learning, reflect and evaluate, use information and communications technology *(optional)*

147a Lesson Planner: Unit 7, Lesson 5

What did you do?

GOAL ➤ **Report progress**

 A Maria's supervisor has asked her to write a progress report about a long-term project she is working on. Read the guidelines he gave her.

Progress Report Guidelines

You write a progress report to inform a supervisor, associate, or customer about progress you've made on a project over a certain period of time. In the progress report, you explain any or all of the following:

• how much of the work is complete,
• what part of the work is currently in progress,
• what work remains to be done,
• what problems or unexpected things, if any, have arisen,
• how the project is going in general.

(Source: Reprinted with permission from David A. McMurrey, author of *Power Tools for Technical Communication*, Boston: Heinle. 2001.)

B Read part of Maria's report. Is she following the guidelines so far?

To: Henry Kim, Human Resources Director
From: Maria Avalos
Date: April 14, 2008
Subject: Program for Employee Training

It seems that many problems have arisen from the employees working such long hours and not being able to communicate effectively with one another. It was proposed that I put together a training program for our employees on conflict resolution.

So far, I have been conducting research on whether it is better to bring in an outside training organization or do the training ourselves. I have concluded that it would be more cost-effective for us to do the training ourselves. So, I am currently working on putting together a training manual that can be used for the conflict-resolution training. I foresee that it will take me another two weeks to complete the manual. Once it has been completed, we will need to choose several people to conduct the training and train them to be effective leaders.

 C What does Maria still need to include in her report? (Answers will vary.)

1. How much of the manual has been completed

2. How she will choose the trainers and the conflict-resolution leaders

LESSON 5 **GOAL** ➤ **Report progress**

D Study the chart with your classmates and teacher.

Noun Clauses as Objects		
Subject + Verb	**Noun clause**	**Explanation**
I did	*what* I was asked.	• A noun clause starts with a question word or *that* and is followed by a subject and verb. • In these examples, the noun clauses are the objects of the sentences.
She knows	*how* the computer works.	
They decided	*where* the location would be.	
My boss asked	*who* would be best for the job.	
I hope	*that* they work as a team.	

E Complete each of the sentences below with an appropriate noun clause from the list. More than one noun clause may be appropriate.

> how the filing system worked   where the files were
> ~~what she told me to~~   who got to receive the training
> that they would be promoted   how to complete the progress report
> that we knew what we were doing   who wanted to be the team leader

1. I did _what she told me to_

2. She found _where the files were_

3. The supervisor asked _how the filing system worked_

4. He explained _how to complete the progress report_

5. Our team showed _that we knew what we were doing_

6. Sari asked _who wanted to be the team leader_

7. Jared and Giulia hoped _that they would be promoted_

8. The representative chose _who got to receive the training_

F Complete each sentence with a noun clause of your own. (Answers will vary.)

1. I asked _when lunch would be served_

2. I hoped _that the report was well-written_

3. I decided _who would assist me on the oral report_

4. I explained _where the files were stored_

148   Unit 7   Lesson 5

Presentation 2

5-10 mins. ■■■

D Study the chart with your classmates and teacher.

Practice 2

15-20 mins. ■■

Note: Shorter classes can do this exercise for homework.

E Complete each of the sentences below with an appropriate noun clause from the list. More than one noun clause may be appropriate.

F Complete each sentence with a noun clause of your own.

Evaluation 2

10-15 mins. ■■

Go over the answers to Exercise E as a class by asking volunteers to read each sentence out loud. Discuss if there is more than one appropriate answer. Then, ask volunteers to read their sentences from Exercise F.

Activity Bank

Unit 7, Lesson 5, Worksheet 1: Noun Clauses

Refer students to *Stand Out 5 Grammar Challenge*, Unit 7, Challenge 5 for practice with noun clauses as objects of verbs.

There are also two Grammar Challenge extensions. Extension Challenge 1 offers practice with indirect and reported speech. Extension Challenge 2 gives more practice with noun clauses using *whether* and *if*.

Lesson Planner: Unit 7, Lesson 5 **148a**

Presentation 3   5 mins. ■■■

Go over the instructions for Exercise G.

Practice 3   15–20 mins. ■

Note: Shorter classes can do this exercise for homework.

(G) Maria reports that she has encountered a few more problems in addition to those she mentioned in her report in Exercise B.

Write a paragraph from Maria's perspective. Add the problems mentioned above to her report. Include what she might suggest as solutions.

Evaluation 3   5–10 mins. ■

Walk around the classroom and help students as needed. Make suggestions for how to improve their paragraphs. Ask a few students whom you think have written good paragraphs to read them out loud.

Application   10–20 mins. ■■■

(H) Write a progress report using the guidelines from page 147. Use the format of Maria's report. Use the information below for your report.

Using the examples in Exercises D and E, include a few noun clauses in your report.

Activity Bank 💿

Unit 7, Lesson 5, Worksheet 2: Progress Reports

LESSON 5 **GOAL** ➤ **Report progress**

G Maria reports that she has encountered a few more problems in addition to those she mentioned in her report in Exercise B.

- The employees do not want this training.
- None of the supervisors who could be trainers want to lead the training.

Write a paragraph from Maria's perspective. Add the problems mentioned above to her report. Include what she might suggest as solutions. (Answers will vary. Sample answer is given.)

In doing my research, I discovered two more problems. First, I know that the employees do not want this training. They feel that they are overworked as it is. Second, I hoped that supervisors would lead the training. The supervisors have decided that none of them want to lead the training. I suggest that both the employees and the supervisors be offered an incentive for doing the training.

H **Write a progress report using the guidelines from page 147. Use the format of Maria's report. Use the information below for your report.** (Answers will vary.)

Project: Organize the files for the entire company

Work completed: Half of the stacks of papers in all the offices have been organized

Doing now: Currently organizing the other half of the stacks

To do: Still need to create labels for hanging files and file folders

Problems: Employees don't want me to come into their offices

Progress: Good

Using the examples in Exercises D and E, include a few noun clauses in your report.

Review

A Read the instructions for setting up an MP3 player and answer the questions that follow. (Lesson 1)

> ### Setting Up Your MP3 Player
>
> Step 1: Charge the battery.
> Step 2: Install the software.
> Step 3: Import music to your computer.
> Step 4: Connect the MP3 player to your computer and transfer music.
> Step 5: Play music.

1. What do you need to do before you import music to your computer?

   <u>Charge the battery and install the software.</u>

2. What can you do after you have transferred music?

   <u>Play music.</u>

3. What is the first thing you must do?

   <u>Charge the battery.</u>

4. What must you do in order to be able to transfer music?

   <u>Connect the MP3 player to your computer.</u>

B Read the tips and troubleshooting advice for the MP3 player. Then, choose the best answer. (Lesson 2)

> Most problems can be resolved by resetting your MP3 player.
>   To reset your MP3 player:
>
>   1. Connect it to a power outlet using the power adaptor.
>   2. Toggle the hold switch on and off.
>   3. Press and hold the menu button for at least 10 seconds.
>
> If your player won't turn on or respond:
>
>   • Make sure the hold switch is off.
>   • If you're using the remote, make sure the remote's hold switch is off.
>   • Recharge your battery.

1. How can you solve most problems with your MP3 player?
   a. Recharge the battery.   b. Turn it on and off.   c. Reset it.

2. What button do you hold down when resetting the player?
   a. Hold   b. Menu   c. Power Adaptor

3. What's the first thing you should do to reset your player?
   a. Make sure the hold switch is off.
   b. Connect it to a power outlet.
   c. Hold down the menu button.

Objectives: All unit objectives
Grammar: All unit grammar
Academic Strategy: Reviewing
Vocabulary: All Unit 7 vocabulary

RESOURCES

Stand Out 5 Assessment CD-ROM with Exam*View*®

■ 1.5 hour classes ■ 2.5 hour classes ■ 3⁺ hour classes

AGENDA

Discuss unit objectives.
Complete the review.
Use unit vocabulary.

Warm-up and Review   5-10 mins.

Talk about progress reports. Ask students how many of them have written one before or might be asked to write one in the future. For students who don't work, ask them for some other situations in their lives where they might write a progress report.

Introduction   5-10 mins.

Ask students as a class to try to recall all the objectives of this unit without looking back in their books. The objectives for this unit include identifying and using technology, resolving technology, establishing an organizational system, identifying and resolving problems at work, and reporting progress. Write all the objectives on the board from Unit 7. Show students the first page of the unit and mention the five objectives.

State the objective: *Today we will be reviewing everything we have learned in this unit and preparing for the team project.*

Presentation 1   10-15 mins.

This presentation will cover the first three pages of the review. Quickly go to the first page of each lesson. Discuss the objective of each. Ask simple questions to remind students of what they have learned.

Note: Since there is little presentation in the review, you can assign the review exercises that don't require collaboration with a partner or group for homework and go over them in class the following day.

Practice 1   20-25 mins.

Note: There are two ways to do the review:

1. Go through the exercises one at a time and, as students complete each one, go over the answers.

2. Quickly go through the instructions of each exercise, let students complete all of the exercises at once, and then go over the answers.

(A) Read the instructions for setting up an MP3 player and answer the questions that follow. (Lesson 1)

(B) Read the tips and troubleshooting advice for the MP3 player. Then, choose the best answer. (Lesson 2)

Evaluation 1   10-15 mins.

Go around the classroom and check on students' progress. Help individuals when needed. If you see consistent errors among several students, interrupt the class and give a mini-lesson or review to help students feel comfortable with the concept.

STANDARDS CORRELATIONS

CASAS: 7.2.1 (See CASAS Competency List on pages 187–193.)
SCANS: Resources Allocate time
Information Acquire and evaluate information
Interpersonal Participate as a member of a team, teach others, negotiate to arrive at a decision, work with cultural diversity
Systems Monitor and correct performance
Basic Skills Reading, writing, arithmetic, listening, speaking

Thinking Skills Think creatively, make decisions, solve problems, see things in the mind's eye
Personal Qualities Responsibility, sociability, self-management
EFF: **Communication** Read with understanding, convey ideas in writing, speak so others can understand, listen actively, observe critically
Interpersonal Cooperate with others, guide others
Lifelong Learning Take responsibility for learning, reflect and evaluate

Practice 1 *(continued)*   15–20 mins. ■■■

C Alphabetize the following items. (Lesson 3)

D How would you organize these items in an office? Write a brief explanation.

E Answer the following questions about the conflict-resolution article. (Lesson 4)

F Name the five things a progress report should include. (Lesson 5)

Evaluation 1 *(continued)*   10–15 mins. ■■■

Go around the classroom and check on students' progress. Help individuals when needed. If you see consistent errors among several students, interrupt the class and give a mini-lesson or review to help students feel comfortable with the concept.

Teacher Tip

Recycling/Review

The review exercises, the research activity, and the team project are part of the recycling/review process. Students often need to be reintroduced to concepts to solidify what they have learned. Many concepts are learned and forgotten when students are engaged in learning other new concepts. This is because students learn but are not necessarily ready to acquire language concepts.

Therefore, it becomes very important to review material with students and to show them how to review it on their own. It is also important to recycle the new concepts in different contexts.

C Alphabetize the following items. (Lesson 3)

> 9 paper shredder   1 business telephone   12 scanner
> 6 flash drive   7 label maker   4 external hard drive
> 8 LCD projector   3 computer   11 printer
> 2 cables   5 fax machine   10 power adaptors

D How would you organize these items in an office? Write a brief explanation. (Answers will vary.)

Each employee should have a business telephone and a computer. A paper shredder, fax machine, scanner, printer and label maker should be kept in a central location. Extra flash drives, cables, external hard drives, and power adapters should be kept with the LCD projector in a locked technology cabinet.

E Answer the following questions about the conflict-resolution article. (Lesson 4)

1. What are the three benefits to resolving conflict?
   a. Increased understanding
   b. Increased group cohesion
   c. Improved self-knowledge

2. What are the five different conflict styles in Thomas and Kilmann's theory?
   a. Competitive
   b. Collaborative
   c. Compromising
   d. Accommodating
   e. Avoiding

3. What are the six steps of the IBR approach?
   a. Good relationships are the first priority.
   b. Keep people and problems separate.
   c. Pay attention to interests presented.
   d. Listen first; talk second.
   e. Set out the "facts."
   f. Explore options together.

4. What are the five steps for resolving conflict?
   a. Set the scene
   b. Gather information
   c. Agree on the problem
   d. Brainstorm possible solutions.
   e. Negotiate a solution

F Name the five things a progress report should include. (Lesson 5)

VOCABULARY REVIEW

 G Put each word below in the correct column according to its part of speech: *noun, verb,* or *adjective.*

cost-effective	reorganize	organize	hanging files	fan
feed	effective	splotchy	paper jam	long-term
obstructions	force	faded	toner	power supply

Noun
1. obstructions
2. hanging files
3. paper jam
4. toner
5. power supply

Verb
1. feed
2. reorganize
3. force
4. organize
5. fan

Adjective
1. cost-effective
2. effective
3. splotchy
4. faded
5. long-term

H Use words from Exercise G to complete the sentences. Not all the words are used.

1. Did you get a chance to put the _____ hanging files _____ in alphabetical order?

2. The computer wasn't working because the _____ power supply _____ wasn't plugged in.

3. If you _____ fan _____ out the paper, it shouldn't stick together so much.

4. It doesn't seem _____ cost-effective _____ to have so many computers running at the same time. That wastes a lot of energy.

5. Tim, can you _____ reorganize _____ these files? They seem to have gotten out of order.

6. If you _____ force _____ the paper into the feeder, it will probably cause a _____ paper jam _____.

7. When I opened up the fax machine, I couldn't see any _____ obstructions _____.

8. We need a/an _____ effective _____ solution to this disorganized supply closet.

9. Is there any more _____ toner _____ in the supply closet? These copies are _____ splotchy _____ and _____ faded _____.

10. I wonder why the paper won't _____ feed _____ through the printer correctly?

Practice 1 (continued)   25–30 mins.   ■■■□

Vocabulary Review

(G) Put each word below in the correct column according to its part of speech: *noun, verb,* or *adjective.*

(H) Use words from Exercise G to complete the sentences. Not all the words are used.

Evaluation 1 (continued)   5–15 mins.   ■■■□

Go around the classroom and check on students' progress. Help individuals when needed. If you see consistent errors among several students, interrupt the class and give a mini-lesson or review to help students feel comfortable with the concept.

TB Assessment (optional)   ■■■□

Use the Stand Out 5 Assessment CD-ROM with Exam*View*® to create a post-test for Unit 7.

Objective: Research careers
Academic Strategy: Research
Vocabulary: *earnings, related occupations*

RESOURCES

Activity Bank CD-ROM: Research: PDF files on retail and office careers

Internet access

AGENDA

Research jobs.
Research salary, training/
qualifications, and related
occupations.

Academic Feature: Research

Each unit will have a research page where students are required to complete a task by conducting research. Options will be given for students to use the Internet as well as printed resource materials. The printed resource materials can be found on the Activity Bank CD-ROM.

Introduction   5-10 mins.

Ask students to raise their hands if they work in a retail store. Ask students to raise their hands if they work in an office. Ask students who didn't raise their hands what type of environment they work in.

State the objective: *Today you will research different careers associated with the retail world and the office world.*

Presentation   10-15 mins.

(A) In the past two units, you have learned about two different areas of work: the retail setting and the office. In a group, brainstorm a list of jobs that might be found in each of these areas.

(B) Look back at your two lists. Circle the jobs that you think earn the most money.

Practice   10-15 mins.

(C) Using the Internet or printed materials from your teacher, research jobs and see if you can add any more to your lists above.

(D) Now choose two or three jobs that seem the most interesting to you and find out the following information.

Evaluation   5-10 mins.

Have students share their research with the class.

Activity Bank

Unit 7, Research: PDF Files on Retail and Office Careers

STANDARDS CORRELATIONS

CASAS: 4.9.3, 7.2.1, 7.4.4, 7.4.5, 7.4.6 (See CASAS Competency List on pages 187–193.)
***SCANS:* Information** Acquire and evaluate information, organize and maintain information, interpret and communicate information, use computers to process information *(optional)*
Interpersonal Participate as a member of a team, teach others, negotiate to arrive at a decision, work with cultural diversity
Systems Understand systems
Technology Select technology, apply technology to a task, maintain and troubleshoot technology *(optional)*

Basic Skills Reading, writing
Thinking Skills Think creatively, make decisions, see things in the mind's eye
Personal Qualities Responsibility, sociability, self-management
***EFF:* Communication** Read with understanding, convey ideas in writing, observe critically
Decision Making Solve problems and make decisions, plan
Lifelong Learning Take responsibility for learning, reflect and evaluate, learn through research, use information and communications technology *(optional)*

Research Project

A In the past two units, you have learned about two different areas of work: the retail setting and the office. In a group, brainstorm a list of jobs that might be found in each of these areas. (Answers will vary.)

Retail jobs	Office jobs
clerk	supervisor
supervisor	office manager
manager	facilities manager
stock assistant	administrative assistant
owner	information systems manager
buyer	vice president
assistant buyer	receptionist

B Look back at your two lists. Circle the jobs that you think earn the most money.
(Answers will vary.)

C Using the Internet or printed materials from your teacher, research jobs and see if you can add any more to your lists above.
(Answers will vary.)

D Now choose two or three jobs that seem the most interesting to you and find out the following information.
(Answers will vary.)

Job title	Salary	Training/Qualifications required	Related occupations

Team Project

Set up a typical business office.

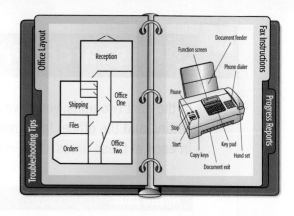

1. Form a team with four or five students. Choose positions for each member of your team.

POSITION	JOB DESCRIPTION	STUDENT NAME
Student 1: **Project Leader**	See that everyone speaks English. See that everyone participates.	
Student 2: **Secretary**	Take notes on your team's ideas.	
Student 3: **Designer**	Design layout of the office.	
Student 4: **Tech Writer**	Write up instructions for use and troubleshooting tips for two pieces of technology in the office.	
Student 5: **Documenter**	Write a progress report about the process.	

2. Decide what kind of office your team will create (what you do, how many employees you have, etc.).

3. Make an alphabetized inventory list of all the items in your office and how many of each item your office has.

4. Draw a diagram of your office and indicate where everything is located.

5. Choose two pieces of technology in your office and write up instructions for use as well as troubleshooting tips.

6. Write a progress report explaining what you did. Include any conflicts you may have had with team members while completing the project.

7. As a team, present your office documents to the class. Be prepared to explain why you set up the office the way you did.

Set up a typical business office.

Each team will create an office. They will decide what kind of an office they create and draw a layout of it, which will include where all the technology is located. They will write up detailed instructions on how to use and troubleshoot two of the technology items. Finally, they will write a progress report.

The team project is the final application for the unit. It gives students a chance to show that they have mastered all of the Unit 7 objectives.

Note: Shorter classes can extend this project over two class meetings.

Stage 1   5 mins.

Form a team with four or five students. Choose positions for each member of your team.

Have students decide who will lead each step as described on the student page. Provide well-defined directions on the board for how teams should proceed. Explain that all the students do every step as a team. Teams shouldn't go to the next stage until the previous one is complete.

Stage 2   5 mins.

Decide what kind of office your team will create (what you do, how many employees you have, etc.).

Give students a few minutes to come up with this information and then ask for the spokesperson of each team to report to the class.

Stage 3   10-15 mins.

Make an alphabetized inventory list of all the items in your office and how many of each item your office has.

Briefly discuss this stage with students, pointing out that each office will have a different list of items, depending on the type of business it is. For example, a printing company will have a lot of paper and printers. On the other hand, a service company may have more computers and phones.

Stage 4   10-15 mins.

Draw a diagram of your office and indicate where everything is located.

Stage 5   5 mins.

Choose two pieces of technology in your office and write up instructions for use as well as troubleshooting tips.

Stage 6   15-20 mins.

Write a progress report explaining what you did. Include any conflicts you may have had with team members while completing the project.

Optional Computer Activities: Students may want to use the computer to design office layouts as well as write their progress reports.

Stage 7   15-20 mins.

As a team, present your office documents to the class. Be prepared to explain why you set the office up the way you did.

Help teams prepare for their presentations. Suggest that each member choose a different part of the project to present.

STANDARDS CORRELATIONS

CASAS: 4.8.1, 4.8.5, 4.8.6 (See CASAS Competency List on pages 187-193.)
SCANS: Resources Allocate time
Information Acquire and evaluate information, organize and maintain information, interpret and communicate information, use computers to process information
Systems Understand systems, improve and design systems
Technology Select technology, apply technology to exercise
Basic Skills Writing
Thinking Skills Think creatively, make decisions, solve problems, see things in the mind's eye, use reasoning

Personal Qualities Responsibility, self-esteem, self-management, integrity
EFF: Communication Read with understanding, convey ideas in writing, speak so others can understand, listen actively, observe critically
Decision Making Solve problems and make decisions, plan
Interpersonal Cooperate with others, advocate and influence, resolve conflict and negotiate, guide others
Lifelong Learning Take responsibility for learning, reflect and evaluate, learn through research, use information and communications technology (optional)

Objective: Introduce new vocabulary
Academic Strategies: Making inferences, categorizing vocabulary, using a dictionary
Vocabulary: See lesson.

RESOURCES

Dictionaries: It is recommended that each student in class have an ESL learner's dictionary or that there be dictionaries available in the classroom for students to use. Dictionaries that will be referred to in this book

are the *Heinle's Newbury House Dictionary of American English* and the *Collins Cobuild Intermediate* or *Advanced Dictionary of American English.*

Academic Feature: Vocabulary Builder

Each unit will begin with a vocabulary-building section. The purpose of this two-page section is to introduce students to many of the words they will be using in the unit lessons. Students will have a chance to see how much they already know, and they will get exposure to the new vocabulary found in the unit.

Note: All of the exercises on these two pages should be done in class, no matter the class length. Longer classes can do this lesson and then move onto Lesson 1 during the same class meeting; shorter classes may have to devote one whole class meeting to this lesson.

Introduction   5–10 mins.

State the objective: *Today we will be identifying and working with the vocabulary you will learn in this unit.*

Presentation 1   10–15 mins.

Write this sentence on the board: *Born and raised in Hong Kong, she moved to the U.S. and was naturalized is 2002.* Ask students what part of speech *naturalized* is (verb). Then, ask them what they think the word means. Write all their ideas on the board. Then ask a volunteer to look it up in a dictionary and read the definition out loud. Explain that this process of guessing what a word means is also called making an inference.

Practice 1   10–15 mins.

(A) Guessing the meaning of a word from the context of its sentence is called *making an inference*. Read each sentence and guess the meaning of the italicized word and its part of speech. Then, look it up in a dictionary to check if you got it right.

UNIT 8
Civic Responsibility

GOALS

➤ Identify requirements for establishing residency and citizenship

➤ Understand your rights

➤ Identify local civic organizations

➤ Interpret information about environmental issues

➤ Communicate your opinion

Vocabulary Builder

(A) Guessing the meaning of a word from the context of its sentence is called *making an inference*. Read each sentence and guess the meaning of the italicized word and its part of speech. Then, look it up in a dictionary to check if you got it right. (Answers will vary.)

1. The judge gave an *impartial* verdict that did not favor either side.

   Part of speech: __adj.__ Meaning: doesn't favor one side or the other

   Dictionary definition: not partial; unprejudiced

2. There are so many *commuters* on the roads today that there is always a lot of pollution and noise.

   Part of speech: __n.(pl.)__ Meaning: people who drive back and forth

   Dictionary definition: a person who travels regularly from one place to another

3. We all must *conserve* energy so our kids don't have to worry when they get older.

   Part of speech: __v.__ Meaning: retain or keep

   Dictionary definition: to protect from loss or depletion

4. During the war, many *refugees* went to safer countries to try to live better lives.

   Part of speech: __n.(pl.)__ Meaning: people who leave a country because of problems

   Dictionary definition: a person who flees to find refuge or safety

5. She runs a *charitable* organization that gives food to homeless people.

   Part of speech: __adj.__ Meaning: giving of things to the poor

   Dictionary definition: generous in giving money or other help

Vocabulary Builder

B Each sentence in Exercise A reflects the topic of a lesson in this unit. Look at each sentence and guess what you think the lesson will be about. (*Hint:* Look at the goals listed at the top of page 155.)

1. Rights
2. Environmental issues
3. Environmental issues/Communicate opinion
4. Requirements for establishing residency
5. Civic organizations

C Look at the list of terms below and categorize each word or phrase by writing it under the correct lesson title. (Answers may vary.)

alien	conserve	punishment	reusable
bear arms	eligible	refugee	slavery
believe	naturalization	peaceably assemble	social welfare
capital crime	opinion	resource	status
civic	protect		

Identify requirements for establishing residency and citizenship	Identify your rights	Identify local civic organizations	Interpret information about environmental issues	Communicate your opinion
alien eligible naturalization refugee status	bear arms capital crime/believe protect punishment peaceably assemble slavery	civic social welfare	conserve resource reusable	believe opinion

D Write your own sentence for each of the words below. (Answers may vary.)

1. naturalization: He went through the naturalization process to become a citizen.

2. punishment: Her punishment was to pay a fine.

3. civic: His civic duty was to vote in every election.

4. reusable: I think some garbage is reusable.

5. resource: Water is an important resource in all countries.

B Each sentence in Exercise A reflects the topic of a lesson in this unit. Look at each sentence and guess what you think the lesson will be about. (*Hint:* Look at the goals listed at the top of page 155.)

Evaluation 1   10-15 mins.

Go over the answers as a class.

Presentation 2   5-10 mins.

Go over the instructions for Exercises C and D. Do a few examples if necessary. Tell students that they can use a dictionary for both exercises if they need to.

Vocabulary

When teaching students new vocabulary, pronounce each word for them several times and ask them to repeat it. Often, students may be familiar with the words you are introducing but have never seen them spelled out. By pronouncing the words for students, you allow students to make a connection between the words' spellings and their sounds. It is also important that students learn the correct pronunciation of new words so they feel comfortable using their new vocabulary inside and outside of the classroom.

Practice 2   10-15 mins.

C Look at the list of terms below and categorize each word or phrase by writing it under the correct lesson title.

D Write your own sentence for each of the words below.

Evaluation 2   10-15 mins.

Go over the answers to Exercise C as a class. Although there is a suggested answer key, some words may fit under more than the lesson title.

Ask volunteers to write their original sentences from Exercise D on the board. As a class, analyze the sentences to make sure the words have been used correctly.

Objective: Identify requirements for establishing residency and citizenship

Academic Strategies: Active reading, evaluating situations

Vocabulary: *permanent resident, eligible, petition, alien, admitted, asylee, refugee, naturalization*

RESOURCES

Activity Bank: Unit 8, Lesson 1, Worksheet 1 and Citizenship PDF

 1.5 hour classes ■ 2.5 hour classes ■ 3+ hour classes

AGENDA

Read and discuss resident status requirements.

Listen to an immigration officer talk about citizenship requirements.

Discuss naturalization.

Grammar Challenge 5: Unit 8, Challenge 1

Audio: CD Track 34

Stand Out 5 Assessment CD-ROM with Exam*View*®

Pre-assessment *(optional)*

Use the Stand Out 5 Assessment CD-ROM with Exam*View*® to create a pre-test for Unit 8.

Warm-up and Review   5–10 mins.

Write the objective of this lesson on the board. Identify requirements for establishing residency and citizenship. Ask students to come up with a list of vocabulary from the previous lesson that would fit into this objective. Have them work with a small group to define each word on their lists.

Introduction   10–15 mins.

Dictation:

1. Their entire family applied to become permanent residents three years ago.
2. His employer likes him so much that he filed a visa petition, so Joe could stay here to work.
3. We are still waiting to hear if our application has been approved.
4. Now that he has been a resident for five years, he is applying for citizenship.

State the objective: *Today we will be identifying requirements for establishing residency and citizenship.*

Presentation 1   10–15 mins.

(A) How can an immigrant become a permanent resident of the United States? Make a list of your ideas below.

Have students work in small groups to discuss the questions and then write all their ideas on the board. Don't comment on students' discussions at this stage.

Practice 1   5–10 mins.

(B) Several students in Mrs. Morgan's class want to become permanent residents of the United States. Read about each nonresident below and decide if you think he or she is eligible to become a permanent resident. Write *yes* or *no*.

Tell students they will just be making guesses based on what they think they know.

Evaluation 1   5–10 mins.

Have students discuss their answers with a partner and see if they can come to a consensus. The real answers will be revealed in the next practice.

STANDARDS CORRELATIONS

CASAS: 5.3.6 (See CASAS Competency List on pages 187–193.)

SCANS: **Information** Acquire and evaluate information, organize and maintain information, interpret and communicate information

Interpersonal Participate as a member of a team, teach others, serve clients and customers, exercise leadership, negotiate to arrive at a decision, work with cultural diversity

Systems Monitor and correct performance

Technology Select technology, apply technology to a task *(optional)*

Basic Skills Reading, writing, listening, speaking

Thinking Skills Make decisions, see things in the mind's eye

Personal Qualities Responsibility, sociability, self-management

EFF: **Communication** Read with understanding, convey ideas in writing, speak so others can understand, listen actively, observe critically

Decision Making Solve problems and make decisions

Interpersonal Cooperate with others, advocate and influence, resolve conflict and negotiate, guide others

Lifelong Learning Take responsibility for learning, reflect and evaluate, learn through research, use information and communications technology *(optional)*

LESSON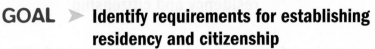

Investigating citizenship

GOAL ➤ **Identify requirements for establishing residency and citizenship**

Vocabulary | Grammar
Life Skills
Academic | Pronunciation

A How can an immigrant become a permanent resident of the United States? Make a list of your ideas below. (Answers will vary. Sample answers are given.)

1. Live in the U.S. a long time on a visa and then apply.

2. Marry a U.S. citizen.

3. Get a job in the United States with a work visa.

4. Join a family member who is already a citizen.

B Several students in Mrs. Morgan's class want to become permanent residents of the United States. Read about each nonresident below and decide if you think he or she is eligible to become a permanent resident. Write *yes* or *no*. (Answers will vary.)

1. Hanh has been living in the U.S. since 1985. She recently became engaged to a U.S. citizen. Is she eligible? _____

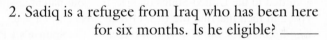

2. Sadiq is a refugee from Iraq who has been here for six months. Is he eligible? _____

3. Ella is 35 and her mother just became a permanent resident. Is she eligible? _____

4. Phillipe has lived in the U.S. since 1965. Is he eligible? _____

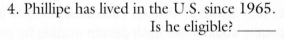

5. Enrique's wife just became a permanent resident. Is he eligible? _____

GOAL ➤ **Identify requirements for establishing residency and citizenship**

 C Read the following information found on the Web site of U.S. Citizenship and Immigration Services (www.uscis.gov).

You may be *eligible* to apply for adjustment to permanent resident status if you are already in the United States *and* if one or more of the following categories apply to you.

Family Member 1.You are the spouse, parent, unmarried child under age 21, the unmarried son or daughter over age 21, the married son or daughter, or the brother or sister of a United States citizen and have a visa petition approved in your behalf. 2. You are the spouse or unmarried son or daughter of any age of a lawful permanent resident and you have a family-based visa petition approved in your behalf.

Employment You are an alien who has an approved visa petition filed in your behalf by a United States employer.

Fiancé You were a fiancé who was admitted to the United States on a K-1 visa and then married the U.S. citizen *who applied for the K-1 visa for you.* Your unmarried, minor children are also eligible for adjustment of status. If you did not marry the U.S. citizen who filed the K-1 petition in your behalf, or if you married another U.S. citizen or lawful permanent resident, you are not eligible to adjust status in the United States.

Asylee You are an asylee or refugee who has been in the United States for at least a year after being given asylum or refugee status and still qualify for asylum or refugee status.

Diversity Visa You received notice from the Department of State that you have won a visa in the Diversity Visa Lottery.

U.S. Resident Since Before 01/01/72 You have been a continuous resident of the United States since before January 1, 1972.

Parent's Lawful Permanent Resident (LPR) Status Your parent became a lawful permanent resident after you were born. You may be eligible to receive following-to-join benefits if you are the unmarried child under age 21 of the lawful permanent resident. In these cases, you may apply to adjust to permanent resident status at the same time that your parent applies for following-to-join benefits for you.

Spouse's LPR Status Your spouse became a lawful permanent resident after you were married. You may be eligible to receive following-to-join benefits. In these cases, you may apply to adjust to permanent resident status at the same time that your spouse applies for following-to-join benefits for you.

D Look back at each of the nonresidents in Exercise B. Do you need to change some of your answers? Discuss each situation with a partner and decide what specific details would make each person eligible for permanent resident status.

(Answers may vary.)

1. No, if her fiancé did not apply for a K–1 visa for her.
2. No, he needs to have been here for at least one year.
3. Yes, if she is an unmarried daughter over 21.
4. Yes, he has been a continuous U.S. resident since before 01/01/72.
5. Yes, he may be eligible to receive "following-to-join" benefits.

Presentation 2   15–20 mins.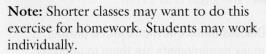

C Read the following information found on the Web site of U.S. Citizenship and Immigration Services (www.uscis.gov).

Have students read silently to themselves. Then go over each section together, making sure students completely understand the eligibility requirements.

Note: If you have Internet access in your classroom and students want to get more detailed information, have them go to the USCIS Web site.

Practice 2   10–15 mins. ■■

Note: Shorter classes may want to do this exercise for homework. Students may work individually.

D Look back at each of the nonresidents in Exercise B. Do you need to change some of your answers? Discuss each situation with a partner and decide what specific details would make each person eligible for permanent resident status.

Do the first one together as a class.

Evaluation 2   10–15 mins. ■■

Discuss each person. As a class, decide if he or she is eligible. If not, ask what would make him or her eligible.

Instructor's Notes

Presentation 3 5-10 mins. ▪▪▪▫

Have students briefly read through the information in Exercise E. Have them guess at the missing words.

Practice 3 15-20 mins. ▪

 E **Listen to the immigration officer talk about how to become a citizen. Fill in the missing words.**

Play the recording once. Have students share their answers with a partner. If students are able to come up with most of the answers in pairs, go on to the evaluation. If you think your students need to hear the recording one more time, play it again and have them continue to share with their partners until they have most of the blanks filled in.

🎧 Listening Script *CD Track 34*

United States (U.S.) citizenship carries many responsibilities with it . The decision to become a U.S. citizen is a very important one. Being granted U.S. citizenship is known as naturalization. In most cases, a person who wants to naturalize must first be a permanent resident. By becoming a U.S. citizen, you gain many rights that permanent residents or others do not have, including the right to vote. To be eligible for naturalization, you must first meet certain requirements set by U.S. law.

What are the basic requirements to apply for naturalization?
Generally, to be eligible for naturalization you must:

- *Be age 18 or older; and*
- *Be a permanent resident for a certain amount of time (usually 5 years); and*
- *Be a person of good moral character; and*
- *Have a basic knowledge of U.S. history and government; and*
- *Have a period of continuous residence and physical presence in the U.S.; and*
- *Be able to read, write, and speak basic English. There are exceptions to this rule for someone who:*
  - *Is 55 years old and has been a permanent resident for at least 15 years; or*
  - *Is 50 years old and has been a permanent resident for at least 20 years; or*
  - *Has a physical or mental impairment that makes them unable to fulfill these requirements.*

(continued)

When can I apply for naturalization?
You may be able to apply for naturalization if you are at least 18 years of age and have been a permanent resident of the U.S.:

- *For at least 5 years; or*
- *For at least 3 years during which time you have been, and continue to be, married to and living in marriage with your U.S. citizen husband or wife; or*
- *Have honorable service in the U.S. military. Certain spouses of U.S. citizens and members of the military may be able to file for naturalization sooner than noted above previously.*

Evaluation 3 5-10 mins. ▪

Go over the answers as a class.

 F **Discuss these questions with a partner: How many requirements are there to apply for naturalization? What are they?**

Application 10-20 mins. ▪▪▪▫

 G **Think about people you know who have become permanent residents or citizens. Write short paragraphs about them following the example below.**

If students are comfortable sharing, ask volunteers to read their short paragraphs out loud.

Activity Bank 🔊

Unit 8, Lesson 1, Worksheet 1: Can you become a resident? (listening)

PDF Documents
Citizenship Flash Cards
Citizenship Answers
Citizenship Questions

📖 **Refer students to** *Stand Out 5 Grammar Challenge*, **Unit 8, Challenge 1 for practice with articles:** *a, an,* **and** *the.*

  E Listen to the immigration officer talk about how to become a citizen. Fill in the missing words.

CD
TR 34

United States (U.S.) citizenship carries many ___responsibilities___ with it. The decision to become a U.S. citizen is a very important one. Being granted U.S. citizenship is known as ___naturalization___. In most cases, a person who wants to naturalize must first be a ___permanent___ resident. By becoming a U.S. citizen, you gain many ___rights___ that permanent residents or others do not have, including the ___right to vote___. To be eligible for naturalization, you must first meet certain ___requirements___ set by U.S. law.

What are the basic requirements to apply for naturalization?
Generally, to be eligible for naturalization you must:
• Be age ___18___ or older; and
• Be a permanent resident for a certain amount of time (usually 5 years); and
• Be a person of good ___moral___ character; and
• Have a basic knowledge of U.S. ___history___ and government; and
• Have a period of ___continuous___ residence and physical presence in the U.S.; and
• Be able to read, ___write___, and speak basic English. There are exceptions to this rule for someone who:
 – Is ___55___ years old and has been a permanent resident for at least 15 years; or
 – Is ___50___ years old and has been a permanent resident for at least 20 years; or
 – Has a physical or mental impairment that makes them unable to ___fulfill___ these requirements.

When can I apply for naturalization?
You may be able to apply for naturalization if you are at least 18 years of age and have been a permanent resident of the U.S.:
• For at least ___5___ years; or
• For at least ___3___ years during which time you have been, and continue to be, married to and living in marriage with your U.S. citizen husband or wife; or
• Have honorable service in the U.S. military. Certain ___spouses___ of U.S. citizens and members of the military may be able to file for naturalization sooner than noted above previously.

(*Source:* www.uscis.gov)

F Discuss these questions with a partner: How many requirements are there to apply for naturalization? What are they? Six main requirements with three exceptions. (See document in Exercise E.)

G Think about people you know who have become permanent residents or citizens. Write short paragraphs about them following the example below.

My cousin has been living in the U.S. for ten years. Two years ago, her employer filed a visa petition for her to become a permanent resident, so she could stay and work for the company. The petition was approved and she got her green card last year.

LESSON 2

Rights

GOAL ➤ **Understand your rights**

> *"A bill of rights is what the people are entitled to against every government on earth, general or particular, and what no just government should refuse, or rest on inference."*
>
> —Thomas Jefferson

A **What do you think this quotation means?** The list of rights is a natural group of rights that all people on Earth should have that is more important than their governments. No government should deny these rights or simply imply that the people have these rights. In other words, these rights should be written down.

B **In 1791 the Bill of Rights was added to the United States Constitution. It is composed of the Constitution's first ten amendments. Read the Bill of Rights below. In a small group, paraphrase each amendment.**

Amendment I Congress shall make no law respecting an establishment of religion, or prohibiting the free exercise thereof; or abridging the freedom of speech, or of the press; or the right of the people peaceably to assemble, and to petition the government for a redress of grievances.

Amendment II A well regulated militia, being necessary to the security of a free state, the right of the people to keep and bear arms, shall not be infringed.

Amendment III No soldier shall, in time of peace be quartered in any house, without the consent of the owner, nor in time of war, but in a manner to be prescribed by law.

Amendment IV The right of the people to be secure in their persons, houses, papers, and effects, against unreasonable searches and seizures, shall not be violated, and no warrants shall issue, but upon probable cause, supported by oath or affirmation, and particularly describing the place to be searched, and the persons or things to be seized.

Amendment V No person shall be held to answer for a capital, or otherwise infamous crime, unless on a presentment or indictment of a grand jury, except in cases arising in the land or naval forces, or in the militia, when in actual service in time of war or public danger; nor shall any person be subject for the same offense to be twice put in jeopardy of life or limb; nor shall be compelled in any criminal case to be a witness against himself, nor be deprived of life, liberty, or property, without due process of law; nor shall private property be taken for public use, without just compensation.

Amendment VI In all criminal prosecutions, the accused shall enjoy the right to a speedy and public trial, by an impartial jury of the state and district wherein the crime shall have been committed, which district shall have been previously ascertained by law, and to be informed of the nature and cause of the accusation; to be confronted with the witnesses against him; to have compulsory process for obtaining witnesses in his favor, and to have the assistance of counsel for his defense.

Amendment VII In suits at common law, where the value in controversy shall exceed twenty dollars, the right of trial by jury shall be preserved, and no fact tried by a jury, shall be otherwise reexamined in any court of the United States, than according to the rules of the common law.

Amendment VIII Excessive bail shall not be required, nor excessive fines imposed, nor cruel and unusual punishments inflicted.

Amendment IX The enumeration in the Constitution, of certain rights, shall not be construed to deny or disparage others retained by the people.

Amendment X The powers not delegated to the United States by the Constitution, nor prohibited by it to the states, are reserved to the states respectively, or to the people.

Objective: Identify your rights
Academic Strategy: Paraphrasing
Vocabulary: *entitled, just, establishment, abridge, peaceably assemble, bear arms, quartered, seizure, capital crime, indictment, impartial, trial by jury, bail, fines, excessive, cruel, punishment, slavery, involuntary servitude*

RESOURCES

Activity Bank: Unit 8, Lesson 2, Worksheets 1–2

Grammar Challenge 5: Unit 8, Challenge 2

■ 1.5 hour classes ■ 2.5 hour classes ■ 3⁺ hour classes

AGENDA

Read the Bill of Rights.
Paraphrase amendments.
Create a Bill of Rights for school or classroom.

Warm-up and Review   10–15 mins. ■■■

Ask students to write down what they can remember about becoming a resident or a citizen without looking back in their books. When they have finished, ask students to pair up with one or two students who wrote about the same topic. See if they can add anything to their notes. Then, have them look back in their books for more clarification.

Introduction   15–20 mins. ■■■

Dictation: Quotes about civil rights by famous Americans

1. It was we, the people; not we, the white male citizens; nor yet we, the male citizens; but we, the whole people, who formed the Union. (Susan B. Anthony)
2. Freedom and the power to choose should not be the privilege of wealth. They are the birthright of every American. (George Herbert Walker Bush)
3. If we don't believe in freedom of expression for people we despise, we don't believe in it at all. (Noam Chomsky)
4. Honest difference of views and honest debate are not disunity. They are the vital process of policy among free men. (Herbert Hoover)

State the objective: *Today we will identify the rights of U.S. citizens by interpreting some of the amendments of the Constitution.*

Presentation 1   10–15 mins. ■■■

Ⓐ **What do you think this quotation means?**

Present the quotation to students and have a class discussion about it. (More information about the Bill of Rights and Thomas Jefferson can be found on the Activity Bank CD-ROM.)

Practice 1   15–25 mins. ■■■

Ⓑ **In 1791, the Bill of Rights was added to the United States Constitution. It is composed of the Constitution's first ten amendments. Read the Bill of Rights below. In a small group, paraphrase each amendment.**

Explain to students that this exercise may be very difficult. The wording of each amendment is from the original document so encourage students to look for key words rather than to try to understand every word.

Evaluation 1   10–15 mins. ■■■

Go over the answers as a class.

STANDARDS CORRELATIONS

CASAS: 5.2.2, 5.3.2 (See CASAS Competency List on pages 187–193.)
SCANS: **Information** Acquire and evaluate information, organize and maintain information, interpret and communicate information, use computers to process information *(optional)*
Interpersonal Participate as a member of a team, teach others, exercise leadership, negotiate to arrive at a decision, work with cultural diversity
Systems Monitor and correct performance, improve and design systems
Technology Apply technology to a task *(optional)*
Basic Skills Reading, writing, listening, speaking
Thinking Skills Think creatively, make decisions, solve problems, see things in the mind's eye

Personal Qualities Responsibility, sociability, self-management
EFF: **Communication** Read with understanding, convey ideas in writing, speak so others can understand, listen actively, observe critically
Decision Making Solve problems and make decisions, plan
Interpersonal Cooperate with others, advocate and influence, resolve conflict and negotiate, guide others
Lifelong Learning Take responsibility for learning, reflect and evaluate, learn through research

Presentation 2   10–15 mins. ■■■□

C Match each amendment with the right it guarantees.

If you think students can do this exercise by themselves, have them try it first before you do it together. This is another opportunity for you to explain the amendments in the Bill of Rights.

Practice 2   5–10 mins. ■■□

Note: Shorter classes can do this exercise for homework.

D Read each situation. Then, decide which amendment describes your rights. Write the amendment number on the line.

Evaluation 2   5 mins. ■■□

Go over the answers as a class.

C Match each amendment with the right it guarantees.

1. The first amendment guarantees __d__.

2. The second amendment guarantees __f__.

3. The third amendment guarantees __h__.

4. The fourth amendment guarantees __e__.

5. The fifth amendment guarantees __b__.

6. The sixth amendment guarantees __a__.

7. The seventh amendment guarantees __i__.

8. The eighth amendment guarantees __j__.

9. The ninth amendment guarantees __c__.

10. The tenth amendment guarantees __g__.

a. a speedy and public trial by an impartial jury

b. the right to be charged by a grand jury if accused of a serious crime

c. people have other rights not listed in the Bill of Rights

d. freedom of religion

e. people, homes, and belongings are protected from unreasonable search and seizure

f. right to keep and bear arms

g. people have all the rights not given to the government by the Constitution

h. that government cannot force people to house soldiers during times of peace

i. a trial by jury in civil cases (dispute between private parties or between the government and a private party)

j. no excessive bail or fines will be imposed and that punishment will not be cruel and unusual

D Read each situation. Then, decide which amendment describes your rights. Write the amendment number on the line.

1. Your friend is Christian and celebrates Easter, but you are Jewish. __first (I)__

2. You have a registered gun in your house, locked up in a safe. __second (II)__

3. The police can't come into your home without a warrant. __fourth (IV)__

4. If you are convicted of a crime, your punishment will not be cruel. __eighth (VIII)__

5. If you are accused of a crime, you will get a fair trial. __fifth (V)__

E There are currently 27 amendments to the Constitution. Read some of these other important amendments and answer the questions that follow.

Amendment XIII (1865)
Neither slavery nor involuntary servitude, except as a punishment for crime whereof the party shall have been duly convicted, shall exist within the United States, or any place subject to their jurisdiction.

Amendment XV (1870)
The right of citizens of the United States to vote shall not be denied or abridged by the United States or by any state on account of race, color, or previous condition of servitude.

Amendment XIX (1920)
The right of citizens of the United States to vote shall not be denied or abridged by the United States or by any state on account of sex.

Amendment XXVI (1971)
The right of citizens of the United States, who are 18 years of age or older, to vote, shall not be denied or abridged by the United States or any state on account of age.

---

1. What does the thirteenth amendment guarantee? <u>Slavery is illegal.</u>

2. The fifteenth, nineteenth, and twenty-sixth amendments are all about the same right. What is it? <u>the right to vote</u>

3. What is the difference between these three amendments?

   <u>The 15th prevents discrimination in voting because of race, the 19th prevents</u>

   <u>voting discrimination based on gender, and the 26th gives the voting right to</u>
   <u>citizens 18 years old and older.</u>

4. In the original Constitution, why do you think so many groups of people were not given the right to vote? <u>Women and people of color were not allowed to</u>

   <u>vote formerly because they weren't considered legally responsible people.</u>

F **Discuss the following questions with a small group.** (Answers will vary.)

Do any of the rights identified in this lesson affect your life? Which ones? In what ways?

G **Create a Bill of Rights for your classroom or school.** (Answers will vary.)

Presentation 3
5-10 mins. ■■■□

Go over the amendments together and then have students answer the questions by themselves.

Practice 3
15-20 mins. ■□□□

Note: Shorter classes can do this exercise for homework.

(E) There are currently 27 amendments to the Constitution. Read some of these other important amendments and answer the questions that follow.

Evaluation 3
5-10 mins. ■□□□

Go over the answers as a class.

(F) Discuss the following questions with a small group.

Do any of the rights identified in this lesson affect your life? Which ones? In what ways?

Application
10-20 mins. ■■■□

(G) Create a Bill of Rights for your classroom or school.

Put students in small groups or have students work as one large group. You may need to help students get started by brainstorming one or two ideas.

Optional Computer Activity: Have students create their Bill of Rights on the computer.

Activity Bank

Unit 8, Lesson 2, Worksheet 1: Quotes from Famous People

Unit 8, Lesson 2, Worksheet 2: Thomas Jefferson and the Bill of Rights

📖 Refer students to *Stand Out 5 Grammar Challenge*, Unit 8, Challenge 2 for practice with using definite articles *vs.* nothing.

Objective: Identify local civic organizations
Vocabulary: *civic, charitable, social welfare*

RESOURCES

Activity Bank: Unit 8, Lesson 3, Worksheet 1
Grammar Challenge 5: Unit 8, Challenge 3

 1.5 hour classes ■ 2.5 hour classes ■ 3⁺ hour classes

AGENDA

*Read about the Mothers' Club
of Northville, MI.*
Read about and discuss civic organizations.
Create a civic organization.

Warm-up and Review   10–20 mins.

Ask students to take out a piece of paper and
number it from 1 to 10. Ask them to write down
the ten amendments from the Bill of Rights in
their own words. Give them about ten minutes
before letting them look in their books.

Introduction   5–10 mins. ■■■

Dictation:

1. We raise money to help low-income schools
   continue their music and arts programs.
2. Our group conducts environmental awareness
   seminars in the community.
3. She started a group that brings hot meals to
   families who have loved ones in the hospital.
4. Every year, we have a live and silent auction
   to raise scholarship money for high school
   students.

State the objective: *Today we will talk about local
civic organizations and, by the end of class, you
will have created your own organization.*

Presentation 1   10–15 mins. ■■■

**(A) Read about the Mothers' Club
of Northville, Michigan.**

Have students read about the Mothers' Club.
Then ask them the following questions: *What
is the name of the organization? What is their
purpose? What do they do for community service?
How much money do they donate per year?*

Go over the definition of a civic organization.

Practice 1   5–10 mins.

**(B) Answer the following questions with a partner.
Share your answers with others in your class.**

Evaluation 1   5–10 mins. ■■■

Go over the answers as a class. Ask pairs to share
about civic organizations in their community.

STANDARDS CORRELATIONS

CASAS: 5.6.2 (See CASAS Competency List on pages 187–193.)
SCANS: **Resources** Allocate time, allocate materials and facility
resources, allocate human resources
Information Acquire and evaluate information, organize and maintain
information, interpret and communicate information
Interpersonal Participate as a member of a team, teach others, exercise
leadership, negotiate to arrive at a decision, work with cultural diversity
Systems Monitor and correct performance
Basic Skills Reading, writing, arithmetic, listening, speaking

Thinking Skills Think creatively, make decisions, solve problems, see
things in the mind's eye
Personal Qualities Responsibility, sociability, self-management
EFF: **Communication** Read with understanding, speak so others can
understand, listen actively, observe critically
Decision Making Solve problems and make decisions, plan
Interpersonal Cooperate with others, advocate and influence, resolve
conflict and negotiate, guide others
Lifelong Learning Take responsibility for learning

Getting involved

GOAL ➤ Identify local civic organizations

A Read about the Mothers' Club of Northville, Michigan.

The Mothers' Club is a group of 35 dynamic women working to help Northville school children excel by providing enrichment materials and opportunities.

History

In 1935, a group of 12 women decided to meet regularly for enlightenment and social activities. During the Depression of the 1930's, the Mothers' Club held a fundraiser to purchase milk for school children to drink with their lunches. The Club's fundraising has now grown to three events each year, enabling the Club to donate approximately $30,000 annually to student enrichment programs and activities.

Fundraising

A. Fall: Mothers' Club hosts a booth during Northville's Victorian Festival.

B. Winter: *All Aglow* is an opportunity to honor or remember someone by purchasing a light on the community Christmas tree, located in front of the bandshell in downtown Northville.

C. Spring: *Hands to the Future*, a dinner and auction held annually in March, alternates every other year with... *The Community Telephone Directory*, distributed biannually to every household in the Northville School District

Community Service

Mothers' Club performs service projects at the public school buildings on a rotating cycle, working at two or three schools each year.

Social

1. Book club
2. Lunch and movie afternoons
3. Evening socials
4. Weekend getaways

(*Source:* Reprinted by permission of the City of Northville, MI. Web site: http://www.ci.northville.mi.us)

This club is an example of a *civic organization*. A civic organization is a group of people who come together for educational or charitable purposes, including the promotion of community welfare. The money generated by these clubs is devoted exclusively to charitable, educational, recreational, or social welfare purposes.

B Answer the following questions with a partner. Share your answers with others in your class.

(Answers will vary. Sample answers are given.)

1. What makes the Mothers' Club a civic organization?

   They perform charitable tasks in the community.

2. Can you think of any civic organizations in your community?

   Boy and Girl Scouts, Rotary Clubs, Lions, Elks, Odd Fellow, Knights of Columbus Clubs

C Read about these civic organizations and answer the questions on the next page.

American Legion

Purpose: To provide care for veterans and their families at hospitals and homes in the community
Members: Relatives of veterans
Annual Dues: $12

Boy Scouts

Purpose: To promote self-confidence, service to others, citizenship, and outdoor skills
Members: Boys only, at least 11 years old
Volunteer Scoutmasters: Male and female scoutmasters needed
Annual Dues: $25

Friends of the Library

Purpose: To promote and support the local public library
Members: All welcome
Annual Dues: $15

Hiking Club

Purpose: To enjoy the forest and also help raise public awareness of issues that face the present-day forest
Members: Anyone who enjoys hiking
Annual Dues: $10

Garden Club

Purpose: To share experiences in gardening
Members: Anyone who enjoys gardening
Annual Dues: $15
Special Events: Plant sale

Rotary Club

Purpose: To provide humanitarian service, encourage high ethical standards in all vocations, and help build goodwill and peace in the world
Members: To become a Rotarian, you must be invited to join a Rotary Club by a member of that club. A qualified candidate for Rotary-Club membership is an adult of good character and good business, professional, or community reputation.
Annual Dues: Amounts vary

Presentation 2

5-10 mins. ■■□

Go over the different organizations in Exercise C.

Practice 2

10-15 mins. ■□

Note: Shorter classes can do this exercise for homework.

C Read about these civic organizations and answer the questions on the next page.

Evaluation 2

10-15 mins. ■□

Go over the answers as a class. Ask a number of students to share their answers to the fifth question on page 165.

Presentation 3　　　　5-10 mins. ■■■□

Go over the instructions and scenario in
Exercise D with the class. Then, put them into
groups or have them select their own groups to
complete the exercise.

Practice 3　　　　　15-20 mins. ■□□□

Note: Shorter classes can do this exercise
for homework.

(D) Some of the students from Mrs. Morgan's
class want to create a civic organization. They
have come together because they have common
interests. Read about the students below and then
come up with an idea for an organization.

Evaluation 3　　　　10-15 mins. ■□□□

Ask each group to present its organization
to the class.

Application　　　　10-20 mins. ■■□□

(E) Follow the directions for creating a civic
organization.

Step 1. Get together with a few students
from your class and create a new civic
organization. Complete the information
about your organization below.

Step 2. Now recruit members for your
organization. You need at least ten members
to be a true organization.

Have students walk around the classroom and
tell other students about their organization.
Then, have them write down any students that
want to join. Tell them they can be seated when
they have at least ten members.

Activity Bank

Unit 8, Lesson 3, Worksheet 1: Civic Organizations

Refer students to *Stand Out 5 Grammar
Challenge*, Unit 8, Challenge 3 for more
practice with *the* and demonstrative
determiners.

GOAL ➤ Identify local civic organizations

1. Which clubs would you join if you liked nature? _Hiking Club/Garden Club_

2. Which clubs can you join if you are a woman? _All of the clubs. Of special interest might be American Legion and Garden Clubs._

3. Which club has the highest dues? _Boy Scouts_

   The lowest? _Hiking Club_

4. Which clubs provide community service? _All of them, but Boy Scouts and Rotary Club in particular._

5. If you could join one club, which one would it be? _(Answers will vary.)_

   Why? _____

D Some of the students from Mrs. Morgan's class want to create a civic organization. They have come together because they have common interests. Read about the students below and then come up with an idea for an organization. (Answers will vary.)

Hanh, Sadiq, Ella, Phillipe, and Enrique have just found out that many students at their school can't afford to buy books. There are over 100 students a year who attend class without textbooks. Hanh, Sadiq, Ella, Phillipe, and Enrique have one thing in common—they are all very creative. Sadiq takes beautiful photographs. Hanh and Ella both knit; they can make anything from hats to sweaters and blankets. Phillipe is an accomplished musician and songwriter, and Enrique paints oil paintings of flowers and animals.

Name of civic organization: _____

Purpose: _____

Members: _____

Annual dues: _____

Special events: _____

E Follow the directions for creating a civic organization.

Step 1. Get together with a few students from your class and create a new civic organization. Complete the information about your organization below.

- Name of civic organization
- Purpose
- Members
- Annual dues
- Special events

Step 2. Now recruit members for your organization. You need at least ten members to be a true organization.

LESSON 4

Saving the environment

GOAL ➤ Interpret information about environmental issues

A Look at the list of ways to create less trash. Which ones do you do? Put a check (✔) next to them. (Answers will vary.)

Create Less Trash

☐ Buy items in bulk from loose bins when possible to reduce the packaging wasted.
☐ Avoid products with several layers of packaging when only one is sufficient.
☐ Buy products that you can reuse.
☐ Maintain and repair durable products instead of buying new ones.
☐ Check reports for products that are easily repaired and have low breakdown rates.
☐ Reuse items like bags and containers when possible.
☐ Use cloth napkins instead of paper ones.
☐ Use reusable plates and utensils instead of disposable ones.
☐ Use reusable containers to store food instead of aluminum foil and cling wrap.
☐ Shop with a canvas bag instead of using paper and plastic bags.
☐ Buy rechargeable batteries for devices used frequently.
☐ Reuse packaging cartons and shipping materials. Old newspapers make great packaging material.
☐ Buy used furniture—there is a surplus of it, and it is much cheaper than new furniture.

(*Source:* Used with permission from Sustainable Environment for Quality of Life, www.seql.org)

B Interview your partner to find out how he or she conserves energy at home. Put a check (✔) next to the ones he or she does. (Answers will vary.)

In Your Home—Conserve Energy

☐ Clean or replace air filters on your air-conditioning unit at least once a month.
☐ Lower the thermostat on your water heater to 120°F.
☐ Wrap your water heater in an insulated blanket.
☐ Turn down or shut off your water heater when you will be away for extended periods.
☐ Turn off unneeded lights even when leaving a room for a short time.
☐ Set your refrigerator temperature at 36 to 38°F and your freezer at 0 to 5°F.
☐ When using an oven, minimize door opening while it is in use.
☐ Clean the lint filter in your dryer after every load so that it uses less energy.
☐ Unplug seldom-used appliances.
☐ Use a microwave whenever you can instead of a conventional oven or stove.
☐ Wash clothes with warm or cold water instead of hot.
☐ Turn off lights, computers, and other appliances when not in use.
☐ Use compact fluorescent lightbulbs to save money and energy.
☐ Keep your thermostat at 68°F in winter and 78°F in summer.
☐ Use cold water instead of warm or hot water when possible.
☐ Connect your outdoor lights to a timer.

(*Source:* Used with permission from Sustainable Environment for Quality of Life, www.seql.org)

Objective: Interpret information about environmental issues

Academic Strategies: Reading for understanding, brainstorming

Vocabulary: *sufficient, reusable, commuters, auto emissions*

RESOURCES

Activity Bank: Unit 8, Lesson 4, Worksheet 1 and PDFs

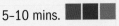 1.5 hour classes 2.5 hour classes 3⁺ hour classes

Grammar Challenge 5: Unit 8, Challenge 4

AGENDA

Find out how to create less trash.
Interview partner about conserving energy.
Read about SEQL's action item.
Brainstorm community programs.
Develop a program.

Warm-up and Review   10-15 mins.

Ask volunteers to present their civic organization to the class and list the ten members who they recruited in the previous lesson.

Introduction   5-10 mins.

Dictation:

1. Learn about alternatives to household cleaning items that do not use hazardous chemicals.
2. Take your car to a car wash instead of washing it in the driveway.
3. Use an electric-powered lawn mower instead of a gas-powered one.
4. Turn off lights, computers, and other appliances when not in use.

When you have finished the dictation, ask students how following each of these suggestions would help the environment.

State the objective: *Today we will talk about ways to save the environment and create an action plan for something you can do in this community.*

Presentation 1   10-15 mins.

(A) Look at the list of ways to create less trash. Which ones do you do? Put a check (✓) next to them.

Go over each item as a class and have students put checks next to the ones they do. If there are certain items that most students don't do, ask them *why.* Try to come up with some ways that would make it easier to follow some of the suggestions.

Practice 1   10-15 mins.

(B) Interview your partner to find out how he or she conserves energy at home. Put a check (✓) next to the ones he or she does.

Evaluation 1   5-10 mins.

Have each pair sit down once they've finished their interview and discuss the ways that they conserve energy. Have them come up with some suggestions on how to do more of the items on the list.

 There is a list of one hundred ways to save the environment on the Activity Bank CD-ROM.

Presentation 2

5-10 mins.

Write the word *carpooling* on the board and ask the following questions:

1. What is carpooling?
2. What are some examples of places you can carpool to?
3. Are there special lanes on the highways here for people who carpool?
4. Are there special parking places for people who carpool?
5. Do you think carpooling is a good idea? Why or why not?

Go over the instructions for Exercise C.

Practice 2

10-15 mins.

Note: Shorter classes can do this exercise for homework.

C Sustainable Environment for Quality of Life (SEQL) has put together several action items that they would like to see accomplished in their communities in North and South Carolina. Read their plan for carpooling.

Evaluation 2

10-15 mins.

On the Activity Bank, there is a worksheet related to this reading that you can give students to see if they have understood what they've read. You can also do an oral evaluation by asking the following questions:

1. *Why is carpooling good?* (reduces vehicle trips and miles traveled, which, in turn, reduces auto emissions)
2. *How can people who carpool save money?* (spend less on gas, auto maintenance, and parking)
3. *How long would it take to implement a carpooling program?* (a few months)
4. *Name two groups of people who need to be involved in the carpooling plan.* (businesses, transit providers, private parking lot owners, employees)

Activity Bank

Unit 8, Lesson 4, Worksheet 1: Carpooling

Instructor's Notes

LESSON 4

GOAL ➤ Interpret information about environmental issues

Ⓒ Sustainable Environment for Quality of Life (SEQL) has put together several action items that they would like to see accomplished in their communities in North and South Carolina. Read their plan for carpooling.

Carpooling: What is it?

Vanpooling/carpooling is an arrangement by a group of commuters to ride together from home or a prearranged meeting place in a van or a car to their destinations in a single round trip, with the driver as a fellow commuter. Vanpools/carpools usually consist of individuals who live near each other and are employees of the same company, or are employees of different companies located only a short distance apart, and have the same work hours. The great advantage of vanpools and carpools is that it reduces vehicle trips, reduces vehicle miles traveled, and therefore reduces auto emissions that result in poor air quality.

Shared Impact and Benefits
- Car- and vanpooling reduce overall auto emissions by reducing vehicle miles traveled, and by doing so, improve air quality. Ground-level ozone formation is reduced through the reduced levels of oxides of nitrogen from auto exhaust.
- The American Lung Association reports that low levels of ground-level ozone adversely affect nearly one-third of our population. So improvements in air quality result in improvements in public health.
- Peak-hour traffic congestion (and resulting gasoline consumption) are reduced. Nine billion gallons of fuel are wasted in traffic congestion each year—800 times the amount of oil spilled by the ship Exxon Valdez in 1989.
- Employers will be able to offer employees a value-added benefit and take a tax write-off.
- Eight of ten U.S. workers believe commuter benefits are valuable to employees.
- Furthermore, employers that pay for employee parking costs can save money.
- Vanpool/carpool participants save money by sharing commuting costs.

- Vanpool/carpool riders have lower stress commutes to work. Employers will also have more productive employees with higher morale.

Costs
Usually vanpoolers/carpoolers will share the costs of gasoline, maintenance, and/or leasing the vehicles. By offering commuter benefits, including carpooling and vanpooling, a company with 1,000 employees can lower its annual parking expenses by more than $70,000 and save participating employees $13,000 each year in taxes and $160,000 each year in gasoline, parking, and vehicle costs.

How long does this take to implement?
A vanpooling/carpooling program can be implemented within a few months. Once the program is established, individual pools can be set up in less than a few weeks.

The Bottom Line
Carpooling and vanpooling commuters get to work in ways that reduce air pollution and traffic congestion, save employers and employees money, reduce the environmental impacts associated with driving single-passenger vehicles, reduce parking space demand and expenses, and relieve commuter stress.

Who needs to be involved?
- Governing board and/or management (to endorse a vanpool/carpool policy and support a program that provides incentives for employees who participate in a vanpool or carpool)
- Businesses and their human resource or fiscal office staff
- Transit providers and/or private vanpool leasing companies
- Private parking deck and lot owners
- Employees willing to start up their own vanpool or carpool

(*Source:* Used with permission from Sustainable Environment for Quality of Life, www.seql.org)

D Working with a partner, choose one of the following three environmental topics. Come up with a list of programs that might work to improve the environment in your community.

air quality   water resources   sustainable development

(Answers will vary.)

Topic: _____

Possible programs: _____

_____

_____

_____

E Find another pair of students who chose the same topic as you. Work together and share your ideas. Then, choose one program to develop. Think about and decide on the following items.
(Answers will vary.)

Topic: _____

Name of program: _____

Briefly describe how program works: _____

_____

_____

Impact and benefit the environment: _____

_____

_____

Length of time to implement: _____

Cost: _____

People involved: _____

Presentation 3　　　　　5 mins. ▮▮▮▯

Go over the instructions for Exercise D and put students in pairs.

Definitions of Topics:

Improving air quality: making the air we breathe healthier

Protecting water resources: making sure we don't use up so much water that we have a water shortage

Creating sustainable development: making sure we're not taking too many resources from the earth while allowing people to meet basic needs and enjoy a good quality of life without compromising the quality of life for future generations (should be socially desirable, ecologically viable, economically feasible).

Practice 3　　　　　15-20 mins. ▮

Note: Shorter classes can do this exercise individually for homework.

D Working with a partner, choose one of the following three environmental topics. Come up with a list of programs that might work to improve the environment in your community.

Evaluation 3　　　　　5-10 mins. ▮

Write each of the three topics on the board. Ask students to share some of the ideas they came up with.

Application　　　　　10-20 mins. ▮▮▯

Help students get into teams of four and explain what they will be doing. Point out that they will be coming up with information similar to that found on page 167. If possible, allow students to do research. If not, tell them to come up with information that they think is accurate.

E Find another pair of students who chose the same topic as you. Work together and share your ideas. Then, choose one program to develop. Think about and decide on the following items.

Have each team present its program to the class.

Activity Bank

Unit 8, Lesson 4, PDFs:
100 Ways to Save the Environment (PDF)
Kids Can Do Bookmark

 Refer students to *Stand Out 5 Grammar Challenge*, Unit 8, Challenge 4 for practice with demonstrative determiners and pronouns.

Instructor's Notes

_____
_____
_____
_____
_____
_____
_____
_____
_____
_____
_____
_____
_____
_____
_____
_____
_____
_____
_____
_____

Objective: Communicate your opinion
Pronunciation: Express an opinion
Academic Strategy: Writing an opinion paragraph
Vocabulary: *opinion, protect, conserve, resource*

RESOURCES

Activity Bank: Unit 8, Lesson 5, Worksheets 1–2
Grammar Challenge 5: Unit 8, Challenge 5

■ 1.5 hour classes ■ 2.5 hour classes ■ 3⁺ hour classes

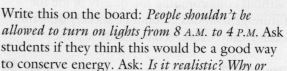

AGENDA

Brainstorm opinions.
Communicate your opinion.
Read and answer questions about Ella's paragraph on water conservation.
Use transitional expressions.
Write a paragraph.

Warm-up and Review   5–10 mins.

Quickly review each program that the students came up with in the previous lesson. Write them on the board. Ask the class to discuss which programs they think are most possible. Vote as a class on the best program.

Introduction   5–10 mins.

Dictation:

1. Recycling means taking a product at the end of its useful life and turning it into a usable raw material to make another product.
2. Curbside recycling is the most convenient means for households to recycle a variety of materials.
3. The most commonly recycled items are aluminum cans, glass bottles, paper, plastic, and steel/tin cans.
4. Not all things are recyclable in all areas of the country.

(*Source:* Excerpted from www.earth911.org)

State the objective: *Today you will practice communicating opinions, verbally and on paper.*

Presentation 1   10–15 mins.

Write this on the board: *People shouldn't be allowed to turn on lights from 8 A.M. to 4 P.M.* Ask students if they think this would be a good way to conserve energy. Ask: *Is it realistic? Why or why not?*

Go over the instructions for Exercises A and B.

Practice 1   10–15 mins.   ■■■

A Everyone has an opinion when it comes to the environment. In a small group, brainstorm some *yes* and *no* opinions for each of the suggestions below.

Review the example together and present the different opinions.

B Practice communicating your opinion to a partner.

Evaluation 1   5 mins.

Walk around the classroom and help students come up with ideas if necessary.

STANDARDS CORRELATIONS

CASAS: 5.1.6, 5.7.1 (See CASAS Competency List on pages 187–193.)
SCANS: **Information** Acquire and evaluate information, organize and maintain information, interpret and communicate information
Interpersonal Participate as a member of a team, teach others, exercise leadership, negotiate to arrive at a decision, work with cultural diversity
Systems Understand systems, monitor and correct performance
Basic Skills Reading, writing, listening, speaking
Thinking Skills Think creatively, make decisions, solve problems, see things in the mind's eye

Personal Qualities Responsibility, sociability, self-management
EFF: **Communication** Read with understanding, convey ideas in writing, speak so others can understand, listen actively, observe critically
Decision Making Solve problems and make decisions, plan
Interpersonal Cooperate with others, advocate and influence, resolve conflict and negotiate, guide others
Lifelong Learning Take responsibility for learning, reflect and evaluate

Expressing yourself

GOAL ➤ Communicate your opinion

A Everyone has an opinion when it comes to the environment. In a small group, brainstorm some *yes* and *no* opinions for each of the suggestions below. (Answers will vary. Sample answers are below.)

EXAMPLE: People should not be permitted to buy large cars that create a lot of pollution.

Yes: *If everyone bought smaller cars, pollution would be significantly reduced.*

No: *Many people need large cars for their families. Large cars are safer and hold more people and more groceries.*

1. Our city should build more carpool lanes.

Yes		**No**	
a.	This will reduce pollution in the air.	a.	These lanes are wasted space.
b.		b.	
c.		c.	

2. Everyone should take his own recyclable items to a recycling center.

Yes		**No**	
a.	All individuals and families should recycle.	a.	The government should provide pick up service.
b.		b.	
c.		c.	

3. Each home should only be allowed to have a certain amount of water per month.

Yes		**No**	
a.	People should be aware of their water use.	a.	There should be no limits on water use.
b.		b.	
c.		c.	

B Practice communicating your opinion to a partner.

EXAMPLE: **A:** *I think our city should build more carpool lanes.*
   B: *I disagree. In my opinion, it is a waste of money because it won't make more people carpool.*

Phrases for Communicating Your Opinion

I think . . .   I believe . . .   In my opinion, . . .   I agree.   I disagree.

C Ella wrote a paragraph communicating her opinion on the environment. Read.

> ### Our Most Precious Resource
>
> There are many things we should do to protect our environment, but I think one of the most important things we can do is to conserve water. Why? Water is one of our most precious resources. I believe this for many reasons. One reason is that the human body is made up of 75% water. We can only live for one week without water; therefore, we need to drink water to survive. Another reason that water is so important is that we need it to clean. We need water to clean our bodies, wash our dishes, flush our toilets, and launder our clothes. Can you imagine not being able to do any of these things? Still another reason is that plants and trees need water to grow and survive. Without plants and trees, humans wouldn't survive because plants give off the oxygen we need in order to breathe. For these reasons, I believe that we need to conserve our most precious resource—water.

D Answer the questions about the sentence types in Ella's paragraph.

1. What is Ella's topic sentence?

   Water is one of our most precious resources.

2. What is Ella's concluding sentence?

   For these reasons, I believe that we need to conserve our most precious resource—water.

3. Ella gives three reasons to support her main idea. For each idea, she gives a supporting detail. What are her reasons and details?

   a. Reason: The human body is 75% water.

   Detail: We can only live one week without water.

   b. Reason: We need water to clean.

   Detail: We clean our bodies, wash dishes, do laundry, and flush toilets.

   c. Reason: Plants and trees need water to grow.

   Detail: We need the oxygen given off by plants to breathe.

Presentation 2   10-15 mins. ■■■

C Ella wrote a paragraph communicating her opinion on the environment. Read.

Have students read Ella's paragraph silently and then read it out loud. Tell them this is an opinion paragraph. Ask students what makes it an opinion paragraph. Ask them if they agree with Ella.

Practice 2   10-15 mins. ■■

Note: Shorter classes can do this exercise for homework.

D Answer the questions about the sentence types in Ella's paragraph.

Evaluation 2   10-15 mins. ■■

Go over the answers as a class.

Presentation 3   5-10 mins.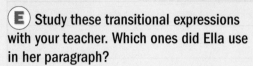

(E) Study these transitional expressions with your teacher. Which ones did Ella use in her paragraph?

Practice 3   15-20 mins. ▪

Note: Shorter classes can do these exercises for homework.

(F) What are some of your ideas about the environment? Use a cluster map like this one to brainstorm your ideas.

(G) Choose one of your ideas. Write three reasons to support that idea.

(H) Come up with at least one detail to support each reason.

Evaluation 3   ▪

Walk around the classroom and help students as needed.

Application   20-30 mins. ▪▪▪

(I) On a separate piece of paper, write a paragraph communicating your opinion about the environment.

You can give these guidelines to students when they are writing the first draft of their opinion paragraphs:

1. Begin with a topic sentence that includes your opinion.
2. Write about three reasons, no more.
3. Use enumeration signals to connect your ideas for the reader.
4. Add supporting details to each reason to make it clearer and more interesting.
5. End with a concluding sentence that restates your opinion.

Activity Bank

Unit 8, Lesson 5, Worksheet 1: Opinions
                    Opinion Paragraphs

Refer students to *Stand Out 5 Grammar Challenge*, Unit 8, Challenge 5 for practice with *such* and demonstrative determiners.

There are also two extension challenges. Extension Challenge 1 offers practice with specific and general determiners. Extension Challenge 2 gives more review practice on demonstrative forms, pronouns, and definite articles.

Instructor's Notes

_____

_____

_____

_____

_____

_____

_____

_____

_____

_____

_____

_____

_____

_____

_____

_____

_____

_____

_____

_____

_____

_____

_____

_____

E   Study these transitional expressions with your teacher. Which ones did Ella use in her paragraph?

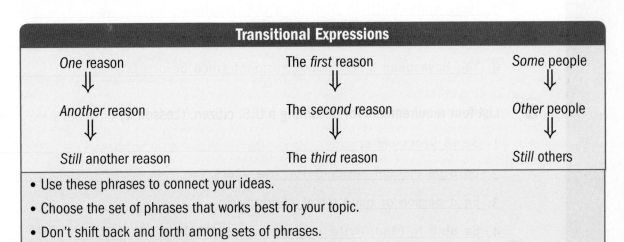

Transitional Expressions		
One reason ⇓	The *first* reason ⇓	*Some* people ⇓
Another reason ⇓	The *second* reason ⇓	*Other* people ⇓
Still another reason	The *third* reason	*Still* others

- Use these phrases to connect your ideas.
- Choose the set of phrases that works best for your topic.
- Don't shift back and forth among sets of phrases.

F   What are some of your ideas about the environment? Use a cluster map like this one to brainstorm your ideas.

(Answers will vary.)

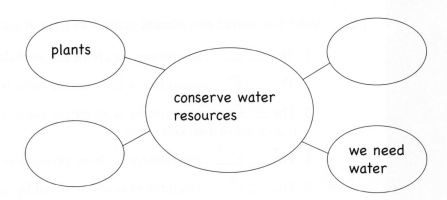

G   Choose one of your ideas. Write three reasons to support that idea. (Answers will vary.)

Reason 1: _____

Reason 2: _____

Reason 3: _____

H   Come up with at least one detail to support each reason. (Answers will vary.)

Detail 1: _____

Detail 2: _____

Detail 3: _____

I   On a separate piece of paper, write a paragraph communicating your opinion about the environment.

Review

(A) List four ways one can become a permanent resident of the United States. **(Lesson 1)**

1. You are the spouse of an LPR who filed a family-based petition.

2. Have a visa petition filed by a U.S. employer.

3. Be an asylee or refugee for at least one year.

4. You have been a continuous resident since before 1/1/72.

(B) List four requirements for becoming a U.S. citizen. **(Lesson 1)** (Answers may vary.)

1. Be 18 years old or older.

2. Be a permanent resident for five years.

3. Be a person of good moral character.

4. Be able to read, write, and speak basic English.

(C) Write the correct amendment number in front of each description. **(Lesson 2)**

1. The ___13th___ amendment is about the abolishment of slavery.

2. The ___19th___ amendment is about the right for women to vote.

3. The ___5th___ amendment is about the right to be charged by a grand jury if accused of a serious crime.

4. The ___4th___ amendment is about protection from unreasonable search and seizure.

5. The ___7th___ amendment is about a trial by jury in civil cases (dispute between private parties or between the government and a private party).

6. The ___6th___ amendment is about a speedy and public trial by an impartial jury.

7. The ___1st___ amendment is about freedom of religion.

8. The ___2nd___ amendment is about the right to keep and bear arms.

9. The ___15th___ amendment is about the right for people of all races to vote.

10. The ___3rd___ amendment is about protection from forced housing of soldiers.

AT-A-GLANCE PREP

Objectives: All unit objectives
Grammar: All unit grammar
Academic Strategy: Reviewing
Vocabulary: All Unit 8 vocabulary

RESOURCES

Stand Out 5 Assessment CD-ROM with Exam*View*®

 1.5 hour classes  2.5 hour classes ▮ 3⁺ hour classes

AGENDA

Discuss unit objectives.
Complete the review.
Use unit vocabulary.

Warm-up and Review   5-10 mins. ▮▮▮

Have students summarize their paragraph about the environment for the class. Encourage students to ask questions to clarify each others' opinions.

Introduction   5-10 mins. ▮▮▮

Ask students as a class to try to recall all the objectives of this unit without looking back in their books. The objectives for this unit include identifying requirements for establishing residency and citizenship, identifying your rights, identifying local civic organizations, interpreting information about environmental issues, and communicating your opinion. Write all the objectives on the board from Unit 8. Show students the first page of the unit and mention the five objectives.

State the objective: *Today we will be reviewing everything we have learned in this unit and preparing for the individual project.*

Presentation 1   10-15 mins. ▮▮▮

This presentation will cover the first three pages of the review. Quickly go to the first page of each lesson. Discuss the objective of each. Ask simple questions to remind students of what they have learned.

Note: Since there is little presentation in the review, you can assign the review exercises that don't require collaboration with a partner or group for homework and go over them in class the following day.

Practice 1   20-25 mins. ▮▮▮

Note: There are two ways to do the review:
1. Go through the exercises one at a time and, as students complete each one, go over the answers.

2. Quickly go through the instructions of each exercise, let students complete all of the exercises at once, and then go over the answers.

Ⓐ List four ways one can become a permanent resident of the United States. (Lesson 1)

Ⓑ List four requirements for becoming a U.S. citizen. (Lesson 1)

Ⓒ Write the correct amendment number in front of each description. (Lesson 2)

Evaluation 1   5-15 mins. ▮▮▮

Go around the classroom and check on students' progress. Help individuals when needed. If you see consistent errors among several students, interrupt the class and give a mini-lesson or review to help students feel comfortable with the concept.

STANDARDS CORRELATIONS

CASAS: 7.2.1 (See CASAS Competency List on pages 187–193.)
SCANS: **Resources** Allocate time
Information Acquire and evaluate information
Interpersonal Participate as a member of a team, teach others, negotiate to arrive at a decision, work with cultural diversity
Systems Monitor and correct performance
Basic Skills Reading, writing, arithmetic, listening, speaking

Thinking Skills Think creatively, make decisions, solve problems, see things in the mind's eye
Personal Qualities Responsibility, sociability, self-management
EFF: **Communication** Read with understanding, convey ideas in writing, speak so others can understand, listen actively, observe critically
Interpersonal Cooperate with others, guide others
Lifelong Learning Take responsibility for learning, reflect and evaluate

Practice 1 *(continued)*   25–30 mins. ■■■□

D Create a civic organization for the following group's problem. (Lesson 3)

E Work with a partner and list ten ways you can help protect and preserve the environment. (Lesson 4)

F Choose one of the ways you and your partner listed in Exercise E and write a paragraph about why it is important. (Lesson 5)

Evaluation 1 *(continued)*   5–15 mins. ■■□□

Go around the classroom and check on students' progress. Help individuals when needed. If you see consistent errors among several students, interrupt the class and give a mini-lesson or review to help students feel comfortable with the concept.

Teacher Tip

Recycling/Review

The review exercises, the research activity, and the individual project are part of the recycling/review process. Students often need to be reintroduced to concepts to solidify what they have learned. Many concepts are learned and forgotten when students are engaged in learning other new concepts. This is because students learn but are not necessarily ready to acquire language concepts.

Therefore, it becomes very important to review material with students and to show them how to review it on their own. It is also important to recycle the new concepts in different contexts.

D Create a civic organization for the following group's problem. (Lesson 3)

A group of children who live in a shelter for homeless families goes to a nearby elementary school. However, the parents of the children don't have any money to buy the required school uniform—blue pants and a white shirt. The volunteers at the shelter want to find a way to raise money for these kids. (Answers will vary.)

Name of organization: _____

Purpose: _____

Members: _____

Annual dues: _____

Special events: _____

E Work with a partner and list ten ways you can help protect and preserve the environment. **(Lesson 4)** (Answers will vary. Sample answers are given.)

1. Drive my car less.   6. Turn down the heat.

2. Use less paper.   7. Drink tap, not bottled, water.

3. Support alternative energies.   8. Walk to the store.

4. Recycle my plastic.   9. Limit building in my town.

5. Compost my vegetable waste.   10. Support environmental organizations.

F Choose one of the ways you and your partner listed in Exercise E and write a paragraph about why it is important. **(Lesson 5)** (Answers will vary.)

_____

_____

_____

_____

_____

_____

VOCABULARY REVIEW

alien	conserve	protect	reusable
bear arms	eligible	punishment	slavery
believe	naturalization	refugee	social welfare
capital crime	opinion	resource	status
civic	peaceably assemble		

G Choose five words from the vocabulary list above. Use each word in a meaningful sentence that reviews an important point or piece of information that you have learned in this unit.

(Answers will vary. Sample answer is given).

1. Slavery is illegal in the U.S.

2. _____

3. _____

4. _____

5. _____

H Use five different words from the list above to write five different opinions you have.

(Answers will vary. Sample answer is given.)

1. I believe I have the right to criticize the government.

2. _____

3. _____

4. _____

5. _____

I Write the correct word in front of each definition below.

1. _____ Alien _____ means resident foreigner.

2. _____ Status _____ means having the right to do or be chosen for something.

3. _____ Punishment _____ means a payment for doing something wrong.

4. _____ Reusable _____ means useful things.

5. _____ Eligible _____ means a legal condition.

Practice 1 (continued) 25–30 mins. ■■■■

Vocabulary Review

(G) Choose five words from the vocabulary list above. Use each word in a meaningful sentence that reviews an important point or piece of information that you have learned in this unit.

(H) Use five different words from the list above to write five different opinions you have.

(I) Write the correct word in front of each definition below.

Evaluation 1 (continued) 5–15 mins. ■■■

Go around the classroom and check on students' progress. Help individuals when needed. If you see consistent errors among several students, interrupt the class and give a mini-lesson or review to help students feel comfortable with the concept.

Assessment (optional) ■■■

Use the Stand Out 5 Assessment CD-ROM with Exam*View®* to create a post-test for Unit 8.

Objective: Research a unit topic
Academic Strategy: Research

RESOURCES

Activity Bank: Unit 8, Internet Activities

AGENDA

Choose topic to research.
Determine best way to conduct research.
Research topic and share information.

Introduction   5-10 mins.

Have students help you make a list on the board of all the different ways they have learned how to conduct research.

State the objective: *Today you will choose something you want to know more about and do some research on it.*

Presentation   10-15 mins.

A Think about the things you have learned in this unit. Imagine that you want to know more about something you have learned. What would be the best way to research it? Write your idea next to each topic.

You can have students do this by themselves and then go over the topics as a class. Alternatively, you could read through each objective and have students call out their ideas of how they might go about researching the objectives.

Practice   15-20 mins.

B Choose one of the topics from Exercise A that you want to research. Make a list of what you want to know more about or questions you want answered.

You might also suggest that students look through their work in the Activity Bank for topics in which they might be interested.

C Research your topic and find the information in your want-to-know list above. Take notes on a separate piece of paper.

In this final unit, students have to figure out how to research something on their own, without being given the resources. If this exercise is something students are unable to complete in class, assign it for homework and have them bring their results back to the next class meeting.

Evaluation   15-20 mins.

D Share what you learned with your classmates.

Have students stand up and tell what they researched, what they wanted to know, and what they found out.

STANDARDS CORRELATIONS

CASAS: 4.9.3, 7.2.1, 7.4.4, 7.4.5, 7.4.6 (See CASAS Competency List on pages 187–193.)
SCANS: **Information** Acquire and evaluate information, organize and maintain information, interpret and communicate information, use computers to process information *(optional)*
Interpersonal Participate as a member of a team, teach others, negotiate to arrive at a decision, work with cultural diversity
Systems Understand systems
Technology Select technology, apply technology to a task, maintain and troubleshoot technology *(optional)*

Basic Skills Reading, writing
Thinking Skills Think creatively, make decisions, see things in the mind's eye
Personal Qualities Responsibility, sociability, self-management
EFF: **Communication** Read with understanding, convey ideas in writing, observe critically
Decision Making Solve problems and make decisions, plan
Lifelong Learning Take responsibility for learning, reflect and evaluate, learn through research, use information and communications technology *(optional)*

Research Project

A Think about the things you have learned in this unit. Imagine that you want to know more about something you have learned. What would be the best way to research it? Write your ideas next to each topic.

1. Becoming a resident or citizen: Take a citizenship class, look online, go to the library

2. The Bill of Rights: Look in a history book, read online, go to the library

3. Civic organizations: Look in the local newspaper or Web site, ask your neighbors

4. Environmental issues: Read online, go to the library

B Choose one of the topics from Exercise A that you want to research. Make a list of what you want to know more about or questions you want answered.
(Answers will vary. Sample answer is given.)

I want to know . . .

1. how my relatives in Albania can become U.S. citizens.

2.

3.

4.

5.

C Research your topic and find the information in your want-to-know list above. Take notes on a separate piece of paper.

D Share what you learned with your classmates.

Individual Project

Give an opinion speech.

In this project, you will work <u>individually</u> to develop an opinion speech supported with details.

1. Look back at everything you have learned in this unit and choose one topic to give a speech about. Remember, this speech should be persuasive. You should not just present facts without giving your opinion. However, you can support your opinion with facts. First, write one sentence that states your opinion.

   Some examples:

   • *I think that someone should be able to become a citizen anytime he or she wants.*

   • *I don't think Americans should have the right to bear arms.*

   • *I think every citizen should have to be a part of a civic organization.*

2. Read your opinion out loud to the class.

3. Come up with reasons to support your opinion and write a speech. Prepare to speak for at least two minutes.

4. Practice your speech. Remember the following tips:

   • Enunciate (speak clearly).

   • Make eye contact with your audience.

   • Practice so you recall your major points without notes.

   • Thank your audience for listening and/or for their time.

5. Give your two-minute opinion speech. At the end of your speech, ask your classmates if they have any questions.

Individual Project

Give an opinion speech.

In this project students will work individually to develop an opinion speech supported with details.

Note: Shorter classes can extend this project over two class meetings.

Stage 1   5 mins.

Look back at everything you have learned in this unit and choose one topic to give a speech about. Remember, this speech should be persuasive. You should not just present facts without giving your opinion. However, you can support your opinion with facts. First, write one sentence that states your opinion.

Go over the examples from the book and give a few more if you think students need some ideas. Tell them they must come up with their own opinion, not use one from the examples in the book.

Stage 2   10–15 mins.

Read your opinion out loud to the class.

Have each student read his or her opinion out loud. Make sure that it is an opinion. If it is not, help the student reword the sentence. Ask the class to help.

Stage 3   20–30 mins.

Come up with reasons to support your opinion and write a speech. Prepare to speak for at least two minutes.

Walk around the classroom and help students as they are writing their speeches.

Stage 4   10–15 mins.

Practice your speech. Remember the following tips:

- Enunciate (speak clearly).
- Make eye contact with your audience.
- Practice so you recall your major points without notes.
- Thank your audience for listening and/or for their time.

Stage 5   5 mins.

Give your two-minute opinion speech. At the end of your speech, ask your classmates if they have any questions.

STANDARDS CORRELATIONS

CASAS: 4.8.1, 4.8.5, 4.8.6. (See CASAS Competency List on pages 187–193.)
SCANS: **Resources** Allocate time
Information Acquire and evaluate information, organize and maintain information, interpret and communicate information, use computers to process information
Systems Understand systems, improve and design systems
Technology Select technology, apply technology to exercise
Basic Skills Writing
Thinking Skills Think creatively, make decisions, solve problems, see things in the mind's eye, use reasoning

Personal Qualities Responsibility, self-esteem, self-management, integrity
EFF: **Communication** Read with understanding, convey ideas in writing, speak so others can understand, listen actively, observe critically
Decision Making Solve problems and make decisions, plan
Interpersonal Cooperate with others, advocate and influence, resolve conflict and negotiate, guide others
Lifelong Learning Take responsibility for learning, reflect and evaluate, learn through research, use information and communications technology (optional)

Give an opinion speech

In this project students will work individually to develop an opinion speech, supported with details.

Note: Shorter classes can extend this project over two class meetings.

Stage 1   5 mins.

Look back at everything you have learned in this unit and choose one topic to give a speech about. Remember, this speech should be persuasive. You should not just present facts without giving your opinion. However, you can support your opinion with facts. First, write one sentence that states your opinion.

Go over the examples from the book and give a few more. If you think students need some ideas, tell them they must come up with their own opinion, not use one from the example in the book.

Stage 2   10-15 mins.

Read your opinion out loud to the class.

Have each student read his or her opinion out loud. Make sure that it is an opinion. If it is not, help the student reword the sentence. Ask the class to help.

Stage 3   20-30 mins.

Come up with reasons to support your opinion and write a speech. Prepare to speak for at least two minutes.

Walk around the classroom and help students as they are writing their speeches.

Stage 4   10-15 mins.

Practice your speech. Remember the following tips:

- Enunciate (speak clearly).
- Make eye contact with your audience.
- Practice so you recall your major points without notes.
- Thank your audience for listening and ask for their time.

Stage 5   5 mins.

Give your two-minute opinion speech. At the end of your speech, ask your classmates if they have any questions.

STANDARDS CORRELATIONS

➤ Think about your knowledge of the goals listed below.
➤ Check if you achieved this goal during the unit.
➤ Write the page number(s) for the goals that you still need to review.
➤ As you work through the text, make a list of your own personal goals.

Pre-Unit: Getting to Know You

Goals	Achieved	Page(s)
Get to know my classmates	☐ Yes ☐ Maybe ☐ No	
Talk about personal interests	☐ Yes ☐ Maybe ☐ No	
Write a personal letter	☐ Yes ☐ Maybe ☐ No	

Unit 1: Balancing Your Life

Goals	Achieved	Page(s)
Identify my learning style	☐ Yes ☐ Maybe ☐ No	
Identify a career path	☐ Yes ☐ Maybe ☐ No	
Balance my life	☐ Yes ☐ Maybe ☐ No	
Identify and prioritize goals	☐ Yes ☐ Maybe ☐ No	
Motivate myself	☐ Yes ☐ Maybe ☐ No	

Unit 2: Personal Finance

Goals	Achieved	Page(s)
Organize your finances	☐ Yes ☐ Maybe ☐ No	
Reduce debt and save money	☐ Yes ☐ Maybe ☐ No	
Identify investment strategies	☐ Yes ☐ Maybe ☐ No	
Maintain good credit	☐ Yes ☐ Maybe ☐ No	
Protect myself against identity theft	☐ Yes ☐ Maybe ☐ No	

Unit 3: Automotive Know-How

Goals	Achieved	Page(s)
Purchase a car	☐ Yes ☐ Maybe ☐ No	
Maintain and repair my car	☐ Yes ☐ Maybe ☐ No	
Interpret an auto insurance policy	☐ Yes ☐ Maybe ☐ No	
Compute mileage and gas consumption	☐ Yes ☐ Maybe ☐ No	
Follow the rules of the road	☐ Yes ☐ Maybe ☐ No	

Unit 4: Housing

Goals	Achieved	Page(s)
Communicate issues by phone	☐ Yes ☐ Maybe ☐ No	
Interpret rental agreements	☐ Yes ☐ Maybe ☐ No	
Identify tenant and landlord rights	☐ Yes ☐ Maybe ☐ No	
Get insurance	☐ Yes ☐ Maybe ☐ No	
Prevent theft	☐ Yes ☐ Maybe ☐ No	

Unit 5: Health

Goals	Achieved	Page(s)
Identify practices that promote mental and physical well-being	☐ Yes ☐ Maybe ☐ No	
Ask about medical bills	☐ Yes ☐ Maybe ☐ No	
Interpret health insurance information	☐ Yes ☐ Maybe ☐ No	
Identify addictions	☐ Yes ☐ Maybe ☐ No	
Interpret procedures for first aid	☐ Yes ☐ Maybe ☐ No	

Unit 6: Retail

Goals	Achieved	Page(s)
Do product research	☐ Yes ☐ Maybe ☐ No	
Purchase goods and services by phone and Internet	☐ Yes ☐ Maybe ☐ No	
Interpret product guarantees and warranties	☐ Yes ☐ Maybe ☐ No	
Return a product	☐ Yes ☐ Maybe ☐ No	
Sell a product	☐ Yes ☐ Maybe ☐ No	

Unit 7: The Office

Goals	Achieved	Page(s)
Identify and use technology	☐ Yes ☐ Maybe ☐ No	
Resolve technological problems	☐ Yes ☐ Maybe ☐ No	
Establish an organizational system	☐ Yes ☐ Maybe ☐ No	
Identify and resolve problems at work	☐ Yes ☐ Maybe ☐ No	
Report progress	☐ Yes ☐ Maybe ☐ No	

Unit 8: Civic Responsibility

Goals	Achieved	Page(s)
Identify requirements for establishing residency and citizenship	☐ Yes ☐ Maybe ☐ No	
Understand my rights	☐ Yes ☐ Maybe ☐ No	
Identify local civic organizations	☐ Yes ☐ Maybe ☐ No	
Interpret information about environmental issues	☐ Yes ☐ Maybe ☐ No	
Communicate my opinion	☐ Yes ☐ Maybe ☐ No	

My Personal Goals	To Achieve By (Date)

Vocabulary List

Pre-Unit
cook, P5
do crossword puzzles, P5
do yoga, P5
draw, P5
knit, P5
lift weights, P5
paint, P5
play soccer, P5
play video games, P5
read, P5
run, P5
swim, P5
take pictures, P5
watch movies, P5
write, P5

Unit 1
achieve, 2, 20
auditory, 1, 2
balance, 2, 20
be flexible, 2, 20
bodily, 2, 6
career path, 1, 2
computer programmer, 1
earning power, 2, 20
educational attainment, 2, 20
evaluate, 2, 20
financial, 1
fun, 1
goal setting, 2
graphic designer, 1
inspire, 2, 20
intelligences, 2
interpersonal, 2, 6
intrapersonal, 2, 6
joy, 1
kinesthetic, 2, 6
learning style, 1, 2
linguistic, 2, 6
logical, 2, 6
long-term, 2, 20
mathematical, 6
monitor, 2, 20
motivate, 2, 20
motivation, 1, 2
multiple, 2
musical, 6
naturalistic, 2, 6
photographer, 1
positive outlook, 2, 20
prioritize, 2, 20
pursue, 2, 20
registered nurse, 1
rhythmic, 2, 6
short-term, 2, 20
spatial, 2, 6

support, 2, 20
tactile, 1, 2
time with family, 1
verbal, 2, 6
visual, 1, 2, 6

Unit 2
bankruptcy, 24
bargain, 42
budget cut, 23
buy in bulk, 23
capital gains, 23, 31
collateral, 24
commit fraud, 23
convert, 31, 42
counterfeit, 42
counterfeit checks, 23
current income, 23
daunting, 24
debt, 42
delinquent, 42
delinquent accounts, 23
dumpster diving, 37
earnings, 42
expense, 42
false pretenses, 23
fraud, 42
inflation, 24, 31
investment, 24
liquid, 24, 31
net appreciation, 31
penalty, 24, 31
periodically, 24
phishing, 37
pretexting, 37
purchasing power, 31
risk, 42
risky, 24, 31
skimming, 37
unauthorized transactions, 23
value, 31
vehicle, 31
worth, 42

Unit 3
accident, 46
air filter, 50
alternator, 50
battery, 50
bodily injury, 46
brake fluid reservoir, 50
change, 46, 62
check, 62
children, 59
choose, 46
collision, 46, 64
commute, 46

convertible, 45
coolant reservoir, 50
coverage, 46
disc brake, 50
distributor, 50
do, 46
exhaust manifold, 50
fatalities, 64
fill, 62
fill up, 46
find, 46
four-door sedan, 45
fuel injection system, 50
imagine, 46
incident, 46
inspect, 62
limits of liability, 46
look at, 46
make, 46
minivan, 45
model, 46
MPG, 64
muffler, 50
odometer, 64
pedestrians, 59
perform, 62
pickup truck, 45
police officer, 59
policy, 46
power steering reservoir, 50
premium, 46, 64
radiator, 50
rear axle, 50
rear suspension, 50
red light, 59
replace, 46, 62
school bus, 59
seat belts, 59
speed limit, 59
sports car, 45
sport utility vehicle (SUV), 45
station wagon, 45
stop sign, 59
timing belt, 50
top off, 62
two-door coupe, 45
uninsured motorist, 46
unrestrained, 64
van, 45
VIN, 46
water pump, 50

Unit 4
abandon, 67
activate, 68
burglarize, 67
burglary, 86

Review: *Be*

Subject	*Past*	Present	Future
I	was	am	will be
you	were	are	will be
he, she, it	was	is	will be
we	were	are	will be
they	were	are	will be

Review: Simple Tenses

Subject	Past	Present	Future	
I	spent	spend	will spend	more time with my brothers.
You	enjoyed	enjoy	will enjoy	being a mother.
He, She, It	studied	studies	will study	English every day.
We	put	put	will put	our studies first.
They	worked	work	will work	too many hours.

Future Perfect Tense

Subject	*will have*	Past participle		Future event—Time expression
I	will have	become	a teacher	by the time my kids are in school.
He	will have	been	a graphic designer (for five years)	when he turns 35.
They	will have	found	a job	by 2015.

We use the future perfect to talk about an activity that will be completed before another time or event in the future. ⊢──── present ──── ✕ ── future to be completed (perfect) ── ✕ ── future event with time expression

Note: The order of events is not important. If the future event with the time expression comes first, use a comma.

Example: *By the time my kids are in school, I will have become a teacher.*

Past Perfect Continuous Tense

	First event in past				Second event in past
Subject	*had*	*been*	**Verb + *-ing***		
Kimla	had	been	buying	designer clothes	before she started bargain shopping.
He	had	been	buying	coffee at a coffee shop	before he began making it at home.
They	had	been	paying	a lower deductible	before they called the insurance company.

- We use the past perfect continuous to talk about an activity that was happening for a while before another event happened in the past. For the most recent event, we use the simple past tense.

- Remember to use a comma if you put the second event as the first part of the sentence. Example: Before she started bargain shopping, Kimla had been buying designer clothes.

Causative Verbs: *Get, Have, Help, Make, Let*

Subject	**Verb**	**Noun/Pronoun**	**Infinitive (Omit *to* except with *get*.)**
He	will get	his handyman	to come.
She	had	her mom	wait for the repairperson.
The landlord	helped	me	move in.
Ming Mei	makes	her sister	pay half of the rent.
Mr. Martin	let	Ming Mei	skip one month's rent.

Adverb Clauses of Concession

Dependent clause	Independent clause
Although he spends a lot of time in Las Vegas,	he says he doesn't have a gambling problem.
Even though her sister spends thousands of dollars a month,	she doesn't think she is a shopaholic.
Though she has to drink two cups of coffee before she can get out of bed in the morning,	she is convinced she isn't addicted to caffeine.
In spite of the fact that he plays video games for three hours a night,	he denies he has a problem.

Explanation: Adverb clauses of concession show a contrast in ideas. The main or independent clauses show the unexpected outcome. The unexpected outcome in the third example is that it is surprising that she thinks she isn't addicted to caffeine.

Note: The clauses can be reversed and have the same meaning. Do not use a comma if the independent clause comes first in the sentence.

Example: *She doesn't think she is a shopaholic even though she spends thousands of dollars a month.*

Appositives

Noun or Noun Phrase	Appositive	Remainder of sentence (Predicate)
The ad,	**the one with all the great pictures,**	makes me want to buy those dishes.
That computer,	**the fastest machine in the store,**	sells for over $2,000.

Explanation:
- An appositive is a noun or noun phrase that renames another noun next to it in a sentence.
- The appositive adds extra descriptive detail, explains, or identifies something about the noun.

Example: *A helpful gift, money is always appreciated by a newly married couple.*
- An appositive can come before or after the noun phrase it is modifying:

Note: Appositives are usually set off by commas.

Noun Clauses as Objects

Subject + Verb	Noun clause	Explanation
I did	*what* I was asked.	• A noun clause starts with a question word or *that* and is followed by a subject and verb.
She knows	*how* the computer works.	
They decided	*where* the location would be.	• In these examples, the noun clauses are the objects of the sentences.
My boss asked	*who* would be best for the job.	
I hope	*that* they work as a team.	

Transitional Expressions

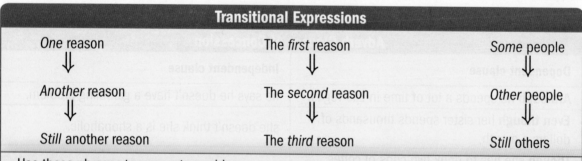

- Use these phrases to connect your ideas.
- Choose the set of phrases that works best for your topic.
- Don't shift back and forth among sets of phrases.

Skills Index

ACADEMIC SKILLS

Brainstorming, 48, 71, 81, 100, 125, 153, 169, 171

Calculations

Annual and monthly expenses, 26

Gas mileage and cost per mile, 56, 57, 58, 62

Categorizing, P5, 18, 67, 75, 156, 166

Charts, graphs, and diagrams, P1, P5, 7, 17, 30, 48, 56, 58, 60, 65, 67, 69, 70, 79, 82, 89, 97, 99, 107, 116, 134, 139, 140, 156, 171

Drawing, 134, 141

Editing, P8, 11, 129

Estimating costs, 78

Grammar

Adverb clauses of concession, 102

Appositives, 126, 129

Causative verbs, 70, 71, 77, 84

Dependent clauses, 102

Future perfect tense, 17, 19

Independent clauses, 102

Noun and verb forms, 68

Noun clauses, 148, 149

Parts of speech, 152

Past perfect continuous tense, 30

Past perfect progressive tense, 40–41

Simple past tense, 40–41

Simple tenses, 10

Transitional expressions, 171

Word families, 89, 134

Group activities, P5, P6, P8, 5, 7, 12, 15, 23, 27, 31, 34, 37, 39, 44, 46, 47, 48, 50, 53, 58, 59, 61, 72, 73, 76, 78, 81, 91, 97, 99, 101, 102, 103, 113, 115, 116, 117, 118, 122, 127, 128, 138, 140, 141, 143, 148, 153, 160, 162, 165, 168, 169, 175

Learning styles, 3–5

Listening

Conversations, P1, P2, P3, 8, 15, 29, 56, 69, 94, 95, 113, 116, 122, 124, 139

Descriptions, 9

Discussion, 7, 37, 48, 78, 83, 91

Explanations, 159

Interviews, 38

Introductions, P3

Lectures, 3, 13, 25

Questions, 122

Sales pitches, 47

Matching, 5, 6, 42, 54, 64, 68, 70, 100, 124, 130, 136, 139, 142, 161

Multiple-choice questions, 38, 55, 121, 140, 150

Partner activities, P2, P3, 4, 6, 8, 9, 10, 11, 14, 15, 17, 25, 28, 32, 36, 49, 50, 51, 54, 62, 65, 69, 71, 74, 75, 77, 84, 86, 95, 96, 97, 100, 105, 106, 119, 121, 125, 128, 129, 130, 135, 137, 144, 158, 159, 163, 166, 168, 169, 173

Prioritizing, 14

Reading

Ads, 28, 125

Articles, 4, 31–32, 34–36, 144–146

Bill of Rights, 160, 161, 162

Catalogs, 116, 128

Charts and graphs, 7, 17, 30, 48, 70, 97, 98, 102, 105, 107, 148

Conversations, P2, 56, 69, 95, 122

Descriptions, 143, 157, 161, 163, 164, 165

Doctor's bills, 96, 106

E-mail messages, P7, P9

Fliers, 12

Instruction manuals, 135, 137, 138, 139, 150

Insurance policies, 53, 63, 79, 85

Introductions, P3

Lists, 23, 27, 31, 71, 75, 101, 114

Main ideas, 34–36

Maintenance and repair guides, 51, 52

Newsletters, 81, 82

Newspaper columns, 92, 93

Noun and verb forms, 68

Paragraphs, 10

Personal letters, P7

Phrases, 64

Plan for carpooling, 167

Product reviews, 114, 115

Rental agreements, 72, 73, 74

Report guidelines, 147

Reports, 147

Research data, 60

Return policies, 123

Scenarios, 41, 54

Sentences, 24, 155, 156

Statements, 16, 53, 101, 126

Tables, 99

Thank-you notes, P8

Warranties and guarantees, 76, 119, 120, 121, 129

Web sites, 29, 44, 117, 158

Worksheets, 26

Research strategies, P10, 21, 43, 48, 65, 87, 109, 118, 131, 153, 175

Selecting responses, 16, 29, 61, 126, 172

Speaking

Answering questions, 8, 10, 86, 105

Asking questions, P6, 8, 11, 19, 49, 86, 97, 115, 128, 129

Conversations, 69, 71, 84, 95, 96, 106, 118

Discussion, P6, 1, 4, 5, 6, 7, 9, 12, 14, 15, 17, 23, 25, 27, 31, 32, 34, 37, 44, 46, 47, 50, 53, 58, 61, 62, 72, 73, 76, 78, 91, 97, 101, 103, 113, 115, 117, 122, 138, 141, 158, 159, 162

Expressing opinions, 169

Instructions, 135

Interviewing, 18, 99, 166

Introductions, P1, P2, P3

Presentations, P6, 37, 61, 73, 127, 140, 175

Sharing with partner, P3

Spelling, 68

Team projects, 22, 44, 66, 88, 110, 132, 154, 176

True/false questions, 29, 86

Vocabulary

Addiction, 100, 108

Balancing your life, 1–2

Careers, 1–2, 6, 20

Cars, 45–46, 50, 64

Civic responsibility, 155–156, 174

Dictionary use, 2, 23, 36, 50, 67, 68, 81, 89–90, 111, 112

Finances, 23–24, 42

First aid, 103–104

Guessing meanings of words, 155

Health, 89–90, 108

Housing, 67–68, 86

Idioms, 23

Learning styles, 1–2

Motivation, 1–2

Office, 133–134, 152

Retail sales, 111–112

Synonyms, 112

Writing

Ads, 127

Alphabetical order, 142, 151

Answers to questions, P3, 11, 12, 13, 25, 28, 39, 41, 51, 60, 63, 70, 80, 81, 85, 90, 93, 94, 107, 115, 118, 119, 122, 127, 128, 138, 144, 151, 163, 164, 165, 170

Bill of Rights, 162

Categorizing, P5

Charts, graphs, and diagrams, P1, 56, 58, 65, 67, 69, 79, 82, 89, 99, 116, 134, 139, 140, 156, 171

CASAS Competencies

0. Basic Communication

0.1 Communicate in interpersonal interactions
0.1.1 Identify or use appropriate non-verbal behavior in a variety of situations (e.g., handshaking)
0.1.2 Identify or use appropriate language for informational purposes (e.g., to identify, describe, ask for information, state needs, command, agree or disagree, ask permission)
0.1.3 Identify or use appropriate language to influence or persuade (e.g., to caution, request, advise, persuade, negotiate)
0.1.4 Identify or use appropriate language in general social situations (e.g., to greet, introduce, thank, apologize, compliment, express pleasure or regret)
0.1.5 Identify or use appropriate classroom behavior
0.1.6 Clarify or request clarification

0.2 Communicate regarding personal information
0.2.1 Respond appropriately to common personal information questions
0.2.2 Complete a personal information form
0.2.3 Interpret or write a personal note, invitation, or letter
0.2.4 Converse about daily and leisure activities and personal interests

1. Consumer Economics

1.1 Use weights, measures, measurement scales, and money
1.1.1 Interpret recipes
1.1.2 Use the metric system (see also 1.1.4, 6.6.1, 6.6.2, 6.6.3, 6.6.4)
1.1.3 Interpret maps and graphs (see also 1.9.4, 2.2.1, 2.2.5)
1.1.4 Select, compute, or interpret appropriate standard measurement for length, width, perimeter, area, volume, height, or weight (see also 1.1.2, 6.6.1, 6.6.2, 6.6.3, 6.6.4, 6.6.5)
1.1.5 Interpret temperatures (see also 6.6.4)
1.1.6 Count, convert, and use coins and currency, and recognize symbols such as ($) and (.) (see also 6.1.1, 6.1.2, 6.1.3, 6.1.4, 6.1.5)
1.1.7 Identify product containers and interpret weight and volume
1.1.8 Compute averages (see also 6.7.5)
1.1.9 Interpret clothing and pattern sizes and use height and weight tables

1.2 Apply principles of comparison-shopping in the selection of goods and services
1.2.1 Interpret advertisements, labels, charts, and price tags in selecting goods and services
1.2.2 Compare price or quality to determine the best buys for goods and services
1.2.3 Compute discounts (see also 6.4.1)
1.2.4 Compute unit pricing
1.2.5 Interpret letters, articles, and information about consumer-related topics

1.3 Understand methods and procedures used to purchase goods and services
1.3.1 Compare different methods used to purchase goods and services
1.3.2 Interpret credit applications and recognize how to use and maintain credit
1.3.3 Identify or use various methods to purchase goods and services, and make returns and exchanges
1.3.4 Use catalogs, order forms, and related information to purchase goods and services
1.3.5 Use coupons to purchase goods and services
1.3.6 Use coin-operated machines
1.3.7 Interpret information or directions to locate merchandise (see also 2.5.4)
1.3.8 Identify common food items
1.3.9 Identify common articles of clothing

1.4 Understand methods and procedures to obtain housing and related services
1.4.1 Identify different kinds of housing, areas of the home, and common household items
1.4.2 Select appropriate housing by interpreting classified ads, signs, and other information
1.4.3 Interpret lease and rental agreements
1.4.4 Interpret information to obtain, maintain, or cancel housing utilities
1.4.5 Interpret information about tenant and landlord rights
1.4.6 Interpret information about housing loans and home-related insurance
1.4.7 Interpret information about home maintenance, and communicate housing problems to a landlord (see also 1.7.4)
1.4.8 Recognize home theft and fire prevention measures

1.5 Apply principles of budgeting in the management of money
1.5.1 Interpret information about personal and family budgets
1.5.2 Plan for major purchases (see also 1.5.1)
1.5.3 Interpret bills (see also 2.1.4)

1.6 Understand consumer protection measures
1.6.1 Interpret food packaging labels (see also 1.2.1, 3.5.1)
1.6.2 Identify consumer protection resources available when confronted with fraudulent practices
1.6.3 Identify procedures the consumer can follow if merchandise or service is unsatisfactory
1.6.4 Check sales receipts

1.7 Understand procedures for the care, maintenance, and use of personal possessions

1.7.1 Interpret product guarantees and warranties
1.7.2 Interpret clothing care labels
1.7.3 Interpret operating instructions, directions, or labels for consumer products (see also 3.4.1)
1.7.4 Interpret maintenance procedures for household appliances and personal possessions
1.7.5 Interpret information to obtain repairs

1.8 Use banking and financial services in the community

1.8.1 Demonstrate the use of savings and checking accounts, including using an ATM
1.8.2 Interpret the procedures and forms associated with banking services, including writing checks
1.8.3 Interpret interest or interest-earning savings plans
1.8.4 Interpret information about the types of loans available through lending institutions
1.8.5 Interpret information on financial agencies and financial planning

1.9 Understand methods and procedures for the purchase and maintenance of an automobile and interpret driving regulations

1.9.1 Interpret highway and traffic signs (see also 2.2.2)
1.9.2 Identify driving regulations and procedures to obtain a driver's license (see also 2.5.7)
1.9.3 Compute mileage and gasoline consumption
1.9.4 Interpret maps related to driving (see also 1.1.3, 2.2.1, 2.2.5)
1.9.5 Interpret information related to the selection and purchase of a car
1.9.6 Interpret information related to automobile maintenance
1.9.7 Recognize what to do in case of automobile emergencies
1.9.8 Interpret information about automobile insurance

2. Community Resources

2.1 Use the telephone and telephone book

2.1.1 Use the telephone directory and related publications to locate information
2.1.2 Identify emergency numbers and place emergency calls (see also 2.5.1)
2.1.3 Interpret information about time zones (see also 2.3.1)
2.1.4 Interpret telephone billings
2.1.5 Interpret telegram rates and procedures
2.1.6 Interpret information about using a pay telephone
2.1.7 Take and interpret telephone messages, leave messages on answering machines, and interpret recorded messages (see also 4.5.4)
2.1.8 Use the telephone to make and receive routine personal and business calls

2.2 Understand how to locate and use different types of transportation and interpret related travel information

2.2.1 Ask for, give, follow, or clarify directions (see also 1.1.3, 1.9.4, 2.2.5)
2.2.2 Recognize and use signs related to transportation (see also 1.9.1)
2.2.3 Identify or use different types of transportation in the community, and interpret traffic information
2.2.4 Interpret transportation schedules and fares
2.2.5 Use maps relating to travel needs (see also 1.1.3, 1.9.4, 2.2.1)

2.3 Understand concepts of time and weather

2.3.1 Interpret clock time (see also 2.1.3, 6.6.6)
2.3.2 Identify the months of the year and the days of the week
2.3.3 Interpret information about weather conditions

2.4 Use postal services

2.4.1 Address letters and envelopes
2.4.2 Interpret postal rates and types of mailing services
2.4.3 Interpret postal service forms and instructions on returned mail
2.4.4 Purchase stamps and other postal items and services
2.4.5 Interpret procedures for tracing a lost letter or parcel
2.4.6 Interpret a postal money order form

2.5 Use community agencies and services

2.5.1 Locate and utilize services of agencies that provide emergency help
2.5.2 Identify how and when to obtain social and governmental services (e.g., low-income housing, Social Security, Medicare), and how to interact with service providers
2.5.3 Locate medical and health facilities in the community (see also 3.1.3)
2.5.4 Read, interpret, and follow directions found on public signs and building directories (see also 1.3.7)
2.5.5 Locate and use educational services in the community, including interpreting and writing school-related communications
2.5.6 Use library services
2.5.7 Interpret permit and license requirements (see also 1.9.2)
2.5.8 (unassigned)
2.5.9 Identify child care services in the community (see also 3.5.7)

2.6 Use leisure time resources and facilities

2.6.1 Interpret information about recreational and entertainment facilities and activities
2.6.2 Locate information in TV, movie, and other recreational listings

2.6.3 Interpret information in order to plan for outings and vacations

2.6.4 Interpret and order from restaurant and fast food menus, and compute related costs

2.7 Understand aspects of society and culture

2.7.1 Interpret information about holidays

2.7.2 Interpret information about ethnic groups, cultural groups, and language groups

2.7.3 Interpret information about social issues (see also 2.7.2)

2.7.4 Interpret information about religion

2.7.5 Interpret literary materials such as poetry and literature

2.7.6 Interpret materials related to the arts, such as fine art, music, drama, and film

3. Health

3.1 Understand how to access and utilize the health care system

3.1.1 Describe symptoms of illness, including identifying parts of the body; interpret doctor's directions

3.1.2 Identify information necessary to make or keep medical and dental appointments

3.1.3 Identify and utilize appropriate health care services and facilities, including interacting with providers (see also 2.5.3)

3.2 Understand medical and dental forms and related information

3.2.1 Fill out medical health history forms

3.2.2 Interpret immunization requirements

3.2.3 Interpret information associated with medical, dental, or life insurance

3.2.4 Ask for clarification about medical bills

3.3 Understand how to select and use medications

3.3.1 Identify and use necessary medications (see also 3.3.2, 3.3.3)

3.3.2 Interpret medicine labels (see also 3.3.1, 3.4.1)

3.3.3 Identify the difference between prescription, over-the-counter, and generic medications (see also 3.3.1)

3.4 Understand basic health and safety procedures

3.4.1 Interpret product label directions and safety warnings (see also 1.7.3, 3.3.2)

3.4.2 Identify safety measures that can prevent accidents and injuries

3.4.3 Interpret procedures for simple first-aid

3.4.4 Interpret information about AIDS and other sexually transmitted diseases (see also 3.1.1)

3.4.5 Recognize problems related to drugs, tobacco, and alcohol and identify where treatment may be obtained

3.5 Understand basic principles of health maintenance

3.5.1 Interpret nutritional and related information listed on food labels (see also 1.6.1)

3.5.2 Select a balanced diet

3.5.3 Interpret food storage information

3.5.4 Identify practices that promote dental health

3.5.5 Identify practices that promote cleanliness and hygiene

3.5.6 Interpret information and identify agencies that assist with family planning (see also 2.5.3, 3.1.3)

3.5.7 Identify child-rearing practices and community resources that assist in developing parenting skills (see also 2.5.9)

3.5.8 Identify practices that promote mental well being

3.5.9 Identify practices that promote physical well being

4. Employment

4.1 Understand basic principles of getting a job

4.1.1 Interpret governmental forms related to seeking work, such as applications for Social Security (see also 2.5.2)

4.1.2 Follow procedures for applying for a job, including interpreting and completing job applications, résumés, and letters of application

4.1.3 Identify and use sources of information about job opportunities such as job descriptions, job ads, and announcements, and about the workforce and job market

4.1.4 Identify and use information about training opportunities (see also 2.5.5)

4.1.5 Identify procedures involved in interviewing for a job, such as arranging for an interview, acting and dressing appropriately, and selecting appropriate questions and responses

4.1.6 Interpret general work-related vocabulary (e.g., experience, swing shift)

4.1.7 Identify appropriate behavior and attitudes for getting a job

4.1.8 Identify common occupations and the skills and education required for them

4.1.9 Identify procedures for career planning, including self-assessment

4.2 Understand wages, benefits, and concepts of employee organizations

4.2.1 Interpret wages, wage deductions, benefits, and timekeeping forms

4.2.2 Interpret information about employee organizations

4.2.3 Interpret employment contract and union agreements

4.2.4 Interpret employee handbooks, personnel policies, and job manuals

4.3 Understand work-related safety standards and procedures

4.3.1 Interpret safety signs found in the workplace (see also 3.4.1)

4.3.2 Interpret work safety manuals and related information

4.3.3 Identify safe work procedures and common safety equipment, including wearing safe work attire

4.3.4 Report unsafe working conditions work-related accidents, injuries, damages

4.4 Understand concepts and materials related to job performance and training

4.4.1 Identify appropriate behavior, attire, attitudes, and social interaction, factors that affect job retention advancement

4.4.2 Identify appropriate skills and education for keeping a job and getting a

4.4.3 Interpret job-related signs, charts, diagrams, forms, and procedures, record information on forms, charts, checklists, etc. (see also 4.2.1, 4.3.4)

4.4.4 Interpret job responsibilities and performance reviews (see also 4.4.2)

4.4.5 Identify job training needs and goals

4.4.6 Interpret work specifications and standards

4.4.7 Demonstrate the ability to apply skills learned in one job situation another

4.4.8 Interpret job-related technical information, such as from service manuals and classes

4.5 Effectively utilize common workplace technology and systems

4.5.1 Identify common tools, equipment, machines, and materials required one's job

4.5.2 Demonstrate simple keyboarding

4.5.3 Demonstrate ability to use a filing or other ordered system (e.g., coded numbered)

4.5.4 Demonstrate use of common business machines (see also 2.1.7, 2.1.8)

4.5.5 Demonstrate basic computer skills use of common software programs, including reading or interpreting computer generated printouts

4.5.6 Demonstrate ability to select, set use tools and machines in order accomplish a task, while operating a technological system

4.5.7 Demonstrate ability to identify resolve problems with machines follow proper maintenance procedures

4.6 Communicate effectively in the workplace

4.6.1 Follow, clarify, give, or provide feedback to instructions; give and respond appropriately to criticism

4.6.2 Interpret and write work-related correspondence, including notes, memos, letters, and e-mail (see also 4.4.3)

4.6.3 Interpret written workplace announcements and notices (see also 4.4.1, 4.4.3)

4.6.4 Report progress on activities, status of assigned tasks, and problems and other situations affecting job completion (see also 4.3.4)

4.6.5 Select and analyze work-related information for a given purpose and communicate it to others orally or in writing

4.7 Effectively manage workplace resources

4.7.1 Interpret or prepare a work-related budget, including projecting costs, keeping detailed records, and tracking status of expenditures and revenue

4.7.2 Identify or demonstrate effective management of material resources, including acquisition, storage, and distribution

4.7.3 Identify or demonstrate effective management of human resources, including assessing skills, making appropriate work assignments, and monitoring performance

4.7.4 Identify, secure, evaluate, process, and/or store information needed to perform tasks or keep records

4.8 Demonstrate effectiveness in working with other people

4.8.1 Demonstrate ability to work cooperatively with others as a member of a team, contributing to team efforts, maximizing the strengths of team members, promoting effective group interaction, and taking personal responsibility for accomplishing goals

4.8.2 Identify ways to learn from others and to help others learn job-related concepts and skills

4.8.3 Demonstrate effective communication skills in working with customers and clients

4.8.4 Demonstrate initiative and resourcefulness in meeting the needs and solving the problems of customers

4.8.5 Demonstrate leadership skills, including effectively communicating ideas or positions, motivating and respecting others, and responsibly challenging existing policies

4.8.6 Demonstrate negotiation skills in resolving differences, including presenting facts and arguments, recognizing differing points of view, offering options, and making compromises

4.8.7 Identify and use effective approaches to working within a multicultural workforce, including respecting cultural diversity, avoiding stereotypes, and recognizing concerns of members of other ethnic and gender groups

4.9 Understand how social, organizational, and technological systems work, and operate effectively within them

4.9.1 Identify the formal organizational structure of one's work environment

4.9.2 Demonstrate how a system's structures relate to its goals

4.9.3 Identify sources of information and assistance, and access resources within a system

4.9.4 Assess the operation of a system or organization and make recommendations for improvement, including development of new systems

5. Government and Law

5.1 Understand voting and the political process
5.1.1 Identify voter qualifications
5.1.2 Interpret a voter registration form
5.1.3 Interpret a ballot
5.1.4 Interpret information about electoral politics and candidates
5.1.5 Interpret information about special interest groups
5.1.6 Communicate one's opinions on a current issue

5.2 Understand historical and geographical information
5.2.1 Interpret information about U.S. history
5.2.2 Identify or interpret U.S. historical documents
5.2.3 Interpret information about world history
5.2.4 Interpret information about U.S. states, cities, geographical features, and points of interest
5.2.5 Interpret information about world geography

5.3 Understand an individual's legal rights and responsibilities and procedures for obtaining legal advice
5.3.1 Interpret common laws and ordinances, and legal forms and documents
5.3.2 Identify individual legal rights and procedures for obtaining legal advice (see also 5.3.1)
5.3.3 Interpret basic court procedures
5.3.4 Interpret laws affecting door-to-door sales (see also 1.6.2)
5.3.5 Interpret information about traffic tickets
5.3.6 Interpret information or identify requirements for establishing residency and/or obtaining citizenship
5.3.7 Identify common infractions and crimes, and legal consequences
5.3.8 Identify procedures for reporting a crime

5.4 Understand information about taxes
5.4.1 Interpret income tax forms
5.4.2 Compute or define sales tax
5.4.3 Interpret tax tables (see also 5.4.1, 5.4.2)
5.4.4 Interpret tax information from articles and publications

5.5 Understand governmental activities
5.5.1 Interpret information about international affairs
5.5.2 Interpret information about legislative activities
5.5.3 Interpret information about judicial activities
5.5.4 Interpret information about executive activities
5.5.5 Interpret information about military activities
5.5.6 Interpret information about law enforcement activities
5.5.7 Interpret information about local policymaking groups
5.5.8 Identify local, state and federal government leaders

5.6 Understand civic responsibilities and activities
5.6.1 Interpret information about neighborhood or community problems and their solutions
5.6.2 Interpret information about civic organizations and public service groups
5.6.3 Interpret civic responsibilities, such as voting, jury duty, taxes

5.7 Understand environmental and science-related issues
5.7.1 Interpret information about environmental issues
5.7.2 Interpret information related to physics, including energy
5.7.3 Interpret information about earth-related sciences
5.7.4 Interpret information about new technologies and scientific issues

5.8 Understand concepts of economics
5.8.1 Interpret economic information and statistics
5.8.2 Interpret information on economic issues and trends
5.8.3 Interpret information on world economic systems

6. Computation

6.0 Demonstrate pre-computation skills
6.0.1 Identify and classify numeric symbols
6.0.2 Count and associate numbers with quantities, including recognizing correct number sequencing
6.0.3 Identify information needed to solve a given problem
6.0.4 Determine appropriate operation to apply to a given problem
6.0.5 Demonstrate use of a calculator

6.1 Compute using whole numbers
6.1.1 Add whole numbers
6.1.2 Subtract whole numbers
6.1.3 Multiply whole numbers
6.1.4 Divide whole numbers
6.1.5 Perform multiple operations using whole numbers

6.2 Compute using decimal fractions
6.2.1 Add decimal fractions
6.2.2 Subtract decimal fractions
6.2.3 Multiply decimal fractions
6.2.4 Divide decimal fractions

6.2.5 Perform multiple operations using decimal fractions

6.2.6 Convert decimal fractions to common fractions or percents

6.3 Compute using fractions

6.3.1 Add common or mixed fractions

6.3.2 Subtract common or mixed fractions

6.3.3 Multiply common or mixed fractions

6.3.4 Divide common or mixed fractions

6.3.5 Perform multiple operations using common or mixed fractions

6.3.6 Convert common or mixed fractions to decimal fractions or percents

6.3.7 Identify or calculate equivalent fractions

6.4 Compute with percents, rate, ratio, and proportion

6.4.1 Apply a percent to determine amount of discount (see also 1.2.3)

6.4.2 Apply a percent in a context not involving money

6.4.3 Calculate percents

6.4.4 Convert percents to common, mixed, or decimal fractions

6.4.5 Use rate to compute increase or decrease

6.4.6 Compute using ratio or proportion (see also 6.4.5)

6.5 Use expressions, equations, and formulas

6.5.1 Recognize and evaluate simple consumer formulas

6.5.2 Recognize and apply simple geometric formulas

6.5.3 Recognize and apply simple algebraic formulas

6.5.4 Recognize and evaluate logical statements

6.6 Demonstrate measurement skills (see also 1.1)

6.6.1 Convert units of U.S. standard measurement and metric system (see also 1.1.2, 1.1.4)

6.6.2 Recognize, use, and measure linear dimensions, geometric shapes, or angles (see also 1.1.2, 1.1.4)

6.6.3 Measure area and volume of geometric shapes (see also 1.1.2, 1.1.4)

6.6.4 Use or interpret measurement instruments, such as rulers, scales, gauges, and dials (see also 1.1.2, 1.1.4, 1.1.5, 4.3.3, 4.4.3)

6.6.5 Interpret diagrams, illustrations, and scale drawings (see also 1.1.4, 4.4.3)

6.6.6 Calculate with units of time

6.6.7 Solve measurement problems in stipulated situations

6.6.8 Interpret mechanical concepts or spatial relationships

6.6.9 Use or interpret switches and controls

6.7 Interpret data from graphs and compute averages

6.7.1 Interpret data given in a line graph (see also 1.1.3)

6.7.2 Interpret data given in a bar graph (see also 1.1.3)

6.7.3 Interpret data given in a picture graph

6.7.4 Interpret data given in a circle graph (see also 1.1.3)

6.7.5 Compute averages, medians, or modes (see also 1.1.8)

6.8 Use statistics and probability

6.8.1 Interpret statistical information used in news reports and articles

6.8.2 Interpret statements of probability

6.9 Use estimation and mental arithmetic

6.9.1 Use computation short cuts

6.9.2 Estimate answers

7. Learning to Learn

7.1 Identify or practice effective organizational and time management skills in accomplishing goals

7.1.1 Identify and prioritize personal, educational, and workplace goals (see also 4.4.5)

7.1.2 Demonstrate an organized approach to achieving goals, including identifying and prioritizing tasks and setting and following an effective schedule

7.1.3 Demonstrate personal responsibility and motivation in accomplishing goals

7.1.4 Establish, maintain, and utilize a physical system of organization, such as notebooks, files, calendars, folders, and checklists (see also 4.5.3)

7.2 Demonstrate ability to use thinking skills

7.2.1 Identify and paraphrase pertinent information

7.2.2 Analyze a situation, statement, or process, identifying component elements and causal and part/whole relationships

7.2.3 Make comparisons, differentiating among, sorting, and classifying items, information, or ideas

7.2.4 Identify or make inferences through inductive and deductive reasoning to hypothesize, predict, conclude, and synthesize; distinguish fact from opinion, and determine what is mandatory and what is discretionary

7.2.5 Evaluate a situation, statement, or process, assembling information and providing evidence, making judgements, examining assumptions, and identifying contradictions

7.2.6 Generate ideas using divergent (brainstorming) and convergent (focus) approaches, and also through creative imagination

7.2.7 Identify factors involved in making decisions, including considering goals, constraints, and consequences, and weighing alternatives

7.3 Demonstrate ability to use problem-solving skills

7.3.1 Identify a problem and its possible causes

7.3.2 Devise and implement a solution to an identified problem

7.3.3 Evaluate the outcome of an implemented solution and suggest modifications to the solution as needed

7.3.4 Utilize problem-solving strategies, such as breaking down the problem into component parts and generating alternative or creative solutions

7.4 Demonstrate study skills

7.4.1 Identify or utilize effective study strategies

7.4.2 Take notes or write a summary or an outline

7.4.3 Identify, utilize, or create devices or processes for remembering information

7.4.4 Identify or utilize appropriate informational resources, including the Internet (see also 4.9.3)

7.4.5 Use reference materials, such as dictionaries and encyclopedias

7.4.6 Use indexes and tables of contents

7.4.7 Identify or utilize test-taking skills

7.4.8 Interpret visual representations, such as symbols, blueprints, flowcharts, and schematics (see also 6.6.5)

7.4.9 Identify personal learning style

7.5 Understand aspects of and approaches to effective personal management

7.5.1 Identify personal values, qualities, interests, abilities, and aptitudes

7.5.2 Identify or use strategies to develop a positive attitude and self-image, and self-esteem

7.5.3 Identify or use strategies to cope with negative feedback

7.5.4 Identify sources of stress, and resources for stress reduction

7.5.5 Identify personal, family, and work responsibilities, and ways to accommodate them and deal with related problems

7.5.6 Identify or use strategies for communicating more successfully

7.5.7 Identify constructive ways of dealing with change, including showing flexibility and adaptability, and updating skills

8. Independent Living

8.1 Perform self-care skills

8.1.1 Recognize and/or demonstrate hygiene and grooming skills (see also 3.5.5)

8.1.2 Recognize and/or demonstrate dressing skills

8.1.3 Recognize and/or demonstrate dining skills and manners

8.1.4 Recognize and/or demonstrate selection and care of clothing and personal property

8.2 Perform home-care skills

8.2.1 Recognize and/or demonstrate meal and snack preparation tasks and activities (see also 1.1.1, 3.5.2)

8.2.2 Recognize and/or demonstrate dishwashing and meal clean-up activities (see also 3.5.5)

8.2.3 Recognize and/or demonstrate housekeeping and house cleaning tasks

8.2.4 Recognize and/or demonstrate laundry skills and related clothing-care skills (see also 1.7.2, 1.7.3)

8.2.5 Recognize and/or demonstrate yard and garden tasks and activities

8.2.6 Recognize and/or demonstrate general household repair and maintenance (see also 1.4.7, 1.7.4)

8.3 Use support services to assist in maintaining independence and achieving community integration

8.3.1 Identify and interact with persons in the home environment who can provide support in achieving goals (e.g., family, friends, caregivers)

8.3.2 Identify and interact with persons in the community who can provide support in achieving goals (e.g., neighbors, contacts from human service agencies and recreation facilities)

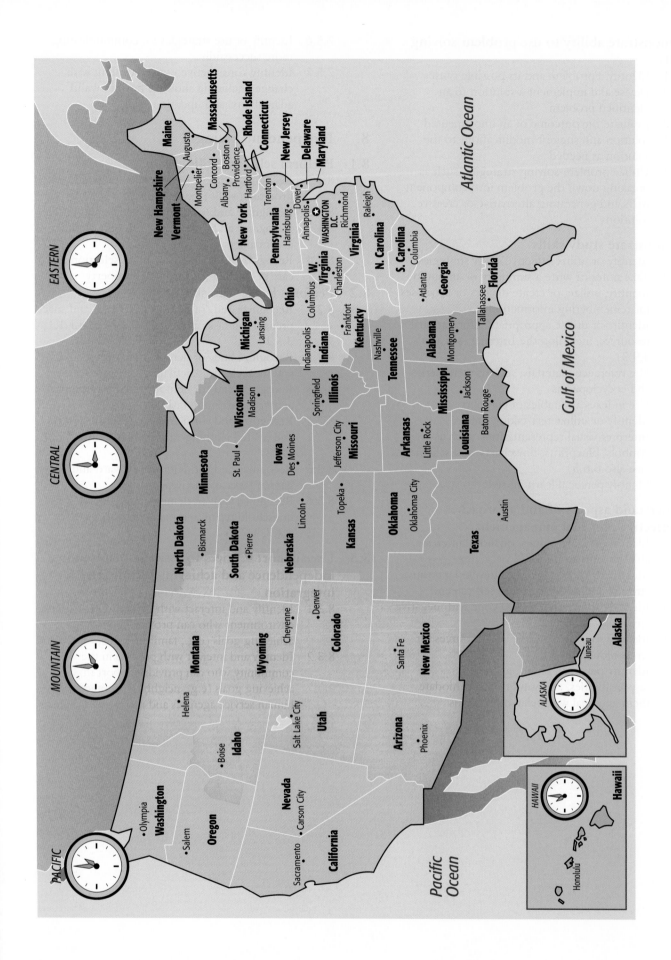

Activity Bank Contents (available on the enclosed CD-ROM)

Pre-Unit	Lesson	Worksheets*	Skill
Getting to Know You	1	1. Introductions 🎧	Listen to conversations and take notes.
	2	1. Personal Interests Conversations 🎧	Listen to conversations and answer questions based on personal interests.
		2. List of Personal Interests	A list of personal interests with suggested activities.
	3	1. Personal Letters	Find mistakes in a personal letter. Write a personal letter.
	Research	• Talking to People	Research by talking to people.

Unit 1	Lesson	Worksheets*	Skill
Balancing Your Life	1	1. Learning Styles	Read about learning styles. Do related activities.
		2. Multiple Intelligences	Read and listen to a lecture on multiple intelligences. Fill in the missing words. Answer questions.
		3. Class Poll	Templates for two class polls: one on learning styles and one on multiple intelligences
	2	1. Choose the Career Path	Match the intelligence to a career. Complete statements about people, suggesting careers or them.
		2. Conversations with Counselors	Listen to students talk to counselors and fill in a chart.
	3	1. Simple Verb Tenses	Complete statements with simple verb tenses.
		2. Balance	Take a true/false quiz on balance.
		3. Suggestions to Improve Writing	a list of suggestions to use for personal writing and peer editing
	4	1. Goal Setting Lecture	Read lecture and answer questions.
		2. Goal Chart	Read Jason's goal chart and decide if they are realistic. Fill out a goal chart.
	5	1. Motivation Checklist and Motivate Yourself	Write goals and motivation technique using checklist.
		2. Future Perfect	Complete statements using the future perfect tense. Complete personal statements using the future perfect tense.
	Research	• (PDF) Career Information from Occupational Outlook Handbook	Do research using government statistics.

* Unit worksheets include low, mid-level, and high-level versions.
• Indicates PDF file or template

Unit 2	Lesson	Worksheets*	Skill
Personal Finance	1	1. Money Out	Calculate and fill in monthly and annual expenses.
		2. Expense Sheets	Two expense sheet templates (one with expenses and one without).
	2	1. Debt Ad Vocabulary	Do exercises with vocabulary expressions from advertisement in the student book.
		2. Saving Money 🎧	Brainstorm things to save money for. Listen to conversations and decide how the person will save money and what they will save it for. Listen to students talk to counselors and fill in a chart.
		3. Past Perfect Progressive	Complete statements with simple past and past perfect progressive.
	3	1. Investing Vocabulary Practice	Complete exercises with *investing* vocabulary.
		2. The Chicken or the Market? Reading Comprehension	Read article and complete comprehension exercises.
	4	1. The Four Keys to Great Credit: Comprehension	Complete comprehension exercises based on article from the student book.
		2. The Four Key's to Great Credit (Outline)	Practice outlining the article from the student book. (Included are an outline template, a partially completed outline, and an outline sample)
	5	1. Identity Theft	Create an outline from an interview on identity theft. Practice asking and answering questions from the interview.
	Research	• Basic information from the FTC and FDIC Web sites (PDF files)	Do research using government information.

Unit 3	Lesson	Worksheets*	Skill
Automotive Know-How	1	1. Car Ad Practice	Answer questions about cars for sale.
		2. Car Buying Plan	Read a sample car-buying plan and fill one out.
	2	1. Auto Maintenance and Repair	Label the parts of a car. Match maintenance tips.
	3	1. Auto Insurance Practice	Answer questions about auto insurance policies.
	4	1. Gas/Mileage Chart	Blank template
		2. Compute Mileage and Gas	Computer trip miles and MPG in a chart. Answer questions about the chart.
		3. Change Your Driving Habits to Save Gas	Read and discuss tips for saving gas.
	5	1. Sample Driving Tests	Take three sample driving tests.
		2. Violation Scenarios 🎧	Listen to the conversations between a police officer and drivers. Record information.

*Unit worksheets include low, mid-level, and high-level versions.
• Indicates PDF file or template

Unit 4	Lesson	Worksheets*	Skill
Housing	1	1. Landlord Tenant Conversations 🎧	Calculate and fill in monthly and annual expenses.
		2. Causative Verbs	Two expense sheet templates (one with expenses and one without)
	2	1. Rental Application	Fill out a rental application and discuss agreement with a small group.
		2. Lease Agreement	Sample lease agreement with teaching ideas
	3	1. Noisy Neighbors	Read an article about noisy neighbors and answer questions.
	4	1. Renter's Insurance	Answer questions about a renter's insurance quote.
		2. Homeowner's Insurance	Answer questions about a homeowner's insurance policy.
	5	1. Theft Prevention—Compare and Contrast	Compare two lists of theft prevention tips.

Unit 5	Lesson	Worksheets*	Skill
Health	1	1. Give Advice	Come up with health related problems and advice. Work with a partner to ask for advice.
		2. Write an Article	brainstorming worksheet to help students write a health-related article.
	2	1. Conversations with the Doctor's Office	Listen to conversations between a patient and doctor's office and fill out a chart with information from the conversations.
		2. Medical Bill	Answer questions about a medical bill.
	3	1. Doing Research	Do research about health insurance coverage.
		• Bar Graph	Use bar graphs with Worksheet 1 to illustrate date gathered. (templates folder)
		• Health Insurance Coverage (PDF)	Article
	4	1. Substance Abuse and Addiction	Read an article on substance abuse and addiction. Answer questions and discuss.
		2. Adverb Clauses of Concession	Write sentences using adverb clauses of concession.
	5	1. First Aid Kit	Discuss a first aid kit checklist. Gather items for a first aid kit.

* Unit worksheets include low, mid-level, and high-level versions.
• Indicates PDF file or template

Unit 6	Lesson	Worksheets*	Skill
Retail	1	1. Product Reviews	Read product reviews and guess what product is being reviewed. Write a review for a restaurant or hotel.
		2. Product Research	Do research on a cell phone company by taking to classmates. (Blank research template also included)
	2	1. Catalog Shopping	Complete a form with information from a catalog (Catalogs needed to do this activity. Ask students to bring in catalogs received in the mail.)
	3	1. Warranties	Read an article from ftc.gov on warranties. Discuss questions and do a class presentation.
		2. Complaint Letter	Write a letter to complain about a product.
	4	1. Returns and Exchanges	Read and practice conversations about returning a product. Write a conversation and present it to the class.
		1. Radio Ads	Listen to radio ads and write down the information you hear. Then write an ad based on the information from one of the radio ads.
	5	1. Appositives	Practice finding and creating appositives.

Unit 7	Lesson	Worksheets*	Skill
The Office	1	1. Technology Instructions	Put technology instructions in order. Write instructions for a piece of technology from the classroom.
	2	1. Troubleshoot Technology	Read conversations from the student book and answer questions. Listen to more conversations and write down the problems and solutions.
	3	1. Organize It!	Come up with a plan to organize bookshelves and someone's desk.
	4	1. Conflict Resolution	A reading
		2. Build Vocabulary	Complete vocabulary exercises related to the reading on conflict resolution.
		3. Resolve Conflict: Scenarios	Resolve conflict in two different scenarios.
	5	1. Noun Clauses	Complete exercises with noun clauses.
		2. Progress Reports	Write a progress report.
	Research	• Retail and Office Careers (PDF files)	Do research on information related to retail and office careers. Use with the student book page 153.

* Unit worksheets include low, mid-level, and high-level versions.
• Indicates PDF file or template

Unit 8	Lesson	Worksheets*	Skill
Civic Responsibility	1	1. Can You Become a Resident?	Review residency requirements. Listen to people talk about themselves and decide if they are eligible or not to because a resident.
		• Citizenship Q & A (PDF)	A list of 96 questions and answers for the citizenship oral exam
		• Citizenship Flashcards (PDF)	Flashcards of the citizenship questions
		• Citizenship Detailed Answers (PDF)	Detailed answers for the citizenship questions
	2	1. Quotes from Famous People	Interpret quotes from famous people. Research the famous people.
		2. Thomas Jefferson and the Bill of a Rights	Brief reading on the history of the Bill of Rights
	3	1. Create a Civic Organization	Using a given scenario, create a civic organization.
	4	1. Carpooling	Using SEQL reading from the student book, answer questions on carpooling.
		• 100 Ways to Save the Environment	List
		• "Kids Can Do" (Bookmark)	A bookmark with a list of ten things kids can do to help save the environment
	5	1. Opinions	Agree or disagree with opinions related to the environment. Write an opinion paragraph
		• Paragraph Editing	(Templates folder)

* Unit worksheets include low, mid-level, and high-level versions.
• Indicates PDF file or template

Photo Credits